奥数精选题库

国际小学数学竞赛试题解答

（第二版）

朱华伟　孙文先　编译

科学出版社
北京

内 容 简 介

本书收录了第 1 届 (2003 年) 至第 14 届 (2016 年) 国际小学数学竞赛全部试题,对每一道试题均给出详细解答,有些题还给出了多种解法与评注,以使读者开阔眼界,加深对问题的理解,从中得到有益的启发,培养举一反三的能力.

本书可供小学数学资优生、准备参加各级小学数学竞赛的选手、小学数学教师、高等师范院校数学教育专业师生、数学爱好者及数学研究工作者参考.

图书在版编目(CIP)数据

国际小学数学竞赛试题解答/朱华伟,孙文先编译. —2 版. —北京:科学出版社,2018.5
(奥数题库精选)
ISBN 978-7-03-056424-5

Ⅰ. ①国… Ⅱ. ①朱… ②孙… Ⅲ. ①小学数学课–题解 Ⅳ. ①G624.505

中国版本图书馆 CIP 数据核字(2018)第 015975 号

责任编辑:李 敏/责任校对:彭 涛
责任印制:肖 兴/封面设计:黄华斌

科 学 出 版 社 出版
北京东黄城根北街 16 号
邮政编码:100717
http://www.sciencep.com

文林印务有限公司 印刷
科学出版社发行 各地新华书店经销

*

2014 年 3 月第 一 版　开本:720×1000　1/16
2018 年 5 月第 二 版　印张:19 1/2
2018 年 5 月第一次印刷　字数:460 000

定价:96.00 元
(如有印装质量问题,我社负责调换)

主要作者简介

朱华伟,二级教授,特级教师,博士生导师

美国加利福尼亚州立大学洛杉矶分校高级访问学者.湖北省十大杰出青年.享受国务院政府特殊津贴专家.

兼任国际教育数学协会常务副理事长,国际数学竞赛学术委员会副主席,国际中小学生数学能力检测学术委员会副主席,中国教育数学学会常务副理事长兼秘书长,全国华罗庚金杯赛主试委员. 多次参与中国数学奥林匹克、全国高中数学联赛、女子数学奥林匹克、西部数学奥林匹克及青少年数学国际城市邀请赛的命题工作.曾任国际数学奥林匹克中国队领队、主教练,率中国队获团体冠军.

在国内外学术期刊上发表论文 100 余篇,出版著作 100 余部.

张景中谈奥数

华伟教授认为，竞赛数学是教育数学的一部分．这个看法是言之成理的．数学要解题，要发现问题、创造方法．年复一年进行的数学竞赛活动，不断地为数学问题的宝库注入新鲜血液，常常把学术形态的数学成果转化为可能用于教学的形态．早期的国际数学奥林匹克试题，有不少进入了数学教材，成为例题和习题．竞赛数学与教育数学的关系，于此可见一斑．

写到这里，忍不住要为数学竞赛说几句话．有一阵子，媒体上面出现不少讨伐数学竞赛的声音，有的教育专家甚至认为数学竞赛之害甚于黄、赌、毒．我看了有关报道后第一个想法是，中国现在值得反对的事情不少，论轻重缓急还远远轮不到反对数学竞赛吧．再仔细读这些反对数学竞赛的意见，可以看出来，他们反对的实际上是某些为牟利而又误人子弟的数学竞赛培训．就数学竞赛本身而言，是面向青少年中很小一部分数学爱好者而组织的活动．这些热心参与数学竞赛的数学爱好者 (还有不少数学爱好者参与其他活动，例如青少年创新发明活动、数学建模活动、近年来设立的丘成桐中学数学奖)，估计不超过约两亿中小学生的百分之五．从一方面讲，数学竞赛培训活动过热产生的消极影响，和升学考试体制以及教育资源分配过分集中等多种因素有关，这笔账不能算在数学竞赛头上；从另一方面看，大学招生和数学竞赛挂钩，也正说明了数学竞赛活动的成功因而得到认可．对于青少年的课外兴趣活动，积极的对策不应当是限制堵塞，而是开源分流．发展多种课外活动，让更多的青少年各得其所，把各种活动都办得像数学竞赛这样成功并且被认可，数学竞赛培训活动过热的问题自然就化解或缓解了．

摘自《走进教育数学》丛书总序

第二版前言

我们都知道数学是科学之母，在科技神速发展的今日，数学的重要性尤为彰显．在太空科技、电子通信、金融贸易、生物化学等领域处处都深切需要数学，唯有借助数学的渗透才能使这些领域蓬勃发展．近几年来，地球暖化、环境变迁与物价波动、金融危机等周遭切身的问题，促使全球科学家绞尽脑汁寻求解决方案，而数学的理论与方法在其间有着很重大的影响．在现今可以说是数学领导着科学之发展，数学的思维与数学的方法促使科学研究进入新的境界．由于人们深刻了解到数学的重要性，也体认到应尽早培养学生对数学的兴趣与数学思维的习惯，因此，人们举办了许多内容丰富的数学活动，而数学竞赛就是这些多姿多彩的活动之一．

在学校里的考试，是测试学生应该掌握的知识．但是在数学竞赛中，试题不仅限于学校数学课程的范围．考生们将见到一些新颖的问题，以开阔他们的视野．许多亚洲国家，学生的课业压力沉重，学生对数学只专注于它的功利价值，而忽视了它迷人的面貌．让学生体认数学之美当然是有益的，但这绝对不应是首要的考虑．更重要的，应该鼓励年轻人重建对数学的热情．

国际小学数学竞赛（Elementary Mathematics International Contest（EMIC））是由泰国 Dr. Kajornpai Pramote 于 2003 年所创办的，当年的竞赛活动得到泰国教育部与泰国佛教寺院团体全力支持，如今本竞赛参赛国家与地区已经达 30 多个，遍布五大洲．

创立国际小学数学竞赛有以下的目标：

(1) 可提供各国小学生一个竞技的场合，借以促进各国小学生数学能力之提升．

(2) 经由数学竞赛可以检视各国数学课程之状况，作为各国教育改革之参考．

(3) 新颖且有创意的竞赛试题可让小学生享受深思的乐趣，欣赏数学之美．

(4) 可学习如何与他人通力合作，通过互相讨论，齐心协力共同解决难题．

(5) 可接触来自世界各地不同的文化与生活习俗，增广见闻，学习互相包容，促进世界和平．

2004 年的国际小学数学竞赛由印度接办；2005 年由菲律宾主办；2006 年则由印度尼西亚教育部主办；2007 年在中国香港举行；2008 年又回到泰国清迈，由泰国教育部主办；2009 年由菲律宾数学教育研究会、菲律宾科技部、菲律宾教育部 Iloilo 市政府合办；2010 年在韩国仁川举办；2011 年由印度尼西亚教育部在巴厘岛主办；2012 年由财团法人台北市九章数学教育基金会在中国台湾台北市举办；2013 年在保加利亚举办；2014 年在韩国举办；2015 年在中国长春举办；2016 由泰国教育部在清迈主办．

2008 年泰国教育部首度将国际小学数学竞赛与青少年数学国际城市邀请赛(IWYMIC)合并举办并改称为国际数学竞赛(International Mathematics Competition(IMC))，保加利亚于 2013 年 6 月 30 日至 7 月 5 日在 Burgas 市举行 BIMC 2013．主办单位为保加利亚教育部、Burgas 市政府、Burgas 市政府教育处、保加

第二版前言

利亚数学联合会.

国际小学数学竞赛出题模式为：由世界各国参赛队伍邀请该国专家学者提供个人赛和队际赛试题各5题，早期阶段由领队在领队会议上挑选合适的试题，最近几年则由国际小学数学竞赛主试委员会委员选定并修改试题. 国际小学数学竞赛的试题，内容涵盖广泛，设计新颖，生动有趣，充分展现了数学之美.

国际小学数学竞赛的比赛项目分个人赛和队际赛. 参加个人赛的选手必须在1小时30分内完成15道题，每题10分，总分150分. 队际赛共10道题，每题40分，分两部分进行，须在1小时内完成. 其中第一部分，全队4名选手首先在10分钟内商议分配其中8个试题，在35分钟内独立完成各自分配到的试题，每位成员至少完成1题；第二部分比赛时间15分钟，由全队4名队员合作共同完成余下的2道试题. 邀请赛不但要求学生有一定的逻辑思维和独立解题的能力，而且讲求团队合作精神.

本书收录了第1届(2003年)至第14届(2016年)国际小学数学竞赛的全部试题，对每一道试题均给出了详细解答，有些题还给出了多种解法与评注，目的是使读者加深对问题的理解，从中得到有益的启发.

在本书编写过程中，编者参阅了许多中外文文献资料，在此向原作者表示衷心的谢意. 在本书的编校过程中，广州市教育研究院郑焕博士提供了很大的帮助，在此向他表示真诚的感谢. 对于本书存在的问题，热忱希望读者不吝赐教.

朱华伟 孙文先 谨志
2018年11月于广州

第一版前言

我们都知道数学是科学之母,在科技神速发展的今日,数学的重要性尤为彰显. 在太空科技、电子通信、金融贸易、生物化学等领域处处都深切需要数学,唯有借助数学的渗透才能使这些领域得以蓬勃发展. 近几年来,地球变暖、环境变迁与物价波动、金融危机等周遭切身的问题,促使全球科学家绞尽脑汁寻求解决方案,而数学的理论与方法在其间有着很重大的影响. 在现今可以说是数学领导着科学之发展,数学的思维与数学的方法促使科学研究进入新的境界. 由于人们深刻了解到数学的重要性,也体会到应尽早培养学生对数学的兴趣与数学思维的习惯,因此,人们举办了许多内容丰富的数学活动,数学竞赛就是这些多姿多彩的活动之一.

在学校里的考试,是测试学生应该掌握的知识. 但是在数学竞赛中,试题不仅限于学校数学课程的范围. 考生们将见到一些新颖的问题,以开阔他们的视野. 许多亚洲国家,学生的课业压力沉重,学生对数学只专注于它的功利价值,而忽视了它迷人的面貌. 让学生体会数学之美当然是有益的,但这绝对不应是首要的考虑,更重要的是鼓励年轻人重建对数学的热情.

国际小学数学竞赛 (Elementary Mathematics International Contest, EMIC) 是由泰国 Dr. Kajornpai Pramote 于 2003 年所创办的,当年的竞赛活动得到泰国教育部与泰国佛教寺院团体全力支持,如今本竞赛参赛国家与地区已经达三十余国,遍布五大洲.

创立国际小学数学竞赛有以下的目标：

(1) 可提供各国小学生一个竞技的场合，借以促进各国小学生数学能力之提升．

(2) 经由数学竞赛可以检视各国数学课程之状况，作为各国教育改革之参考．

(3) 新颖且有创意的竞赛试题可让小学生享受深思的乐趣，欣赏数学之美．

(4) 可学习如何与他人通力合作，通过互相讨论，齐心协力共同解决难题．

(5) 可接触来自世界各地不同的文化与生活习俗，增广见闻，学习互相包容，促进世界和平．

2004 年的国际小学数学竞赛由印度接办；2005 年由菲律宾主办；2006 年则由印度尼西亚教育部主办；2007 年在中国香港举行；2008 年又回到泰国清迈，由泰国教育部主办；2009 年由菲律宾数学教育研究会、菲律宾科技部、菲律宾教育部 Iloilo 市政府合办；2010 年在韩国仁川举办；2011 年由印度尼西亚教育部在巴厘岛主办；2012 年由财团法人台北市九章数学教育基金会在中国台湾台北市举办；2013 年在保加利亚举办．

2008 年泰国教育部首度将国际小学数学竞赛 (EMIC) 与青少年数学国际城市邀请赛 (IWYMIC) 合并举办并改称为"国际数学竞赛 (International Mathematics Competition，IMC)"，保加利亚于 2013 年 6 月 30 日至 7 月 5 日在 Burgas 市举行 BIMC 2013. 主办单位为保加利亚教育部、Burgas 市政府、Burgas 市政府教育处、保加利亚数学联合会．

第一版前言

国际小学数学竞赛出题模式为：由世界各国参赛队伍邀请该国专家学者提供个人赛和队际赛试题各五题，早期阶段由领队在领队会议上挑选合适的试题，最近几年则由国际小学数学竞赛主试委员会委员选定并修改试题．国际小学数学竞赛的试题，内容涵盖广泛、设计新颖、生动有趣、充分展现了数学之美．

国际小学数学竞赛的比赛项目分个人赛和队际赛．参加个人赛的选手必须在 90 分钟内完成 15 道试题；队际赛分两部分进行，需在 1 小时内完成．其中第一部分时间 35 分钟，由全队四名选手首先在 10 分钟内商议分配其中 8 个试题，要求队员独立完成各自分配到的试题，每位成员至少完成 1 道题；第二部分比赛时间 15 分钟，由全队四名队员合作共同完成余下的 2 道试题．队际赛不但要求队员有一定的逻辑思维和独立解题的能力，而且讲求团队合作精神．

本书收录了第 1 届 (2003 年) 至第 11 届 (2013 年) 国际小学数学竞赛的全部试题，对每一道试题均给出了详细解答，有些题还给出了多种解法与评注，目的是使读者加深对问题的理解，从中得到有益的启发．

在本书编写过程中，编者参阅了许多中外文文献资料，在此向原作者表示衷心的谢意．在本书的编校过程中，广州大学软件研究所博士研究生郑焕给予了很大的帮助，在此向他表示真诚的感谢．对于本书存在的问题，热忱希望读者不吝赐教．

2013 年 11 月于广州大学城

目 录

张景中谈奥数
第二版前言
第一版前言
第1章 2003年第1届国际小学数学竞赛 ·· 1
  1.1 EMIC个人赛英文试题 ·· 1
  1.2 EMIC个人赛中文试题 ·· 3
  1.3 EMIC个人赛试题解答与评注 ·· 5
  1.4 EMIC队际赛英文试题 ·· 12
  1.5 EMIC队际赛中文试题 ·· 14
  1.6 EMIC队际赛试题解答与评注 ·· 16
第2章 2004年第2届国际小学数学竞赛 ······································ 22
  2.1 EMIC个人赛英文试题 ·· 22
  2.2 EMIC个人赛中文试题 ·· 24
  2.3 EMIC个人赛试题解答与评注 ·· 27
  2.4 EMIC队际赛英文试题 ·· 31
  2.5 EMIC队际赛中文试题 ·· 34
  2.6 EMIC队际赛试题解答与评注 ·· 36
第3章 2005年第3届国际小学数学竞赛 ······································ 48
  3.1 EMIC个人赛英文试题 ·· 48
  3.2 EMIC个人赛中文试题 ·· 51
  3.3 EMIC个人赛试题解答与评注 ·· 54
  3.4 EMIC队际赛英文试题 ·· 60
  3.5 EMIC队际赛中文试题 ·· 63
  3.6 EMIC队际赛试题解答与评注 ·· 66
第4章 2006年第4届国际小学数学竞赛 ······································ 73
  4.1 EMIC个人赛英文试题 ·· 73

	4.2	EMIC 个人赛中文试题 ···	75
	4.3	EMIC 个人赛试题解答与评注 ·······································	78
	4.4	EMIC 队际赛英文试题 ···	81
	4.5	EMIC 队际赛中文试题 ···	83
	4.6	EMIC 队际赛试题解答与评注 ·······································	84

第 5 章 2007 年第 5 届国际小学数学竞赛 ·· 89

	5.1	EMIC 个人赛英文试题 ···	89
	5.2	EMIC 个人赛中文试题 ···	91
	5.3	EMIC 个人赛试题解答与评注 ·······································	93
	5.4	EMIC 队际赛英文试题 ···	97
	5.5	EMIC 队际赛中文试题 ···	98
	5.6	EMIC 队际赛试题解答与评注 ·······································	100

第 6 章 2008 年第 6 届国际小学数学竞赛 ·· 105

	6.1	EMIC 个人赛英文试题 ···	105
	6.2	EMIC 个人赛中文试题 ···	108
	6.3	EMIC 个人赛试题解答与评注 ·······································	110
	6.4	EMIC 队际赛英文试题 ···	116
	6.5	EMIC 队际赛中文试题 ···	119
	6.6	EMIC 队际赛试题解答与评注 ·······································	123

第 7 章 2009 年第 7 届国际小学数学竞赛 ·· 130

	7.1	EMIC 个人赛英文试题 ···	130
	7.2	EMIC 个人赛中文试题 ···	132
	7.3	EMIC 个人赛试题解答与评注 ·······································	135
	7.4	EMIC 队际赛英文试题 ···	141
	7.5	EMIC 队际赛中文试题 ···	145
	7.6	EMIC 队际赛试题解答与评注 ·······································	148

第 8 章 2010 年第 8 届国际小学数学竞赛 ·· 157

	8.1	EMIC 个人赛英文试题 ···	157
	8.2	EMIC 个人赛中文试题 ···	159
	8.3	EMIC 个人赛试题解答与评注 ·······································	161
	8.4	EMIC 队际赛英文试题 ···	166

    8.5   EMIC 队际赛中文试题 ·· 168

    8.6   EMIC 队际赛试题解答与评注 ··· 171

第 9 章　2011 年第 9 届国际小学数学竞赛　175

    9.1   EMIC 个人赛英文试题 ·· 175

    9.2   EMIC 个人赛中文试题 ·· 178

    9.3   EMIC 个人赛试题解答与评注 ··· 182

    9.4   EMIC 队际赛英文试题 ·· 185

    9.5   EMIC 队际赛中文试题 ·· 188

    9.6   EMIC 队际赛试题解答与评注 ··· 190

第 10 章　2012 年第 10 届国际小学数学竞赛　197

    10.1   EMIC 个人赛英文试题 ·· 197

    10.2   EMIC 个人赛中文试题 ·· 200

    10.3   EMIC 个人赛试题解答与评注 ·· 202

    10.4   EMIC 队际赛英文试题 ·· 207

    10.5   EMIC 队际赛中文试题 ·· 210

    10.6   EMIC 队际赛试题解答与评注 ·· 213

第 11 章　2013 年第 11 届国际小学数学竞赛　218

    11.1   EMIC 个人赛英文试题 ·· 218

    11.2   EMIC 个人赛中文试题 ·· 221

    11.3   EMIC 个人赛试题解答与评注 ·· 223

    11.4   EMIC 队际赛英文试题 ·· 227

    11.5   EMIC 队际赛中文试题 ·· 229

    11.6   EMIC 队际赛试题解答与评注 ·· 232

第 12 章　2014 年第 12 届国际小学数学竞赛　238

    12.1   EMIC 个人赛英文试题 ·· 238

    12.2   EMIC 个人赛中文试题 ·· 240

    12.3   EMIC 个人赛试题解答与评注 ·· 241

    12.4   EMIC 队际赛英文试题 ·· 245

    12.5   EMIC 队际赛中文试题 ·· 247

    12.6   EMIC 队际赛试题解答与评注 ·· 249

第 13 章 2015 年第 13 届国际小学数学竞赛 255
13.1　EMIC 个人赛英文试题 255
13.2　EMIC 个人赛中文试题 257
13.3　EMIC 个人赛试题解答与评注 259
13.4　EMIC 队际赛英文试题 264
13.5　EMIC 队际赛中文试题 266
13.6　EMIC 队际赛试题解答与评注 268

第 14 章 2016 年第 14 届国际小学数学竞赛 274
14.1　EMIC 个人赛英文试题 274
14.2　EMIC 个人赛中文试题 276
14.3　EMIC 个人赛试题解答与评注 277
14.4　EMIC 队际赛英文试题 281
14.5　EMIC 队际赛中文试题 283
14.6　EMIC 队际赛试题解答与评注 285

第 1 章 2003 年第 1 届国际小学数学竞赛

1.1 EMIC 个人赛英文试题

Elementary Mathematics International Contest 2003
8th September, 2003, Nakhon Pathom, Thailand

Individual Contest

1. M sold some apples and received an amount of money. If M had sold 10 more apples for the same amount of money, the price of one apple would be 2 baht less than the original price. If M had sold 10 less apples for the same amount of money, the price of one apple would be 4 baht more than the original price (Note: Baht is the Thai currency).
   (a) How many apples did M sell?
   (b) What was the price of one apple?

2. Bag A has twice the number of beads in bag B. 12% of beads in bag A are removed and transferred to bag C. 20% of beads in bag B are removed and transferred to bag C. After removing and transferring beads, there are now 488 beads in bag C which is 22% more than the original number of beads in bag C. How many beads were there in the bag A at the beginning?

3. City P is 625 kilometers from City Q. M departed from City P at 5:30 a.m. travelling at 100 kilometers per hour, and arrived at City Q. Fifteen minutes after M left, N departed from City Q and arrived at City P travelling at 80 kilometers per hour. At what time did M and N meet together?

4. Alan has 80% more stamps than Billy. Billy has $\frac{3}{5}$ of the number of Charlie's stamps. If Billy gave 150 stamps to Charlie, then Charlie would now have three times the number of Billy's remaining stamps. What is the total number of stamps they have altogether?

5. A boat is 50 kilometers away from the port. The boat is leaky, so water

flows into the boat at the rate of 2 tons per 5 minutes. If there were 90 tons of water in the boat, the boat would sink. If there is a pump in the boat, pumping out 12 tons of water per hour, what should be the minimum speed of the boat in km/h to avoid the boat from sinking?

6. X is a 2-digit number whose value is $\dfrac{13}{4}$ of the sum of its digits. If 36 is added to X, the result will contain the same digits but in reverse order. Find X.

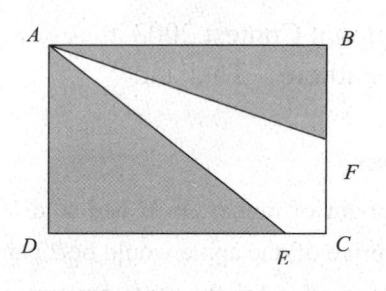

7. Given: $ABCD$ is a rectangle and
$BF = FC$, $DE = 6EC$.
What is the ratio between the unshaded area and the shaded area?

8. Find all 2-digit numbers such that when the number is divided by the sum of its digits the quotient is 4 with a remainder of 3.

9. Calculate the result of
$$1^2 - 2^2 + 3^2 - 4^2 + \cdots + 2001^2 - 2002^2 + 2003^2.$$

10. In the figure right, $\dfrac{EB}{BD} = \dfrac{1}{2}$ and the area of the shaded part is 42 cm^2. Find the area of ABC.

11. A, B and C worked together and received a total wage of 52400 baht. A received 125% of B's wage, but 90% of C's wage (Baht=Currency of Thailand).

(a) Determine who received more: B or C?

(b) What is the difference between the wages of B and C?

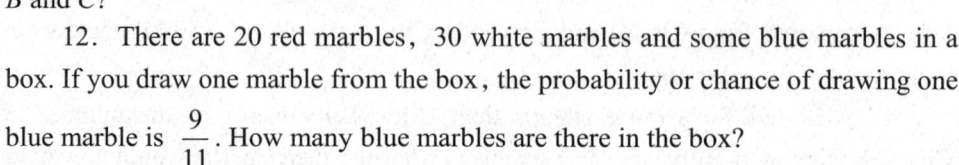

12. There are 20 red marbles, 30 white marbles and some blue marbles in a box. If you draw one marble from the box, the probability or chance of drawing one blue marble is $\dfrac{9}{11}$. How many blue marbles are there in the box?

13. When 31513 and 34369 are each divided by a certain three-digit number, the remainders are equal. Find this remainder.

14. Fill in all the numbers below into circles A, B, C, such that all numbers

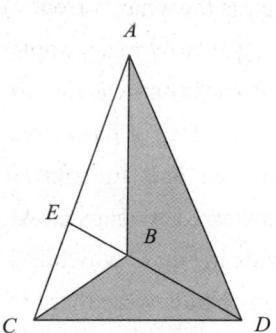

in circle A are divisible by 5, all numbers in circle B are divisible by 2, all numbers in circle C are divisible by 3.

48, 102, 112, 207, 750, 930, 1348, 1605, 1749, 2001, 2025, 2030, 3250, 7893.

15. Fill the digits 1, 2, 3, 4, 5, 6, 7, 8, 9 into the boxes
□□□□×□□□×□,
so that the expression will produce the largest product. (Each digit can be used only once)

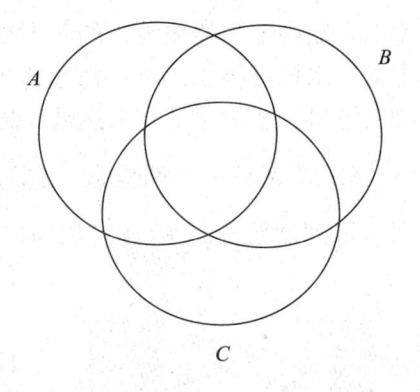

1.2　EMIC个人赛中文试题

2003 年国际小学数学竞赛个人竞赛试题

1. 小明卖出一批苹果得到一笔钱. 如果小明多卖出 10 个苹果且所得到的钱的总数相同, 则每个苹果的售价将比原售价少 2 元. 如果小明少卖出 10 个苹果且所得到的钱的总数相同, 则每个苹果的售价将比原售价多 4 元. 请问

(1) 小明卖出几个苹果?

(2) 每个苹果原来的售价是多少元?

2. A 袋中珠子的数量是 B 袋中的两倍. 若将 A 袋中 12% 的珠子及 B 袋中 20% 的珠子加入 C 袋中, 最后 C 袋中共有 488 颗珠子且比 C 袋中原有珠子的数量增加 22%. 请问 A 袋中原来有多少颗珠子?

3. P、Q 两城市相距 625 km, 小华从 P 市于上午 5:30 出发, 以 100 km/h 的速度驶向 Q 市. 小华出发 15 分钟后, 小安从 Q 市以 80 km/h 的速度驶向 P 市. 请问两人于几点几分在途中相遇?

4. 小恩收集的邮票的数量比小皮的多 80%, 小皮收集的邮票的数量是小喜的 $\frac{3}{5}$. 若小皮给小喜 150 张邮票, 则小喜现有邮票的数量是小皮剩下的邮票的 3 倍. 请问三人共有多少张邮票?

5. 有一艘船距离港口 50 km, 由于船舱漏水, 海水以每 5 分钟 2 吨的速率渗入船内．当船舱渗入的海水总量超过 90 吨时，此船将沉入海中．假若船上的抽水机可将 12 t/h 的海水排出船外．请问此船至少要以多少 km/h 的速度驶向港口，才能保证在抵达港口之前不会沉没？

6. 设 X 是一个两位数，它的值等于它的数码和的 $\frac{13}{4}$．若将 X 加上 36，则所得到的数与 X 的数码相同但两个数码的顺序恰好相反．请问 X 之值是什么？

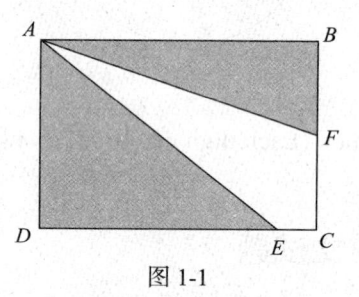

7. 如图 1-1 所示，四边形 $ABCD$ 是矩形，且 $BF=FC$、$DE=6EC$．请问此矩形中未涂阴影部分的面积与涂阴影部分的面积之比是多少？

8. 有一些两位数，将它的数值除以它的数码和，所得到的商是 4，余数是 3．请找出满足上述条件的所有的两位数．

图 1-1

9. 请问 $1^2-2^2+3^2-4^2+\cdots+2001^2-2002^2+2003^2$ 之值是多少？

10. 图 1-2 中，$\frac{EB}{BD}=\frac{1}{2}$ 且阴影部分的面积为 42cm^2．请问 $\triangle ABC$ 的面积为多少 cm^2？

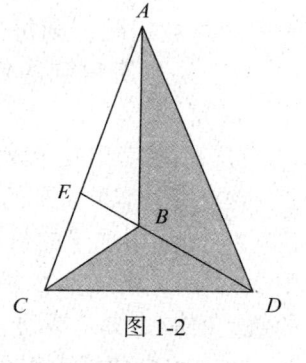

11. A、B、C 三人合作一个工程，三人共得到工资 52400 元．A 所得工资是 B 所得工资的 125%，但只是 C 所得工资的 90%．请问

(1) B 和 C 何人所得的工资较多？

(2) B 和 C 所得的工资相差多少元？

12. 在一个盒子中有 20 颗红珠子、30 颗白珠子及若干颗蓝珠子．若从此盒子中任意摸出一颗珠子，而此珠子恰好是蓝色的概率为 $\frac{9}{11}$．请问在此盒子中有多少颗蓝珠子？

图 1-2

13. 将 31513 与 34369 除以某个三位数，所得到的余数相等．请问此余数是多少？

14. 请将下列所有的 14 个数：48，102，112，207，750，930，1348，1605，1749，2001，2025，2030，3250，7893 全部填到图 1-3 由 A、B、C 三个圆所围成的区域内，使得圆 A 内的每一个数都是 5 的倍数，圆 B 内的每一个数都是 2 的倍数，圆 C 内的每一个数都是 3 的倍数．

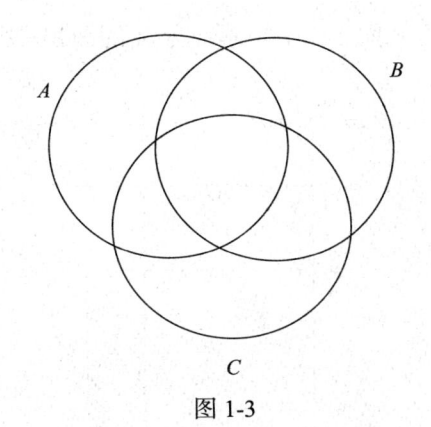

第1章 2003年第1届国际小学数学竞赛

图 1-3

15. 请将数码 1，2，3，4，5，6，7，8，9 填入下式的空格内，
□□□□□×□□□×□
使得所得到的乘积的值为最大. (每个数码恰好使用一次)

1.3 EMIC个人赛试题解答与评注

2003年国际小学数学竞赛个人竞赛试题解答

1. **解法 1** 假设每个苹果原来的售价为 a 元、共卖出 x 个苹果. 由条件"多卖出 10 个苹果且所得到的钱的总数相同,则每个苹果的售价将比原售价少 2 元", 可知图 1-4 中阴影部分 A 的面积=阴影部分 B 的面积, 即 $2x = 10(a-2)$.

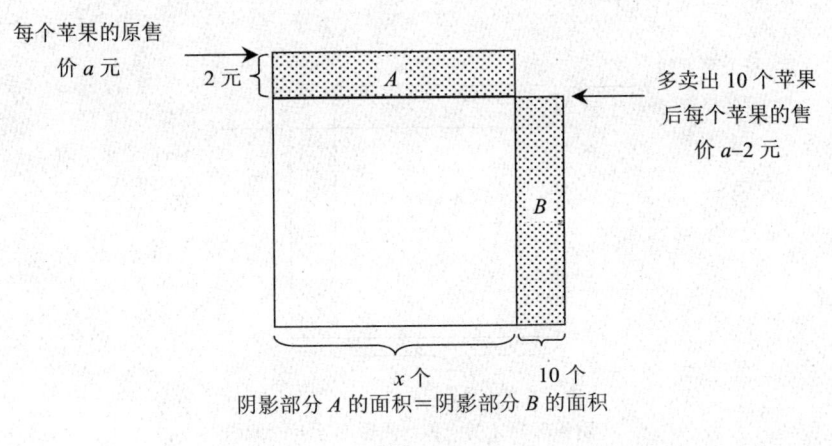

图 1-4

由条件"少卖出 10 个苹果且所得到的钱的总数相同, 则每个苹果的售价

将比原售价多 4 元"可知图 1-5 中阴影部分 A 的面积=阴影部分 B 的面积，即 $10a=4(x-10)$.

将 $2x=10(a-2)$ 代入 $10a=4(x-10)$ 中，知 $10a=20a-40-40$，即 $a=8$，因此 $x=30$.

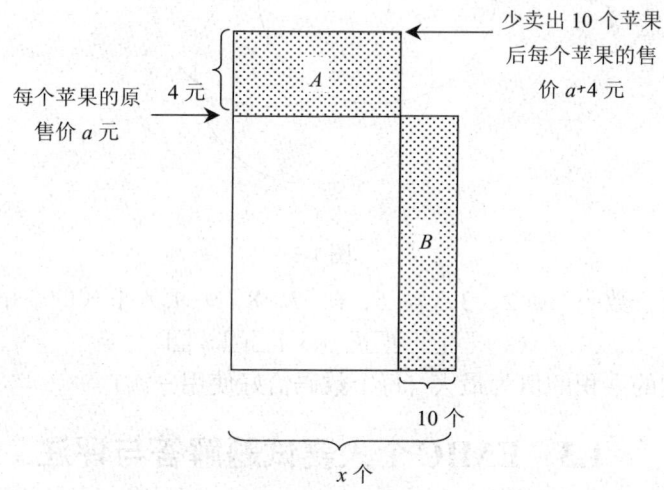

每个苹果的原售价 a 元 → 4 元
少卖出 10 个苹果后每个苹果的售价 $a+4$ 元

10 个
x 个

阴影部分 A 的面积=阴影部分 B 的面积

图 1-5

解法 2 假设共卖出 x 个苹果. 由"多卖出 10 个苹果且所得到的钱的总数相同，则每个苹果的售价将比原售价少 2 元"可知每个苹果原来的售价是 $\dfrac{2x}{10}+2=\dfrac{x}{5}+2$ 元 (图 1-6).

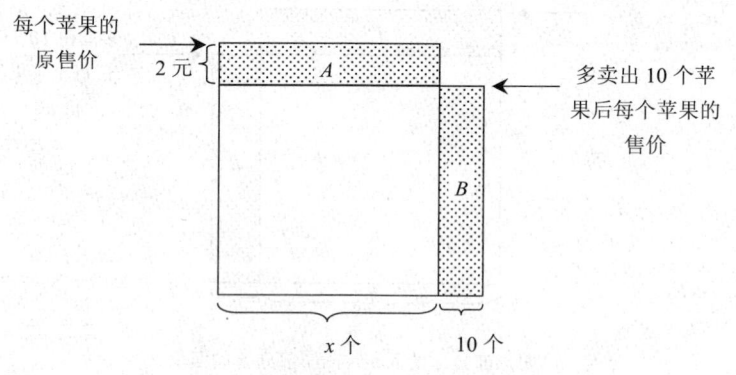

每个苹果的原售价 → 2 元
多卖出 10 个苹果后每个苹果的售价

x 个 10 个

阴影部分 A 的面积=阴影部分 B 的面积

图 1-6

第 1 章　2003 年第 1 届国际小学数学竞赛

由"少卖出 10 个苹果且所得到的钱的总数相同，则每个苹果的售价将比原售价多 4 元"可知每个苹果原来的售价是 $\dfrac{4(x-10)}{10}=\dfrac{2(x-10)}{5}$ 元（图 1-7）.

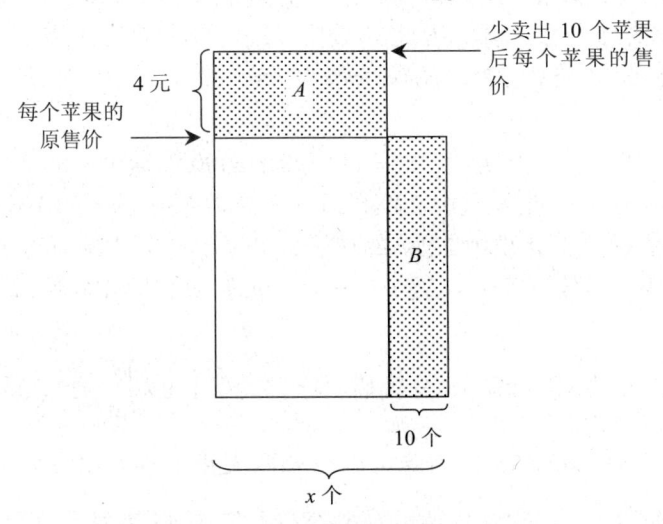

图中标注：
- 每个苹果的原售价
- 4 元
- 少卖出 10 个苹果后每个苹果的售价
- A
- B
- 10 个
- x 个

阴影部分 A 的面积＝阴影部分 B 的面积

图 1-7

因此可知 $\dfrac{x}{5}+2=\dfrac{2(x-10)}{5}$，$x=30$.

每个苹果原来的售价是 $\dfrac{30}{5}+2=8$ 元.

解法 3　假设卖出 x 个苹果，共得到 S 元，则知 $\begin{cases}\dfrac{S}{x-10}-\dfrac{S}{x}=4,\\ \dfrac{S}{x}-\dfrac{S}{x+10}=2.\end{cases}$ 可化简为

$\begin{cases}\dfrac{10S}{x(x-10)}=4,\\ \dfrac{10S}{x(x+10)}=2.\end{cases}\Rightarrow\begin{cases}10S=4x(x-10),\\ 10S=2x(x+10).\end{cases}$

因 $x\neq 0$，故可得 $4(x-10)=2(x+10)$，即 $x=30$.

因此每个苹果售价为 $\dfrac{S}{x}=\dfrac{10S}{10x}=\dfrac{4\times 30\times(30-10)}{300}=8$ 元.

答：(1) 30 个；(2) 8 元

2. **解法1** 可知 C 袋中原有 $488÷(1+22\%)=400$ 颗珠子，因此 A 袋中 12% 的珠子及 B 袋中 20% 的珠子合计共有 $488-400=88$ 颗．再因 A 袋中珠子的数量是 B 袋中的两倍，故可得知 B 袋中 20% 的珠子数与 A 袋中 $20\%÷2=10\%$ 的珠子数一样，因此 A 袋中 12% 的珠子及 A 袋中 10% 的珠子合计 88 颗，即 A 袋中 22% 的珠子数为 88，故 A 袋中原来有 $88÷22\%=400$ 颗珠子．

解法2 可知 C 袋中原有 $488÷(1+22\%)=400$ 颗珠子．A 袋中珠子的数量是 B 袋中的两倍，因此 B 袋中 20% 的珠子等于 A 袋中珠子的 10%，故 C 袋增加的珠子的数量等于 A 袋中 22% 的珠子，也等于 C 袋中原有珠子的 22%．故 A 袋中原来珠子的数量等于 C 袋中原来珠子的数量，即 400 颗．

答: 400 颗

3. **解** 可知小华出发 15 分钟后，已移动了 $100×\dfrac{15}{60}=25$ (km)，即此时两人相距 $625-25=600$ (km)，因此可以得知两人将在小安出发后 $\dfrac{600}{100+80}=\dfrac{10}{3}$ 小时相遇，即 3 小时又 20 分钟后．小安在上午 5：45 出发，故两人将在 9：05 相遇．

答: 9：05

4. **解** 由小皮收集的邮票的数量是小喜的 $\dfrac{3}{5}$，可令小皮收集的邮票的数量为 $3x$、小喜收集的邮票的数量为 $5x$，再由若小皮给小喜 150 张邮票，则小喜现有邮票的数量是小皮剩下的邮票的 3 倍知 $5x+150=3(3x-150)$，可得 $x=150$，因此小皮收集的邮票的数量为 $150×3=450$ 张、小喜收集的邮票的数量为 $150×5=750$ 张、小恩收集的邮票的数量为 $450×(1+80\%)=810$ 张，故三人共有 $450+750+810=2010$ 张邮票．

答: 2010 张

5. **解** 因为抽水机排出 12 t/h 海水，海水以 24 t/h 的速率渗入船内．因此船舱内会增加 $24-12=12$ t/h 的水，故知需在 $90÷12=7.5$ h 内抵达港口，即需 7.5 h 行驶 50 km，故至少要以 $\dfrac{50}{7.5}=\dfrac{20}{3}=6\dfrac{2}{3}$ (km/h) 的速度驶向港口．

答: $6\dfrac{2}{3}$ km/h

第1章 2003年第1届国际小学数学竞赛

6. 解法 1 由 X 的值等于它的数码和的 $\dfrac{13}{4}$ 且 13 为素数，故可以得知 X 为 13 的倍数而 X 的数码和必为 4 的倍数．而 13 的两位数倍数中，仅 13、26、39 的数码和为 4 的倍数，且 13+36=49、26+36=62、39+36=75，故知 X 为 26．

解法 2 可令 $X=\overline{ab}=10a+b$，则由 X 的值等于它的数码和的 $\dfrac{13}{4}$ 可以得知 $10a+b=\dfrac{13}{4}(a+b)$，即 $3a=b$；接着再由将 X 加上 36，则所得到的数与 X 的数码相同但两个数码的顺序恰好相反可以得知 $10a+b+36=10b+a$，即 $a=b-4$．因此 $a=3a-4$，故 $a=2$、$b=6$，即 $X=26$．

答：26

7. 解 连接 AC（图 1-8）．因四边形 $ABCD$ 是矩形且 AC 为其对角线，故知 $\triangle ABC$ 与 $\triangle ADC$ 的面积相等，不妨都令其值为 1．

因 $BF=FC$，故 $\triangle ACF$ 的面积为 $\triangle ABC$ 的面积的 $\dfrac{1}{2}$，即矩形 $ABCD$ 面积的 $\dfrac{1}{4}$．因 $DE=6EC$，故 $\triangle ACE$ 的面积为 $\triangle ADC$ 的面积的 $\dfrac{1}{7}$，即矩形 $ABCD$ 面积的 $\dfrac{1}{14}$．

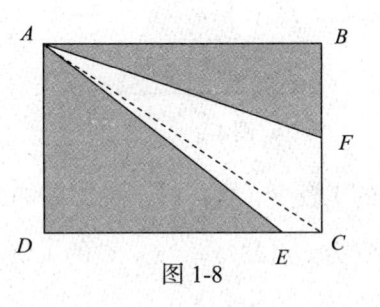

图 1-8

因此可以得知此矩形中未涂阴影部分的面积与涂阴影部分的面积之比为 $\left(\dfrac{1}{4}+\dfrac{1}{14}\right):\left(1-\dfrac{1}{4}-\dfrac{1}{14}\right)=9:19$．

答：9:19

8. 解 令满足题意的两位数为 $\overline{ab}=10a+b$，则由题目所给的条件可知 $10a+b=4(a+b)+3=4a+4b+3$，即 $6a=3b+3$，故得 $b=2a-1$，因此 $(a,b)=(1,1)$、$(2,3)$、$(3,5)$、$(4,7)$ 或 $(5,9)$．而由余数是 3 可知除数需大于 3，即 $a+b>3$，因此满足题意的两位数为 23、35、47 与 59．

答：23、35、47、59

9. 解
$$1^2-2^2+3^2-4^2+\cdots+2001^2-2002^2+2003^2$$
$$=(2003^2-2002^2)+(2001^2-2000^2)+\cdots+(3^2-2^2)+1^2$$
$$=(2003+2002)(2003-2002)+(2001+2000)(2001-2000)+\cdots$$

$$+(3+2)(3-2)+1$$
$$=(2003+2002)+(2001+2000)+\cdots+(3+2)+1$$
$$=\frac{(1+2003)\times 2003}{2}$$
$$=2007006.$$

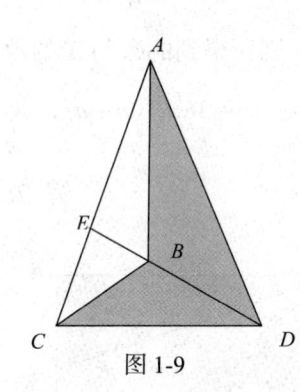

答：2007006

10. 解 因 $\frac{EB}{BD}=\frac{1}{2}$，故知△BCE 面积为△BCD 面积的 $\frac{1}{2}$，以及△ABE 面积为△ABD 面积的 $\frac{1}{2}$. 故 △ABC 的面积为涂阴影部分的面积的 $\frac{1}{2}$，即 $42\times\frac{1}{2}=21(cm^2)$ (图 1-9).

图 1-9

答：21 cm²

11. 解 可知 A 的工资比 B 的工资多，但比 C 的工资少，故 C 的工资比 B 的工资多. 接着可令 A 的工资为 x，则可知 B 的工资为 $x\div 125\%=\frac{4}{5}x$、C 的工资为 $x\div 90\%=\frac{10}{9}x$，因此可知 C 的工资比 B 的工资多了 $\frac{10}{9}x-\frac{4}{5}x=\frac{14}{45}x$ 元. 此时再由三人的工资合计为 52400 元知 $x+\frac{4}{5}x+\frac{10}{9}x=52400$，即 x=18000，因此 C 的工资比 B 的工资多 $\frac{14}{45}\times 18000=5600$ 元.

答：(1) C；(2) 5600 元

12. 解法 1 因任意摸出一颗珠子，而此珠子恰好是蓝色的概率为 $\frac{9}{11}$，故可令此盒子中共有 11x 颗珠子、蓝珠子为 9x 颗，因此不是蓝色的珠子共有 2x=20+30 颗，即 x=25，故蓝珠子共有 225 颗.

解法 2 令此盒子中共有 x 颗蓝珠子，故知 $\frac{x}{x+20+30}=\frac{9}{11}$，化简后可得 11x=450+9x 颗，即 x=225，故蓝珠子共有 225 颗.

答：225 颗

13. 解 因为 31513 与 34369 除以某个三位数后，所得到的余数相等，故

其差 $34369-31513=2856$ 必为这个三位数的倍数. 因 $2856=2^3\times3\times7\times17$, 故此三位数可能为 102、119、136、168、204、238、357、408、476、714 及 952, 任意选择其中一个代入运算可得余数为 97.

答：97

14. **解** 因 48 为 2、3 的倍数但不为 5 的倍数, 故 48 必须填在圆 B、C 的交集内但不能填在圆 A 内；

因 102 为 2、3 的倍数但不为 5 的倍数, 故 102 必须填在圆 B、C 的交集内但不能填在圆 A 内；

因 112 为 2 的倍数但不为 3、5 的倍数, 故 1348 必须填在圆 B 内但不能填在圆 A、C 的圆内；

因 207 为 3 的倍数但不为 2、5 的倍数, 故 207 必须填在圆 C 内但不能填在圆 A、B 的圆内；

因 750 为 2、3、5 的倍数, 故 750 必须填在三圆的交集内；

因 930 为 2、3、5 的倍数, 故 930 必须填在三圆的交集内；

因 1348 为 2 的倍数但不为 3、5 的倍数, 故 112 必须填在圆 B 内但不能填在圆 A、C 的圆内；

因 1605 为 3、5 的倍数而不是 2 的倍数, 故 1605 必须填在圆 A、C 的交集内但不能填在圆 B 内.

因 1749 为 3 的倍数而不是 2、5 的倍数, 故 1749 必须填在圆 C 内但不能填在圆 A 与圆 B 内；

因 2001 为 3 的倍数而不是 2、5 的倍数, 故 2001 必须填在圆 C 内但不能填在圆 A 与圆 B 内；

因 2025 为 3、5 的倍数而不是 2 的倍数, 故 2025 必须填在圆 A、C 的交集内但不能填在圆 B 内；

因 2030 为 2、5 的倍数而不是 3 的倍数, 故 2030 必须填在圆 A、B 的交集内但不能填在圆 C 内；

因 3250 为 2、5 的倍数而不是 3 的倍数, 故 3250 必须填在圆 A、B 的交集内但不能填在圆 C 内；

因 7893 为 3 的倍数而不是 2、5 的倍数, 故 7893 必须填在圆 C 内但不能填在圆 A 与圆 B 内.

综上所述, 可得到如图 1-10 所示的填法.

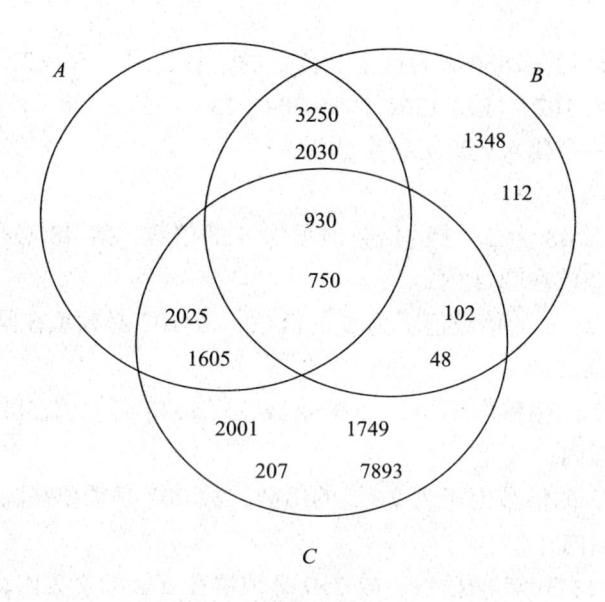

```
              A                              B
                    3250
                    2030              1348
                                      112
                          930
                          750
                 2025            102
                 1605            48
                       2001  1749
                       207   7893
                         C
```

图 1-10

15. **解**　令该式为 $\overline{abcde} \times \overline{fgh} \times k$．可判断出要使乘积为最大必须 a、f、k 是 7、8、9，而 b、g 是 5、6，以及 c、h 是 3、4，此时知 $\overline{de} = 21$．当 k 固定，$\overline{abc}$ 与 $\overline{fgh}$ 两数之和相等时，知此两数越接近时，其乘积越大，故取 $k=9$、$\overline{abc} = 764$、$\overline{fgh} = 853$ 时乘积最大，即乘积最大的乘式为 $76421 \times 853 \times 9$．

答：$76421 \times 853 \times 9$

1.4　EMIC 队际赛英文试题

Elementary Mathematics International Contest 2003
8th September, 2003, Nakhon Pathom, Thailand

Team Contest

1. On quadrilateral $ABCD$, points M, N, P and Q are located on AB, BC, CD and DA, respectively. The ratios of distance are as follows:

　　　$AM : MB = 3 : 5$；　$BN : NC = 1 : 3$；
　　　$CP : PD = 4 : 5$；　$DQ : QA = 1 : 8$.

What is ratio of the area of $MBNPDQ$ to the area of $ABCD$?

第1章 2003年第1届国际小学数学竞赛

2. Peter had 144 books and donated them to four schools. When Peter checked the number of books given to each school, he found out that the difference of the number of books between School *A* and School *B* was 4; between School *B* and School *C* was 3; between School *C* and School *D* was 2. School *A* had the most number of books, but received less than 40 books.

(a) In how many ways could Peter allot the books to School *B* and School *D*, according to all conditions?

(b) How many books will School *B* and School *D* each get?

3. The area of quadrilateral *ABCD* is 6174 cm^2. Points *E* and *F* are the midpoints of *AB* and *CD*, while *G* and *H* are the points on *BC* and *AD* respectively, such that *CG=2GB* and *AH=2HD*. What is the area of *EGFH*?

4. How many trailing zeros are there in the product of $1×2×3×4×5×\cdots×2003$? (Example: 10200000 has 5 trailing zeros)

5. Alloy *M* is composed of 95% bronze, 4% tin and 1% zinc. Alloy *N* is composed of bronze and tin only. If alloy *M* is mixed with alloy *N* in equal proportion, a new alloy is formed, which has 86% bronze, 13.6% tin and 0.4% zinc. What is the percentage of bronze in alloy *N*? (Note: alloy is a mixture of metals)

6. An uncovered tank of water has the capacity 43.12 m^3. The inner diameter of the tank is 2.8 meters. The walls and the base of the tank have a uniform thickness of 0.1 m. If it costs 80 baht per square meter to paint the tank, calculate the cost of painting the total surface area. (Note: Baht is the Thai currency) $\left(\text{Given } \pi = \frac{22}{7} \text{ and answer to 2 decimals places}\right)$ (Hint: Remember to include all surfaces)

7. There are three numbers: 3945, 4686 and 5598. When they are divided by *X*, the remainder is the same for each. What is the sum of the *X* and the common remainder?

8. *ABCD* is a rectangle, with *AB*=4 cm. The area of rectangle *ABCD* is equal to the area of the semicircle with radius *AB*. Find the length *EG*. ($\pi = 3.14$)

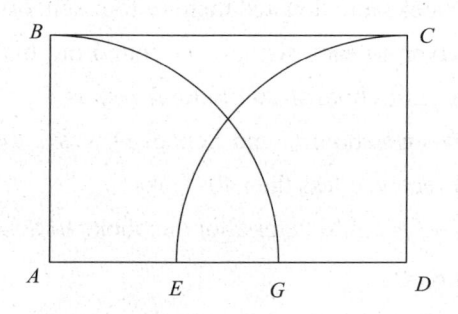

9. In a box of 12 different colored crayons, one of them is black. In how many different ways can the teacher give these crayons to a student so that the student receives at least one black? (Note: A student may receive from 1–12 crayons)

10. How many seven-digit numbers contain the digit '7' at least once?

1.5　EMIC队际赛中文试题

2003 年国际小学数学竞赛队际竞赛试题

1. 在四边形 ABCD 中，点 M, N, P 和 Q 分别是边 AB, BC, CD 和 DA 上的点，且各线段的比如下：

$$AM:MB=3:5, \quad BN:NC=1:3,$$
$$CP:PD=4:5, \quad DQ:QA=1:8.$$

请问六边形 MBNPDQ 与四边形 ABCD 的面积比是什么？

2. 小王将 144 本书捐赠给四所学校．小王清点捐赠给各学校的书的本数时，发现学校 A 与学校 B 相差 4 本，学校 B 与学校 C 相差 3 本，学校 C 和学校 D 相差 2 本．学校 A 得到的书最多但总数不超过 40 本．在满足上述条件下，请问

(1) 小王有多少种不同的方法将书捐给学校 B 和学校 D？

(2) 学校 B 和学校 D 各得到多少本书？

3. 已知四边形 ABCD 的面积是 6174 cm^2，点 E 和 F 分别是 AB 和 CD 边上的中点，G 和 H 分别是 BC 和 AD 边上的点，且有 CG=2GB，AH=2HD．请问四边形 EGFH 的面积为多少 cm^2？

4. 请问乘积 1×2×3×4×5×⋯×2003 的值之末尾共有多少个零？(注：例如，

第1章 2003年第1届国际小学数学竞赛

数 10200000 的末尾一共有 5 个零)

5. 已知合金 M 含铜 95%、含锡 4%、含锌 1%；合金 N 只含有铜和锡．如果将合金 M 与合金 N 混合制成新的合金，在此新的合金中含铜 86%、含锡 13.6%、含锌 0.4%．请问合金 N 中含有百分之多少的铜？（注：合金指的是由不同种金属混合制成的新物质）

6. 有一个容积为 43.12 m³ 的无盖圆桶，它的桶壁和桶底的厚度都是 0.1 m，内部的圆之直径为 2.8 m．如果将此桶漆上油漆，每平方米的费用为 80 元，请问将此桶内部及外部的所有表面都涂上油漆共需要多少元？（令 $\pi = \dfrac{22}{7}$，计算至小数第二位）（请注意：要包括所有的表面积）

7. 已知三个数 3945、4686 和 5598，将它们都除以数 X 时，所得的余数都等于 Y．请问 X+Y 之可能值是什么？

8. 如图 1-11 所示，四边形 ABCD 是矩形，AB=4 cm，矩形 ABCD 的面积等于以 AB 长为半径的圆的面积的一半．请问线段 EG 的长度是多少 cm？（令 $\pi = 3.14$）

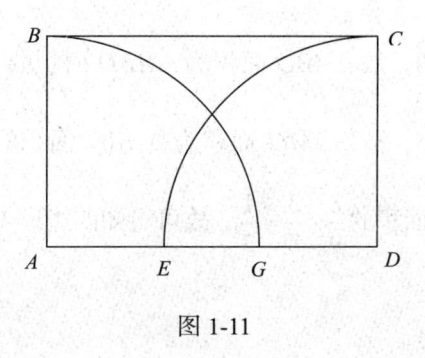

图 1-11

9. 一个盒子中装有 12 支颜色都互不相同的彩色笔，其中 1 支是黑色的，老师欲将这 12 支不同颜色的彩色笔分给小李，若小李得到的彩色笔中必须有一支是黑色的．请问老师有多少种不同的方法将彩色笔分送给小李？（注：小李可能得到 1 至 12 支不同颜色的彩色笔．小李所得到的彩色笔中只要有一支颜色不同就视为是不同的分送方法）

10. 在七位数的正整数中，请问有多少个数的各位数码中至少有一个数码是 7？

1.6 EMIC队际赛试题解答与评注

2003年国际小学数学竞赛队际竞赛试题解答

1. 解法1 如图1-12所示，连接 BQ、BD、BP.

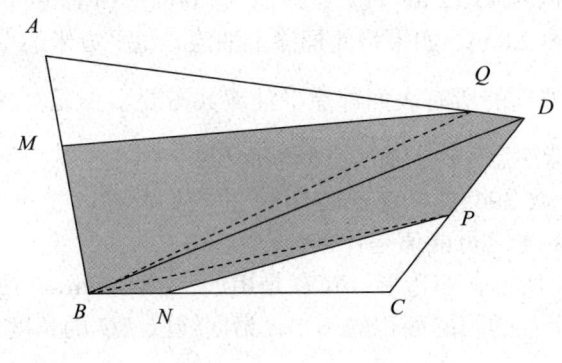

图1-12

因 $QD:AQ=1:8$，故 $\triangle ABQ$ 面积为 $\triangle ABD$ 面积的 $\dfrac{8}{8+1}=\dfrac{8}{9}$；

因 $AM:MB=3:5$，故 $\triangle AMQ$ 面积为 $\triangle ABQ$ 面积的 $\dfrac{3}{3+5}=\dfrac{3}{8}$；由此可知 $\triangle AMQ$ 面积为 $\triangle ABD$ 面积的 $\dfrac{8}{9} \times \dfrac{3}{8}=\dfrac{1}{3}$，故可得知四边形 $MBDQ$ 的面积为 $\triangle ABD$ 面积的 $1-\dfrac{1}{3}=\dfrac{2}{3}$.

因 $CP:PD=4:5$，故 $\triangle BCP$ 面积为 $\triangle BCD$ 面积的 $\dfrac{4}{4+5}=\dfrac{4}{9}$；因 $CN:NB=3:1$，故 $\triangle NCP$ 面积为 $\triangle BCP$ 面积的 $\dfrac{3}{3+1}=\dfrac{3}{4}$；由此可知 $\triangle NCP$ 面积为 $\triangle BCD$ 面积的 $\dfrac{4}{9} \times \dfrac{3}{4}=\dfrac{1}{3}$，故可得知四边形 $BNPD$ 的面积为 $\triangle BCD$ 面积的 $1-\dfrac{1}{3}=\dfrac{2}{3}$.

因此多边形 $MBNPDQ$ 面积为四边形 $ABCD$ 面积的 $\dfrac{2}{3}$，即其面积比为 $2:3$.

解法 2 如图 1-13 所示，连接 BD. 由共角定理知 $\triangle AMQ$ 面积为 $\triangle ABD$ 面积的 $\frac{8}{9} \times \frac{3}{8} = \frac{1}{3}$；$\triangle NCP$ 面积为 $\triangle BCD$ 面积的 $\frac{4}{9} \times \frac{3}{4} = \frac{1}{3}$，故六边形 $MBNPDQ$ 面积为四边形 $ABCD$ 面积的 $1 - \frac{1}{3} = \frac{2}{3}$，即其面积比为 $2：3$.

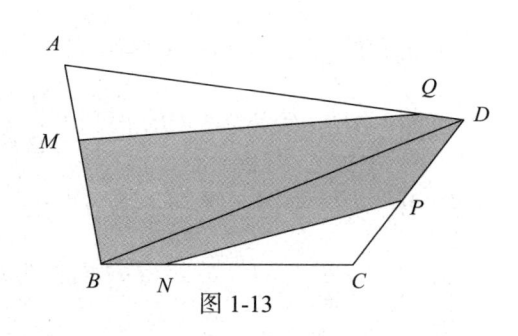

图 1-13

答：$2：3$.

2. 解 可假设学校 A 得到 a 本，且 $a<40$. 因学校 A 得到的书最多，故知学校 B 只可能得到 $a-4$ 本. 此时可依照题意得表 1-1.

表 1-1

学校A得到书数	a			
学校B得到书数	$a-4$			
学校C得到书数	$a-4+3=a-1$		$a-4-3=a-7$	
学校D得到书数	$a-1+2=a+1>a$ (不符合)	$a-1-2$ $=a-3$	$a-7+2$ $=a-5$	$a-7-2$ $=a-9$
合计		$4a-8=144$	$4a-16=144$	$4a-20=144$
a 的值		38	40 (不符合)	41 (不符合)

因学校 A 得到的书最多，故知学校 D 得到 $a+1$ 本的情况不符合；再由 $a<40$ 知学校 D 得到 $a-5$ 本、$a-9$ 本的情况也不符合，故仅学校 D 得到 $a-3$ 本这一种情况可满足条件，即学校 A 得到 38 本、学校 B 得到 38-4=34 本、学校 C 得到 38-1=37 本、学校 D 得到 38-3=35 本.

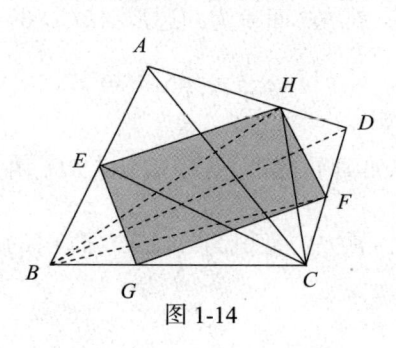

答：(1) 1 种方法；(2) 学校 B 得到 34 本、学校 D 得到 35 本

3. 解法 1 如图 1-14 所示，连接 AC、EC、HC、BD、BH、BF.

可知 $AE：EB=1：1$，故 $\triangle BCE$ 面积为

图 1-14

△ABC 面积的 $\frac{1}{2}$；又因 BG∶GC=1∶2，故△BGE 面积为△BCE 面积的 $\frac{1}{1+2}=\frac{1}{3}$；由此可知△BGE 面积为△ABC 面积的 $\frac{1}{2}\times\frac{1}{3}=\frac{1}{6}$.

因 AH∶HD=2∶1，故△CDH 面积为△ACD 面积的 $\frac{1}{2+1}=\frac{1}{3}$；

因 CF∶FB=1∶1，故△FDH 面积为△CDH 面积的 $\frac{1}{1+1}=\frac{1}{2}$；

由此可知△FDH 面积为△ACD 面积的 $\frac{1}{3}\times\frac{1}{2}=\frac{1}{6}$.

因此△BGE 与△FDH 面积合计为四边形 ABCD 的 $\frac{1}{6}$.

因 AH∶HD=2∶1，故△ABH 面积为△ABD 面积的 $\frac{2}{2+1}=\frac{2}{3}$；可知 AE∶EB=1∶1，故△AEH 面积为△ABH 面积的 $\frac{1}{1+1}=\frac{1}{2}$；由此可知△AEH 面积为△ABD 面积的 $\frac{2}{3}\times\frac{1}{2}=\frac{1}{3}$.

因 CF∶FB=1∶1，故△BCF 面积为△BCD 面积的 $\frac{1}{1+1}=\frac{1}{2}$；可知 BG∶GC=1∶2，故△GCF 面积为△BCF 面积的 $\frac{2}{1+2}=\frac{2}{3}$；由此可知△GCF 面积为△BCD 面积的 $\frac{1}{2}\times\frac{2}{3}=\frac{1}{3}$.

因此△AEH 与△GCF 面积合计为四边形 ABCD 的 $\frac{1}{3}$.

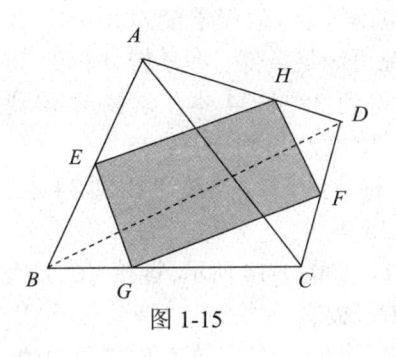

故四边形 EGFH 面积为四边形 ABCD 的 $1-\frac{1}{6}-\frac{1}{3}=\frac{1}{2}$，即 $6174\times\frac{1}{2}=3087$ (cm²).

解法 2 如图 1-15 所示，连接 AC、BD. 由共角定理知△FDH 面积为△ACD 面积的 $\frac{1}{3}\times\frac{1}{2}=\frac{1}{6}$；

图 1-15

第1章 2003年第1届国际小学数学竞赛

△BGE 面积为△ABC 面积的 $\frac{1}{3} \times \frac{1}{2} = \frac{1}{6}$；因此△BGE 与△FDH 面积合计为四边形 ABCD 的 $\frac{1}{6}$.

同理可知△AEH 面积为△ABD 面积的 $\frac{2}{3} \times \frac{1}{2} = \frac{1}{3}$；△GCF 面积为△BCD 面积的 $\frac{1}{2} \times \frac{2}{3} = \frac{1}{3}$. 因此△AEH 与△GCF 面积合计为四边形 ABCD 的 $\frac{1}{3}$.

故四边形 EGFH 面积为四边形 ABCD 的 $1-\frac{1}{6}-\frac{1}{3}=\frac{1}{2}$，即 $6174 \times \frac{1}{2} = 3087$ (cm²).

答：3087 cm²

4．解 要求值的末尾有多少个零即为求出该值的所有因子中，10 的幂次最高为多少．因 10=2×5，而在此乘积的素因子分解式中，明显可知 2 的幂次必多于 5 的幂次，故此乘积的素因子分解式中 5 的幂次即为值的末尾零的个数．

因 2003=5×400+3，故共有 400 个数是 5 的倍数；
因 2003=25×80+3，故共有 80 个数是 $5^2=25$ 的倍数；
因 2003=125×16+3，故共有 16 个数是 $5^3=125$ 的倍数；
因 2003=625×3+128，故共有 3 个数是 $5^4=625$ 的倍数；
因 $5^5>2003$，故不用再考虑 5 的更高次方，且可知此乘积的素因子分解式中 5 的幂次为 400+80+16+3=499.

答：499

5．解 由锌的含量可判断出合金 M 在新的合金中，所占的比值为 $\frac{0.4\%}{1\%} = \frac{4}{10} = \frac{2}{5}$，故知可令合金 M 为 2 单位、合金 N 为 3 单位，则知合金 M 及新的合金中，铜依序为 2×95%=1.9 单位以及 5×86%=4.3 单位，故合金 N 中铜依序为 4.3−1.9=2.4 单位，也由此知合金 N 中含铜 $2.4 \div 3 = 80\%$．

答：80%

6．解 可以得知内圆的面积为 $\pi \times \left(\frac{2.8}{2}\right)^2 = 1.96\pi$ (m²)，内圆的周长为 2.8π m、外圆的面积为 $\pi \times \left(\frac{2.8}{2}+0.1\right)^2 = 2.25\pi$ (m²)，外圆的周长为 (2.8+0.1×

2)π = 3π (m)，故圆桶内的高为 $\frac{43.12}{1.96\pi} = \frac{22}{\pi} = 7$ (m)，接着便可得知内壁的表面积为 $7 \times 2.8\pi = 2.8 \times 22 = 61.6$ (m²)、外壁的表面积为 $(7+0.1) \times 3\pi = \frac{468.6}{7}$ (m²)、上缘的面积为 $2.25\pi - 1.96\pi = 0.29\pi$ (m²). 故可知将此桶内部及外部的所有表面都涂上油漆共需

$$80 \times \left(0.29\pi + 61.6 + \frac{468.6}{7} + 2.25\pi + 1.96\pi\right)$$

$$= 80 \times \left(4.5 \times \frac{22}{7} + \frac{889.8}{7}\right) = 11414.86（元）$$

答：11414.86 元

7. 解　因三个数除以 X 后，所得余数都相等，故知三数彼此相减，都为 X 的倍数，即 X 为 5598−4686=912、5598−3945=1653、4686−3945=741 的公因子．

因 $912 = 2^4 \times 3 \times 19$、$1653 = 3 \times 19 \times 29$、$741 = 3 \times 13 \times 19$，故知 X 可为 1、3、19 或 $3 \times 19 = 57$．

若 $X=1$，则 $Y=0$，即 $X+Y=1$；
若 $X=3$，则 $Y=0$，即 $X+Y=3$；
若 $X=19$，则 $Y=12$，即 $X+Y=31$；
若 $X=57$，则 $Y=12$，即 $X+Y=69$．

答：1、3、31 或 69

8. 解　以 AB 长为半径的圆的面积为 3.14×4^2 (cm²)，故知矩形 $ABCD$ 面积为 $3.14 \times 4^2 \times \frac{1}{2}$ (cm²)，因此可得知 AD 长度为 $3.14 \times 4^2 \times \frac{1}{2} \div 4 = 2 \times 3.14 = 6.28$ (cm)；由图可知 $AG=ED=4$ (cm)，故 EG 长度为 $AG+ED−AD=4+4−6.28=1.72$ (cm)．

答：1.72 cm

9. 解法 1　因小李得到的彩色笔中必须有一支是黑色的，故知
若小李得到 1 支笔，则只有 1 种方法；
若小李得到 2 支笔，则有 $C_{11}^1 = 11$ 种方法；
若小李得到 3 支笔，则有 $C_{11}^2 = \frac{11 \times 10}{2} = 55$ 种方法；
若小李得到 4 支笔，则有 $C_{11}^3 = \frac{11 \times 10 \times 9}{3 \times 2} = 165$ 种方法；

若小李得到 5 支笔，则有 $C_{11}^4 = \dfrac{11 \times 10 \times 9 \times 8}{4 \times 3 \times 2} = 330$ 种方法；

若小李得到 6 支笔，则有 $C_{11}^5 = \dfrac{11 \times 10 \times 9 \times 8 \times 6}{5 \times 4 \times 3 \times 2} = 462$ 种方法；

若小李得到 7 支笔，则有 $C_{11}^6 = \dfrac{11 \times 10 \times 9 \times 8 \times 6}{5 \times 4 \times 3 \times 2} = 462$ 种方法；

若小李得到 8 支笔，则有 $C_{11}^7 = \dfrac{11 \times 10 \times 9 \times 8}{4 \times 3 \times 2} = 330$ 种方法；

若小李得到 9 支笔，则有 $C_{11}^8 = \dfrac{11 \times 10 \times 9}{3 \times 2} = 165$ 种方法；

若小李得到 10 支笔，则有 $C_{11}^9 = \dfrac{11 \times 10}{2} = 55$ 种方法；

若小李得到 11 支笔，则有 $C_{11}^{10} = 11$ 种方法；

若小李得到 12 支笔，则只有 1 种方法．

合计共有 1+11+55+165+330+462+462+330+165+55+11+1=2048 种不同的方法．

解法 2 因小李得到的彩色笔中必须有一支是黑色的，故知对于其他 11 支笔，都有可能分给小李或不分给小李两种情况，故知共有 $2^{11} = 2048$ 种不同的方法．

答: 2048 种

10. **解** 可知七位数的正整数共有 9999999 − 999999 = 9000000 个，其中完全没有 7 的正整数个数可利用以下方式来考虑：因首位数不可为 0 与 7，故首位数有 8 种选择，而其余的位数不可为 7，故有 9 种选择．故完全没有 7 的正整数共有 8×9×9×9×9×9×9 = 4251528 个．由此知共有 9000000 − 4251528 = 4748472 个数且它的各位数码中至少有一个数码是 7．

答: 4748472 个

第 2 章 2004 年第 2 届国际小学数学竞赛

2.1 EMIC 个人赛英文试题

Elementary Mathematics International Contest 2004
10th September, 2004, Lucknow, India

Individual Contest

1. There are 5 trucks. Trucks A and B each carry 3 tons. Trucks C and D each carry 4.5 tons. Truck E carries 1 ton more than the average load of all the trucks. How many tons does truck E carry?

2. Let
$$A=200320032003\times 2004200420042004 \text{ and}$$
$$B=200420042004\times 2003200320032003.$$
Find $A-B$.

3. There are 5 boxes. Each box contains either green or red marbles only. The numbers of marbles in the boxes are 110, 105, 100, 115 and 130 respectively. If one box is taken away, the number of green marbles in the remaining boxes will be 3 times the number of red marbles. How many marbles are there in the box that is taken away?

4. Find the smallest natural number which when multiplied by 123 will yield a product that ends in 2004.

5. Peter has a weigh balance with two pans. He also has one 200 g weight and one 1000 g weight. He wants to take 600 g of sugar out of a pack containing 2000 g of sugar. What is the minimum number of moves to accomplish this task?

6. It takes 6 minutes to fry each side of a fish in a frying pan. Only 4 fish can be fried at a time. What is the minimum number of minutes needed to fry 5 fish on both sides?

7. John and Carlson take turns to pick candies from a bag. John picks 1 candy,

第2章 2004年第2届国际小学数学竞赛

Carlson 2 candies, John 3, Carlson 4 and so forth. After a while there are too few candies to continue and so the boy whose turn it is, takes all the remaining candies. When all the candies are picked, John has 1012 candies in total. What was the original number of candies in the bag?

8. There are five positive numbers. The sum of the first and the fifth number is 13. The second number is one-third of the sum of these five numbers, the third number is one-fourth of this sum and the fourth number is one-fifth of this sum. What is the value of the largest number?

9. In a class of students, 80% participated in basketball, 85% participated in football, 74% participated in baseball, 68% participated in volleyball. What is the minimum percent of the students who participated in all the four sports events?

10. Three digit numbers such as 986, 852 and 741 have digits in decreasing order. But 342, 551, 622 are not in decreasing order. Each number in the following sequence is composed of three digits:

$$100, 101, 102, 103, \cdots, 997, 998, 999.$$

How many three digit numbers in the given sequence have digits in decreasing order?

11. In the following figure, the black ball moves one position at a time clockwise. The white ball moves two positions at a time counter-clockwise. In how many moves will they meet again?

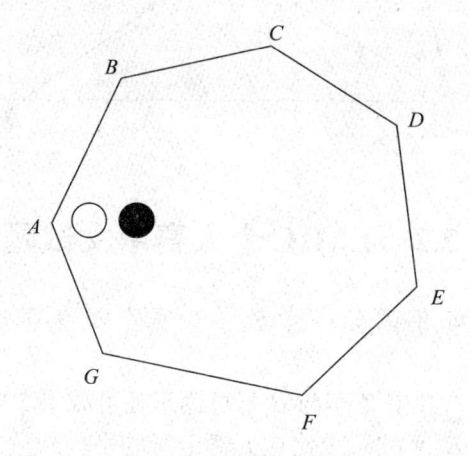

12. Compute: $1^2 - 2^2 + 3^2 - 4^2 + \cdots - 2002^2 + 2003^2 - 2004^2 + 2005^2$.

13. During recess one of the five pupils wrote something nasty on the blackboard. When questioned by the class teacher, they answered in following order:

A: "It was B and C."

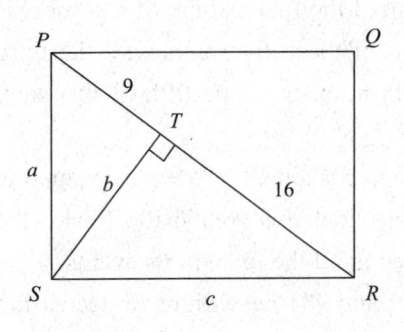

B: "Neither E nor I did it."

C: "A and B are both lying."

D: "Either A or B is telling the truth."

E: "D is not telling the truth."

The class teacher knows that three of them never lie while the other two may lie. Who wrote it?

14. In the figure below, PQRS is a rectangle. What is the value of $a+b+c$?

15. In the following figure, if $CA=CE$, what is the value of x?

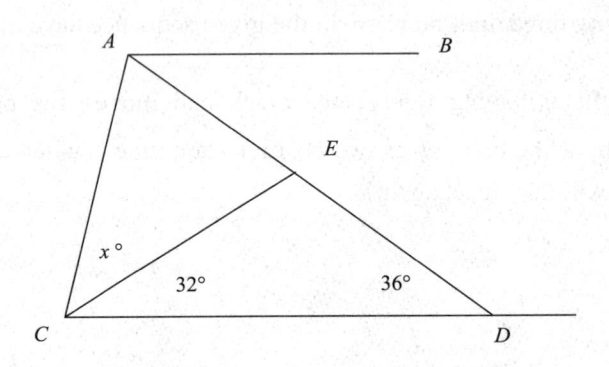

2.2 EMIC个人赛中文试题

2004年国际小学数学竞赛个人竞赛试题

1. 有五辆卡车，其中 A 车与 B 车每辆车各可载重 3 吨，C 车与 D 车每辆车各可载重 4.5 吨，E 车的载重比这五辆卡车的平均载重多 1 吨. 请问 E 车的载重是多少吨？

第 2 章 2004 年第 2 届国际小学数学竞赛

2. 令
$$A=200320032003×2004200420042004$$ 且
$$B=200420042004×2003200320032003.$$
请问 $A-B$ 的值是多少？

3. 有五个箱子，箱内只装有红色或绿色珠子，每个箱子内所装的珠子的数量分别为 110、105、100、115 及 130 颗．若从中拿走一个箱子，则剩下的四个箱子内绿色珠子的总数是红色珠子的总数的三倍．请问拿走的箱子内共有多少颗珠子？

4. 将一个正整数 x 乘以 123 所得的乘积的最后四位数为 2004．请问满足上述条件的数中，x 的最小值是多少？

5. 彼得有一座两臂天平、一个 200 克的砝码及一个 1000 克的砝码．他想从一袋 2000 克的糖中取出 600 克的糖，若将天平平衡时视为称一次，请问他最少要使用此天平称几次？

6. 一个平底锅可以同时煎四条鱼，要煎熟一条鱼的其中一面需费时 6 分钟．现欲将五条鱼的两个面都用这个锅子煎熟，请问最少需要多少分钟？

7. 小杰及小克轮流从一个纸袋内取糖，先由小杰开始取 1 颗糖，接着由小克取 2 颗糖，然后小杰取 3 颗糖，小克取 4 颗糖，…．若袋子内所剩的糖果的颗数少于应取的数量时，则可将剩下的这些糖全部取走．当纸袋内的糖全部分完后，小杰共取得 1012 颗糖．请问纸袋内原有多少颗糖？

8. 有五个正整数，第一个数与第五个数之和为 13；第二个数是这五个数总和的 $\frac{1}{3}$；第三个数是这五个数总和的 $\frac{1}{4}$；第四个数是这五个数总和的 $\frac{1}{5}$．请问这五个正整数中最大的数是多少？

9. 某班的学生中，有 80% 的学生参加篮球赛；有 85% 的学生参加足球赛；有 74% 的学生参加棒球赛；有 68% 的学生参加排球赛．请问这四种球赛都参加的学生至少有百分之多少？

10. 像 986、852 及 741 这样的三位数，它们的各位数码越来越小，我们称这种数为"吉祥数"，而 342、551 及 622 则不是"吉祥数"．请问在 100、101、102、103、…、997、998、999 的三位数中总共有多少个"吉祥数"？

11. 在图 2-1 中，黑球每次依顺时针方向移动一个位置；白球每次依逆时针方向移动两个位置．若此两球同时由 A 点出发，请问移动多少次之后它们会再度相遇于同一点上？

图2-1

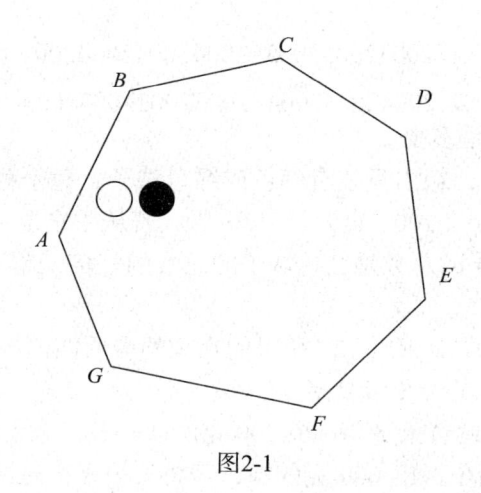

12. 请问 $1^2 - 2^2 + 3^2 - 4^2 + \cdots - 2002^2 + 2003^2 - 2004^2 + 2005^2$ 的值是多少?

13. 下课时五位同学之一在黑板上写了一些脏话,当老师质问这五位学生时,他们依序作了以下的回答:

A:"是 B 或 C 写的."

B:"不是 E 也不是我写的."

C:"A 和 B 两个人都说谎."

D:"A 或 B 说实话."

E:"D 没有说实话."

老师知道这些学生中有三位从来都不说谎,而其他两位则可能说谎. 请问黑板上的脏话是谁写的?

14. 在图2-2中,PQRS 是个矩形. 请问 $a+b+c$ 的值是多少?

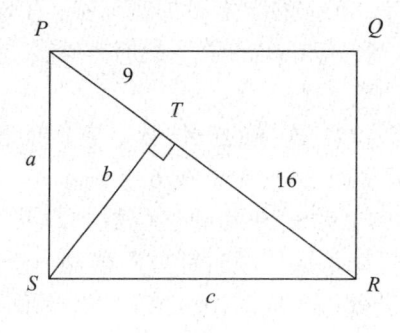

图2-2

第 2 章　2004 年第 2 届国际小学数学竞赛

15. 在图2-3中，若 $CA=CE$，请问 x 的值是多少？

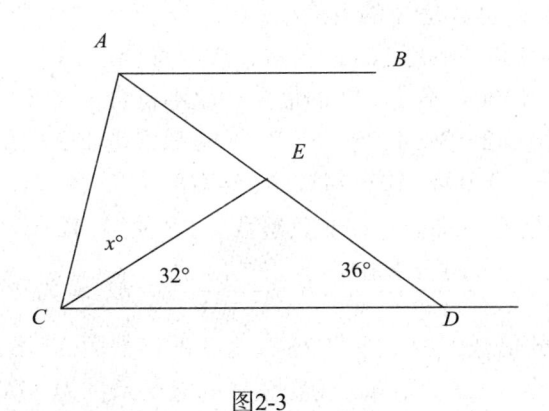

图2-3

2.3　EMIC个人赛试题解答与评注

2004 年国际小学数学竞赛个人竞赛试题解答

1. **解**　由 E 车的载重比这五辆卡车的平均载重多 1 吨可知其余四车的总载重比平均载重的 4 倍少 1 吨，所以知平均载重为 $\frac{3+3+4.5+4.5+1}{4}=\frac{16}{4}=4$ 吨，故 E 车的载重为 4+1=5 吨.

答：5 吨

2. **解**　可知

$$A = 2003 \times 100010001 \times 2004 \times 1001000010001$$
$$= 2003 \times 2004 \times 100010001 \times 1001000010001,$$
$$B = 2004 \times 100010001 \times 2003 \times 1001000010001$$
$$= 2003 \times 2004 \times 100010001 \times 1001000010001,$$

故知 $A-B=0$.

答：0

3. **解**　因绿色珠子的总数是红色珠子的总数的三倍，故珠子总数为 4 的倍数. 因 110+105+100+115+130=560 也是 4 的倍数，故拿走的箱子内部装有的珠子数也必为 4 的倍数，故知拿走的箱子内总共有 100 颗珠子.

答：100颗

4. **解法 1** 若 x 的值最小，则其乘积 $123x = A \times 10^4 + 2004$ 的值也最小，其中 A 为非负整数，也就是 A 的值最小．

当 $A=0$ 时，2004 不是 123 的倍数，故不符合．

当 $A=1$ 时，12004 不是 123 的倍数，故不符合．

同样地，当 $A=2$、3、4、5、6、7、8 时都不是 123 的倍数，故都不符合．

而当 $A=9$ 时，$92004 \div 123 = 748$，故 $x=748$．

解法 2 由题意可知必存在非负整数 A、B 使得 $123x = A \times 10^4 + 2004$，移项后即可得知 $x = \dfrac{A \times 10^4 + 2004}{123} = B + \dfrac{37A + 36}{123}$，故 x 为正整数的充要条件为 $37A+36$ 为 123 的倍数．因 123 与 36 都为 3 的倍数而 37 不是，故知 A 必须为 3 的倍数，即可令 $A=3K$，则知 x 为正整数的充要条件为 $37K+12$ 为 41 的倍数；因 41 的倍数依序为 41、82、123、…，其中最小可写成 $37K+12$ 这形式的数为 $123 = 37 \times 3 + 12$，故知 $K=3$、$A=9$，此时 $x = \dfrac{92004}{123} = 748$．

答：748

5. **解** 因将天平平衡时视为称一次，则可先将 1000 克砝码置于左秤、200 克的砝码与 2000 克的糖置于右秤，此时天平必不平衡，若要平衡则是两边各重 1600 克，故可将右秤的部分糖取出置于左秤，平衡时即加了 1600−1000=600 克的糖至左秤，此时便已取出 600 克的糖，故称一次即可．

答：1 次

6. **解** 五条鱼都要煎熟的总时数为 $(6+6) \times 5 = 60$ 分钟，而在锅子都摆满了四条鱼同时煎时，相当于每分钟有煎四分钟的效率，因此所需使用时间最少为 $60 \div 4 = 15$ 分钟．

令这五条鱼的正面分别为 A、B、C、D、E，反面分别为 a、b、c、d、e，则可利用以下方式用 15 分钟煎熟：$(A、B、C、D)$，$(B、C、D、E)$，$(c、d、E、A)$，$(d、e、a、b)$，$(e、a、b、c)$ 各煎 3 分钟．

答：15 分钟

7. **解** 可知小杰取的个数除了最后一次以外，其余为从 1 开始的连续奇数．因从 1 开始的连续奇数和为一个完全平方数，且计算后知 $31^2 = 961 < 1012 < 32^2 = 1024$，故知小杰的倒数第二次为他第 31 次取糖，亦即他倒数第二次取了 $2 \times 31 - 1 = 61$ 颗糖，小杰最后一次取 1012−961=51 颗，且可推知小克最后一次取 62 颗．因此纸袋内原有

28

第 2 章 2004 年第 2 届国际小学数学竞赛

$$(1+2+3+\cdots+60+61+62)+51 = \frac{62\times 63}{2}+51 = 2004 \text{ 颗}.$$

答：2004颗

8. 解 由题目所述条件知可令五个数总和为 $60A$，则第二个数为 $20A$、第三个数为 $15A$、第四个数为 $12A$，故第一个数与第五个数之总和为 $60A-20A-15A-12A=13A$，即知 $A=1$，因此知第二个数为 20，而其他的数都小于 20，所以这五个数中最大数为 20.

答：20

9. 解 由 80% 的学生参加篮球赛、85%的学生参加足球赛知至少有 85%–(1–80%) =65%的学生同时参加篮球赛与足球赛，再由已知有 74%的学生参加棒球赛知至少有 74%–(1–65%) =39%的学生同时参加篮球赛、足球赛与棒球赛，接着再由有 68%的学生参加排球赛知至少有 68%– (1–39%) =7%的学生同时参加四种球赛.

答：7%

10. 解法1 令 $\overline{abc}$ 为三位数的吉祥数. 可知 $1 \leqslant b \leqslant 8$：

若 $b=1$，则 a 只能是 2、3、4、…、9 这 8 种选择而 c 只能是 0 这 1 种选择，即共有 8×1=8 个这样的吉祥数；

若 $b=2$，则 a 只能是 3、4、5、…、9 这 7 种选择而 c 只能是 0、1 这 2 种选择，即共有 7×2=14 个这样的吉祥数；

若 $b=3$，则 a 只能是 4、5、…、9 这 6 种选择而 c 只能是 0、1、2 这 3 种选择，即共有 6×3=18 个这样的吉祥数；

若 $b=4$，则 a 只能是 5、6、7、8、9 这 5 种选择而 c 只能是 0、1、2、3 这 4 种选择，即共有 5×4=20 个这样的吉祥数；

若 $b=5$，则 a 只能是 6、7、8、9 这 4 种选择而 c 只能是 0、1、2、3、4 这 5 种选择，即共有 4×5=20 个这样的吉祥数；

若 $b=6$，则 a 只能是 7、8、9 这 3 种选择而 c 只能是 0、1、2、3、4、5 这 6 种选择，即共有 3×6=18 个这样的吉祥数；

若 $b=7$，则 a 只能是 8、9 这 2 种选择而 c 只能是 0、1、2、3、4、5、6 这 7 种选择，即共有 2×7=14 个这样的吉祥数；

若 $b=8$，则 a 只能是 9 这 1 种选择而 c 只能是 0、1、2、3、4、5、6、7 这 8 种选择，即共有 1×8=8 个这样的吉祥数.

因此共有 8+14+18+20+20+18+14+8=120 个吉祥数.

解法 2 从 0、1、2、…、8、9 十个数码中任意选三个不相同的数码,然后再将这三个数码由大至小排列,即可得到一个"吉祥数",故共有 $\frac{10 \times 9 \times 8}{3 \times 2}$ = 120 个"吉祥数".

答:120 个

11. **解法 1** 逐次记下移动时两球所在的位置:(黑球,白球):$(B, F) \to (C, D) \to (D, B) \to (E, G) \to (F, E) \to (G, C) \to (A, A)$,故知需移动 7 次才会使两球再度相遇于同一点上.

解法 2 对黑球来说,可将两球在同一点时视为在顺时针方向相距 7 个位置,则知每一次移动两球的距离在顺时针方向都减少 3 个位置. 因 3 与 7 互素,故知需移动 7 次才会使两球再度相遇于同一点上.

答:7 次

12. **解** 原式可改写为

$$2005^2 - 2004^2 + 2003^2 - 2002^2 + \cdots + 3^2 - 2^2 + 1^2$$
$$= (2005 + 2004)(2005 - 2004) + (2003 + 2002)(2003 - 2002)$$
$$\quad + \cdots + (3 + 2)(3 - 2) + 1$$
$$= 2005 + 2004 + 2003 + 2002 + \cdots + 3 + 2 + 1$$
$$= \frac{2006 \times 2005}{2}$$
$$= 2011015.$$

答:2011015

13. **解** 若是 A 写的,则 A 说谎、B 说实话、C 说谎、D 说实话、E 说谎,共 3 人说谎,不符合;

若是 B 写的,则 A 说实话、B 说谎、C 说谎、D 说实话、E 说谎,共 3 人说谎,不符合;

若是 C 写的,则 A 说实话、B 说实话、C 说谎、D 说实话、E 说谎,共 2 人说谎;

若是 D 写的,则 A 说谎、B 说实话、C 说谎、D 说谎、E 实话,共 3 人说谎,不符合;

若是 E 写的,则 A 说谎、B 说实话、C 说实话、D 说谎、E 说实话,共 3 人说谎,不符合.

故可推知是 C 写的.

答: C

14. 解 利用勾股定理可知
$$a^2 = b^2 + 9^2,$$
$$c^2 = b^2 + 16^2,$$
$$(9+16)^2 = a^2 + c^2,$$

故知 $25^2 = 2b^2 + 9^2 + 16^2$，即 $b^2 = \dfrac{25^2 - 9^2 - 16^2}{2} = 144$，由此可知
$$a^2 = b^2 + 9^2 = 144 + 81 = 225,$$
$$c^2 = b^2 + 16^2 = 144 + 256 = 400,$$

所以 $b=12$、$a=15$、$c=20$，因此 $a+b+c=47$.

答: 47

15. 解 可知 $\angle AEC=32°+36°=68°$. 因 $CA=CE$，故 $\angle EAC=\angle AEC=68°$，此时便可得知 $\angle ACE=180°-68°-68°=44°$，故 $x=44$.

答: 44

2.4　EMIC 队际赛英文试题

Elementary Mathematics International Contest 2004
10th September, 2004, Lucknow，India

Team Contest

1. There are three people: grandfather, father and so on. The grandfather's age is an even number. If you invert the order of the digits of the grandfather's age, you get the father's age. When adding the digits of the father's age together, you get the son's age. The sum of the three people's ages is 144. The grandfather's age is less than 100. How old is the grandfather?

2. Three cubes of volume 1 cm³, 8 cm³ and 27 cm³ are glued together at their faces. Find the smallest possible surface area of the resulting configuration.

3. A rectangle is 324 m in length and 141 m in width. Divide it into squares

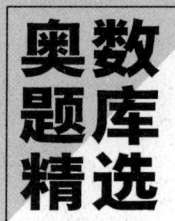

with sides of 141 m, and leave one rectangle with a side less than 141 m. Then divide this new rectangle into smaller squares with sides of the new rectangle's width, leaving a smaller rectangle as before. Repeat until all the figures are squares. What is the length of the side of the smallest square?

4. We have assigned different whole numbers to different letters and then multiplied their values together to make the values of words. For example, if $F=5$, $O=3$ and $X=2$, then $FOX=30$.

Given that $TEEN=52$, $TILT=77$ and $TALL=363$, what is the value of $TATTLE$?

5. If $A=1\times2+2\times3+3\times4+\cdots+98\times99$ and $B=1^2+2^2+3^2+\cdots+97^2+98^2$, what is the value of $A+B$?

6. Nine chairs in a row are to be occupied by six students and Professors Alpha, Beta and Gamma. These three professors arrive before the six students and decide to choose their chairs so that each professor will be between two students. In how many ways can Professors Alpha, Beta and Gamma choose their chairs?

7. Compute: $\dfrac{3}{1}+\dfrac{3}{1+2}+\dfrac{3}{1+2+3}+\cdots+\dfrac{3}{1+2+3+\cdots+100}$.

8. How many different three-digit numbers can satisfy the following multiplication problem?

$$\begin{array}{r} \square\,\square\,\square \\ \times \quad 9\,\square \\ \hline \square\,2\,\square\,\square \end{array}$$

9. There are 16 containers of various shapes in the 4 × 4 array below. Each container has a capacity of 5 litres, but only contains the number of litres as shown in the diagram. The numbers on the sides indicate the total amount of water in the corresponding line of containers. Redistribute the water from only one container to make all the totals equal.

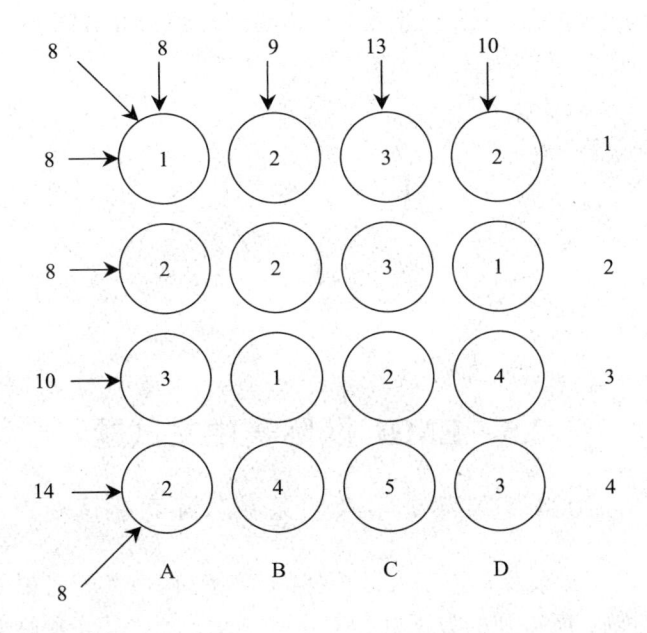

第 2 章 2004 年第 2 届国际小学数学竞赛

```
         8    8    9   13   10
         ↓    ↓    ↓    ↓    ↓
  8  →  (1)  (2)  (3)  (2)      1
  8  →  (2)  (2)  (3)  (1)      2
 10  →  (3)  (1)  (2)  (4)      3
 14  →  (2)  (4)  (5)  (3)      4
         ↑
         A    B    C    D
         8
```

Show your answer by writing the new number of litres in each of the containers in the diagram below.

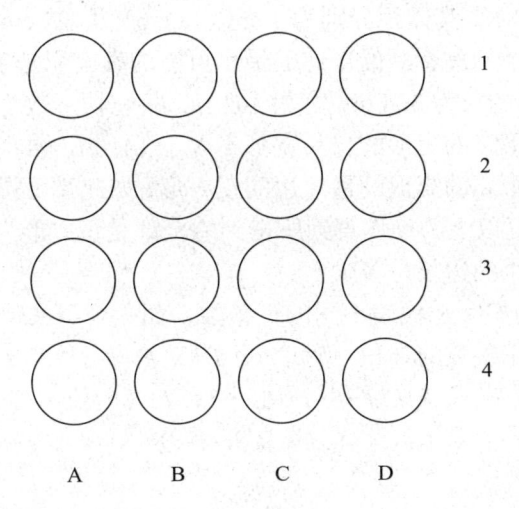

```
  ○    ○    ○    ○     1
  ○    ○    ○    ○     2
  ○    ○    ○    ○     3
  ○    ○    ○    ○     4
  A    B    C    D
```

10. How many possible solutions are there in arranging the digits 1 to 9 into each closed area so that the sum of the digits inside every circle is the same. Each

33

closed area contains only one digit and no digits are repeated. Draw all the possible solutions.

2.5　EMIC队际赛中文试题

2004年国际小学数学竞赛队际竞赛试题

1. 有祖父、父亲及儿子三人，祖父的年龄是偶数．若将祖父年龄的两个数码之顺序对调，所得到的数正好是父亲的年龄；若将父亲年龄的两个数码相加，所得到的值正好是儿子的年龄．假设这三个人年龄的总和为144岁，且祖父的年龄小于100岁，请问祖父的年龄为多少岁？

2. 三个正立方体，其体积分别为 1 cm³、8 cm³ 及 27 cm³，若将其沿表面互相黏合在一起．请问黏合后的形体的最小可能的表面积是多少 cm²？

3. 有一个矩形的长为324 m，宽为141 m．将它切下数个边长为141 m的正方形后，使得剩下来的矩形的长与宽都不大于141 m．再将这个新的矩形切下数个边长等于这个新的矩形的最短边的正方形，如此又可得到一个边长较小的矩形．不断地重复以上的操作直到所得到的全部是正方形为止，请问所得到的这些正方形中最小的边长是多少？

4. 我们用不同的字母代表不同的正整数，而一个英文单词的值等于它的所有字母所代表的正整数的乘积．例如，设 F=5、O=3 且 X=2，则 FOX=30．已知 TEEN=52，TILT=77 及 TALL=363，请问 TATTLE 的值为多少？

5. 令 $A=1\times2+2\times3+3\times4+\cdots+98\times99$ 且 $B=1^2+2^2+3^2+\cdots+97^2+98^2$．请问 A+B 之值为多少？

6. 将九个椅子排成一列，并安排教授 A、B、C 及六位学生坐到这些椅子上．由这三位教授先行选择座位，但要求他们都必须坐在两位学生之间．请问

第2章 2004年第2届国际小学数学竞赛

这三位教授共有多少种不同选择座位的方法?

7. 请问 $\dfrac{3}{1}+\dfrac{3}{1+2}+\dfrac{3}{1+2+3}+\cdots+\dfrac{3}{1+2+3+\cdots+100}$ 之值为多少?

8. 请问共有多少个不同的三位数被乘数可以满足下列的乘式?

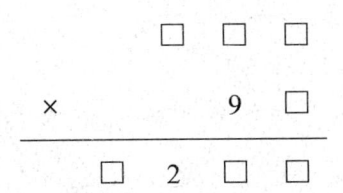

```
      □ □ □
  ×         9 □
  ─────────────
    □ 2 □ □
```

9. 有 16 个容量为 5 升的水桶,将它们排成 4×4 的方阵,并将每个水桶内所装的水之升数写在圆圈内,如图2-4 所示. 图中左侧及上方的数指出在该行或该列或该对角在线各个水桶内装的水之总和. 现只允许挑选其中的一个水桶将其装盛的水任意倒入若干个水桶内,使得每行、每列及每条对角在线各个水桶内装的水之总和都相等.

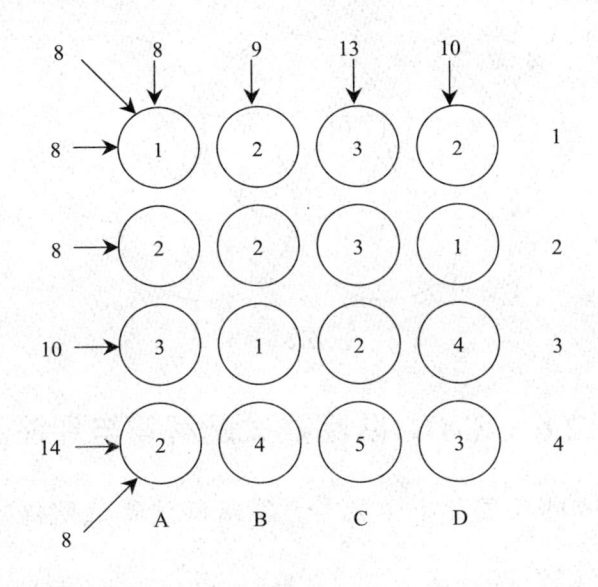

图2-4

请将倒完后各个水桶内装的水之升数填写在图2-5 中.

○ ○ ○ ○ 1
○ ○ ○ ○ 2
○ ○ ○ ○ 3
○ ○ ○ ○ 4
A B C D

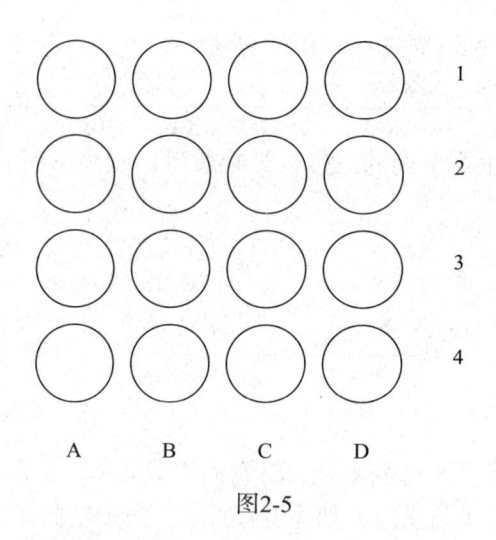

图2-5

10. 将数 1—9 不重复地填入图2-6 由五个圆圈所围的九个区域中，每个区域内只能恰填入一个数，使得每个圆圈内数的总和都相等．请问共有多少组不同的答案？并请画出所有可能的答案．

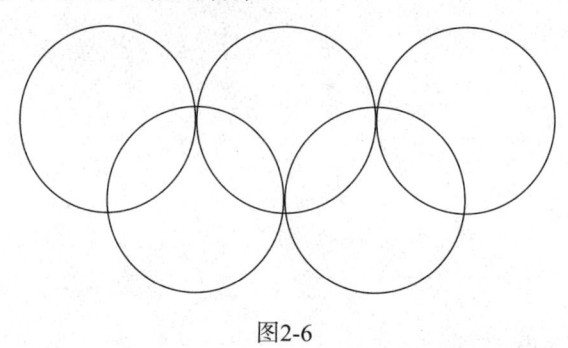

图2-6

2.6　EMIC队际赛试题解答与评注

2004 年国际小学数学竞赛队际竞赛试题解答

1. **解**　可令祖父的年龄为 $\overline{ab}$，其中 b 为偶数，则由题意知父亲的年龄为 $\overline{ba}$、儿子的年龄为 $b+a$．此时由祖父与父亲的年龄可再推知 $a>b$，并由三个人的年龄的总和为 144 岁知

第2章 2004年第2届国际小学数学竞赛

$$\overline{ab} + \overline{ba} + b + a = 144,$$
$$10a + b + 10b + a + b + a = 144,$$
$$a + b = 12.$$

此时仅 $a=8$、$b=4$ 可满足条件，故知祖父的年龄为 84 岁.

答: 84岁

2. **解法 1** 可知三个正立方体的边长由小至大依序为 1 cm、2 cm、3 cm. 因所求为最小可能的表面积，故知黏合的面越多越好. 如图2-7 所示，此为黏合最多面的情形之一，此时其表面积为 $5 \times 3^2 + 4 \times 2^2 + 4 \times 1^2 + (3^2 - 2^2 - 1^2) + (2^2 - 1^2) = 72 \, \text{cm}^2$.

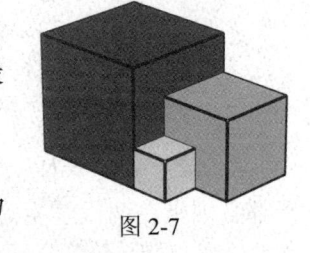

图 2-7

解法 2 分别从左、右边看去，可见到表面积为 9cm^2 与 $9 \, \text{cm}^2$；

分别从前、后边看去，可见到表面积为 $13 \, \text{cm}^2$ 与 $13 \, \text{cm}^2$；

分别从上、下边看去，可见到表面积为 $14 \, \text{cm}^2$ 与 $14 \, \text{cm}^2$.

故其表面积为 $9+9+13+13+14+14=72 \, \text{cm}^2$.

答: $72 \, \text{cm}^2$

3. **解法 1** 因 $324=141\times2+42$，故第一次操作时会切下 2 个边长 141 m 的正方形，剩下一个长为 141 m、宽为 42 m 的长方形；

因 $141=42\times3+15$，故第二次操作时会切下 3 个边长 42 m 的正方形，剩下一个长为 42 m、宽为 15 m 的长方形；

因 $42=15\times2+12$，故第三次操作时会切下 2 个边长 15 m 的正方形，剩下一个长为 15 m、宽为 12 m 的长方形；

因 $15=12\times1+3$，故第三次操作时会切下 1 个边长 12 m 的正方形，剩下一个长为 12 m、宽为 3 m 的长方形；

因 $12=3\times4$，故第四次操作时会切下 4 个边长 3 m 的正方形而没有剩下.

解法 2 不断重复以上的操作直到所得到的全部是正方形为止，即求 324 与 141 最大公因子，故为 3 m.

答: 3 m

4. **解** 由 $77 = 7 \times 11$ 可知 $T=1$，故 $52=TEEN=EEN$、$363=TALL=ALL$；

接着便可由 $52 = 2^2 \times 13$ 知 $E=2$、$N=13$，以及由 $363 = 3 \times 11^2$ 知 $A=3$、$L=11$. 故 $TATTLE=1\times3\times1\times1\times11\times2=66$.

答: 66

5. 解
$$A = (1\times1 + 2\times2 + 3\times3 + \cdots + 98\times98)+(1+2+3+\cdots+98)$$
$$= (1^2 + 2^2 + 3^2 + 4^2 + \cdots + 97^2 + 98^2)+(1+2+3+\cdots+98),$$
$$A + B = 2(1^2 + 2^2 + 3^2 + \cdots + 98^2) + (1+2+3+\cdots+98)$$
$$= \frac{2\times 98\times 99\times 197}{6} + \frac{98\times 99}{2}$$
$$= 33\times 49\times (197\times 2 + 3)$$
$$= 641949.$$

答：641949

6. 解 先让六位学生排成一列，然后将三位教授插入其间，由于要求教授都必须坐在两位学生之间，可知教授可从五个空隙中选择三个空隙插入，因此共有 $C_5^3 = \frac{5\times 4}{2} = 10$ 种选择，而对于每一种选择，因为三位教授就座的顺序可不同，故知会有 3×2×1=6 种可能的坐法，所以这三位教授共有 6×10=60 种不同选择座位的方法。

答：60种

7. 解 可知原式中每一项的分母皆为从 1 开始的连续正整数之和，因此对于第 n 项，可化简成 $\dfrac{3}{\frac{n(n+1)}{2}} = \dfrac{6}{n(n+1)}$，故原式可写成

$$\frac{3}{1}+\frac{3}{1+2}+\frac{3}{1+2+3}+\cdots+\frac{3}{1+2+3+\cdots+100}$$
$$= 6\times\left(\frac{1}{1\times 2}+\frac{1}{2\times 3}+\frac{1}{3\times 4}+\cdots+\frac{1}{100\times 101}\right)$$
$$= 6\times\left(\frac{1}{1}-\frac{1}{2}+\frac{1}{2}-\frac{1}{3}+\frac{1}{3}-\frac{1}{4}+\cdots+\frac{1}{100}-\frac{1}{101}\right)$$
$$= 6\times\left(1-\frac{1}{101}\right)$$
$$= 6\times\frac{100}{101}=\frac{600}{101}=5\frac{95}{101}.$$

答：$\dfrac{600}{101}=5\dfrac{95}{101}$

第 2 章　2004 年第 2 届国际小学数学竞赛

8．解　令此乘式为

$$\begin{array}{r} a\ b\ c \\ \times\ \ \ \ 9\ d \\ \hline e\ 2\ f\ g \end{array}$$

由积为四位数可知 $\overline{abc}<112$，即 $a=1$、$b=1$ 或 0，否则 $\overline{abc}\times\overline{9d}\geqslant 112\times 90=10080$，即积必为五位数；此时可知 $e=9$，且可进一步推得 $\overline{abc}<104$，即 $a=1$、$b=0$，否则 $\overline{abc}\times\overline{9d}\geqslant 104\times 90=9360$，积的百位数必不为 2．因此 $\overline{abc}$ 的可能值为 100、101、102 或 103．

当 $\overline{abc}=100$，则可取 $\overline{9d}=92$；

当 $\overline{abc}=101$，则可取 $\overline{9d}=92$；

当 $\overline{abc}=102$，则可取 $\overline{9d}=91$；

当 $\overline{abc}=103$，则可取 $\overline{9d}=90$．

故共有 4 个不同的三位数可以满足．

答：4 个

9．解　可知这 16 个水桶共装有 40 升的水，要求每行、每列及每条对角在线各个水桶内装的水之总和都相等，即要求每行、每列及每条对角在线各个水桶内装的水之总和都是 10，因此原先总和为 10 行与列的便不需要改变 (图2-8)．

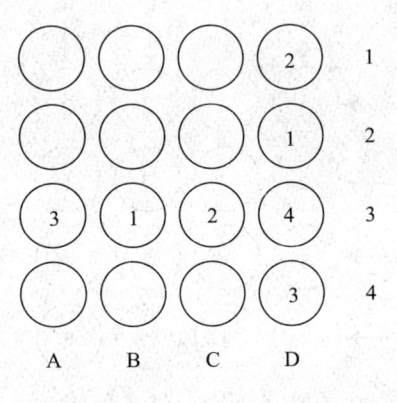

图2-8

而因原先总和超过 10 的行与列分别为第 C 列与第 4 行，故挑选位于 4C 的水桶将其装盛的水倒入其他的水桶内，且由 C 的水桶内装有 5 升的水知最多

39

有 5 桶可加水 1 升. 此时若不考虑 4C 的水量，每行、每列及每条对角在线各个水桶 (图2-9) 内装的水之总和的情形为

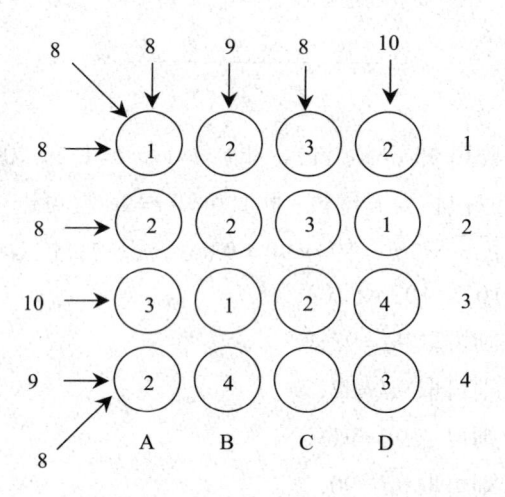

图2-9

观察第 1 行、第 A 列与左上至右下的对角线知只要在其交点 A1 的桶内加入 2 升的水，即可使这三条线都符合所求 (图2-10)，则此时的情形为

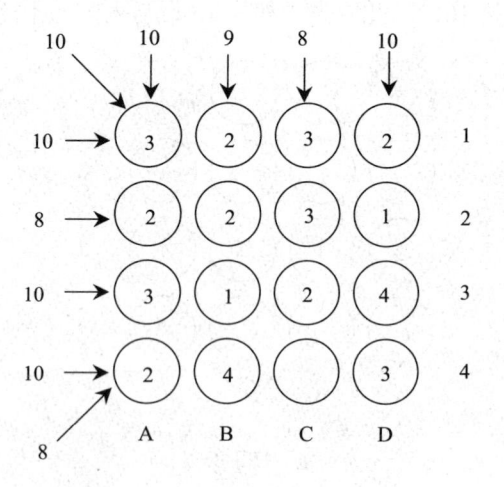

图2-10

观察第 2 行、第 C 列与左下至右上的对角线知只要在其交点 C2 的桶内加入 2 升的水,即可使这三条线都符合所求 (图2-11),则此时的情形为

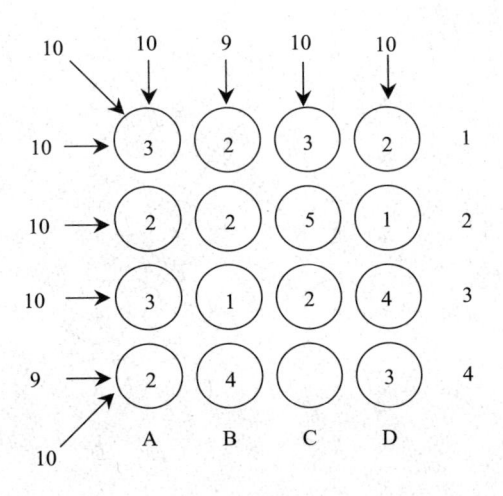

图2-11

观察第 4 行、第 B 列知只要在其交点 B4 的桶内加入 1 升的水,即可使这两条线都符合所求,则此时得到一组答案 (图 2-12)

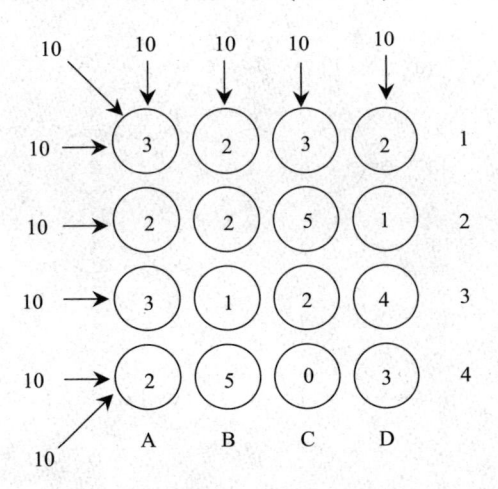

图2-12

观察第 1 行、第 2 行、第 B 列、第 C 列与左上至右下的对角线知只要在

它们的交点 A1、C1、B2、C2 的桶内各加入 1 升的水，即可使这五条线都符合所求 (图2-13)，则此时的情形为

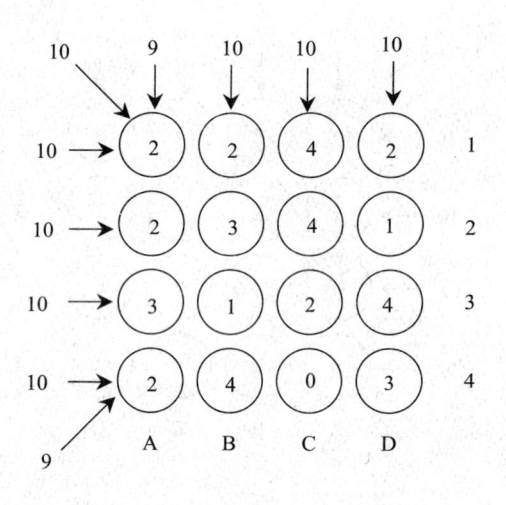

```
      10   9   10  10  10
       ↓   ↓   ↓   ↓   ↓
10 →  (2) (2) (4) (2)   1
10 →  (2) (3) (4) (1)   2
10 →  (3) (1) (2) (4)   3
10 →  (2) (4) (0) (3)   4
       ↑
       9   A   B   C   D
```

图2-13

现只需在 A4 再加入 1 升的水，即可得到另一组答案 (图2-14)

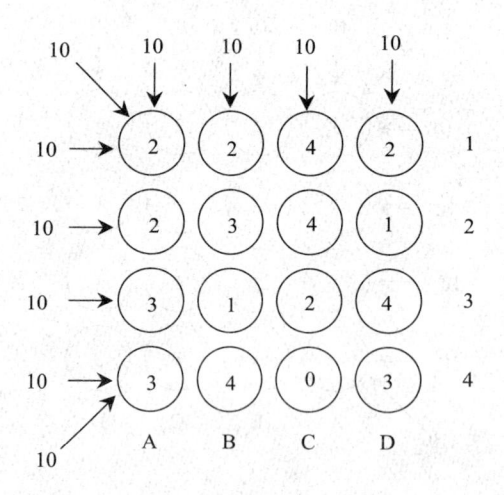

```
      10  10  10  10  10
       ↓   ↓   ↓   ↓   ↓
10 →  (2) (2) (4) (2)   1
10 →  (2) (3) (4) (1)   2
10 →  (3) (1) (2) (4)   3
10 →  (3) (4) (0) (3)   4
       ↑
      10   A   B   C   D
```

图2-14

故知共有两组解 (图2-15)：

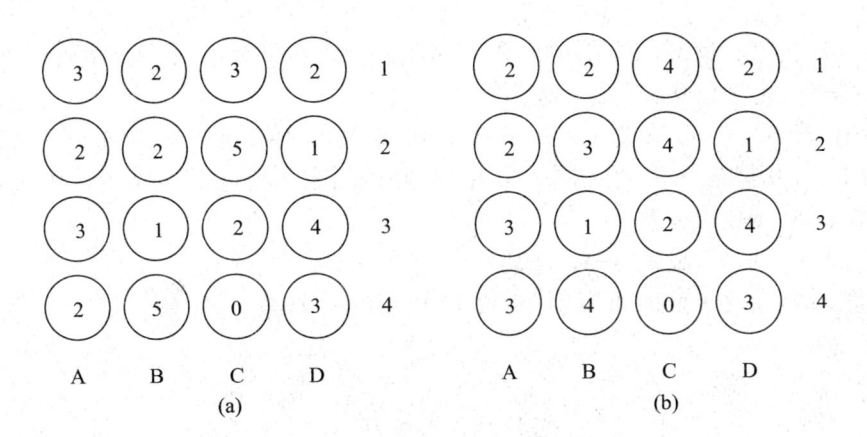

第 2 章 2004 年第 2 届国际小学数学竞赛

```
(a)                                    (b)
  3   2   3   2   1         2   2   4   2   1
  2   2   5   1   2         2   3   4   1   2
  3   1   2   4   3         3   1   2   4   3
  2   5   0   3   4         3   4   0   3   4
  A   B   C   D             A   B   C   D
```

图 2-15

10. **解** 如图 2-16 所示，令 a、b、c、d、e、f、g、h、i 为各区域填入的数，且 K 为完成后每一个圆中的数之总和，则

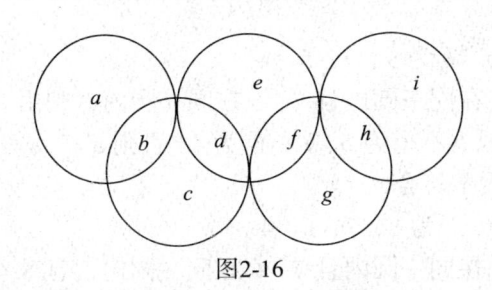

图 2-16

$5K = (a+b) + (b+c+d) + (d+e+f) + (f+g+h) + (h+i) = 45 + b + d + f + g$，

即 $K = 9 + \dfrac{b+d+f+h}{5}$。

因 $10 = 1+2+3+4 \leqslant b+d+f+h \leqslant 6+7+8+9 = 30$，所以可推得 $11 \leqslant K \leqslant 15$；由于对称关系，不失一般性可令 $b+d \leqslant f+h$。

(1) 若 $K=15$，即 $b+d+f+h=30$，故 $c+g = 45-(a+b+d+e+f+h+i) = 45-15\times 3 = 0$，矛盾；故 $K=15$ 不符合。

(2) 若 $K=14$，即 $b+d+f+h=25$，故 $c+g = 45-(a+b+d+e+f+h+i) = 45-14\times 3=3$，因此知 c、g 为 1、2 且 $a+e+i=45-25-3=17$，所以只需考虑 $25=9+8+5+3=9+7+6+3=9+7+5+4=8+7+6+4$ 这四种情况。

(i) 若 b、d、f、h 为 9、8、5、3。
可判断出 9、3 必在同一圆内且 8、5 必在同一圆内，则由 $9+3=12$、$8+5=13$

43

可知 $c=2$、$g=1$；此时因 b 不得为 9、h 不得为 5，否则 $a=5$、$i=9$，矛盾．故知 $d=9$、$f=5$，此时 $e=0$，矛盾．故不符合．

(ii) 若 b、d、f、h 为 9、7、6、3．可知 9、3 必在同一圆内而 7、6 在同一圆内，且 9 与 7、6 不可在同一圆内，否则该圆之和超过 15．故知 $b=9$、$d=3$，由此知 $a=5$、$c=2$、$g=1$．

若 $f=6$、$h=7$，此时 $e=5$，矛盾；

若 $f=7$、$h=6$，此时可得到如图2-17 所示的一个解．

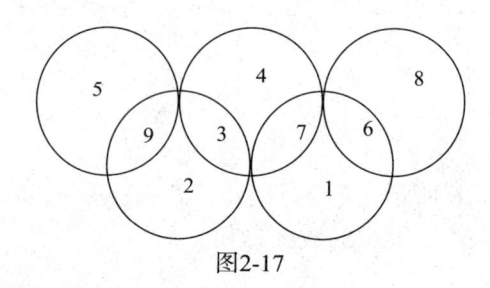

图2-17

(iii) 若 b、d、f、h 为 9、7、5、4．

可判断出 9、4 在同一圆内且 7、5 在同一圆内，则由 $9+4=13$、$7+5=12$ 可知 $c=2$、$g=1$；此时因 b 不得为 5、h 不得为 4，否则 $a=5$、$i=9$，矛盾．故知 $b=7$，此时 $a=7$，矛盾．故不符合．

(iv) 若 b、d、f、h 为 8、7、6、4．

可判断出 8、4 在同一圆内且 7、6 在同一圆内，且 8 与 7、6 不可在同一圆内，故知 $b=8$、$d=4$，此时可知 $a=6$，矛盾．故不符合．

(3) 若 $K=13$，即 $b+d+f+h=20$，故 $c+g=45-(a+b+d+e+f+h+i)=45-13\times 3=6$，$a+e+i=39-20=19$．

因 $6=5+1=4+2$，故 $\{1,2\}$、$\{1,4\}$、$\{2,5\}$、$\{4,5\}$ 不可同时出现在 $\{b,d,f,h\}$ 中，即仅需讨论以下六种情况：

$20=9+7+3+1=9+6+3+2=8+7+3+2=8+6+5+1=8+6+4+2=7+6+4+3$．

(i) 若 b、d、f、h 为 9、7、3、1．

若 9、3 在同一圆内且 7、1 在同一圆内，则由 $9+3=12$ 可知 $g=1$，矛盾；

若 9、1 在同一圆内且 7、3 在同一圆内，由 $9+1=7+3=10$ 知 $c=g=3$，矛盾．故不符合．

(ii) 若 b、d、f、h 为 9、6、3、2．

若 9、2 在同一圆内且 6、3 在同一圆内，则由 $9+2=11$ 可知 $g=2$，矛盾．故不符合.

若 9、3 在同一圆内且 6、2 在同一圆内，若 $b=2$、$d=6$ 则 $a=11$，矛盾. 故可知 $b=6$、$d=2$、$f=3$、$h=9$，此时 $a=7$、$c=5$、$e=8$、$g=1$、$i=4$，可得到如图 2-18 所示的一个解.

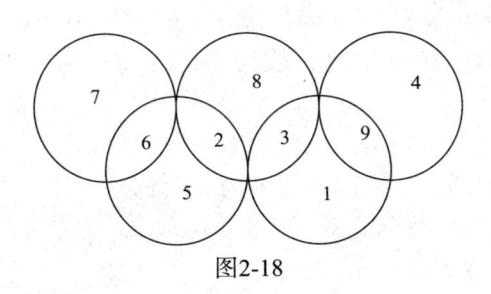

图 2-18

(iii) 若 b、d、f、h 为 8、7、3、2.

若 8、3 在同一圆内且 7、2 在同一圆内，则由 8+3=11 可知 $g=2$，矛盾；

若 8、2 在同一圆内且 7、3 在同一圆内，由 8+2=7+3=10 可知 $c=g=3$，矛盾. 故不符合.

(iv) 若 b、d、f、h 为 8、6、5、1.

若 8、5 在同一圆内且 6、1 在同一圆内，则由 8+5=12 可知 $g=1$，矛盾；

若 8、1 在同一圆内且 6、5 在同一圆内，则知 $b=8$、$d=1$，此时 $a=5$，矛盾. 故不符合.

(v) 若 b、d、f、h 为 8、6、4、2.

若 8、4 在同一圆内且 6、2 在同一圆内，则由 6+2=8、8+4=12 可知 $c=5$，故可判断出 $b=6$、$d=2$、$f=8$、$h=4$，此时可得到如图 2-19 的一个解.

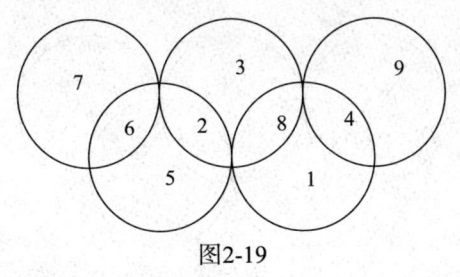

图 2-19

若 8、2 在同一圆内且 6、4 在同一圆内，由 8+2=6+4=10 可知 $c=g=3$，矛盾. 故不符合.

(vi) 若 b、d、f、h 为 7、6、4、3.

45

若 7、6 在同一圆内且 4、3 在同一圆内，则由 7+6=13 可知 $g=0$，矛盾；

若 7、4 在同一圆内且 6、3 在同一圆内，则由 6+3=9 可知 $c=4$，矛盾；

若 7、3 在同一圆内且 6、4 在同一圆内，由 7+3=6+4=10 可知 $c=g=3$，矛盾. 故不符合.

(4) 若 $K=12$，即 $b+d+f+h=15$，故 $c+g=45-(a+b+d+e+f+h+i)=45-12\times 3=9$、$a+e+i=36-15=21$. 故仅需讨论 21=9+8+4=9+7+5=8+7+6 这三种情况.

(i) 若 a、e、i 为 9、8、4.

若 4 不在中央的圆内，则由 b 或 h 为 8，矛盾；

若 4 在中央的圆内，对称关系，可令 $a=9$、$i=8$，则 h 为 4，矛盾. 故不符合.

(ii) 若 a、e、i 为 9、7、5.

若 5 不在中央的圆内，则由 b 或 h 为 7，矛盾；

若 5 在中央的圆内，对称关系，可令 $a=9$、$i=7$，则 h 为 5，矛盾. 故不符合.

(iii) 若 a、e、i 为 8、7、6.

若 6 不在中央的圆内，则由 b 或 h 为 6，矛盾；

若 6 在中央的圆内，对称关系，可令 $a=8$、$i=7$，则 $b=4$、$h=5$、$e=6$、$d+f=6=5+1=4+2$，矛盾. 故不符合.

故 $K=12$ 时无解.

(5) 若 $K=11$，即 b、d、f、h 为 1、2、3、4.

若 1、2 在同一圆内且 3、4 在同一圆内，则由 3+4=7 可知 $g=4$，矛盾.

若 1、3 在同一圆内且 2、4 在同一圆内，则可知 $b=3$、$d=1$，因此 $a=8$、$c=7$，若 $f=2$、$h=4$ 则 $e=10$，矛盾. 故 $f=4$、$h=2$，此时 $e=6$、$i=9$、$g=5$，可得到如图 2-20 所示的一解.

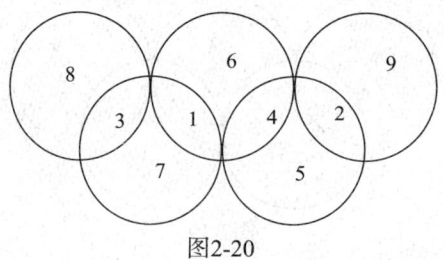

图2-20

若 1、4 在同一圆内且 2、3 在同一圆内，由 1+4=2+3=5 可知 $c=g=6$，矛盾. 故不符合.

故知共有四个解 (图2-21).

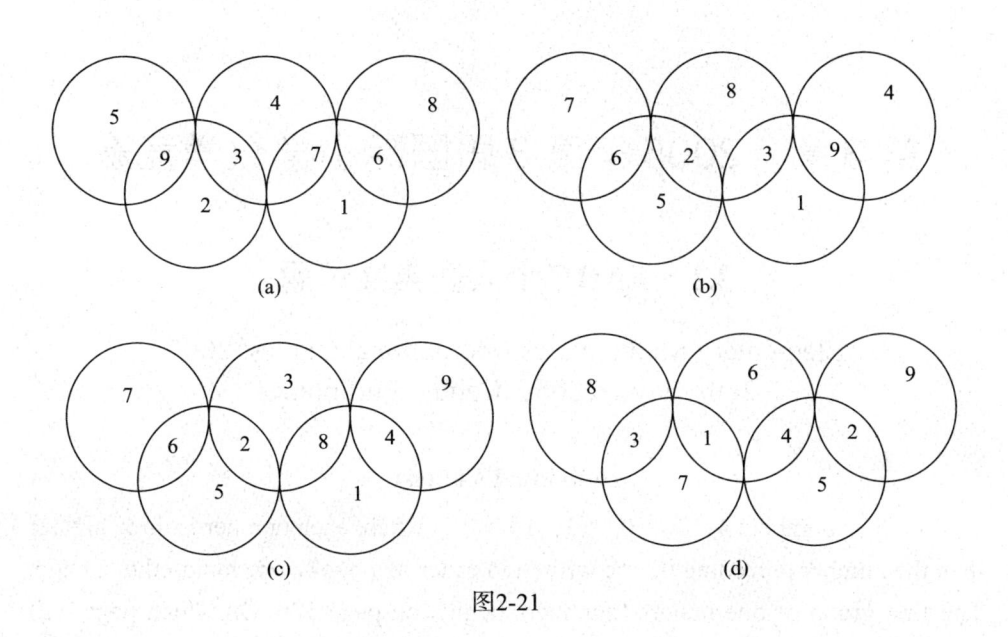

第 2 章 2004 年第 2 届国际小学数学竞赛

(a)

(b)

(c)

(d)

图2-21

第3章 2005年第3届国际小学数学竞赛

3.1 EMIC个人赛英文试题

Elementary Mathematics International Contest 2005
26th May, 2005, Cebu, Philippines

Individual Contest

1. The numbers 4, 7, 10, 13, 16, ⋯, where each number is three greater than the number preceding it, are written in order in a book, one hundred to a page. The first group of one hundred numbers begins on page 526. On which page will the number 2005 be located?

2. The numbers a, b, c, d, e, f and g are consecutive non-zero whole numbers arranged in increasing order. If $a+b+c+d+e+f+g$ is a perfect cube and $c+d+e$ is a perfect square, find the smallest possible value of d? (An example of a perfect cube is 8 because $8=2^3$) (An example of a perfect square is 9 because $9=3^2$)

3. If each large ball weighs $1\frac{1}{3}$ times the weight of each little ball, what is the minimum number of balls that need to be added to the right-hand side to make the scale balance? You may not remove balls, but only add small and/or large balls to the right-hand side.

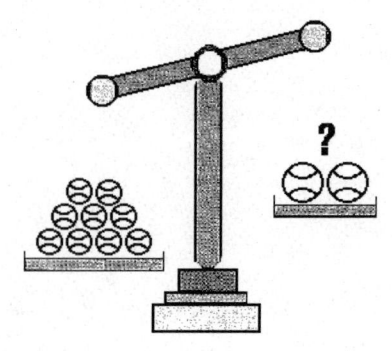

4. The different triangular symbols represent different digits from 1 to 9. The symbols represent the same digits in both examples. Find the two-digit number represented by ?.

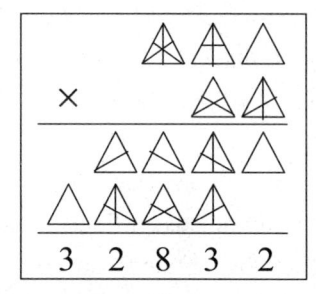

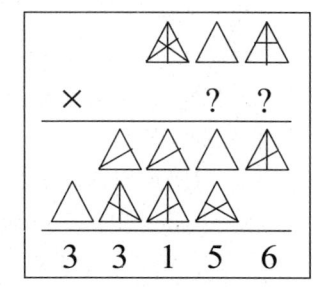

5. The following table shows the number of mathematics books sold over a period of five days. Find the number of books sold on Tuesday.

Monday, Tuesday & Wednesday	115
Wednesday & Thursday	85
Tuesday & Thursday	90
Monday & Friday	70
Thursday & Friday	80

6. Fractions in the form $\dfrac{a}{b}$ are created such that a and b are positive whole numbers and $a+b=333$. How many such fractions are less than one and cannot be simplified? (Cannot be simplified means that the numerator and denominator have no common factor)

7. Four friends were racing side by side down a dusty staircase. Peter went down two steps at a time, Bruce three steps at a time, Jessica four steps at a time, and Maitreyi five steps at a time. If the only steps with all four footprints were at

the top and the bottom, how many steps had only one person's footprint?

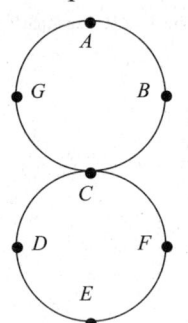

8. In the diagram, there are two touching circles, each of radius 2 cm. An ant starts at point *A* and walks around the figure 8 path *ABCDEFCGA* in that order. The ant repeats the figure 8 walk, again and again. After the ant has walked a distance of 2005π cm it becomes tired and stops. The ant stops at a point in the path. What letter point is it?

9. A basket and 16 potatoes are placed in a straight line at equal intervals of 6 meters, with the basket fixed at one end. What is the shortest possible time for Jose to bring the potatoes one by one into the basket, if he starts from where the basket is and runs at an average speed of 3 meters per second?

10. A sequence of digits is formed by writing the digits from the natural numbers in the order that they appear. The sequence starts:

123456789101112⋯.

What is the 2005th digit in the sequence?

11. While *B* is riding a bicycle from Point *X* to Point *Y*, *C* is driving a car from Point *Y* to Point *X*, each at a steady speed along the same road. They start at the same time and, after passing each other, *B* takes 25 times longer to complete the journey as *C*. Find the ratio of the speed of the bicycle to the speed of the car.

12. Ten whole numbers (not necessarily all different) have the property that if all but one of them are added, the possible sums (depending on which one is omitted) are: 82, 83, 84, 85, 87, 89, 90, 91, 92. The 10th sum is a repetition of one of these. What is the sum of the ten whole numbers?

13. A sequence of squares is made of identical square tiles. The edge of each square is one tile length longer than the edge of the previous square. The first three squares are shown. How many more tiles does the 2005th square have than the 2004th?

14. Lucky, Michael, Nelson and Obet were good friends. Obet had no money. Michael gave one-fifth of his money to Obet. Lucky gave one-fourth of his money to Obet. Finally, Nelson gave one-third of his money to Obet. Obet received the same amount of money from each of them. What fraction of the group's total money did Obet have at the end?

15. Each of the numbers from 1 to 9 is placed, one per circle, into the pattern shown. The sums along each of the four sides are equal. How many different numbers can be placed in the middle circle to satisfy these conditions?

3.2　EMIC个人赛中文试题

2005年国际小学数学竞赛个人竞赛试题

1. 等差数列 4、7、10、13、16、⋯的公差为 3，将数列中的数依序每 100 个写在同一页纸上．若最前的 100 个数写在第 526 页上，请问 2005 这个数出现在第几页？

2. 已知 a、b、c、d、e、f 与 g 为由小至大排列的连续正整数，若 $a+b+c+d+e+f+g$ 为一个完全立方数，且 $c+d+e$ 为一个完全平方数，请问 d 最小的可能值是什么？

3. 图 3-1 中每个大球的重量是小球重量的 $1\frac{1}{3}$ 倍，请问在天平的右秤总共最少要加入几个球才能使得天平平衡？你不可以从原天平的秤上移走球，但可以同时加入大球或小球在天平的右秤内．

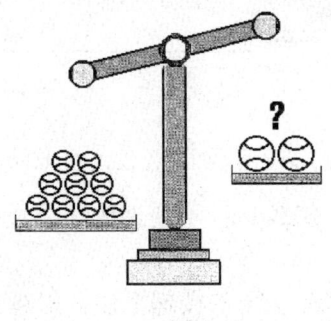

图 3-1

4. 图 3-2 的算式中，不同的记号代表 1—9 不同的数码，在两算式中相同的记号所代表的数码都相同．请问"？？"处的两位数是什么？

(a)

(b)

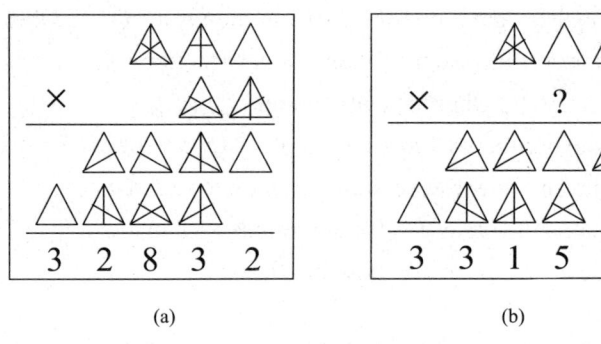

图 3-2

5. 下列表 3-1 显示某五天数学书的销售量．请问数学书在星期二的销售量为多少本 (图 3-3)？

表3-1

星期一，星期二，星期三	115本
星期三，星期四	85本
星期二，星期四	90本
星期一，星期五	70本
星期四，星期五	80本

图3-3

6. 具有 $\frac{a}{b}$ 形式的分数中，a、b 为正整数，且 $a+b=333$．请问满足上述条件并且小于 1 的既约分数共有多少个？(所谓既约分数是指分子和分母没有公因子)

7. 四个人肩并肩从一水泥未干的楼梯下楼，甲每步下二阶，乙每步下三阶，丙每步下四阶，丁每步下五阶．假若他们只有在最顶的一阶及最底的一阶

52

第3章 2005年第3届国际小学数学竞赛

同时有四个人的脚印,请问有几个阶上恰好只有一个脚印?

8. 如图 3-4 所示,两个半径都是 2 cm 的圆互相外切. 一只蚂蚁由 A 开始依 ABCDEFCGA 的顺序沿着圆周上的八段路径绕行. 蚂蚁在这八段路径上不断地爬行,直到行走 2005π cm 后才停下来. 请问最后这只蚂蚁停在哪一个点?

9. 将一个篮子及 16 个苹果排成一直线,它们之间相邻两个都相距 6 m,篮子固定放置在最前端. 小周从篮子所在处开始以每秒钟行走 3 m 的速度将苹果一次一个地放入篮子中. 请问小周将所有的苹果都放入篮子中至少要费时多少秒?

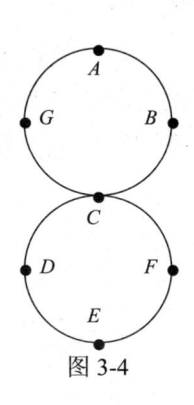

图 3-4

10. 将正整数依下列形式不断地写下去:
$$12345678910111213\cdots.$$
请问第 2005 个数码是什么?

11. 甲由点 X 骑自行车到点 Y,乙由点 Y 开汽车到点 X. 他们各自都以匀速沿着同一条公路行驶. 从他们相遇以后算起,甲抵达点 Y 所费的时间等于乙抵达点 X 所费的时间的 25 倍. 请问自行车的速度与汽车的速度之比是什么?

12. 有十个正整数 (不必全相异) 具有以下性质:若我们每次删除一个数,将剩下的九个数相加,所得的总和可能为 82、83、84、85、87、89、90、91、92 (要看删除哪一个数),第十个总和与上述之一数相同. 请问这十个正整数的总和是多少?

13. 一系列的正方形都是由单位正方形所拼成. 每个正方形的边长都比前一个正方形的边长多一个单位,最前的三个正方形如图 3-5 所示. 请问第 2005 个正方形比第 2004 个正方形多几个单位正方形?

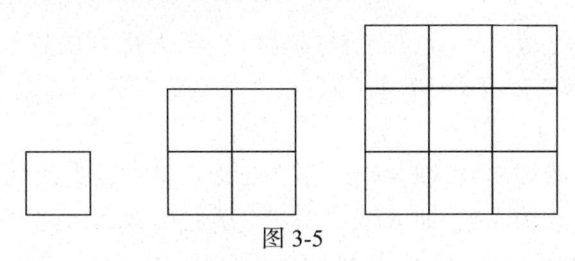

图 3-5

14. L、M、N 及 O 四人是好朋友,O 身上没有钱,M 把自己身上所有的钱的五分之一给 O;L 把自己身上所有的钱的四分之一给 O;N 把自己身上所有的钱的三分之一给 O. 他们给 O 的金额都相同,请问 O 最后所有的钱占他们四人之中总钱数的几分之几?

15. 将数 1—9 不重复的填入图 3-6 的圆圈中，每个圆圈中恰填入一个数，使得四条边上的数之和都相等．请问满足上述的条件下，最中间的圆圈内可填入的数有多少种不同的值？

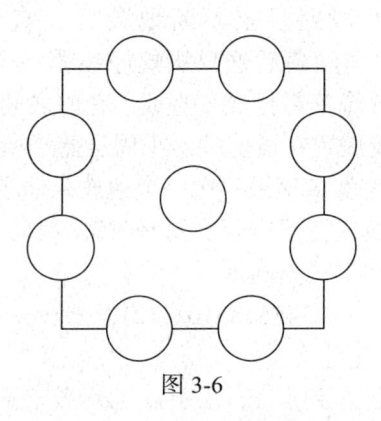

图 3-6

3.3 EMIC 个人赛试题解答与评注

2005 年国际小学数学竞赛个人竞赛试题解答

1. **解** 因 2005=1+3×668，故 2005 是这个等差数列里的第 668 项．因依序每 100 个数写在同一页纸上，且 668=100×6+68，所以 2005 出现在写这些数的第 6+1=7 页．再因最前的 100 个数写在第 526 页上，故 2005 出现在第 526+7−1=532 页上．

答：第 532 页

2. **解** 因 a、b、c、d、e、f 与 g 为由小至大排列的连续正整数，故知 $a+b+c+d+e+f+g=7d$、$c+d+e=3d$，即 $7d$ 为一个完全立方数、$3d$ 为一个完全平方数，因此可令 $7d=A^3$、$3d=B^2$．

因 $7d=A^3$，故知 $7|A$，即 $A=7x$，其中 x 为正整数，由此可得 $d=7^2x^3$；
因 $3d=B^2$，故知 $3|B$，即 $B=3y$，其中 y 为正整数，由此可得 $d=3y^2$；
此时可知 $7^2x^3=3y^2$，故 $3|x$ 且 $7|y$，因此 $d=3^3×7^2×M$，其中 M 为正整数．故知 d 最小的可能值发生在 $M=1$ 时，即 1323．

答：1323

3. **解** 可知小球与大球的重量比为 $1:1\frac{1}{3}=3:4$，故可令小球重量为 3、

第3章 2005年第3届国际小学数学竞赛

大球重量为4,则知右秤的2个大球的重量为8而左秤9个小球的重量为27,因此若左秤不加入球时,右秤加入球的总重量需为19.现再令右秤需加入a个小球、b个大球,则得知$3a+4b=19$,且$b<5$,即$a=\dfrac{19-4b}{3}=6-b+\dfrac{1-b}{3}$,可观察知$\dfrac{1-b}{3}$为整数仅发生在$b=1$、4时,其中当$b=1$时,$a=5$;当$b=4$时,$a=1$,即至少右秤需加入1个小球、4个大球共5个球才能平衡.

答: 5个

4. **解** 可将算式改写成如下算式:

	a	b	c				a	c	b
×		d	e			×		?	?
	f	g	h	c			f	f	c	e
c	h	d	e			c	h	e	d
3	2	8	3	2		3	3	1	5	6

由左式可知 $c=2$、$e=6$:

	a	b	2				a	2	b
×		d	6			×		?	?
	f	g	h	2			f	f	2	6
2	h	d	6			2	h	6	d
3	2	8	3	2		3	3	1	5	6

因右式中 $2+d \leqslant 2+9=11$,故右式中 $2+d=5$,可得 $d=3$;

因左式中 $h+6 \geqslant 1+6=7$,故左式中乘积的十位数为3仅能发生在 $h+6=13$ 时,可得 $h=7$;

	a	b	2				a	2	b
×		3	6			×		?	?
	f	g	7	2			f	f	2	6
2	7	3	6			2	7	6	3
3	2	8	3	2		3	3	1	5	6

因右式中 $f+6 \geq 1+6=7$，故左式中乘积的百位数为 1 仅能发生在 $f+6=11$ 时，可得 $f=5$；

因左式中 $g+3 \leq 9+3=12$ 且左式的十位数有进位，故右式中积的百位数为 8 仅能发生在 $g+3+1=8$ 时，可得 $g=4$；

		a	b	2
×			3	6
		5	4	7	2
	2	7	3	6
	3	2	8	3	2

		a	2	b
×			?	?
		5	5	2	6
	2	7	6	3
	3	3	1	5	6

此时便可得知 $\overline{ab2}=32832 \div 36 = 912$，即 $a=9$、$b=1$，故 $\overline{a2b}=921$，因此所求为 $33156 \div 921 = 36$.

答：36

5. **解法 1** 令 (1)、(2)、…、(5) 分别代表星期一、星期二、…、星期五的销量，则可知 (3)−(5)=85−80=5、(2)−(5)=90−80=10，故由星期一、星期二、星期三合计的销量为 115 本，知 (1)+2×(5)=115−5−10=100 本，再因 (1)+(5)=70，知 (5)=100−70=30，即可得知星期一卖了 40 本、星期二卖了 40 本、星期三卖了 35 本、星期四卖了 50 本.

解法 2 由第一列与第五列知星期一至星期五的总销量为 115+80=195 本、由第二、三、四列知星期一至星期五的销量再加上星期四的销量总共为 85+90+70=245 本. 故由星期四的销量为 50 本，再由第三列即可得知星期二卖了 40 本.

答：40 本

6. **解** 若 a、b 有公因子 d，则 d 必为 333 的因子，故考虑与 333 互素的数. 因 $333=3^2 \times 37$，故小于 333 且与 333 互素的数共有 $333-\dfrac{333}{3}-\dfrac{333}{37}+\dfrac{333}{3 \times 37}=216$ 个. 因 $\dfrac{a}{b}<1$，故知 $a<b$，且再由 $a+b=333$ 可知当 a 的值决定后，b 的值也就决定，故知共有 $216 \div 2=108$ 个.

答：108 个

7. **解法 1** 因已知只有在最顶的一阶及最底的一阶同时有四个人的脚印，

56

第 3 章　2005 年第 3 届国际小学数学竞赛

故知这一个楼梯共有[2，3，4，5]=60 个阶梯．因 4 为 2 的倍数，故知丙踩过的阶梯甲必踩过，故先考虑这个阶梯甲、乙、丁所踩过的阶梯(图 3-7).

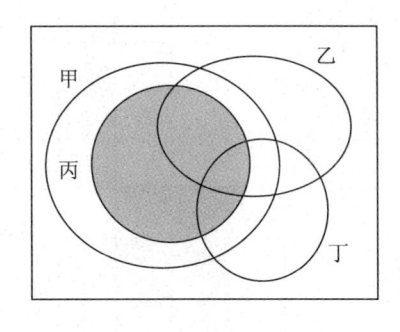

图 3-7

因 $\dfrac{60}{2\times 3\times 5}=2$，故知有 2 个阶梯是甲、乙、丁都踩过的；

因 $\dfrac{60}{2\times 3}=10$，故知有 10 个阶梯是甲、乙都踩过的；

因 $\dfrac{60}{2\times 5}=6$，故知有 6 个阶梯是甲、丁都踩过的；

因 $\dfrac{60}{3\times 5}=4$，故知有 4 个阶梯是乙、丁都踩过的；

因 $\dfrac{60}{2}=30$，故知有 30 个阶梯是甲踩过的；

因 $\dfrac{60}{3}=20$，故知有 20 个阶梯是乙踩过的；

因 $\dfrac{60}{5}=12$，故知有 12 个阶梯是丁踩过的．

故知共有 12+20+30−4−6−10+2=44 个阶梯是甲、乙或丁所踩过的阶梯，其中只有乙或丁一个人踩过的阶梯共有 44−30−4+2=12 个、三人中只有甲踩过的阶梯共有 44−20−12+4= 16 个．因 4=2×2，故甲每踩 2 个阶梯便有 1 个是丙所踩的，故只有甲踩过而丙没有踩过的阶梯共有 $\dfrac{16}{2}=8$ 个．故共有 12+8=20 个阶梯是只有一个人踩过，即 20 个阶上恰好只有一个脚印．

解法 2　因已知只有在最顶的一阶及最底的一阶同时有四个人的脚印，故知这一个楼梯共有[2，3，4，5]=60 个阶梯 (表 3-2).

表 3-2

阶梯	0	1	2	3	4	5	6	7	8	9	10	11	12	13
阶梯上留下脚印的人	甲		甲		甲		甲		甲		甲		甲	
	乙			乙			乙			乙			乙	
	丙				丙				丙				丙	
	丁					丁					丁			

阶梯	14	15	16	17	18	19	20	21	22	23	24	25	26	27	28	29
阶梯上留下脚印的人	甲		甲		甲		甲		甲		甲		甲		甲	
		乙			乙			乙			乙			乙		
			丙				丙				丙				丙	
		丁					丁					丁				

阶梯	30	31	32	33	34	35	36	37	38	39	40	41	42	43	44	45
阶梯上留下脚印的人	甲		甲		甲		甲		甲		甲		甲		甲	
	乙			乙			乙			乙			乙			乙
			丙				丙				丙				丙	
	丁					丁					丁					丁

阶梯	46	47	48	49	50	51	52	53	54	55	56	57	58	59	60	61
阶梯上留下脚印的人	甲		甲		甲		甲		甲		甲		甲		甲	
		乙			乙			乙			乙			乙		
			丙				丙				丙				丙	
					丁					丁					丁	

此时可看出只有在灰色部分阶梯是只有一个脚印，合计共 20 个阶梯．

答：20 个

8. **解** 可知蚂蚁所走路径的相邻两点间的距离为 $\dfrac{2^2\pi}{4}=\pi$(cm)，且每次循环所走的长度为 8π cm. 因 $2005\pi=8\pi\times 250+5\pi$，故知这只蚂蚁所停的位置为出发后抵达的第五个点，即 F 点．

答：F 点

第3章 2005年第3届国际小学数学竞赛

9．解　可知小周每将一个苹果放入篮子，即至少走了篮子至这个苹果所在位置的2倍，因此小周至少共走了

$$2\times6\times(1+2+3+4+\cdots+15+16)=2\times6\times\frac{17\times16}{2}=1632\,(\text{m}),$$

故至少共花费了 $\frac{1632}{3}=544\,(秒).$

答：544秒

10．解　可知一位数共享了9个数码、两位数共享了 $90\times2=180$ 个数码，至此共享了189个数码，因此还需填 $2005-189=1816$ 个数码．因 $1816=3\times605+1$，故第2005个数码为第606个三位数的百位数，即7．

答：7

11．解　可知在距离相同时，时间比的反比即为速度比．可令两人从出发到相遇处所花的时间为 x，乙从相遇处至抵达点 X 所花费的时间为 a，则甲从相遇处至抵达点 Y 所花费的时间为 $25a$．此时可知从相遇处至点 X，甲、乙所用的时间比为 $x:a$，故速度比为 $a:x$；而从相遇处至点 Y，甲、乙所用的时间比为 $25a:x$，故速度比为 $x:25a$．由此知 $a:x=x:25a$，即 $x^2=25a^2$，故 $x=5a$，且速度比为 $a:5a=1:5$．

答：1 : 5

12．解　可知若将这10个总和相加，其必为9的倍数．因为已知的9个总和之和为 $82+83+84+85+87+89+90+91+92=783=9\times87$ 为9的倍数，故第十个总和也必为9的倍数．因已知的可能值中，仅90为9的倍数，故第十个总和为90，且十个数的总和为 $(783+90)\div9=97$．

答：97

13．解法1　观察可以发现，第 a 个正方形都是第 $a-1$ 个正方形的相邻两边往外增加一个宽为 1 单位、长为 $a-1$ 单位的长方形，主对角在线再增加 1 个单位正方形，故知第 a 个正方形比第 $a-1$ 个正方形多 $2(a-1)+1=2a-1$ 个单位正方形．由此可知第 2005 个正方形比第 2004 个正方形多 $2\times2005-1=4009$ 个单位正方形．

解法2　因边长为 a 单位的正方形是由 a^2 个单位正方形所拼成，故可以得知第 2005 个正方形比第 2004 个正方形多 $2005^2-2004^2=(2005+2004)\times(2005-2004)=4009$ 个单位正方形．

答：4009

14. **解** 可令三人给O的钱数为A，则知M原有5A、L原有4A、N原有3A，故知O最后所有的钱占他们四人之中总钱数的 $\dfrac{3A}{5A+4A+3A}=\dfrac{3}{12}=\dfrac{1}{4}$.

答：$\dfrac{1}{4}$

15. **解** 因要求四条边上的数之和都相等，故填在四条边上的8个数之总和必为4的倍数. 因子1—9的总和为45=4×11+1，故满足题意的选法为将数1—9里被4除后余数为1的数选出填在中间的圆圈，即有1、5、9这三种不同的值，其填法分别如图3-8所示.

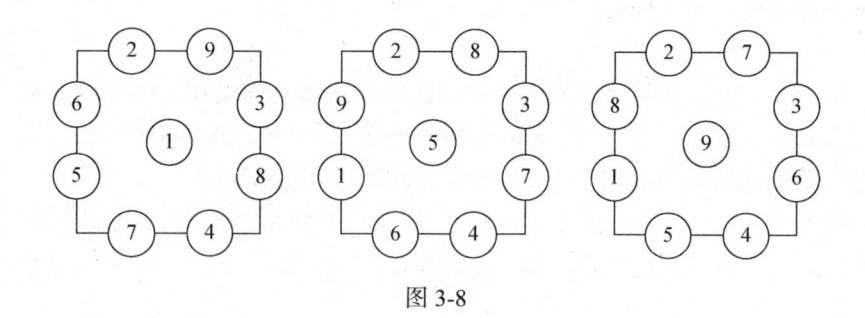

图 3-8

答：3种

3.4 EMIC 队际赛英文试题

Elementary Mathematics International Contest 2005
26th May, 2005, Cebu, Philippines

Team Contest

1. In parallelogram $ABCD$, $BE=EC$. The area of the shaded region is 2 cm^2. What is the area of parallelogram $ABCD$, in cm^2?

2. Refer to the diagram at the right. The length of one side of the large square is 4 cm and the length of one side of the small square is 3 cm. Find the area of the shaded region, in cm^2.

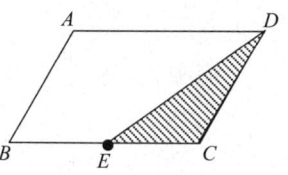

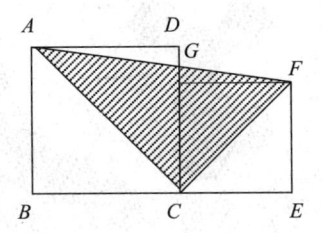

第3章 2005年第3届国际小学数学竞赛

3. The circle below is divided into six equal parts. 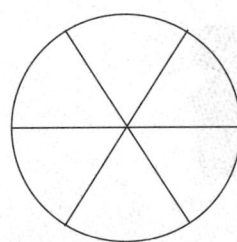 Suppose you paint one or more of these parts black, how many different patterns can you form? Any rotation of a pattern will be counted once.

4. Let $n=9+99+999+\cdots+99999\cdots9$, where the last number to be added consists of 2005 digits of 9. How many times will the digit 1 appear in n?

5. A merchant had ten barrels of oil which he arranged as a pyramid, as shown. Every barrel bore a different number. You can see that he had accidentally arranged them so that for each side the numbers add up to 16. Rearrange them so that for each side, the numbers add up to the smallest sum possible. The sum must be the same for all three sides.

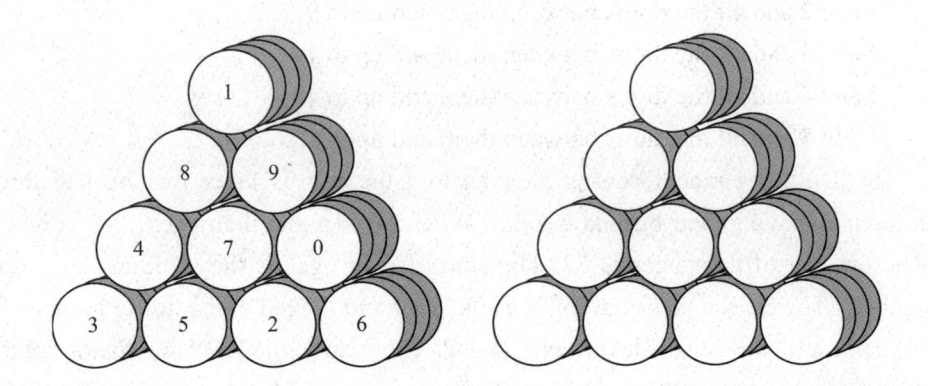

6. Find a route from a top cell to a bottom cell of this puzzle that gives 175 as a total. When your route passes any cell adjacent to zero, your total reduces to zero. Each cell may be used only once.

7.

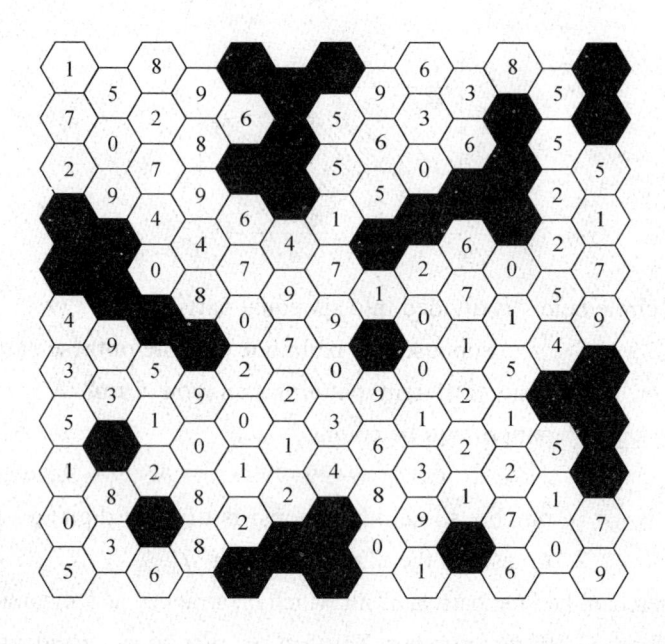

◯◯◯◯◯◯◯◯◯

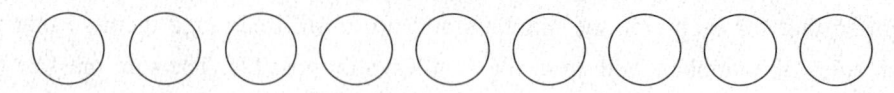

Arrange the digits 1—9 in the circles in such a way that:

1 and 2 and all the digits between them add up to 9.

2 and 3 and all the digits between them add up to 19.

3 and 4 and all the digits between them add up to 45.

4 and 5 and all the digits between them add up to 18.

8. During a recent census, a man told the census taker that he had three children all having their birthdays today. When asked about their ages, he replied, "The product of their ages is 72. The sum of their ages is the same as my house number." The census taker ran towards the door and looked at the house number. "I still can't tell" the census taker complained. The man replied, "Oh, that's right. I forgot to tell you that the oldest one likes ice cream." The census taker promptly wrote down the ages of the three children. How old were they?

9. Digits of the multiplication operation below have been replaced by either a circle or a square. Circles hide odd digits, and squares hide even digits. Fill in the squares and the circles with the missing digits.

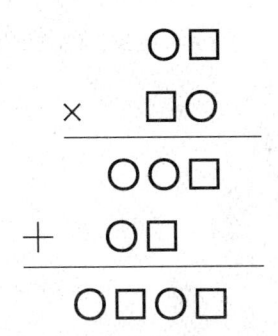

$$\begin{array}{r} \bigcirc\square \\ \times\ \square\bigcirc \\ \hline \bigcirc\bigcirc\square \\ +\ \bigcirc\square \\ \hline \bigcirc\square\bigcirc\square \end{array}$$

10. Donuts are sold only in boxes of 7, 13, or 25. To buy 14 donuts you must order two boxes of 7, but you cannot buy exactly 15 since no combination of boxes contains 15 donuts. What is the largest number of donuts that cannot be ordered using combinations of these boxes?

3.5 EMIC队际赛中文试题

2005年国际小学数学竞赛队际竞赛试题

1. 图 3-9 的平行四边形 ABCD 中，BE=EC. 若阴影部分的面积为 2 cm²，请问平行四边形 ABCD 的面积为多少 cm²？

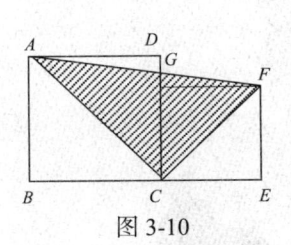

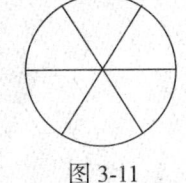

图 3-9

2. 如图 3-10 所示，大正方形的边长为 4 cm，小正方形的边长为 3 cm. 请问阴影部分的面积为多少 cm²？

图 3-10

3. 将一个圆如图 3-11 所示形式分割为六区域. 允许您在图中任何一区域或一区域以上涂黑，请问您可以得到多少种不同的图案？经旋转后相同的图案只能算为一种.

图 3-11

4. 令 $n = 9 + 99 + 999 + \cdots + \underbrace{99999\cdots 9}_{2005 \text{个} 9}$. 将 n 的数值写下，请问其中有多少个数码为 1？

5. 一位商人有 10 桶汽油，排列成如图 3-12 (a) 所示的三角形. 每个桶都标记一个不同的数. 你会发现图 3-12 (a) 的排列方式使得三角形每边上的数之总和恰好都等于 16. 请重新排列这些桶, 使得三角形每边上的数之总和都相等, 并使这个总和最小.

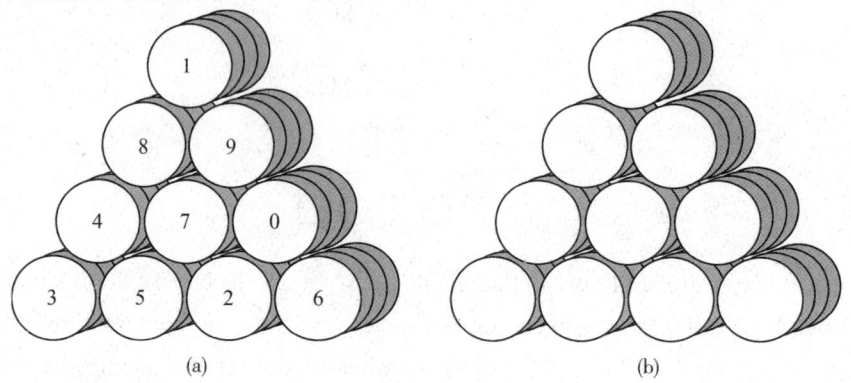

图 3-12

6. 请画出一条由上方的格子通到下方的格子的路径, 使得路径经过的格子上的数之总和等于 175. 任何一个格子只允许至多通过一次. 当路径通过与标记 0 的格子相邻的格子时, 你的总和将归为 0 (图 3-13).

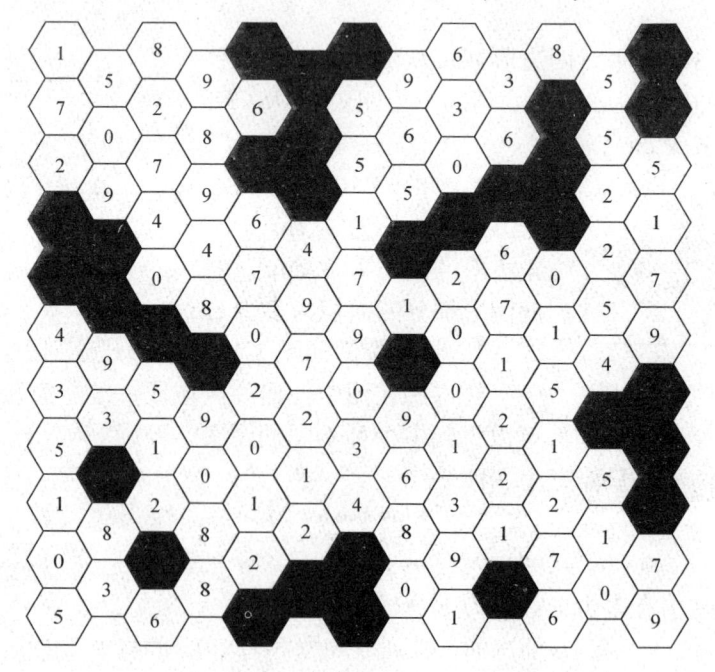

图 3-13

第3章　2005年第3届国际小学数学竞赛

7.

○ ○ ○ ○ ○ ○ ○ ○ ○

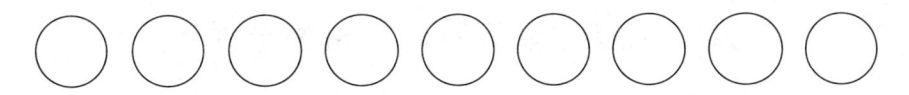

将数码 1—9 不重复地填入圆圈内，每个圆圈内恰填一个数码：

数码 1 和 2 及它们之间的数码的总和为 9.

数码 2 和 3 及它们之间的数码的总和为 19.

数码 3 和 4 及它们之间的数码的总和为 45.

数码 4 和 5 及它们之间的数码的总和为 18.

8. 在最近一次人口调查时，王先生告诉人口调查员说他有三位小孩，正好都是今天生日．当调查员问这些小孩子的年龄时，王先生回答说："我的三位小孩的岁数的乘积为 72，而他们岁数的总和正好等于我家的门牌号码."听完他的话，这位调查员就走出门外看看他家的门牌号码．这位调查员抱怨道："我仍然无法判断出他们的确实年龄."王先生回答说："噢，对不起，我忘了告诉您，我岁数最大的小孩非常喜欢吃冰淇淋."聪明的调查员立刻判断出这三位小孩的岁数并记录下来．请问这三位小孩的岁数分别为多少？

9. 下列算式中，每个数码都被圆纸板和方纸板盖住．圆纸板盖住的数码为奇数，方纸板盖住的数码为偶数．请写出此算式．

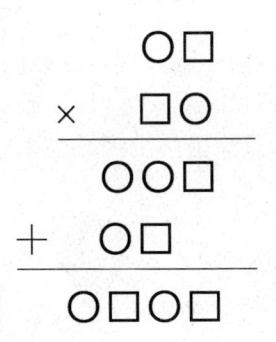

$$
\begin{array}{r}
\bigcirc \square \\
\times\ \square \bigcirc \\
\hline
\bigcirc \bigcirc \square \\
+\ \bigcirc \square\ \ \ \\
\hline
\bigcirc \square \bigcirc \square
\end{array}
$$

10. 甜甜圈只以每盒 7 个、13 个及 25 个的包装销售．当您欲购买 14 个甜甜圈时，您可以购买两盒 7 个包装的，但您不能恰好购买 15 个，因为您无法用以上三种不同的包装组合出 15 个甜甜圈．请问不能用以上三种包装组合出的甜甜圈的最大的个数是多少？

3.6 EMIC 队际赛试题解答与评注

2005 年国际小学数学竞赛队际竞赛试题解答

1. **解** 连接 BD，则由 $BE=EC$ 知 $\triangle BED$ 的面积与阴影部分的面积相同，故 $\triangle BCD$ 的面积为 4 cm^2. 因 $ABCD$ 为平行四边形且 BD 为其对角线，故知 $\triangle BCD$ 的面积为平行四边形 $ABCD$ 的一半，故平行四边形 $ABCD$ 的面积为 8 cm^2.

答: 8 cm^2

2. **解法 1** 延长 AD、EF，令其交点为 H，则知四边形 $ABEH$ 的面积为 $(4+3)\times 4=(28\text{cm}^2)$、$\triangle ABC$ 的面积为 $\frac{1}{2}\times 4\times 4=8\,(\text{cm}^2)$、$\triangle CEF$ 的面积为 $\frac{1}{2}\times 3\times 3=\frac{9}{2}\,(\text{cm}^2)$、$\triangle AFH$ 的面积为 $\frac{1}{2}\times(4+3)\times(4-3)=\frac{7}{2}\,(\text{cm}^2)$，故阴影部分的面积为 $28-8-\frac{9}{2}-\frac{7}{2}=12\text{ cm}^2$.

解法 2 $\angle ACD=\angle FCD=45°$，所以 $\angle FCA=90°$，故得知阴影部分的面积为 $4\times 3=12\,(\text{cm}^2)$.

答: 12cm^2

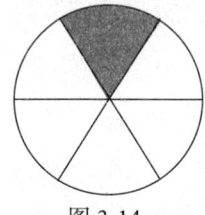

图 3-14

3. **解** 因经旋转后相同的图案只能算为一种，可知:
若只涂黑一个区域，则有 1 种涂法 (图 3-14);
若只涂黑两个区域，则有 3 种涂法 (图 3-15);

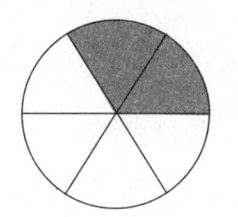

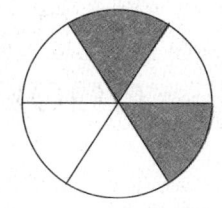

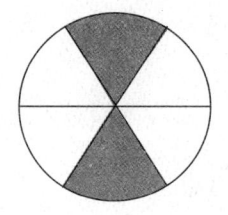

图 3-15

若只涂黑三个区域，则有 4 种涂法 (图 3-16);

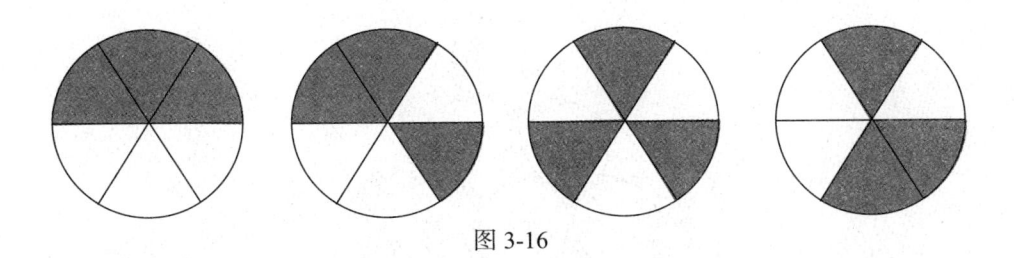

第3章 2005年第3届国际小学数学竞赛

图 3-16

若只涂黑四个区域，则可将涂黑两个区域的情况黑白互换，故知有 3 种涂法；

若只涂黑五个区域，则可将涂黑一个区域的情况黑白互换，故知有 1 种涂法；

若是将六个区域都涂黑，则有 1 种涂法 (图 3-17).

合计共 1+3+4+3+1+1=13 种涂法．

答：13种

图 3-17

4．解

$$n = 9 + 99 + 999 + \cdots + \underbrace{99999\cdots 9}_{2005\text{个}9}$$

$$= (10-1) + (100-1) + (1000-1) + \cdots + (\underbrace{1000\cdots 0}_{2005\text{个}0} - 1)$$

$$= \underbrace{111\cdots 1}_{2005\text{个}1} 0 - 2005$$

$$= \underbrace{111\cdots 1}_{2001\text{个}1} 00000 + 11110 - 2005$$

$$= \underbrace{111\cdots 1}_{2001\text{个}1} 00000 + 9105$$

$$= \underbrace{111\cdots 1}_{2001\text{个}1} 09105.$$

合计共 2001+1=2002 个 1．

答：2002个

5．解 令图 3-18 为所排好桶的情形．因要求三条边上的数之总和都相等，则知填在三条边上的 9 个数之总和必为

67

图 3-18

$(a+b+d+g) + (g+h+i+j) + (j+f+c+a) = 45-e+ (a+g+j)$.

因 10 个数之总和 45 为 3 的倍数，故从中选出 1 个数填在中间的圆圈、其余 9 个数填在三条边上而使总和最小的情形为将数 9 填在中间的圆圈，a、g、j 这三个位置放 0、1、2，此时每边的总和为 $\dfrac{45-9+0+1+2}{3}=13$，以下为其中 2 种摆法 (图 3-19).

(a)   (b)

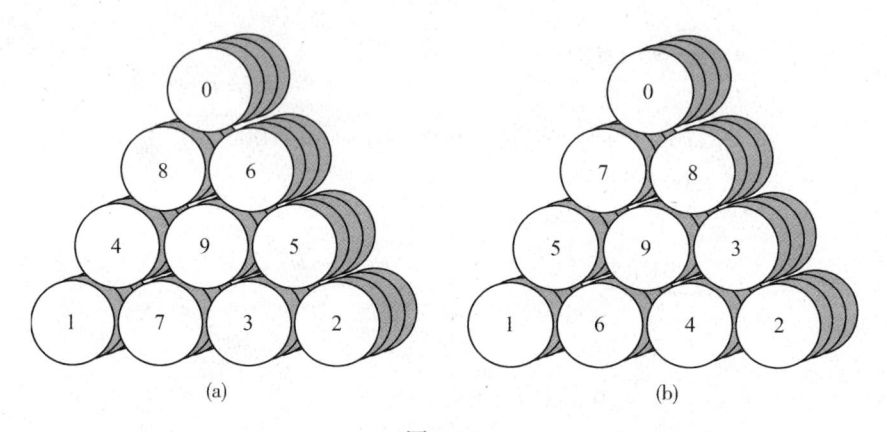

图 3-19

图 3-19 (a) 的 8 与 4、5 与 6、7 与 3 的位置可互换，而图 3-19 (b) 的 8 与 3、6 与 4、7 与 5 的位置可互换.

6. 解 可知不能通过与 0 相邻的格子，故先将 0 及与 0 相邻的格子涂色，可得图 3-20.

此时可得到必走的几段路径：

68

第 3 章　2005 年第 3 届国际小学数学竞赛

(1) 8→9，总和为17；
(2) 8→9→6→4，总和为27；
(3) 1→5→5→9→6→3→8→5→5，总和为47；
(4) 1→7→9→4→5→1，总和为27；
(5) 3→6→4→2→2→8→6，总和为31.

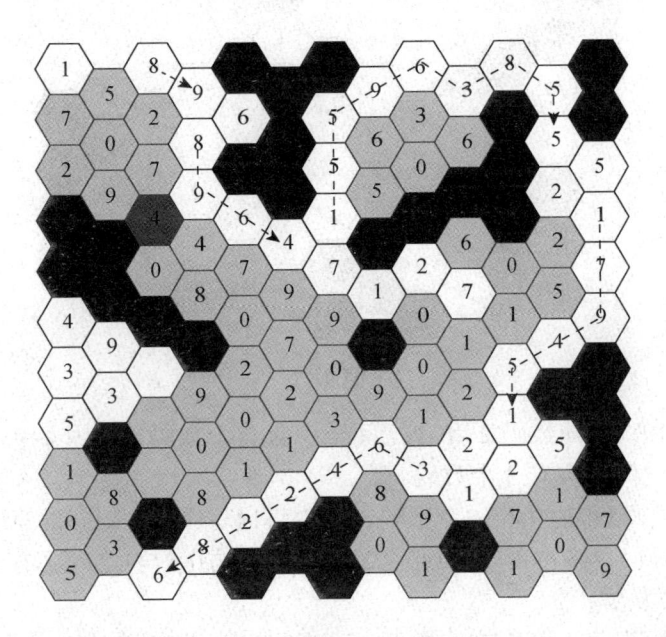

图 3-20

以上必走的路径之总和为 17+27+47+27+31=149，故衔接这几段的格子总和需为 175−149=26，可衔接的格子总和为 6+7+2+5+5+2+2+1=30，因此知 6、7、5、5 皆需保留，故需删去两个 2. 考虑 6、7、5、5 的位置后，便可得到路径如图 3-21 所示.

7. **解**　因子码 3 和 4 及它们之间的数码的总和为 45，此即为数码 1 至 9 的总和，故 3、4 必填入两端；再由题意可知：

数码 1 和 2 之间的数码的总和为 9−1−2=6.
数码 2 和 3 之间的数码的总和为 19−2−3=14.
数码 4 和 5 之间的数码的总和为 18−4−5=9.
因 6=1+5=2+4=1+2+3，故知数码 1 和 2 之间的数码必只有一个数码 6；

69

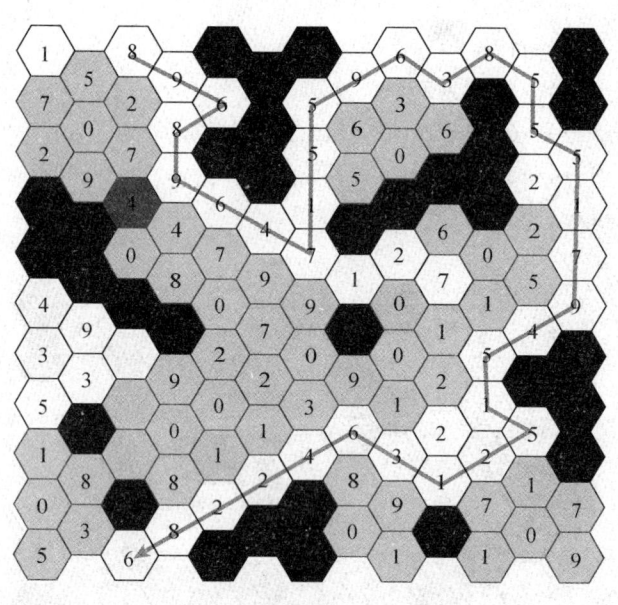

图 3-21

因 14>10，故知数码 2 和 3 之间至少有 2 个数码；再因 1+4+5+6>14，故数码 2 和 3 之间至多有 3 个数码：

(1) 若数码2和3之间有3个数码，则由将14写成不含2与3的3项加式仅可为9+4+1、8+5+1、7+6+1可得知1必在2、3之间，再由2与1之间必有6知2与3之间必有数码6、1、7；

(2) 若数码2和3之间有2个数码，则由将14写成2项加式仅可为9+5、8+6，再由2与1之间必有6知8+6不符合，即2与3之间必有数码9、5，此时再由4、5之间的数码总和9可以知道9必在3与5之间、1与6必在2与4之间，即4与5之间的数为1、6、2，其和恰为9，故知4与5之间已没有其他的数码9．但此时仍有数码为8、7未决定位置，故不符合．

至此，仍未决定相对位置的数码为 5、8、9，其中仅 4、5 之间填 9 可满足条件，故知 5 与 2 之间为 8．因此可由 3、4 位于两端的对称情况得到两组解：

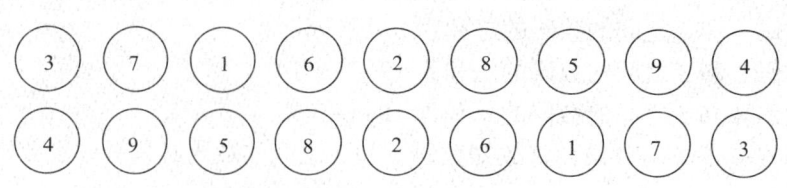

③ ⑦ ① ⑥ ② ⑧ ⑤ ⑨ ④

④ ⑨ ⑤ ⑧ ② ⑥ ① ⑦ ③

第3章 2005年第3届国际小学数学竞赛

8. 解 因调查员看了门牌号码后仍无法判定年龄,故知三个小孩的岁数总和固定时,三个小孩的岁数仍有不同的可能. 现已知小孩的岁数的乘积为 $72 = 2^3 \times 3^2$,故可依岁数总和分类如表3-3所示.

表 3-3

岁数总和	三个小孩的岁数			岁数总和	三个小孩的岁数		
74	1	1	72	18	1	8	9
37	1	2	36	17	2	3	12
27	1	3	24	15	2	4	9
23	1	4	18	14	2	6	6
22	2	2	18		3	3	8
19	1	6	12	13	3	4	6

可发现其中仅岁数总和为 14 时,有两种可能而无法判定三个小孩的岁数. 接着再由父亲的回答可知年纪最大的只有一个,因此便可以判断出三个小孩子的岁数为 8 岁、3 岁、3 岁.

答:8岁、3岁、3岁

9. 解 可将此算式改写为

$$
\begin{array}{r}
A \quad b \\
\times \quad c \quad D \\
\hline
E \quad F \quad g \\
+ \quad H \quad i \\
\hline
J \quad k \quad L \quad g
\end{array}
$$

其中 A、D、E、F、H、J、L 为奇数,其余为偶数. 此时可直接判断出 $J=1$.

现利用奇偶性可知:

(1) 由 E、H、k 的奇偶性可得知 $F+i$ 没有进位;

(2) 由 A、D、F 的奇偶性可得知 $b \times D$ 的十位数为0或偶数;

(3) 由 A、c、H 的奇偶性可得知 $b \times c$ 的十位数为奇数;

(4) 由 $A \times c < 10$ 且 A 为奇数知 $A=1$ 或 3.

若 $A=3$,则 $c=2$,且可判断出 $H=7$. 此时再由 $\overline{Ab} \times \overline{cD} \leqslant 38 \times 29 = 1102$ 可知 $k=0$,接着由 (1) 可知 $E=3$. 现已知算式如下:

$$\begin{array}{r} 3\ b \\ \times\quad 2\ D \\ \hline 3\ F\ g \\ +\quad 7\ i \\ \hline 1\ 0\ L\ g \end{array}$$

现由 (3) 可知 $b=6$ 或 8，此时可知 $D=9$，否则 $\overline{Ab} \times D \leq 38 \times 7 = 266 < 300$，与 $E=3$ 矛盾．但 $36 \times 29 = 1044$、$38 \times 29 = 1102$ 都与 L 为奇数矛盾，故不符合．

因此可知 $A=1$．由 $\overline{Ab} \times D \leq 18 \times 9 = 162$ 知 $E=1$；因 $10 \leq E+H = 1+H$，故可判断出 $H=9$、$k=0$．现已知算式如下：

$$\begin{array}{r} 1\ b \\ \times\quad c\ D \\ \hline 1\ F\ g \\ +\quad 9\ i \\ \hline 1\ 0\ L\ g \end{array}$$

现由 $90 \leq \overline{1b} \times c \leq 98$ 知 $(b,c)=(2,8)$ 或 $(6,6)$．若 $(b,c)=(2,8)$ 则由 (2) 知 $D=1$ 或 3，但由 $\overline{Ab} \times D = 12 \times D \geq 100$ 知 $D=9$，矛盾，故知 $(b,c)=(6,6)$，再由 (2) 知 $D=1$ 或 7，但由 $\overline{Ab} \times D = 16 \times D \geq 100$ 知 $D \geq 7$，故知 $D=7$，此时可得算式如下：

$$\begin{array}{r} 1\ 6 \\ \times\quad 6\ 7 \\ \hline 1\ 1\ 2 \\ +\quad 9\ 6 \\ \hline 1\ 0\ 7\ 2 \end{array}$$

10．解 观察可得若能够找到连续 7 个正整数的数量可用 7 个、13 个及 25 个的包装组合出来，则知这 7 个正整数的数量之后的所有正整数的数量都可用 7 个、13 个及 25 个的包装组合出来．

因 $45 = 7 \times 1 + 13 \times 1 + 25 \times 1$、$46 = 7 \times 1 + 13 \times 3 + 25 \times 0$、$47 = 7 \times 3 + 13 \times 2 + 25 \times 0$、$48 = 7 \times 5 + 13 \times 1 + 25 \times 0$、$49 = 7 \times 7 + 13 \times 0 + 25 \times 0$、$50 = 7 \times 0 + 13 \times 0 + 25 \times 2$、$51 = 7 \times 0 + 13 \times 2 + 25 \times 1$，故知 45 个以上的甜甜圈个数都可用这三种包装组合出来；而 44 个无法利用这三种包装组合出来．

答：44 个

第4章 2006年第4届国际小学数学竞赛

4.1 EMIC个人赛英文试题

Elementary Mathematics International Contest 2006
29th May, 2006, Bali, Indonesia

Individual Contest

1. When Anura was 8 years old his father was 31 years old. Now his father is twice as old as Anura is. How old is Anura now?

2. Nelly correctly measures three sides of a rectangle and gets a total of 88 cm. Her brother Raffy correctly measures three sides of the same rectangle and gets a total of 80 cm. What is the perimeter of the rectangle, in cm?

3. Which number should be removed from: 1, 2, 3, 4, 5, 6, 7, 8, 9, 10 and 11 so that the average of the remaining numbers is 6.1?

4. The houses in a street are located in such a way that each house is directly opposite another house. The houses are numbered 1, 2, 3, ⋯ up one side, continuing down the other side of the street. If number 37 is opposite number 64, how many houses are there in the street altogether?

5. There are 6 basketball players and 14 cheerleaders. The total weight of the 6 basket-ball players is 540 kg. The average weight of the 14 cheerleaders is 40 kg. What is the average weight of all 20 people?

6. How many natural numbers less than 1000 are there, so that the sum of its first digit and last digit is 13?

7. Two bikers A and B were 370 km apart traveling towards each other at a constant speed. They started at the same time, meeting after 4 hours. If biker B started $\frac{1}{2}$ hour later than biker A, they would be 20 km apart 4 hours after A started. At what speed was biker A traveling?

8. In rectangle $ABCD$, $AB=12$ cm and $AD=5$ cm. Points P, Q, R and S are all on diagonal AC, so that $AP=PQ=QR=RS=SC$. What is the total area of the shaded region, in cm^2?

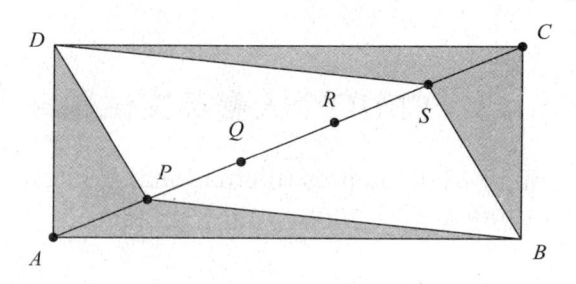

9. In triangle ABC, $AP=AQ$ and $BQ=BR$. Determine angle PQR, in degrees.

10. In the equation below, N is a positive whole number.
$$N=\square+\square-\square.$$

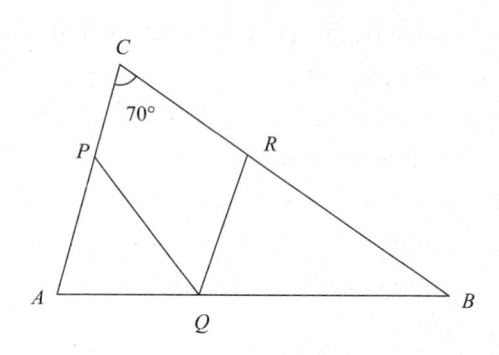

A numbered card is placed in each box. If three cards numbered 1, 2, 3 are used, we get 2 different answers for N, that is 2 and 4. How many different answers for N can we get if four cards numbered 1, 2, 3, and 5 are used?

11. A mathematics exam consists of 20 problems. A student gets 5 points for a correct answer, a deduction of 1 point for an incorrect answer and no points for a blank answer. Jolie gets 31 points in the exam. What is the most number of problems she could have answered (including correct and incorrect answers)?

12. Joni and Dini work at the same factory. After every nine days of work, Joni gets one day off. After every six days of work, Dini gets one day off. Today is Joni's day off and tomorrow will be Dini's day off. At least how many days from today they will have the same day off?

13. In a bank, Bava, Juan and Suren hold a distinct position of director (D), manager (M) and teller (T). The teller, who is the only child in his family, earns the

least. Suren, who is married to Bava's sister, earns more than the manager. What position does Juan hold? Give your answer in terms of D, M or T.

14. The following figures show a sequence of equilateral triangles of 1 square unit. The unshaded triangle in Pattern 2 has its vertices at the midpoint of each side of the larger triangle. If the pattern is continued as indicated by Pattern 3, what is the total area of the shaded triangles in Pattern 5, in square units?

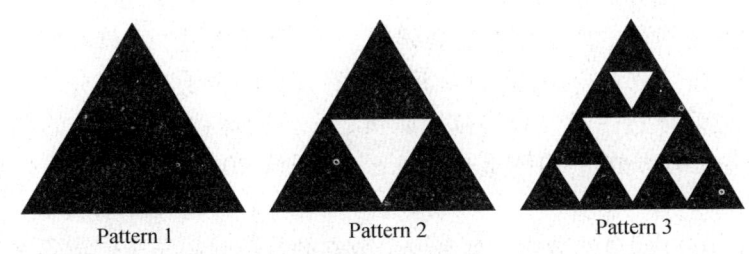

Pattern 1　　Pattern 2　　Pattern 3

15. There are five circles with 3 different diameters. Some of the circles touch each other as shown in the figure below. If the total area of the unshaded parts is 20 cm^2, find the total area of the shaded parts, in cm^2.

4.2　EMIC个人赛中文试题

2006年国际小学数学竞赛个人竞赛试题

1. 当小安8岁时，她的父亲是31岁；今年小安父亲的岁数是小安岁数的两倍．请问小安今年几岁？

2. 小妮在一个长方形中任取三个边长相加，所得值是 88 cm．小诺也在同一个长方形中任取三个边长相加，所得值是 80 cm．请问这个长方形的周长是多少 cm？

3. 从 1、2、3、4、5、6、7、8、9、10 及 11 中取出一个数，使得剩下的数的平均值是 6.1，请问这个被取出的数是什么？

4. 某条街道上，每一间房子正好与另一间房子隔街相对着，门牌的排列方式是从街头的一侧开始按 1，2，3，…的顺序编号，编到街尾的最后一间房子时再继续由其正对面的房子接着连续编号，直到街头为止．已知在此街道上 37 号房子的正对面是 64 号．请问此街道上共有多少间房子？

5. 有 6 位篮球选手及 14 位拉拉队员，6 位篮球选手的体重的总和为 540kg，14 位拉拉队员的平均体重是 40 kg．请问这 20 个人体重的总平均是多少 kg？

6. 在小于 1000 的自然数中，有多少个数它的首位数码与末位数码之和等于 13？

7. A、B 两人相距 370 km，他们骑着自行车以匀速相向而行．若他们在同一时刻出发，则会在 4h 后相遇．若 B 比 A 晚 $\frac{1}{2}$ h 出发，则在 A 出发 4 h 后他们两人相距 20 km．请问 A 骑自行车的速度为多少？

8. 在长方形 ABCD 中，AB=12 cm，AD=5 cm，点 P、Q、R 及 S 都在对角线 AC 上，且 AP=PQ=QR=RS=SC．请问阴影部分的总面积为多少 cm（图 4-1）？

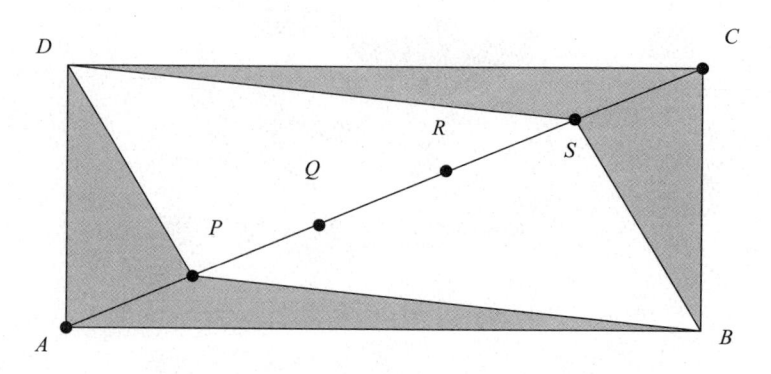

图 4-1

9. 在△ABC中，AP=AQ 且 BQ=BR (图 4-2). 请问∠PQR 是多少度？

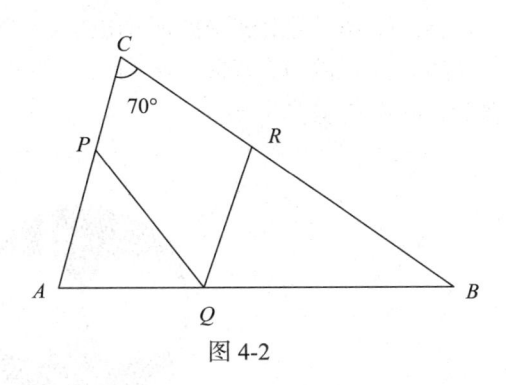

10. 在以下的等式中，N 是正整数.

$N=\Box+\Box-\Box$.

现于每一个小方格内放入一张数卡，如果三张数卡上的数分别为 1、2、3 时，则可能会得出 2 和 4 两种不同的 N 值. 若有四张数卡上的数分别为 1、2、3 及 5，则可得出多少种不同的 N 值？

图 4-2

11. 某次数学考试共有 20 道试题. 每答对一题得 5 分，每答错一题倒扣 1 分，未作答的题目得 0 分. 小朱在此次考试的成绩为 31 分，请问她最多可能总共作答了多少道试题？(包括答对的与答错的)

12. 小宗及小迪在同一间工厂工作. 小宗每连续工作 9 天便休假一天，小迪则每连续工作 6 天便休假一天. 今天是小宗的休假日，明天则是小迪的休假日. 请问从今天算起，最少再经过几天后他们才会在同一天休假？

13. 在一间银行里，小宝、小端及小伦三人中，有一人的职务是董事 (D)，有一人是经理 (M)，有一人是出纳 (T). 已知这位出纳是家中唯一的孩子，且收入是三者中最少的. 小伦与小宝的妹妹结婚，且小伦的收入比经理还多. 请问小端在这间银行里担任什么职务？ (答案请用 D、M 或 T 表示)

14. 在图 4-3 中，最大的正三角形的面积都是 1 平方单位. 图 4-3 (a) 中未涂上阴影部分的三角形的顶点是上一个图中较大三角形的中点. 依照相同的规律继续画出第三个及以后的图形，请问在第五个图形中，阴影部分的总面积为多少平方单位？

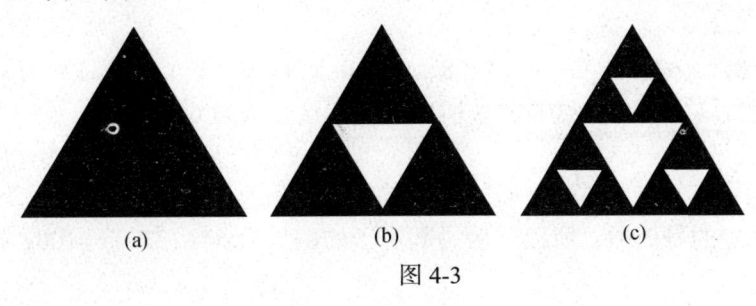

(a)   (b)   (c)

图 4-3

15. 图 4-4 是由五个圆所构成的，其中总共有 3 种不同长度的直径，且有部分的圆彼此相切．若最大圆内白色部分的总面积是 20 cm²，请问最大圆内阴影部分的面积是多少 cm²？

图 4-4

4.3 EMIC 个人赛试题解答与评注

2006 年国际小学数学竞赛个人竞赛试题解答

1. **解** 可知两人岁数差了 31−8=23 岁．因今年小安父亲是小安岁数的两倍，可知小安今年的岁数就是两人岁数之间的差，故知小安今年 23 岁．

答：23 岁

2. **解** 令这个长方形的长为 a cm、宽为 b cm．可知若在一个长方形中任取三个边，则这三个边一定是两边为长、一边为宽或两边为宽、一边为长．因小妮与小诺取出的三边长之和不相同，故知两人所取出的情况恰为一人一种，故若将两人所得的值相加，便可得 $(2a+b)+(2b+a)=168$，即 $a+b=56$．故此长方形的周长为 $2(a+b)=112$ (cm)．

答：112 cm

3. **解** 1、2、3、4、5、6、7、8、9、10 及 11 这 11 个数的总和为 66，而取出一个数后总和为 6.1×10=61，所以取出的这个数为 66−61=5．

答：5

4. **解法 1** 可知最后一号房子与 64 号房子之间隔的号码差恰为 37 号房子与 1 号房子之间隔的号码差，所以最后一间房子的编号为 64+(37−1)=100，即共有 100 间房子．

78

第4章 2006年第4届国际小学数学竞赛

解法2 依照这样编号的方式,易观察出任何一间房子与其正对面的房子的编号总和都相同. 已知此街道上 37 号房子的正对面是 64 号,故此总和为 37+64=101,而最后一间房子的正对面是 1 号,所以最后一间房子的编号为 101−1=100 号.

答: 100间

5. **解** 可知 14 位拉拉队员的体重总和为 40×14=560 (kg),故这 20 个人体重的总平均为 (560+540)÷20=55 (kg).

答: 55 kg

6. **解** 令 A<1000 且它的首位数码与末位数码之和等于 13.

若 A 为两位数 $\overline{ab}$,则知 $a+b$=13,共有 94、85、76、67、58、49 这 6 个数;

若 A 为三位数 $\overline{abc}$,则知 $a+c$=13 且 b 为任意的数码,故共有 6×10=60 个数.

因此共有 60+6=66 个数.

答: 66个

7. **解** 可知 B 在 $\frac{1}{2}$ h 内可行驶 20 (km),即 B 的速率为 40 (km/h),故两人同时出发,4 h 后相遇时 B 共走了 4×40=160 (km),此时 A 走了 370−160=210 (km),故 A 的速率为

$$\frac{210}{4} = 52\frac{1}{2} \text{ (km/h)}.$$

答: $52\frac{1}{2}$ km/h

8. **解** 可知长方形 $ABCD$ 的面积为 $5 \times 12 = 60$ (cm^2),故 △ABC 的面积为 $60 \div 2 = 30$ (cm^2). 因 $AP = CS = \frac{1}{5}AC$,所以 △APD、△APB、△CSD、△CSB 的面积都是 △ABC 面积的 $\frac{1}{5}$,即 $30 \times \frac{1}{5} = 6$ (cm^2),因此阴影部分的面积为 6+6+6+6=24 (cm^2).

答: 24 cm^2

9. **解法1** 由 $AP=AQ$ 可令 ∠APQ = ∠AQP=α,由 $BQ=BR$ 可令 ∠BRQ= ∠BQR=β,且可得 ∠PAQ=180°−2α、∠RBQ=180°−2β 以及 ∠PQR=180°−α−β.

由 70°+180°−2α+180°−2β=180° 知 α+β=125,所以 ∠PQR=180°−α−β=180°−

125°=55°.

解法 2 令 $\angle CAB = \gamma$，$\angle ABC = \delta$，可得知 $\gamma + \delta = 180° - 70° = 110°$．又可得
$\angle AQP = (180° - \gamma) \div 2$、$\angle BQR = (180° - 2\delta) \div 2$ 以及
$\angle PQR = 180° - \angle AQP - \angle BQR = 180° - 90° + \gamma/2 - 90° + \delta/2$
$= \gamma/2 + \delta/2 = 110 \div 2 = 55°$．

答：55°

10. 解 可知 N 的最大值为 $5+3-1=7$，故 N 的可能值最多可有 7 种，经逐一代入只有 $7=5+3-1$、$6=5+3-2=5+2-1$、$4=5+2-3=5+1-2=3+2-1$、$3=5+1-3$、$2=3+1-2$ 这五个数可能得出，故只有 5 种不同的 N 值．

答：5 种

11. 解 因小朱成绩为 31 分，可知小朱至少答对 7 题，即小朱至多答错 13 题，因此在未倒扣的情形下，小朱成绩至多为 $31+13=44$ 分，故小朱至多答对 8 题．若小朱答对 7 题，则小朱答错 $7 \times 5 - 31 = 4$ 题，即共作答 $7+4=11$ 题；若小朱答对 8 题，则小朱答错 $8 \times 5 - 31 = 9$ 题，即共作答 $8+9=17$ 题．故知小朱最多可能总共作答了 17 题．

答：17 题

12. 解法 1 可将小宗视为 $9+1=10$ 天一循环、小迪视为 $6+1=7$ 天一循环，则从今天算起，距离两人同时休假的天数为 10 的倍数与 7 的倍数加 1．因 10 的倍数中同时等于 7 的倍数加 1 的最小值为 $50=7 \times 7 + 1$，故最少再经过 50 天后他们才会在同一天休假．

解法 2 如表 4-1 所示，列出两人的休假日，其中第 0 天为今天．

表 4-1

日数	0	1	2	3	4	5	6	7	8	9	10	11	12	13	14	15
休假人	宗										宗					
		迪							迪							迪

日数	16	17	18	19	20	21	22	23	24	25	26	27	28	29	30	31	32	33
休假人					宗										宗			
		迪					迪							迪				

日数	34	35	36	37	38	39	40	41	42	43	44	45	46	47	48	49	50	51
休假人							宗										宗	
			迪							迪							迪	

可知再经过 50 天后他们才会在同一天休假．

答：50 天

13．**解** 因小宝有妹妹，故小宝不是出纳；因小伦的收入比经理还多，故小伦是董事而不是出纳；此时便可得知出纳为小端，也因此可知小宝是经理．

答：T

14．**解** 可观察出每一次操作都是将前一个图里每一个最小的阴影正三角形挖去中间的 $\frac{1}{4}$，即每一个图阴影部分的总面积都是前一个图阴影部分的总面积的 $1-\frac{1}{4}=\frac{3}{4}$．因图 4-3 (a) 阴影部分的总面积为 1，故知第五个图阴影部分的总面积为 $1\times\frac{3}{4}\times\frac{3}{4}\times\frac{3}{4}\times\frac{3}{4}=\frac{81}{256}$．

答：$\frac{81}{256}$

15．**解** 由图示可知这三种长度不同的直径由小圆到大圆的长度比为 1：2：3，即由小圆到大圆的面积比为 1：4：9，故可令三种圆的面积由小圆到大圆依序为 S、$4S$ 及 $9S$．因最大圆内白色部分的总面积 20 cm^2，即为 $9S-4S-S+2S=6S$ 而最大圆内阴影部分的面积为 $4S-2S+S=3S=\frac{1}{2}\times 6S$，故知所求为 10 cm^2．

答：10 cm^2

4.4　EMIC 队际赛英文试题

Elementary Mathematics International Contest 2006
29th May，2006，Bali，Indonesia

Team Contest

1. Four different natural numbers, all larger than 3, are placed in the four boxes below.

□+□+□+□=27．

The four numbers are arranged from the smallest to the largest. How many different ways can we fill the four boxes?

2. The number 22 has the following property: the sum of its digits is equal to

the product of its digits. Find the smallest 8-digit natural number that satisfies the given condition.

3. A number X consists of 4 non-zero digits. A number Y is obtained from X reversing the order of its digits. If the sum of X and Y is 14773 and the difference between them is 3177, determine the larger of these two numbers.

4. $ABCD$ is a parallelogram. P, Q, R, and S are points on the sides AB, BC, CD and DA respectively so that $AP=DR$. The area of $ABCD$ is 16 cm^2. Find the area of the quadrilateral $PQRS$.

5. Adi has written a number of mathematical exams. In order to obtain an overall average of 90 points/percentage, he needed to score 100 points/percentage in the final exam. Unfortunately, he achieved only 75 points/percentage in the final exam, resulting in an overall average of 85 points/percentage. How many exams did he write altogether?

6. Annisa used 120 unit cubes to make a parallelepiped (rectangular prism). She painted all six faces of the parallelepiped. Once the paint had dried, she disassembled the cubes and found that 24 of the cubes had not been painted on any face. What is the surface area of the parallelepiped?

7. A number of unit cubes are arranged to build a tower-like shape as shown in the figure below. Note that there is a hole across from the left to the right, from the top to the bottom, and from the front to the back. How many unit cubes are there altogether?

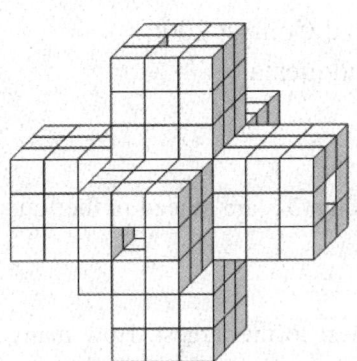

8. When 31513 and 34369 are divided by the same three-digit number, the remainders are equal. What is the remainder?

9. Place any four digits from 1 to 5 in a 2×2 square so that:

(a) in the same row, the digit on the left is greater than that on the right;

(b) in the same column, the digit in the top is greater than that at the bottom.

The diagrams below show two different ways of arranging the digits. How many different ways are there in total?

5	3
4	2

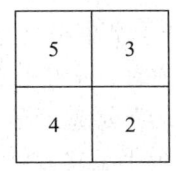

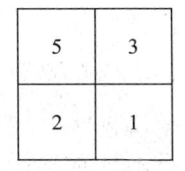

Example 1

5	3
2	1

Example 2

10. Peter uses a remote control to move his robot. The remote control has 3 buttons on it. One button moves the robot 1 step forward, another button moves it 2 steps forward and the third button moves it 3 steps forward. How many different ways are possible to move the robot 8 steps forward?

4.5　EMIC队际赛中文试题

2006年国际小学数学竞赛队际竞赛试题

1. 将四个大于3的相异自然数填入下面的四个空格内，使得等式成立.
$$□+□+□+□=27,$$
已知这四个数是按照由小至大的顺序由左至右分别填入空格内. 请问满足以上条件的填法共有多少种？

2. 数"22"具有以下性质：它的各位数码之和等于它的各位数码之积. 请问满足上述性质最小的八位数是什么？

3. 四位数 X 的各位数码均不等于0. 把 X 的各位数码由后往前写出另一个数 Y. 若 X 与 Y 之和为14773，差为3177. 请问 X 和 Y 这两个数中较大数是什么？

4. 平行四边形 $ABCD$ 中，点 P、Q、R 和 S 分别是 AB、BC、CD 及 DA 边上之点且 $AP=DR$. 现已知 $ABCD$ 的面积是 16 cm^2，请问四边形 $PQRS$ 的面积是多少 cm^2？

5. 本学期举行若干次数学考试. 若小迪欲取得总平均90分的成绩，则他必须于最后一次考试时获得 100 分. 但是最后一次考试他只得到 75 分，因此他的总平均只有 85 分. 请问本学期总共有多少次数学考试？

6. 小安用 120 个单位小正立方体拼成一个长方体. 她在长方体的六个表面上涂上油漆. 当油漆干了以后，她把长方体拆散，她发现共有 24 个小正立方体的任何一个面都没有涂到油漆. 请问小安所拼成的长方体的表面积是多少平方单位？

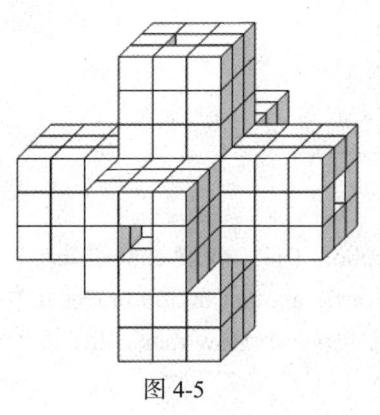

7．用若干个小正立方体拼成如图 4-5 所示的造型，其中有一个小孔分别由左至右、由上至下及由前至后穿透整个造型．请问拼成此造型共需使用多少个小正立方体？

8．将 31513 及 34369 分别除以某个三位数．若所得余数都相同，请问这个余数是什么？

9．从数 1—5 中选四个数填入 2×2 的方格表内，并满足下列条件：

(1) 在同一横列中，在左边的数比右边的数大；

图 4-5

(2) 在同一直行中，在上面的数比下面的数大．

图 4-6 是其中两个例子．请问共有多少种不同的填数方法可满足上述条件？

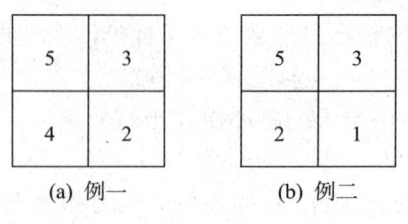

5	3
4	2

(a) 例一

5	3
2	1

(b) 例二

图 4-6

10．彼得使用遥控器操控机器人玩具．遥控器上有 3 个按钮，分别可控制机器人向前走 1 步、2 步或 3 步．若要使机器人向前走 8 步，请问共有多少种不同的操控方法？

4.6　EMIC队际赛试题解答与评注

2006 年国际小学数学竞赛队际竞赛试题解答

1．**解**　令这四个空格由左至右填入的数为 a、b、c、d，则知 $3<a<b<c<d$．但因 $a \geqslant 6$ 时，$a+b+c+d \geqslant 6+7+8+9=30$，故不符合，即 $a=4$ 或 5．

(1) 当 $a=4$ 时，知 $b+c+d=23$ 且 $4<b<c<d$．但因 $b \geqslant 7$ 时，$b+c+d \geqslant 7+8+9=24$，故不符合，即 $b=5$ 或 6．

第4章 2006年第4届国际小学数学竞赛

(i) 当$b=5$时，知$c+d=18$且$5<c<d$，此时 $(c,d) = (6，12)$、$(7，11)$、$(8，10)$这三种情形都满足题意；

(ii) 当$b=6$时，知$c+d=17$且$6<c<d$，此时 $(c,d) = (7，10)$、$(8，9)$ 这两种情形都满足题意.

(2) 当$a=5$时，知$b+c+d=22$且$5<b<c<d$. 因$b \geqslant 7$时，$b+c+d \geqslant 7+8+9 = 24$，故不符合，即$b=6$，此时知$c+d=16$且$6<c<d$，故仅 $(c,d) = (7，9)$ 这一种情形满足题意.

因此一共有 3+2+1=6 种填法.

答: 6种

2. **解** 由题意可知这八位数的数码都不为 0，且因所求为满足条件的最小八位数，故 1 的个数越多越好.

若八位数的 8 个数码都是 1，则各位数码之积为 1 而各位数码之和为 8，不符合；

若八位数里恰有 7 个数码为 1，则令另一个数码为 a，此时各位数码之积为 a 而各位数码之和为 $7+a$，不符合；

若八位数里恰有 6 个数码为 1，则令另两个数码为 a、b，其中 $a \geqslant b$，此时各位数码之积为 ab 而各位数码之和为 $6+a+b$，即得 $ab=6+a+b$，故知

$$ab - a - b = 6, \ ab - a - b + 1 = 7, \ (a-1)(b-1) = 7.$$

因 7 为素数，可得 $a-1 = 7$、$b-1 = 1$，即 $a=8$、$b=2$，故知最小的八位数为 11111128.

若八位数里恰有 5 个或 5 个以下的数码为 1，则其值恒大于 11111128.

答: 11111128

3. **解** X 和 Y 这两个数中较大数为 $\overline{abcd}$，则另一数为 $\overline{dcba}$. 由题意可知

$$\begin{cases} 14773 = \overline{abcd} + \overline{dcba} = 1001(a+d) + 110(b+c), \\ 3177 = \overline{abcd} - \overline{dcba} = 999(a-d) + 90(b-c). \end{cases}$$

$$\Leftrightarrow \begin{cases} 1343 = 91(a+d) + 10(b+c), \\ 353 = 111(a-d) + 10(b-c). \end{cases}$$

观察 $1343 = 91(a+d) + 10(b+c)$ 这一式子的个位数，可知 $a+d = 3$ 或 13；

观察 $353 = 111(a-d) + 10(b-c)$ 这一式子的个位数，可知 $a-d = 3$、$b-c = 2$；

因 $a-d = 3$ 且各位数码均不等于 0，故知 $a+d = 13$，因此 $a=8$、$d=5$ 以

85

及 $b+c=(1343-91\times13)\div10=16$，故可再继续判断出 $b=9$、$c=7$，即所求为 8975.

答: 8975

4. **解** 如图 4-7 所示，连接 PR. 因 $AP=DR$，且 $AP//DR$，故 $APRD$ 为平行四边形，故 $\triangle SPR$ 面积为平行四边形 $APRD$ 面积的一半.

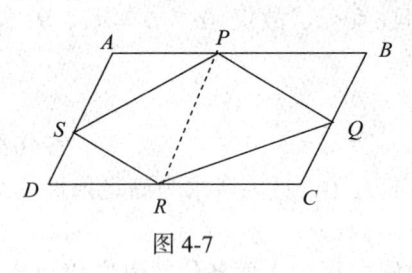

因 $AP=DR$，故 $BP=CR$，且再由 $BP//CR$ 知 $PRCB$ 为平行四边形，所以 $\triangle PQR$ 面积为平行四边形 $PRCB$ 面积的一半.

故四边形 $PQRS$ 的面积为平行四边形 $ABCD$ 的一半，即 $8\ cm^2$.

图 4-7

答: $8\ cm^2$

5. **解** 因小迪在最后一次考试时比目标少得了 $100-75=25$ 分，而总平均便比目标少了 $90-85=5$ 分，故知一共举行了 $25\div5=5$ 次数学考试.

答: 5次

6. **解法 1** 令所拼成的长方体之长、宽、高分别为 a、b、c，其中 a、b、c 皆为正整数，则由题意可知

$$abc=120=2^3\times3\times5,$$
$$(a-2)(b-2)(c-2)=24=2^3\times3.$$

由 $(a-2)(b-2)(c-2)=24$ 知 a、b、c 中不可能有任何一个数超过 26；此时再由 $abc=2^3\times3\times5$ 可判断知 a、b、c 中有一数为 5、10、15 或 20，即 $a-2$、$b-2$、$c-2$ 中有一数为 3、8、13 或 18，接着再由 $(a-2)(b-2)(c-2)=2^3\times3$ 知其中仅 $a-2$、$b-2$、$c-2$ 中有一数为 3 或 8 可能发生，即 a、b、c 中有一数为 5、10.

若 $a-2$、$b-2$、$c-2$ 中有一数为 8，则知另两数必为 1 与 3，此时 a、b、c 为 3、5、10，即 $abc=150$，不符合；故知 $a-2$、$b-2$、$c-2$ 中有一数为 3，不妨令 $a-2=3$，即 $a=5$. 此时可知

$$bc=2^3\times3,$$
$$(b-2)(c-2)=2^3.$$

由 $(b-2)(c-2)=8$ 知 b、c 中不可能有任何一个数超过 10；此时再由 $bc=2^3\times3$ 可判断知 b、c 中有一数为 3 或 6，即 $b-2$、$c-2$ 中有一数为 1 或 4,

第4章　2006年第4届国际小学数学竞赛

不妨令此数为 $b-2$.

若 $b-2=1$，则 $c-2=8$，故不符合；因此知 $b-2=4$，则 $c-2=2$，故知 $b=6$、$c=4$. 因此拼成的长方体之表面积为

$$2\times(5\times6+5\times4+6\times4)=148 \text{ 平方单位}.$$

解法2　令所拼成的长方体之长、宽、高分别为 a、b、c，其中 a、b、c 都为正整数，则由题意可知

$$abc=120=2^3\times3\times5,$$
$$(a-2)(b-2)(c-2)=24$$
$$=1\times1\times24=1\times2\times12=1\times3\times8$$
$$=1\times4\times6=2\times2\times6=2\times3\times4,$$

即 a、b、c 分别等于 (3，3，26)、(3，4，14)、(3，5，10)、(3，6，8)、(4，4，8)、(4，5，6)，而唯有 (4，5，6) 时 abc=120. 因此拼成的长方体之表面积为 $2\times(5\times6+5\times4+6\times4)=148$ 平方单位.

答：148平方单位

7．解　可知每一条穿透的隧道均是挖去 9 个小正立方体，故最多挖去 9×3 个小正立方体；而观察这三条穿透的隧道位置，可知这三条穿透的隧道均通过中央的点，即此小正立方体被多算了 2 次，故知共使用了 $3\times3\times3\times7-9\times3+1\times2=164$ 个小正立方体.

答：164个

8．解　因 31513、34369 除以某个三位数后所得余数相同，故两数相减后必为此三位数的倍数，即 34369−31513=2856 为此三位数的倍数. 因 $2856=2^3\times3\times7\times17$，最大的三位数因子为 952，故可取 952 为此三位数. 此时因 34369=952×36+97、31513= 952×33+97，故所求为 97.

答：97

9．解　如图 4-8 所示，令 a、b、c、d 为填入各方格的数.

可知 $a>b>d$、$a>c>d$，亦即填入的四个数中，a 必为最大数、d 必为最小数且 b、c 的值互换并仍符合题意. 因五个数中任选四个不同的数共有 5 种选法，故知共有 5×2=10 种不同的填数方法.

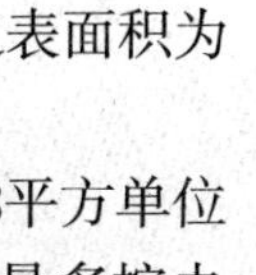

a	b
c	d

图 4-8

答：10

10．解　可令机器人玩具向前走 1 步的位置为 1、向前走 2 步的位置为 2、向前走 3 步的位置为 3、…，以此类推.

再令机器人玩具走到 a 位置的方法数为 $F(a)$. 观察可知机器人玩具要到达 a 位置时，必先经过 $a-1$、$a-2$ 或 $a-3$，即知 $F(a)=F(a-1)+F(a-2)+F(a-3)$，且经由观察易得知 $F(1)=1$、$F(2)=2$、$F(3)=4$，故可得知 $F(4)=1+2+4=7$、$F(5)=2+4+7=13$、$F(6)=4+7+13=24$、$F(7)=7+13+24=44$、$F(8)=13+24+44=81$，即共有 81 种不同的操控方法.

答: 81 种

第5章 2007年第5届国际小学数学竞赛

5.1 EMIC个人赛英文试题

Elementary Mathematics International Contest 2007
31st July, 2007, Hong Kong, China

Individual Contest

1. The product of two three-digit numbers $\overline{abc}$ and $\overline{cba}$ is 396396, where $a>c$. Find the value of $\overline{abc}$.

2. In the figure below, in a right-angled triangle ACD, the area of shaded region is 10 cm^2. $AD=5$ cm, $AB=BC$, $DE=EC$. Find the length of AB, in cm.

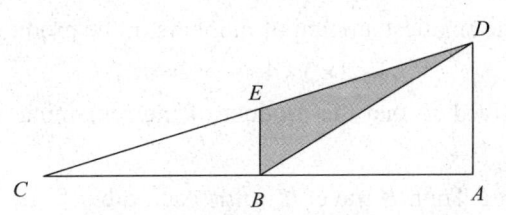

3. A wooden rectangular block, 4 cm×5 cm×6 cm, is painted red and then cut into several 1 cm×1 cm×1 cm cubes. What is the ratio of the number of cubes with two red faces to the number of cubes with three red faces?

4. Eve said to her mother, "If I reverse the two-digits of my age, I will get your age." Her mother said, "Tomorrow is my birthday, and my age will then be twice your age." It is known that their birthdays are not on the same day. How old is Eve?

5. Find how many three-digit numbers satisfy all the following conditions:
if it is divided by 2, the remainder is 1;
if it is divided by 3, the remainder is 2;
if it is divided by 4, the remainder is 3;
if it is divided by 5, the remainder is 4;

if it is divided by 8, the remainder is 7.

6. A giraffe lives in a right-angled triangle. The base and the height of the triangle are 12 m and 16 m respectively. The area is surrounded by a fence. The giraffe can eat the grass outside the fence at a maximum distance of 2 m. What is the maximum area outside the fence, in which the grass can be eaten by the giraffe, in m^2? (Given $\pi = 3.14$ and answer to 2 decimals places)

7. Mary and Peter are running around a circular track of 400 m. Mary's speed equals $\dfrac{3}{5}$ of Peter's. They start running at the same point and the same time, but in opposite directions. 200 seconds later, they have met four times. How many m per second does Peter run faster than Mary?

8. Evaluate $2^{2007} - \left(2^{2006} + 2^{2005} + 2^{2004} + \cdots + 2^2 + 2 + 1\right)$.

9. A, B and C are stamp-collectors. A has 18 stamps more than B. The ratio of the number of stamps of B to that of C is 7 : 5. The ratio of the sum of B's and C's stamps to that of A's is 6 : 5. How many stamps does C have?

10. What is the smallest amount of numbers in the product
$$1 \times 2 \times 3 \times 4 \times \cdots \times 26 \times 27$$
that should be removed so that the product of the remaining numbers is a perfect square?

11. Train A and Train B travel towards each other from Town a and Town b respectively, at a constant speed. The two towns are 1320 km apart. After the two trains meet, Train A takes 5 hours to reach Town b while Train B takes 7.2 hours to reach Town a. How many km does Train A run per hour?

12. Balls of the same size and weight are placed in a container. There are 8 different colors and 90 balls in each color. What is the minimum number of balls that must be drawn from the container in order to get balls of 4 different colors with at least 9 balls for each color?

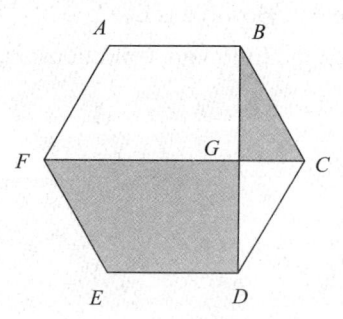

13. In a regular hexagon ABCDEF, two diagonals, FC and BD, intersect at G. What is the ratio of the area of △BCG to that of quadrilateral FEDG?

14. There are three prime numbers. If the sum of their squares is 5070, what is the product of these three numbers?

15. Let *ABCDEF* be a regular hexagon. *O* is the centre of the hexagon. *M* and *N* are the mid-points of *DE* and *OB* respectively. If the sum of areas of △*FNO* and △*FME* is 3 cm^2, find the area of the hexagon, in cm^2.

5.2 EMIC个人赛中文试题

2007年国际小学数学竞赛个人竞赛试题

1. 已知三位数 $\overline{abc}$ 与 $\overline{cba}$ 的乘积为 396396，其中 $a > c$. 请问 $\overline{abc}$ 之值是什么？

2. 直角△*ACD* 中，阴影部分的面积为 10 cm^2，如图 5-1 所示. 已知 *AD*=5cm，*AB*=*BC*，*DE*=*EC*. 请问 *AB* 的长度为多少 cm？

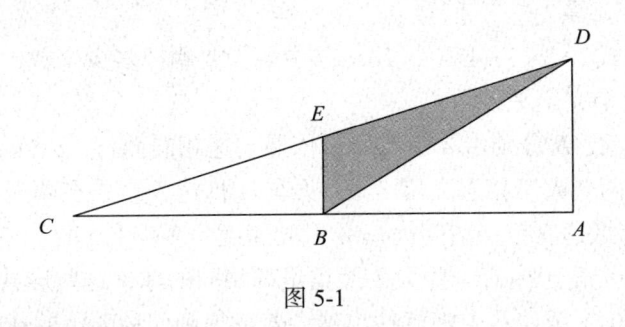

图 5-1

3. 在 4cm×5cm×6cm 的长方体木块的表面涂上红色，然后再将它切成 1cm×1cm×1cm 的小立方块. 请问这些小立方块中，恰好有两面涂有红色的个数与恰好有三面涂有红色的个数之比为何？

4. 尹文对他的妈妈说："若我将我的年龄的两个数码对调，则可得到您的年龄."他妈妈说："明天是我的生日，则我的年龄将是你的年龄的两倍."已知他们两人的生日不在同一天. 请问尹文今年几岁？

5. 请问有多少个三位数满足下列条件？
(1) 若将它除以 2，所得余数为 1；
(2) 若将它除以 3，所得余数为 2；
(3) 若将它除以 4，所得余数为 3；

(4) 若将它除以5，所得余数为4；

(5) 若将它除以8，所得余数为7．

6．一只长颈鹿被关在一个外形为直角三角形的农场里，这个直角三角形农场的两个直角边分别为12 m与16 m，它的四周都用篱笆围起来．长颈鹿最远可以吃到篱笆外2 m的青草．请问这只长颈鹿总共最多可以吃到篱笆外多少 m² 的青草？（令 π = 3.14，计算至小数第二位）

7．玛丽与彼得沿着400 m的圆形跑道跑步．玛丽的速度是彼得速度的 $\frac{3}{5}$．他们同时从跑道上的同一点出发逆向而跑步．200秒钟之后，他们第四次相遇．请问彼得的速度比玛丽的速度每秒钟快多少 m？

8．请问 $2^{2007} - (2^{2006} + 2^{2005} + 2^{2004} + \cdots + 2^2 + 2 + 1)$ 之值是什么？

9．A、B 与 C 三人集邮．A 比 B 多18张邮票，B 的邮票张数与 C 的邮票张数之比是 7：5．B 和 C 的邮票张数之总和与 A 的邮票张数之比是 6：5．请问 C 有多少张邮票？

10．从乘式 $1 \times 2 \times 3 \times 4 \times \cdots \times 26 \times 27$ 中最少要删掉多少个数，才能使得剩下的数的乘积是个完全平方数？

11．火车 A、B 分别由 a 市与 b 市依照匀速相向而行．a、b 两市之距离为1320 km．在两列火车相遇之后5 h，火车 A 抵达 b 市；在两列火车相遇之后7.2 h，火车 B 抵达 a 市．请问火车 A 行驶速度为多少 km/h？

12．在一个箱子内有一些大小及重量都相同的球，这些球共有八种颜色，每种颜色各90个球．从中随意抽出球，若欲得到四种颜色的球，这四种颜色的球每种至少有9个，请问至少要抽出多少个球才能保证一定可以达成目的？

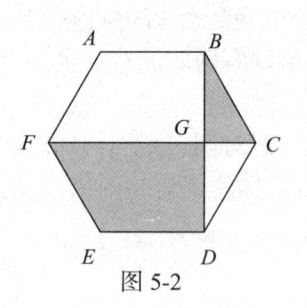

13．在正六边形 ABCDEF 中，对角线 FC 与 BD 相交于点 G．请问△BCG 的面积与四边形 FEDG 的面积之比为多少（图5-2）？

14．有三个不同的素数，已知它们的平方的总和为5070，请问这三个素数的乘积是多少？

15．已知 ABCDEF 是正六边形，O 为其中心．点 M 与点 N 分别为线段 DE 与线段 OB 之中点．已知△FNO 与△FME 的面积之总和为 3cm²，请问此正六边形的面积为多少 cm²？

图5-2

第 5 章　2007 年第 5 届国际小学数学竞赛

5.3　EMIC 个人赛试题解答与评注

2007 年国际小学数学竞赛个人竞赛试题解答

1. **解法 1**　由积的个位数可知 $a \times c$ 的个位数为 6，即 $(a, c) = (9, 4)$、$(8, 2)$、$(8, 7)$、$(6, 1)$ 或 $(3, 2)$.

因 396396<560000=800×700，故知 $(a, c) \neq (8, 7)$；

因 396396>270000=900×300>140000=700×200>120000=400× 300，故知 $(a, c) \neq (8, 2)$、$(6, 1)$ 或 $(3, 2)$；因此 $(a, c) = (9, 4)$，即 $a=9$、$c=4$.

此时由积的十位数以及 $ac=36$ 可知 $9b+4b+3$ 的个位数为 9，即 $13b$ 的个位数为 6，故 $b=2$.

解法 2　396396=396×1001=2×2×3×3×11×7×11×13，故知 $\overline{abc}$ 与 $\overline{cba}$ 都是 11 的倍数. 由积的个位数可知 $a \times c$ 的个位数为 6，即得知 $(a, c) = (9, 4)$、$(8, 2)$、$(8, 7)$、$(6, 1)$ 或 $(3, 2)$. 故知 $\overline{abc}$ =924, 847, 671, 352，经验证其中只有 $\overline{abc}$ =924 符合所求.

答: 924

2. **解法 1**　因 $DE=EC$，故知 $\triangle BED$ 与 $\triangle BEC$ 的面积相同，即 $\triangle BEC$ 的面积为 10 (cm²)，因 BE 为 $\triangle ACD$ 的中点连线，故知 $\triangle ACD$ 的面积为 40 (cm²). 此时因已知 $AD=5$ (cm) 且 AD 为 $\triangle ACD$ 的高，故知 $AC= (40 \times 2) \div 5 =16$ (cm). 再因 $AB=BC$，故 $AB=8$ (cm).

解法 2　因 BE 为直角 $\triangle ACD$ 的中点连线，故知 $BE=AD/2=2.5$ (cm). $\triangle BED$ 的面积为 10 (cm²)，故 $AB = (10 \times 2) \div 2.5 = 8$ (cm).

答: 8 cm

3. **解**　可知三面涂有红色的小立方块需位于原长方体木块的顶点，故知共有 8 个；而恰有两面涂有红色的小立方块需位于原长方体木块的边上但不为顶点，故共有 [(4–2) + (5–2) + (6–2)]×4 =36 个. 故所求个数比为 36 : 8= 9 : 2.

答: 9 : 2

4. **解**　若令尹文的年龄为 $\overline{ab}$，则知他妈妈的年龄为 $\overline{ba}$，且 $\overline{ba}+1 = 2 \times \overline{ab}$，其中 a, b 为正整数且满足 $0 < a \leq 9$、$0 < b \leq 9$. 此时即知

93

$$10b+a+1=2\times(10a+b),$$
$$8b=19a-1,$$

因 a、b 为正整数，a 为奇数且满足 $19a<8\times 9+1=73$ 即 $a\leqslant 3$，但 $a=1$ 不符合，故知仅 $a=3$ 满足，此时 $b=7$.

答：37 岁

5. **解** 可知满足条件的三位数加 1 可分别被 2、3、4、5、8 整除，而 2、3、4、5、8 的最小公倍数为 120，故满足此条件的三位数为 120 的倍数减 1. 而三位数中满足此条件的为 119、239、359、479、599、719、839、959，共 8 个数.

答：8 个

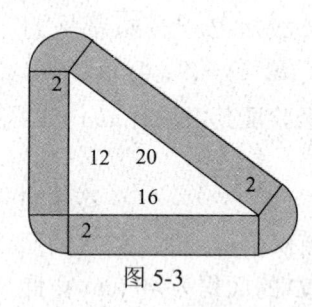

6. **解** 由勾股定理 $12^2+16^2=400=20^2$，可知直角三角形农场的斜边为 20 (m). 如图 5-3 所示，阴影部分即为篱笆外长颈鹿可以吃到青草篱笆. 可知三个扇形部分可构成一个半径为 2 (m)的圆，故知长颈鹿总共最多可以吃到篱笆外 $2\times 12+2\times 16+2\times 20+3.14\times 2^2=108.56$ (m²)的青草.

答：108.56 m²

7. **解** 因两人同时从跑道上的同一点出发逆向而跑，故第四次相遇时，两人合计跑了 4 圈；即两人逆向而跑每 50 秒钟可跑一圈 400 (m)，故两人之速度和为每秒钟 8 (m). 因玛丽的速度是彼得速度的五分之三，可知玛丽的速度是每秒钟 3 (m)，而彼得的速度是每秒钟 5 (m)，因此彼得的速度比玛丽的速度每秒钟快 2 (m).

答：2 m

8. **解法 1** 可知
$$2^{2007}-\left(2^{2006}+2^{2005}+2^{2004}+\cdots+2^3+2^2+2+1\right)$$
$$=2^{2007}-2^{2006}-2^{2005}-2^{2004}-\cdots-2^3-2^2-2-1.$$
因 $2^{2007}=2\times 2^{2006}$，故 $2^{2007}-2^{2006}=2^{2006}$，即原式可改写为
$$2^{2006}-2^{2005}-2^{2004}-\cdots-2^3-2^2-2-1.$$
因 $2^{2006}=2\times 2^{2005}$，故 $2^{2006}-2^{2005}=2^{2005}$，即原式可改写为
$$2^{2005}-2^{2004}-\cdots-2^3-2^2-2-1.$$
……

第5章 2007年第5届国际小学数学竞赛

因 $2^2=2\times 2$,故 $2^2-2=2$,即原式可改写为
$$2-1=1,$$
故所求为 1.

解法2 可知 $2^{2006}+2^{2005}+2^{2004}+\cdots+2^3+2^2+2+1=\dfrac{2^{2007}-1}{2-1}=2^{2007}-1$,故原式可改写为 $2^{2007}-(2^{2007}-1)=1$.

答: 1

9. **解** 因 B 的邮票张数与 C 的邮票张数之比是 7∶5,可令 B 有 7a 张邮票、C 有 5a 张邮票,两人共有 12a 张邮票. 由 B 和 C 的邮票张数之总和与 A 的邮票张数之比是 6∶5,可知 A 有 10a 张邮票. 因已知 A 比 B 多 18 张邮票,即 3a=18,a=6. 故得知 A 有 60 张邮票、B 有 42 张邮票、C 有 30 张邮票.

答: 30张

10. **解** 将 $1\times 2\times 3\times 4\times\cdots\times 26\times 27$ 作素因子分解,它等于
$$2^{23}\times 3^{13}\times 5^6\times 7^3\times 11^2\times 13^2\times 17\times 19\times 23.$$
因要求删除后剩下来的数之乘积为完全平方数,故知其素因子的幂次必为偶数,即必须删除
$2\times 3\times 7\times 17\times 19\times 23=6\times 7\times 17\times 19\times 23$ 或 $3\times 14\times 17\times 19\times 23$ 或 $2\times 21\times 17\times 19\times 23$.

故至少必须删除 5 个数.

答: 5个

11. **解** 可令两列火车出发后行驶 x h 后在 c 地相遇,则知火车 A 从 a 市至 c 地行驶 x h 而火车 B 从 c 地至 a 市行驶 7.2 h,故其速度比为 x∶7.2,以及火车 B 从 b 市至 c 地行驶 x h 而火车 A 从 c 地至 b 市行驶 5 h,故其速度比为 5∶x. 由此可知 x∶7.2=5∶x,即 $x^2=5\times 7.2=36$.

因 x 必为非负整数,故知 $x=6$,即火车 A 共行驶了 6+5=11(h),其行驶 $\dfrac{1320}{11}=120$(km/h).

答: 120 km

12. **解** 可知若有三种颜色的球全部被抽出而其余五种颜色的球各被抽出 8 个时,是无法完成目的的最多球数,故知至少需抽出 90×3+8×5+1=270+40+1=311 个球.

答: 311个

13. **解** 令 O 为 FC 中点，并连接 OE、OD，如图5-4所示。因六边形 $ABCDEF$ 为正六边形，故可知 $\triangle BCG$ 与 $\triangle DCG$ 面积相等，且 $OG=CG=\frac{1}{2}OC=\frac{1}{2}OF=\frac{1}{2}ED$。若令 $\triangle BCG$ 的面积为1，则知 $\triangle DCG$ 与 $\triangle GOD$ 的面积都为1，也由此知 $\triangle OED$ 与 $\triangle OFE$ 的面积都为 $1+1=2$，故 $\triangle BCG$ 的面积与四边形 $FEDG$ 的面积之比为

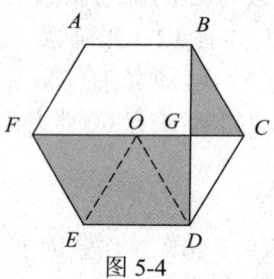

$$1 : (1+2+2) = 1 : 5.$$

图 5-4

答：1∶5

14. **解** 因 5070 为偶数，故这三个素数中，必有一个为偶数2，否则三个奇数的平方和必为奇数，矛盾，故可令这三个素数为 2、p 及 q，且知 $p^2+q^2=5070-2^2=5066$。

此时观察个位数，因除了5以外的所有素数平方的个位数都是1或9，故若两个奇素数的平方和之个位数要为6，仅可能其中一个素数为5，故此时可令 $p=5$，且知 $q^2=5066-25=5041=71^2$，即 $q=71$。故这三个素数的乘积为 $2\times 5\times 71=710$。

答：710

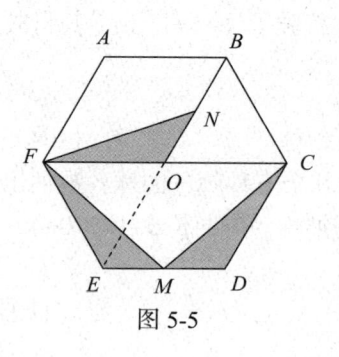

15. **解** 由题意可画出图 5-5。因六边形 $ABCDEF$ 为正六边形，故可知 $OF=CD$、$ON=DM$ 且 $\angle FON=\angle CDM=120°$，即 $\triangle FON$ 与 $\triangle CDM$ 面积相等。连接 OE，则知 $\triangle FCM$ 的面积是 $\triangle FOE$ 面积的2倍。而再由六边形 $ABCDEF$ 为正六边形知四边形 $CDEF$ 的面积为 $\triangle FOE$ 面积的3倍，故知 $\triangle FOE$ 的面积即为四边形 $CDEF$ 的面积扣掉 $\triangle FCM$ 的面积，即 $\triangle FEM$ 与 $\triangle CDM$ 的面积和，

图 5-5

故知其值为 3cm². 因此正六边形 ABCDEF 的面积为 3×6=18 (cm²).

答: 18 cm²

5.4 EMIC 队际赛英文试题

Elementary Mathematics International Contest 2007
31st July 2007, HongKong, China

Team Contest

1. Town A and Town B are connected by a highway which consists of an uphill and a downhill section. A car's speed is 20 km/h and 35 km/h for the uphill and downhill sections respectively. It takes 9 hours from A to B but $7\frac{1}{2}$ hours from B to A. What is the downhill distance (in km) from A to B?

2. The houses on one side of a street are numbered using consecutive odd numbers, starting from 1. On the other side, the houses are numbered using consecutive even numbers starting from 2. In total 256 digits are used on the side with even numbers and 404 digits on the side with odd numbers. Find the difference between the largest odd number and the largest even number.

3. As shown in the figure below, $ABCD$ is a parallelogram with area of 10 cm². If $AB=3$ cm, $BC=5$ cm, $AE=BF=AG=2$ cm, GH is parallel to EF, find the area of $EFHG$, in cm².

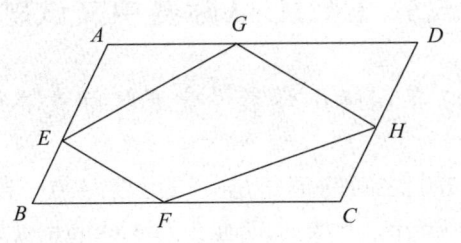

4. Find the two smallest integers which satisfy the following conditions:
(1) The difference between the integers is 3.
(2) In each number, the sum of the digits is a multiple of 11.

5. A four-digit number can be formed by linking two different two-digit prime numbers together. For example, 13 and 17 can be linked together to form

a four-digit number 1317 or 1713. Some four-digit numbers formed in this way can be divided by the average of the two prime numbers. Give one possible four-digit number that fulfills the requirement. (Please be reminded that 1317 and 1713 in the example above do not fulfill the requirement, because they are not divisible by 15)

6. How many prime factors does the number $2 + 2^2 + 2^3 + \cdots + 2^{15} + 2^{16}$ have?

7. A pencil, an easer, and a notebook together cost 100 dollars. A notebook costs more than two pencils, three pencils cost more than four erasers, and three erasers cost more than a notebook. How much does each item cost (assuming that the cost of each item is a whole number of dollars)

8. There are 8 pairs of natural numbers which satisfy the following condition. The product of the sum of the numbers and the difference of the numbers is 1995. Which pair of numbers has the greatest difference?

9. A land with a dimension 52 m×24 m is surrounded by fence. An agricultural scientist wants to divide the land into identical square sections for testing, using fence with total length 1172 m. The sides of the square sections must be parallel to the sides of the land. What is the maximum number of square testing sections that can be formed?

10. Find the total number of ways that 270 can be written as a sum of consecutive positive integers.

5.5　EMIC队际赛中文试题

2007年国际小学数学竞赛队际竞赛试题

1. 在 A 市与 B 市之间的道路是一段上坡路与一段下坡路．有一辆车上坡时的速度为 20 km/h，下坡时的速度为 35 km/h．已知从 A 市到 B 市需时 9 h，从 B 市到 A 市只需 7.5h．请问从 A 市到 B 市的下坡路段的长度为多少 km？

2. 道路的一侧从 1 号开始编上连续奇数的号码，另一侧则从 2 号开始编上连续偶数的号码．已知在编上奇数号的这一侧共使用 404 个数码，在编上偶数号的这一侧共使用 256 个数码，请问这条道路上编号最大的奇数与编号最大

第 5 章 2007 年第 5 届国际小学数学竞赛

的偶数之差为多少?

3. 平行四边形 ABCD 的面积为 10cm², 若 AB=3cm, BC=5cm, AE=BF=AG=2cm, GH 平行于 EF, 如图 5-6 所示. 请问四边形 EFHG 的面积为多少 cm²?

图 5-6

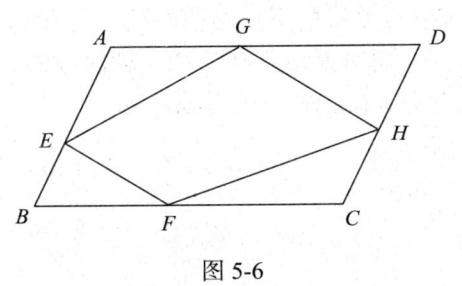

4. 请求出两个最小的正整数满足以下条件:
(1) 这两个正整数之差为 3;
(2) 对每一个正整数而言, 它的各位数码和都可被 11 整除.

5. 将两个相异的两位数的素数合并可以组成一个四位数, 例如, 将 13 与 17 合并可组成四位数 1317 和 1713. 用此方法组成的四位数中, 某些数可以被组成它的两个素数的平均数整除. 请找出任何一个满足上述条件的四位数. **(请注意**上面所给出的例子中, 1317 和 1713 并未满足所要求的条件, 因为它们不可被 15 整除**)**

6. 请问 $2+2^2+2^3+\cdots+2^{15}+2^{16}$ 的值共有多少个素因子?

7. 一支铅笔、一个橡皮擦及一本笔记的总价为 100 元. 一本笔记的价格大于两支铅笔的价格, 三支铅笔的价格大于四个橡皮擦的价格, 三个橡皮擦的价格大于一本笔记的价格. 若这三种物品的单价都是正整数元, 请问这三种物品的单价分别为多少元?

8. 有八组数对满足以下条件: 数对中的两个数之和与差的乘积为 1995.
请问在这八组数对中, 哪一组数对的两个数之差最大?

9. 一块 52 m×24 m 的矩形田地, 它的外围已经用篱笆围住. 一位农技专家想在这块田地的内部用篱笆将它分隔成许多全等的小正方形以进行实验, 小正方形的各边必须平行于矩形田地的各边. 已知他共使用 1172 m 长的篱笆来分隔, 请问他最多可以围出多少个小正方形?

10. 将 270 表示为两个以上的连续正整数之和, 请问共有多少种不同的方法?

5.6　EMIC队际赛试题解答与评注

2007年国际小学数学竞赛队际竞赛试题解答

1. **解法1**　令 A 市到 B 市的下坡路段的长度为 a (km)、A 市到 B 市的上坡路段的长度为 b (km)，则知 B 市到 A 市的上坡路段的长度为 a (km)、B 市到 A 市的下坡路段的长度为 b (km)，且可得知

$$\begin{cases} \dfrac{a}{35}+\dfrac{b}{20}=9, \\ \dfrac{a}{20}+\dfrac{b}{35}=7\dfrac{1}{2}=\dfrac{15}{2} \end{cases} \Leftrightarrow \begin{cases} 4a+7b=9\times 140=1260, \\ 7a+4b=\dfrac{15}{2}\times 140=1050, \end{cases}$$

故知 11 $(a+b)$ =2310，即 $a+b$=210，故知

$$a=(1050-840)\div 3=70,\qquad b=(1260-840)\div 3=140.$$

解法2　距离与时间成正比，速度与时间成反比，假设从 A 市到 B 市的上坡路段的长度为 m、从下坡路段的长度为 n，则从 A 市到 B 市与从 B 市到 A 市所需的时间比为 $\dfrac{7m+4n}{4m+7n}=\dfrac{9}{7.5}=\dfrac{6}{5}$，可得知 m=2n．又从 A 市到 B 市上坡所用的时间与下坡所用的时间比为 $\dfrac{7m}{4n}=\dfrac{14}{4}=\dfrac{7}{2}$，所以上坡用 7 h，下坡用 2 h.

故从 A 市到 B 市的下坡路段的长度为 35×2=70 (km)．

答：70 km

2. **解法1**　从 1 至 9 共有 5 个奇数，用 5 个数码；从 11 至 99 有 45 个奇数，共享 90 个数码；故三位数的奇数共享 404–5–90=309 个数码，即编号最大的奇数为第 309÷3=103 个三位数奇数，即 305.

从 2 至 8 共有 4 个偶数，合计用了 4 个数码；从 10 至 98 共有 45 个偶数，合计用了 90 个数码；因此三位数的偶数共享了 256–4–90=162 个数码，即编号最大的偶数为第 162÷3=54 个三位数偶数，即 208．因此所求为 305–208=97．

解法2　从 1 至 9 有 5 个奇数、4 个偶数；从 10 至 99 奇数与偶数个数一样多．故三位数的奇数比偶数多 (404–256–1)÷3=49 个，所以编号最大的奇数与编号最大的偶数之差为 49×2–1=97.

答：97

3. **解法1**　连接 GF．因 AG=BF=2 (cm)，且 AG//BF，故 $ABFG$ 为平行四

第 5 章　2007 年第 5 届国际小学数学竞赛

边形 (图 5-7)，且其面积为 $\frac{2}{5} \times 10 = 4\ \text{cm}^2$，故 △$GEF$ 的面积为 $\frac{1}{2} \times 4 = 2\ (\text{cm}^2)$；同理 $GFCD$ 为平行四边形，且其面积为 $\frac{3}{5} \times 10 = 6 (\text{cm}^2)$，故 △$GHF$ 的面积为 $\frac{1}{2} \times 6 = 3\ (\text{cm}^2)$；因此四边形 $EFGH$ 的面积为 2+3=5 (cm^2).

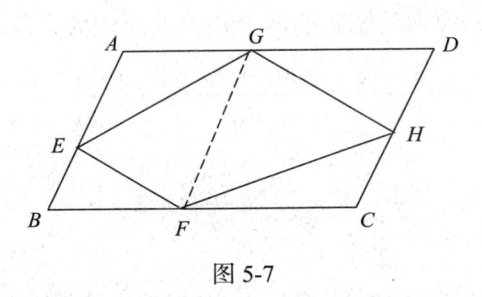

图 5-7

解法 2 连接 GF. 因 $AG=BF=2$ (cm)，且 $AG//BF$，故 $ABFG$ 与 $GFCD$ 都是平行四边形，则 △EFG 的面积为平行四边形 $ABFG$ 面积的一半；△FGH 的面积为平行四边形 $GFCD$ 面积的一半. 因此四边形 $EFHG$ 的面积为平行四边形 $ABCD$ 面积的一半，即 5 (cm^2).

答：5 cm^2

4. 解 令这两个正整数为 A、$A+3$，而 A 的各位数码和为 S.

若 A 的个位数为 0、1、2、3、4、5、6，则 $A+3$ 的各位数码和恒为 $S+3$. 因 S 与 $S+3$ 不可能同时为 11 的倍数，故此情形不可能发生，即 A 的个位数为 7、8、9.

若 A 的十位数不是 9，则 $A+3$ 的各位数码和为 $S-6$. 因 S 与 $S-6$ 不可能同时为 11 的倍数，故此情形不可能发生. 即 A 的十位数为 9，此时 $A+3$ 会进位 1 至百位数且十位数为 0.

若 A 的百位数不是 9，则 $A+3$ 的各位数码和为 $S-15$. 因 S 与 $S-15$ 不可能同时为 11 的倍数，故此情形不可能发生，即 A 的百位数为 9.

若 A 的千位数不是 9，则 $A+3$ 的各位数码和为 $S-24$. 因 S 与 $S-24$ 不可能同时为 11 的倍数，故此情形不可能发生. 即 A 的千位数为 9，此时 $A+3$ 会进位 1 至万位数且十位数、百位数、千位数为 0.

若 A 的万位数不是 9，则 $A+3$ 的各位数码和为 $S-33$. 因 S 与 $S-33$ 同时为 11 的倍数发生在 S 为 11 的倍数时. 因此时已知 $S \geq 9+9+9+7 = 34$，故知 $S=44$、

55、….

因 A、$A+3$ 为满足题意的最小两个正整数，故只考虑 $S=44$，且可令 $A=\overline{a999b}$，则知 $a+b=44-27=17$，故可得知 $a=8$、$b=9$，即满足题意的最小两个正整数为 89999、90002.

答：89999、90002

5. **解** 令 p、q 为满足题意的两个相异的两位数素数，则知

$$\frac{\frac{100p+q}{p+q}}{2} = \frac{200p+2q}{p+q} = 2 + \frac{198p}{p+q} \text{ 及}$$

$$\frac{\frac{100q+p}{p+q}}{2} = \frac{200q+2p}{p+q} = 2 + \frac{198q}{p+q}$$

为正整数，再因 p、q 为素数可推得 $p+q$ 为 198 的因子. 此时由 p、q 为两个相异的两位数素数知 $11+13=24 \leqslant p+q \leqslant 186 = 89+97$ 且 $p+q$ 为偶数，故 $p+q$ 的值为 66. 接着我们必须找出和为 66 的两个素数. 可知当其中一个素数为 11、17、31 时，则另一个数不为素数.

若其中一个素数为 13，则另一个素数为 53，此四位数为 1353 或 5313；
若其中一个素数为 19，则另一个素数为 47，此四位数为 1947 或 4719；
若其中一个素数为 23，则另一个素数为 43，此四位数为 2343 或 4323；
若其中一个素数为 29，则另一个素数为 37，此四位数为 2937 或 3729.

答：1353、5313、1947、4719、2343、4323、2937、3729 共 8 个

6. **解** 可知 $2+2^2+2^3+\cdots+2^{15}+2^{16} = \frac{2(2^{16}-1)}{2-1} = 2 \times (2^{16}-1)$，故原式可改写为 $2 \times (2^8+1) \times (2^4+1) \times (2^2+1) \times (2+1) \times (2-1) = 2 \times 3 \times 5 \times 17 \times 257$，共有 5 个素因子.

答：5 个

7. **解** 令一本笔记 a 元、一支铅笔 b 元、一个橡皮擦 c 元，则由题意知

第5章 2007年第5届国际小学数学竞赛

$$\begin{cases} a+b+c=100, \\ a>2b, \\ 3b>4c, \\ 3c>a. \end{cases} \Leftrightarrow \begin{cases} a+b+c=100, \\ a>2b, \\ b>\dfrac{4}{3}c, \\ c>\dfrac{1}{3}a. \end{cases}$$

故可判断出 $a>b>c$.

(1) 因 $a+b+c=100<a+b+b=a+2b$ 且 $a>2b$，故知 $a>50$；

(2) 因 $a+b+c=100>2b+\dfrac{4}{3}c+c>\dfrac{8}{3}c+\dfrac{4}{3}c+c=5c$，故知 $c<20$；

(3) 因 $c>\dfrac{1}{3}a$ 且 $a>50$，故知 $c>16$.

故可知 $c=17$、18 或 19：

若 $c=17$，则 $3c=51>a>50$，即 a 不为正整数，不符合；

若 $c=18$，由 $3c=54>a>2b$ 知 $b<27$，故 $b+c\leqslant 26+18=44$，即 $a\geqslant 100-44=56$，矛盾；

故 $c=19$，此时 $a+b=100-19=81>2b+b=3b$，知 $b<27$. 又由 $3b>4c$，知 $3b>76$，即 $b>25$. 故 $b=26$，$a=55$. 所以一本笔记 55 元、一支铅笔 26 元、一个橡皮擦 19 元.

答：一本笔记55元、一支铅笔26元、一个橡皮擦19元

8. **解** 令 a、b 为满足条件的一组数对，其中 $a>b$，则知 $(a+b)(a-b)=1995$. 此时两数差最大发生在 $a-b=1995$、$a+b=1$ 时，将两式相加后化简即可知 $a=998$、两式相减后化简即可知 $b=-997$.

答：$(998, -997)$

9. **解** 可令所围出的小正方形边长为 a m，则共有 $\dfrac{52}{a}-1$ 条篱笆与长度为 24 m 的边平行、$\dfrac{24}{a}-1$ 条篱笆与长度为 52 m 的边平行，故专家所用的篱笆总长度为 $24\times\left(\dfrac{52}{a}-1\right)+52\times\left(\dfrac{24}{a}-1\right)$ (m)，即 $24\times\left(\dfrac{52}{a}-1\right)+52\times\left(\dfrac{24}{a}-1\right)=1172$，化简后即可得 $2\times\dfrac{24\times 52}{a}=1172+52+24=1248$，故知 $a=2$，共围出 $\dfrac{52\times 24}{2\times 2}=312$ 个小正方形.

答：312个小正方形

10. **解法1** 令 270 可写成 a、$a+1$、$a+2$、$\cdots$、$a+k$ 这 $k+1$ 个连续正整数之和，其中 a、k 为正整数，则知 $270 = \dfrac{(2a+k)(k+1)}{2}$，即 $(2a+k)(k+1) = 540 = 2^2 \times 3^3 \times 5$。因 $2a+k > k+1$，且 $2a+k$ 与 $k+1$ 的奇偶性必不相同，故可列表 5-1 如下。

表 5-1

$2a+k$	$k+1$	k	a	270
180	3	2	89	89+90+91
135	4	3	66	66+67+68+69
108	5	4	52	52+53+54+55+56
60	9	8	26	26+27+28+29+30+31+32+33+34
45	12	11	17	17+18+19+20+21+22+23+24+25+26+27+28
36	15	14	11	11+12+13+14+15+16+17+18+19+20+21+22+23+24+25
27	20	19	4	4+5+6+7+8+9+10+11+12+13+14+15+16+17+18+19+20+21+22+23

故共有 7 种方法。

解法2 一个矩形方格表若其中有一个边长为大于 1 的奇数，则它可以沿网格线切为两片全等的阶梯状，每片阶梯状可视为连续的正整数。$540 = 2^2 \times 3^3 \times 5$，它共有 $(1+3) \times (1+1) = 8$ 个奇因子，故有 7 种不同的矩形其中的一个边长为大于 1 的奇数且其面积为 540，它们分别是 3×180、4×135、5×108、9×60、12×45、15×36、20×27。每个这样的矩形都可以沿网格线切为两片全等的阶梯状，故 270 共有 7 种不同的方法表示为两个以上的连续正整数之和。

答：7 种

第6章 2008年第6届国际小学数学竞赛

6.1 EMIC个人赛英文试题

Elementary Mathematics International Contest 2008
28th October, 2008, Chiang Mai, Thailand

Individual Contest

1. Starting from the central circle 2, move between two tangent circles. What is the number of ways of covering four circles with the numbers 2, 0, 0 and 8 inside, in that order?

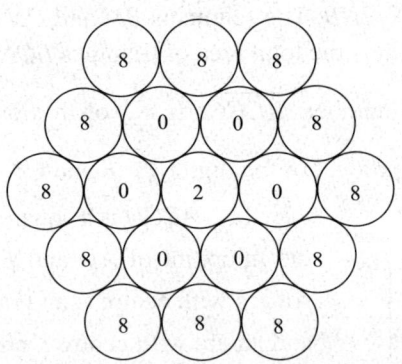

2. Each duck weighs the same, and each duckling weighs the same. If the total weight of 3 ducks and 2 ducklings is 32 kilograms, the total weight of 4 ducks and 3 ducklings is 44 kilograms, what is the total weight, in kilograms, of 2 ducks and 1 duckling?

3. If 25% of the people who were sitting stand up, and 25% of the people who were standing sit down, then 70% of the people are standing. How many percent of the people were standing initially?

4. A sedan of length 3 metres is chasing a truck of length 17 metres. The sedan is travelling at a constant speed of 110 kilometres per hour, while the truck is

travelling at a constant speed of 100 kilometres per hour. From the moment when the front of the sedan is level with the back of the truck to the moment when the front of the truck is level with the back of the sedan, how many seconds would it take?

5. Consider all six-digit numbers consisting of each of the digits '0', '1', '2', '3', '4' and '5' exactly once in some order. If they are arranged in ascending order, what is the 502nd number?

6. How many seven-digit numbers are there in which every digit is '2' or '3', and no two '3' are adjacent?

7. The six-digit number $\overline{abcabc}$ has exactly 16 positive divisors. What is the smallest value of such numbers?

8. How many five-digit multiples of 3 have at least one of its digits equal to '3'?

9. ABCD is a parallelogram. M is a point on AD such that AM=2MD, N is a point on AB such that AN=2NB. The segments BM and DN intersect at O. If the area of ABCD is 60 cm^2, what is the total area of triangles BON and DOM?

10. The four-digit number $\overline{ACCC}$ is $\frac{2}{5}$ of the four-digit number $\overline{CCCB}$. What is the value of the product of the digits A, B and C?

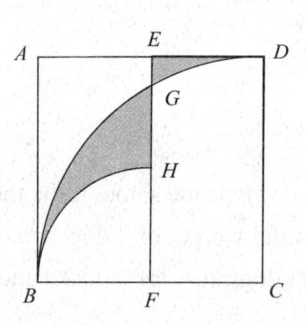

11. ABCD is a square of side length 4 cm. E is the midpoint of AD and F is the midpoint of BC. An arc with centre C and radius 4cm cuts EF at G, and an arc with centre F and radius 2 cm cuts EF at H. The difference between the areas of the region bounded by GH and the arcs BG and BH and the region bounded by EG, DE and the arc DG is of the form $m\pi - n$ cm^2, where m and n are integers. What is the value of m+n?

12. In a chess tournament, the number of boy participants is double the number of girl participants. Every two participants play exactly one game against each other. At the end of the tournament, no games were drawn. The ratio between the number of wins by the girls and the number of wins by the boys is 7 : 5. How many boys

were there in the tournament?

13. In the puzzle every different symbol stands for a different digit.

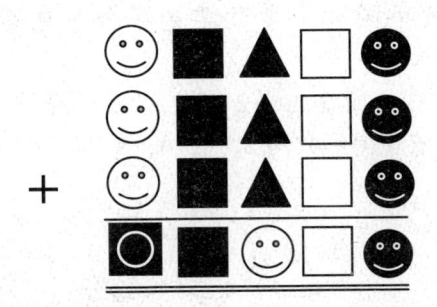

☺■▲□☺
+ ☺■▲□☺
  ☺■▲□☺
─────────
  ◯■☺□☺

What is the answer of this expression which is a five-digit number?

14. In the figure below, the positive numbers are arranged in the grid follow by the arrows' direction.

```
              Column
          1     2     3     4     5
      1 │ 1  →  2     6  →  7    ...
      2 │ 3     5     8    ...
Row   3 │ 4     9    ...
      4 │ 10   ...
      5 │ ...
```

For example,

'8' is placed in Row 2, Column 3.

'9' is placed in Row 3, Column 2.

Which Row and which Column that '2008' is placed?

15. As I arrived at home in the afternoon. The 24-hour digital clock shows the time as below (HH: MM: SS). I noticed instantly that the first three digits on the platform clock were the same as the last three, and in the same order. How many times in twenty four hours does this happen?

| 13: 21: 32 |

Note: The clock shows time from 00: 00: 00 to 23: 59: 59.

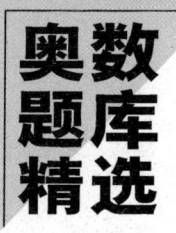

6.2　EMIC个人赛中文试题

2008 年国际小学数学竞赛个人竞赛试题

1. 从图 6-1 中的中心所在的圆 2 出发，每一步都移动到所相接触的圆上，请问要经过四个圆而依序得到数码 2，0，0，8 共有多少种不同的方法？

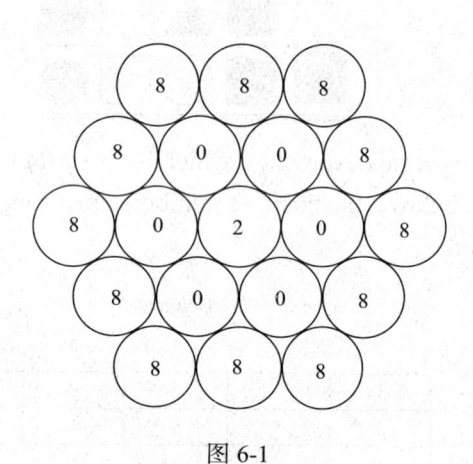

```
        8  8  8
      8  0  0  8
    8  0  2  0  8
      8  0  0  8
        8  8  8
```

图 6-1

2. 农场里所有大鸭子的重量都互相相等，所有小鸭子的重量都互相相等．已知 3 只大鸭子和 2 只小鸭子共重 32 kg，4 只大鸭子和 3 只小鸭子共重 44 kg，请问 2 只大鸭子和 1 只小鸭子共重多少 kg？

3. 操场上有一群人，其中一部分人坐在地上，其余的人站着．如果站着的人中的 25%坐下，同时原先坐着的人中 25%站起来，那么站着的人数占总人数的 70%．请问原先站着的人占总人数的百分比是多少？

4. 在高速公路上一辆长 3 m 的小轿车以 110 km/h 的速度超过一辆长 17 m 以 100 km/h 的速度行驶的卡车．请问小轿车从追到超越卡车的整个超车过程用了多少秒？

5. 用数码 0，1，2，3，4 和 5 组成各位数码都不相同的六位数，并按从小到大顺序排列，请问第 502 个数是什么？

6. 一个七位数，其数码只能是 2 或 3，且没有两个 3 是相邻的．请问这样的七位数共有多少个？

108

7. 若六位数 $\overline{abcabc}$ 恰有 16 个正约数，请问满足此条件的 $\overline{abcabc}$ 的最小值是什么？

8. 请问至少出现一个数码 3，并且是 3 的倍数的五位数共有多少个？

9. 平行四边形 ABCD 中，点 M、N 分别在边 AD、AB 上，且 AM=2MD、AN=2NB，线段 DN 与 BM 相交于点 O. 已知的四边形 ABCD 面积为 60 cm²，请问 △BON 与 △DOM 之面积总和为多少 cm²？

10. 两个四位数 $\overline{ACCC}$ 和 $\overline{CCCB}$ 满足 $\dfrac{\overline{ACCC}}{\overline{CCCB}} = \dfrac{2}{5}$，请问 $A \times B \times C$ 的值是什么？

11. 如图 6-2 所示，ABCD 是一边长为 4 cm 的正方形，点 E、F 分别为边 AD、BC 的中点. 以点 C 为圆心，作半径为 4 cm 的四分之一圆交 EF 于 G；以点 F 为圆心，作半径为 2 cm 的四分之一圆交 EF 于 H 点. 若图中两块阴影部分的面积之差为 $m\pi - n$ cm²（其中 m，n 为正整数），请问 $m+n$ 之值为何？

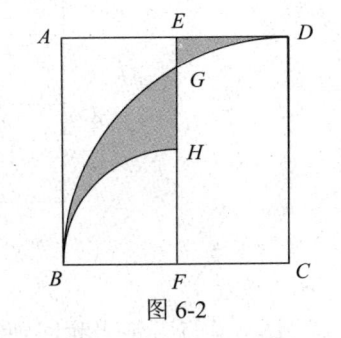

图 6-2

12. 有 2n 名男生和 n 名女生参加象棋比赛，参赛的任两人都要互相比赛一场. 全部比赛结束后，发现比赛中没有平局，且女生赢得的比赛总场数与男生赢得的比赛总场数之比为 7：5. 请问共有多少名男生参加比赛？

13. 在以下数字谜中，不同的图案代表不同的数码 (图 6-3).

图 6-3

请问此算式之和是什么？

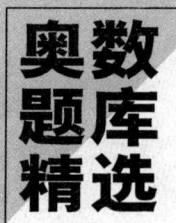

14. 在图 6-4 中，将正整数依照箭头所指示的方式依序填入小方格中，例如，

　　　　　数 8 填入第二行 (Row) 第三列 (Column)；

　　　　　数 9 填入第三行第二列.

请问数 2008 应填入第几列第几行？

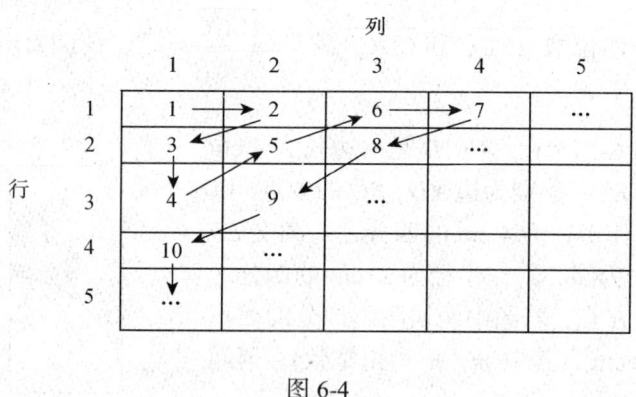

	1	2	3	4	5
1	1	2	6	7	…
2	3	5	8	…	
3	4	9	…		
4	10	…			
5	…				

图 6-4

15. 某日下午当我回到家时，我发现 24 h 制的数字钟显示以下的数字：

$$13:21:32$$

钟面上的前三位数码正好与后三位数码相同，且其顺序也相同. 请问在一天 24 h 之中这个数字钟共会出现多少次这种情况？ (注：此数字钟一天中所显示的数码从 00:00:00 到 23:59:59，它的前两位数代表"时"；中间两位数代表"分"；后两位数代表"秒")

6.3　EMIC 个人赛试题解答与评注

2008 年国际小学数学竞赛个人竞赛试题解答

1. **解**　从中心的 2 出发到 0 共有六种不同的方法，从 0 出发到 0 共有两

第6章　2008年第6届国际小学数学竞赛

种不同的方法，从0出发到8共有三种不同的方法，由乘法原理共有6×2×3=36种不同的方法．

答: 36种

2. **解法 1**　令大鸭子、小鸭子的重量分别为 x (kg)、y (kg)．由题意得知 $3x+2y=32$、$4x+3y=44$，即 $9x+6y=96$、$8x+6y=88$，两式相减则可得 $x=8$，代入又可得 $y=4$，故知 2 只大鸭子和 1 只小鸭子共重 $2\times 8+4=20$ (kg)．

解法 2　由题意得知 6 只大鸭子和 4 只小鸭子共重 64 (kg)，从中扣除 4 只大鸭子和 3 只小鸭子之总重 44 (kg)，即得知 2 只大鸭子和 1 只小鸭子共重 64−44=20 (kg)．

答: 20 kg

3. **解法 1**　用 A 表示原先站着的人数，B 表示原先坐着的人数，C 表示现在站着的人数，则 $C=75\%\times A+25\%\times B=70\%\times A+70\%\times B$，可得 $A:B=9:1$，所以 $\dfrac{A}{A+B}=\dfrac{9}{9+1}=90(\%)$．

解法 2　令原先站着的人占总人数之 x %，则原先坐着的人占总人数之 $(100-x)$ %，由题意可得知 $70\%=75\%\times x\%+25\%\times(100-x)\%$，即 $280=3x+100-x$，解得 $x=90$．故原先站着的人占总人数之 90 %．

答: 90 %

4. **解**　小轿车相对于卡车的速度为 10 (km/h)，即每秒以 $\dfrac{10\times 1000}{60\times 60}=\dfrac{100}{36}$ (m) 靠近．超车过程即轿车从卡车后面行驶到卡车前面的过程，共行驶了 17+3=20 (m)．所以超车用时为

$$t=20\div \dfrac{100}{36}=\dfrac{36}{5}=7.2 \text{ (s)}.$$

答: 7.2秒

5. **解**　首位是 1、2、3、4 的六位数各有 120 个，共 480 个．以 50 开头的六位数有 24 个，即 504321 是第 504 个数．所以第 503 个数是 504312，第 502 个数是 504231．

答: 504231

6. **解法 1**　由表 6-1 可知每次都添加一个数码 2 在 $n-1$ 位数之前及添加数码 32 在 $n-2$ 位数之前而得到满足条件的 n 位数．

111

表 6-1

末位数	满足条件的数					
	一位数	两位数	三位数	四位数	五位数	六位数
2	2	22	222	2222	22222	222222
						322222
				3222	32222	232222
			322	2322	22322	223222
						323222
						222322
						322322
					32322	232322
		32	232	2232	22232	222232
						322232
					32232	232232
				3232	23232	223232
						323232
3	3	23	223	2223	22223	222223
						322223
					32223	232223
				3223	23223	223223
						323223
			323	2323	22323	222323
						322323
					32323	232323

考虑具有所给性质的所有正整数数,用递推的方法.

首位是 2 的七位数的个数与六位数的个数相同;

首位是 3 的十位数必定是以 32 开头的,与五位数的个数相同,即七位数的个数是六位数个数加上五位数的个数.这个规律与斐波那契数列的规律相同.令 $f(n)$ 代表满足条件的 n 位数的个数,我们有 $f(n) = f(n-1) + f(n-2)$,所以 $f(5) = 13$、$f(6) = 21$、$f(7) = 34$.

第 6 章　2008 年第 6 届国际小学数学竞赛

解法 2　因不能有两个以上的 3 相邻，可在决定 2 的个数后，在其间插入 3，而最多只能有 4 个 3. 具有所给性质的所有正整数可分为以下情况：

(a) 假设它没有任何数码 3，则只有 22222222 的 1 种情况；

(b) 若 1 个 3，则有 6 个 2 且共有 $C_{6+1}^1 = 7$ 种情况；

(c) 若 2 个 3，则有 5 个 2 且共有 $C_{5+1}^2 = 15$ 种情况；

(d) 若 3 个 3，则有 4 个 2 且共有 $C_{4+1}^3 = 10$ 种情况；

(e) 若 4 个 3，则有 3 个 2 且只有 3232323 的 1 种情况.

因此共有 1+7+15+10+1=34 个七位数.

答：34

7. 解　因为 $\overline{abcabc} = 1001 \times \overline{abc} = 7 \times 11 \times 13 \times \overline{abc}$ 恰有 16 个正约数，故它等于 $7^3 \times 11 \times 13$、$7 \times 11^3 \times 13$、$7 \times 11 \times 13^3$ 或是 $7 \times 11 \times 13 \times \overline{abc}$（其中 $\overline{abc}$ 是三位数的素数），因 101 是素数而 11^2、13^2 均大于 101 且 7^2 非三位数，即 $\overline{abc}$ 最小是 101.

所以，$\overline{abcabc}$ 的最小值是 101101.

答：101101

8. 解　首先我们考虑有多少个五位数是 3 的倍数但不含有数码 3. 首位数码有 8 种选择，第二、三、四位数码都有 9 种选择. 当前四位的数码和被 3 除余数为 0 时，第五位数码只能取 0、6、9；当余数为 1 时，第五位数码只能取 2、5、8；当余数为 2 时，第五位数码只能取 1、4、7，故五位数中是 3 的倍数但不含有数码 3 共有 8×9×9×9×3=17496 个，而是 3 的倍数的五位数共有 30000 个，故满足条件的五位数共有

30000−17496=12504.

答：12504

9. 解　因为 $S_{\triangle ABM} = S_{\triangle ADN} = \dfrac{1}{3} S_{ABCD}$，所以 $S_{\triangle NBO} = S_{\triangle DMO}$. 设 $S_{\triangle NBO} = S_{\triangle DMO} = x$，则 $S_{\triangle ANO} = 2S_{\triangle NBO} = 2x$、$S_{\triangle AMO} = 2S_{\triangle DMO} = 2x$、$S_{\triangle ABM} = 5x$、$S_{ABCD} = 15x$.

所以 △NBO 与 △MDO 的面积总和（图 6-5）为 60÷15×2=8(cm²).

答：8 cm²

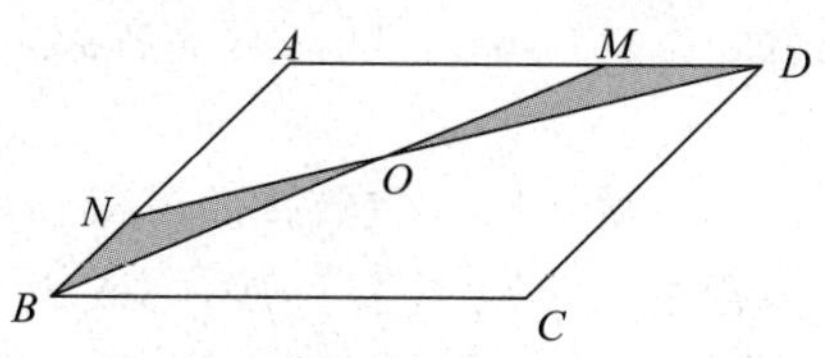

图 6-5

10. 解　由题意，$\overline{ACCC} = 1000A + 111C$、$\overline{CCCB} = 1110C + B$，所以 $2(1110C + B) = 5(1000A + 111C)$，化简可得

$1665C+2B=5000A$.

由上式知 B 为 5 的倍数，若 $B=0$，则 A 与 C 无法同时为整数；若 $B=5$，则 $333C=1000A-2$. $333\times 9+2>1000A$，即 $3>A$，为了使 $1000A-2$ 可被 3 整除，故只有 $A=2$ 满足条件，所以 $A=2$、$B=5$、$C=6$，即 $A\times B\times C=60$.

答：60

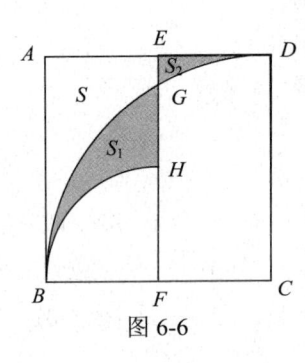

11. **解** 如图 6-6 所示.

$$S+S_1=2\times 4-2\times 2\times \pi\div 4=8-\pi,$$
$$S+S_2=4\times 4-4\times 4\times \pi\div 4=16-4\pi,$$

所以

$$S_1-S_2=(8-\pi)-(16-4\pi)=3\pi-8,$$

故 $m+n=3+8=11$.

答：11

图 6-6

12. **解** 用 k 表示女生赢男生的场数，W 表示女生赢的总场数，M 表示男生赢的总场数. 于是总比赛场数为 $\dfrac{3n(3n-1)}{2}$；男生和女生的比赛场数为 $2n^2$，$k\leqslant 2n^2$；男生间的比赛场数为 $\dfrac{2n(2n-1)}{2}$；女生间的比赛场数为 $\dfrac{n(n-1)}{2}$.

由已知条件得

$$\dfrac{\dfrac{3n(3n-1)}{2}}{k+\dfrac{n(n-1)}{2}}=\dfrac{3n(3n-1)}{2k+n(n-1)}=\dfrac{2(M+W)}{2W}=\dfrac{M}{W}+1=\dfrac{12}{7}.$$

故知 $\dfrac{17n^2-3n}{8}=k\leqslant 2n^2$，化简即 $17n^2-3n\leqslant 16n^2$，故 $n\leqslant 3$.

当 $n=1$ 时，k 不是整数；当 $n=2$ 时，k 也不是整数，当 $n=3$ 时，$k=18$ 满足题意. 所以，$n=3$，即共有 3 名女生和 6 名男生参加比赛.

答：6名

13. **解** 从末位数我们可得知 ☺=0 或 ☺=5.

若 ☺=5，则 3□+1=10+□ 或 3□+1=20+□，但此情况都不可能.

因此 ☺=0 并且 □=5. 从首位数我们可得知 ☺≤3.

关注千位数我们可得知 ■≠5 且 ≠0 并知 3■+1=20+■ 或 3■+2=20+■ 或 3■+1=10+■ 或 3■+2=10+■，而只有以下两种可能满足的情况，即 ■=4 ⇒ (3×4+2=14) 或

114

第6章 2008年第6届国际小学数学竞赛

■=9 ⇒ (3×9+2=29). 无论何种情况都是有进二到万位数，因此▲>6，▲ ≠ 0，且 3▲+1 之和的末位数等于☺，因而必须小于3，也就是说3▲的末位数等于1或2，而只有▲=7可能.

进一步得知☺=2. 此时若■=4，则◉=7，而已知▲=7，所以不可能. 因此只能是■=9，◉=8. 最后我们得到此算式为

$$29750+29750+29750=89250.$$

答: 89250

14. **解** 在第2、4、6、⋯、2k行第1列或在第1、3、5、⋯、2k+1列第1行上的数都是三角形数，即为 $\frac{n(n+1)}{2}$=1+2+3+⋯+n. 我们欲找到最大的 x 使得

$$1+2+3+4+\cdots+x<2008<1+2+3+4+\cdots+x+(x+1).$$

经计算得知 $\frac{62\times63}{2}$=1953<2008< $\frac{63\times64}{2}$<2016，故 x=62 且知 1+2+3+4+⋯+x=1953.

因此，1953 是第62行第1列上的数，接着1954位于第63行第1列，1955位于第62行第2列，⋯⋯. 易算出2008位于第2008−1953=55列第64−55=9行.

答: 第9列第55行

评注 若正整数 n 位于第 r 行第 c 列，我们用记号 n=(r, c) 代表，则

(1) 若 $r+c$ 为偶数，则 $n=\frac{(r+c-2)(r+c-1)}{2}+c$；

(2) 若 $r+c$ 为奇数，则 $n=\frac{(r+c)(r+c-1)}{2}-c+1$.

15. **解** 假设钟面显示 A_1B_1: C_1A_2: B_2C_2，其中首两位数码 A_1B_1 显示"时"，它可以是 00、01、02、⋯、23；中间两位数码 C_1A_2 显示"分"，它可以是 00、01、02、⋯、59；末两位数码 B_2C_2 显示"秒"，它可以是 00、01、02、⋯、59. 故数码 A_1 只能取值 0、1、2；数码 A_2 能取值 0、1、2、⋯、9；数码 B_1 能取值 0、1、2、⋯、9；数码 B_2 只能取值 0、1、2、⋯、5；数码 C_1 能取值 0、1、2、3、4、5；数码 C_2 能取值 0、1、2、⋯、9.

因为 A_1=A_2、B_1=B_2、C_1=C_2，因此 A_1=A_2 只能取值 0、1 或 2；数码 B_1=B_2 只能取值 0、1、2、3、4、5；数码 C_1=C_2 只能取值 0、1、2、3、4、5.

但是当 A_1=2 时，B_1 只能取值 0、1、2 或 3，因此我们分以下两种情况讨论:

(1) 若数码 A_1=A_2=0 或 1 时，数码 B_1=B_2 只能取值 0、1、2、3、4、5，而

数码 $C_1=C_2$ 也是只能取值 0、1、2、3、4、5，所以共出现 2×6×6=72 次.

(2) 若数码 $A_1=A_2=2$ 时，数码 $B_1=B_2$ 只能取值 0、1、2、3，而数码 $C_1=C_2$ 只能取值 0、1、2、3、4、5，由此共出现 1×4×6=24 次这种情况.

所以共出现 72+24=96 次这种情况.

答：96

6.4　EMIC 队际赛英文试题

Elementary Mathematics International Contest 2008
28th October，2008，Chiang Mai，Thailand

Team Contest

1. N is a 5-digit positive integer. P is a 6-digit integer constructed by placing a digit '1' at the right-hand end of N. Q is a six-digit integer constructed by placing a digit '1' at the left–hand end of N. If $P=3Q$，find the five-digit number N.

2. In a triangle ABC，X is a point on AC such that $AX=15$ cm，$XC=5$ cm，$\angle AXB=60°$ and $\angle ABC=2\angle AXB$. Find the length of BC，in cm.

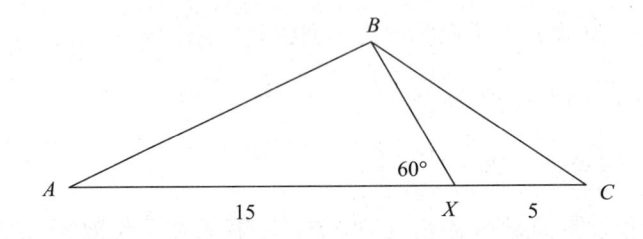

3. A track AB is of length 950 metres. Todd and Steven run for 90 minutes on this track，starting from A at the same time. Todd's speed is 40 metres per minute while Steven's speed is 150 metres per minute. They meet a number of times，running towards each other from opposite directions. At which meeting are they closest to B?

4. The numbers in group A are $\dfrac{1}{6}$，$\dfrac{1}{12}$，$\dfrac{1}{20}$，$\dfrac{1}{30}$ and $\dfrac{1}{42}$. The numbers in group B are $\dfrac{1}{8}$，$\dfrac{1}{24}$，$\dfrac{1}{48}$ and $\dfrac{1}{80}$. The numbers in group C are 2.82，2.76，2.18

and 2.24. One number from each group is chosen and their product is computed.

What is the sum of all 80 products?

5. On the following 8×8 board, draw a single path going between squares with common sides so that

(a) it is closed and not self-intersecting;

(b) it passes through every square with a circle, though not necessarily every square;

(c) it turns (left or right) at every square with a black circle, but does not do so on either the square before or the one after;

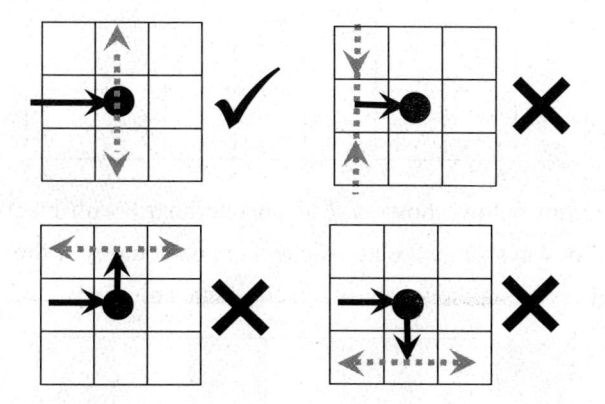

(d) it does not turn (left or right) at any square with a white circle, but must do so on either the square before or the one after, or both.

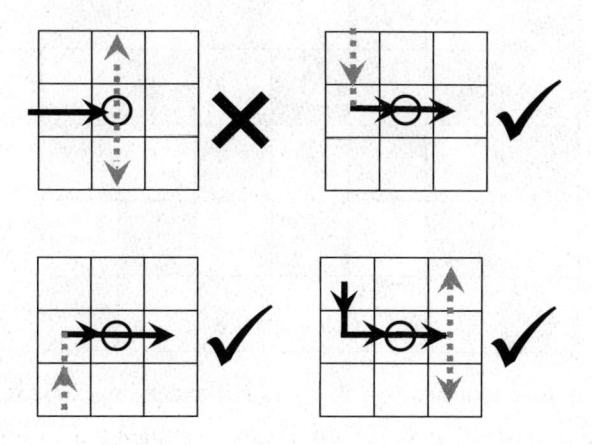

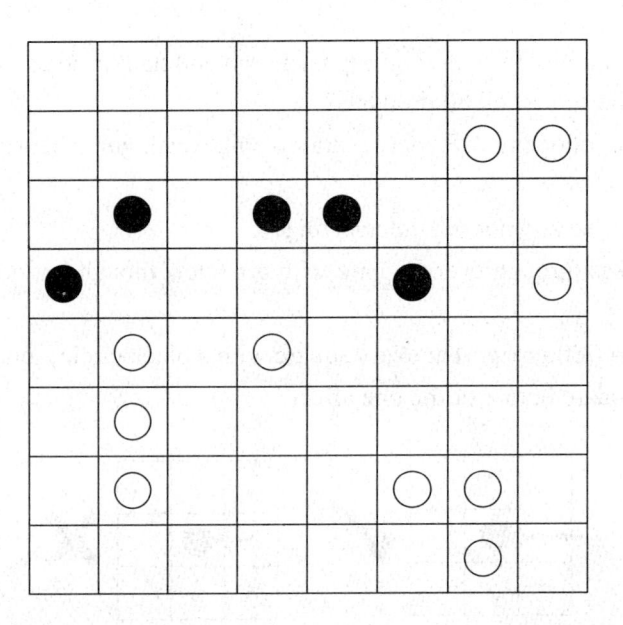

6. The diagram below shows a 7×7 checkerboard with black squares at the corners. How many ways can we place 6 checkers on squares of the same colour, so that no two checkers are in the same row or the same column?

7. How many different positive integers not exceeding 2008 can be chosen at most such that the sum of any two of them is not divisible by their difference?

8. A 7×7×7 cube is cut into any 4×4×4, 3×3×3, 2×2×2, or 1×1×1 cubes. What is the minimum number of cubes which must be cut out?

9. Place the numbers 0 through 9 in the circles in the diagram below without repetitions, so that for each of the six small triangles which are pointing up (shaded triangles), the sum of the numbers in its vertices is the same.

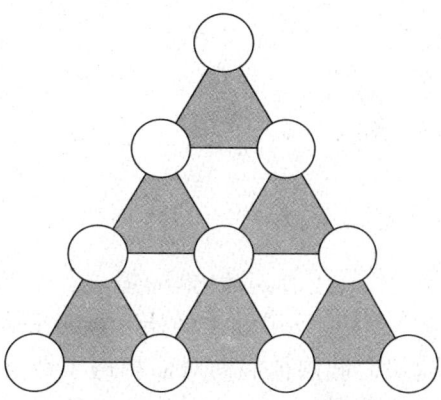

10. A frog is positioned at the origin (which label as 0) of a straight line. He can move in either positive (+) or negative (−) direction. Starting from 0, the frog must get to 2008 in exactly 19 jumps. The lengths of his jump are 1^2, 2^2, $\cdots$, 19^2 respectively (i.e. 1st jump=1^2, 2nd jump=2^2, $\cdots$, and so on). At which jump is the smallest last negative jump?

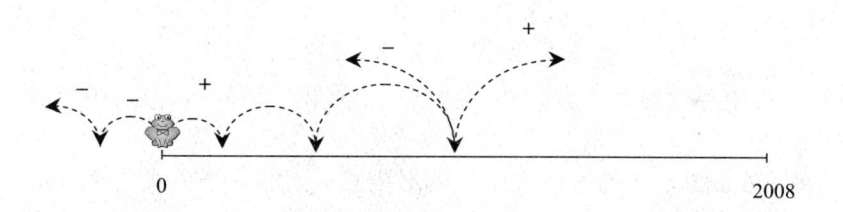

6.5 EMIC队际赛中文试题

2008年国际小学数学竞赛队际竞赛试题

1. 已知正整数 N 是一个五位数，在 N 的最右侧添加一个数码"1"而得到一个六位数 P；在 N 的最左侧添加一个数码"1"而得到另一个六位数 Q。已知 P=3×Q，请问这个五位数 N 是什么？

2. 图 6-7 的△ABC 中，点 X 在边 AC 上，已知∠AXB=60°、∠ABC=2∠AXB 且 AX=15 cm、XC=5 cm，请问边 BC 之长度为多少 cm？

图 6-7

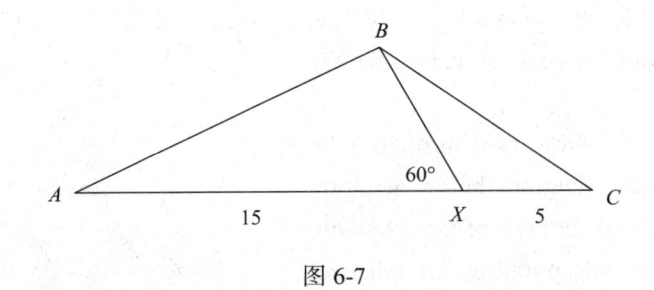

3. A、B 两地相距 950 m，甲、乙两人同时从 A 地出发，往返 A、B 两地跑步 90 分钟．甲跑步的速度是每分钟 40 m；乙跑步的速度是每分钟 150m．在这段时间内他们面对面相遇了数次，请问在第几次相遇时他们离 B 点的距离最近？

4. 有 A、B、C 三组数，

$$A = \left\{\frac{1}{6},\frac{1}{12},\frac{1}{20},\frac{1}{30},\frac{1}{42}\right\},$$

$$B = \left\{\frac{1}{8},\frac{1}{24},\frac{1}{48},\frac{1}{80}\right\},$$

$$C = \{2.82, 2.76, 2.18, 2.24\}.$$

从每一组中各取出一个数，相乘得到一个乘积．请问所有这 80 个乘积的总和是多少？

5. 在图 6-8 的 8×8 的方格表中，绘出绕成一圈的一条折线，使得

(1) 此折线仅与小方格的边平行或垂直，且不与自身相交；

(2) 此折线经过每个小方格至多一次，且必须经过所有标记有小圈的小方格，但不一定要经过没标记的小方格；

(3) 此折线在每一个有黑圈的小方格处必须转一个直角弯，但在黑圈之前或之后的一个小方格处不可以转弯；

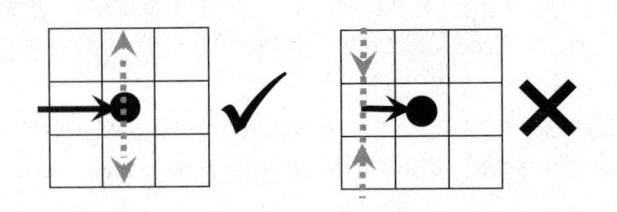

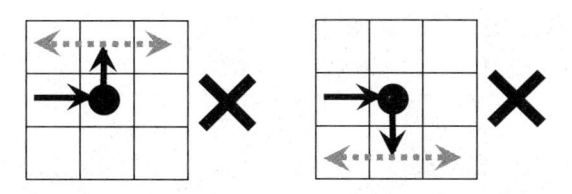

第 6 章　2008 年第 6 届国际小学数学竞赛

(4) 此折线在经过有白圈的小方格之前或之后（或两者）的一个小方格处，都必须转一个直角弯，但在有白圈的小方格处都不可以转弯.

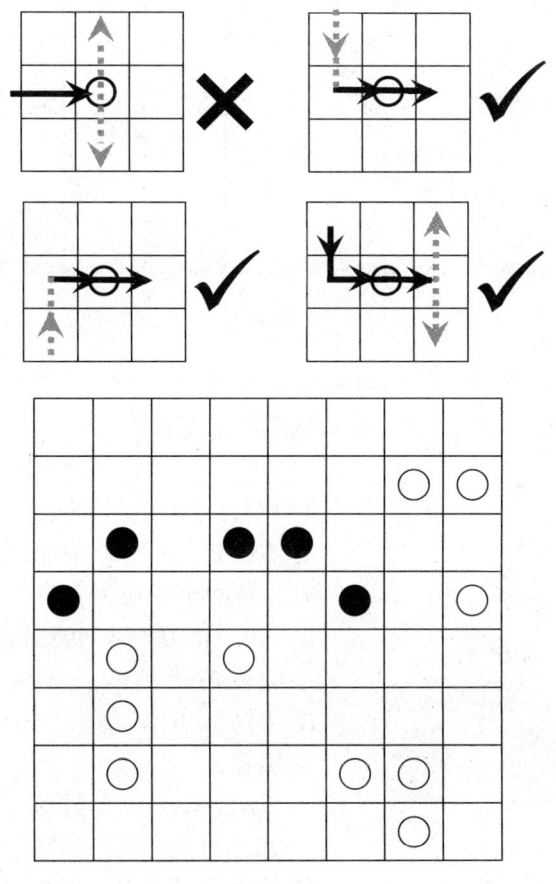

图 6-8

6. 如图 6-9 所示，在 7×7 灰白相间涂色的棋盘中放置六枚相同的棋子，所有的棋子都必须放在同一种颜色的方格中，且没有两枚棋子放在同一行或同一列. 请问共有多少种不同的放法？

图 6-9

7. 请问从 1、2、3、…、2008 这 2008 个正整数中至多可以取出多少个数,使得取出的数中任两数之和不能被这两数之差整除?

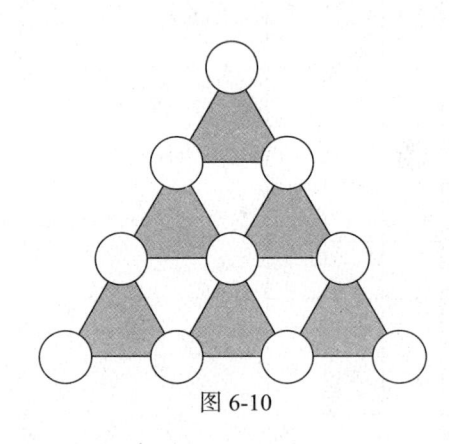

8. 将一个 7×7×7 的正立方体切成一些 4×4×4,3×3×3,2×2×2 或 1×1×1 的小正方体,要求切出的小正方体个数越少越好,请问至少切出多少个?

9. 将 0-9 不重复地在图 6-10 的每个小圆圈内恰填入一个数,使得每个朝上(涂阴影)的三角形三个顶点上的数之和都相等.

图 6-10

10. 有一只青蛙位于一条东西向的直线上,每次可以选择向东跳 (+) 也可以选择向西跳 (−).青蛙第一次跳 1^2 cm,第二次跳 2^2 cm,第三次跳 3^2 cm,…,第十八次跳 18^2 cm,第十九次跳 19^2 cm.若跳完这 19 次后,青蛙必须到达位于原来位置东方 2008 cm 处.假设青蛙达成此任务的方案中最后一次向西跳的距离是 n^2 cm,请问所有可能的 n 值中的最小值是多少 (图 6-11)?

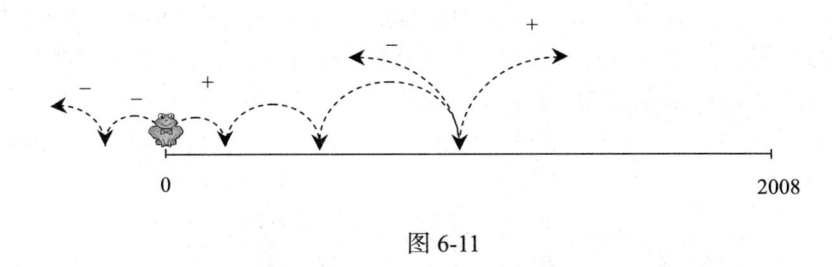

第 6 章 2008 年第 6 届国际小学数学竞赛

图 6-11

6.6 EMIC 队际赛试题解答与评注

2008 年国际小学数学竞赛队际竞赛试题解答

1. **解** 因 P 是在 N 的最右侧添加一个数码"1"而得到的数，故 P=10N+1.
因 Q 是在 N 的最左侧添加一个数码"1"而得到的数，故 Q=100000+N.
因 P=3×Q，可知 10N+1=3 (100000+N)，即 10N+1=300000+3N，因此 7N=299999，即 N=42857.

答: 42857

2. **解** 因 ∠ABC=2∠AXB 以及 ∠AXB=60°，故知 ∠ABC=120°. 因 ∠BXC=180°−∠AXB=120°，所以 ∠ABC=∠BXC. 故在 △ABC 与 △BXC 中，∠ABC=∠BXC 且 ∠C 为共同角，即 △ABC 与 △BXC 为相似三角形，因此 $\dfrac{AC}{BC} = \dfrac{BC}{XC}$.

因 AC=AX+XC=15+5=20，故 $\dfrac{20}{BC} = \dfrac{BC}{5}$，即 $BC^2 = 20 \times 5 = 100$，所以 BC=10cm.

答: 10cm

3. **解** 甲、乙两人同时从 A 地出发，两人第一次面对面相遇是在乙跑到 B 地折返 A 地的途中，两人共跑了全程的两倍，即 1900 (m)，用时 1900÷(40+150)=10 分钟，以后也是每十分钟面对面相遇一次.

他们跑步 90 分钟共面对面相遇 9 次，第一次面对面相遇时两人距 B 地 950−40×10=550 (m)；第二次面对面相遇时距 B 地 950−40×20=150 (m)；第三次面对面相遇时距 B 地 40×30−950=250(m)；第四次面对面相遇时距 B 地 40×40−950=650 (m)；第五次面对面相遇时距 B 地 950×3−40×50=850 (m)；第六次面对面相遇时距 B 地 2850−40×60=450(m)；第七次面对面相遇时距 B 地

2850−40×70=50 (m)；第八次面对面相遇时距 B 地 40×80−2850=350 (m)；第九次面对面相遇时距 B 地 40×90−2850=750(m)，所以他们在第 7 次面对面相遇时离 B 点的距离最近，距离为 50 (m).

答：第7次

4. 解

$$\frac{1}{6} \times \frac{1}{8} \times 2.82 + \frac{1}{6} \times \frac{1}{8} \times 2.76 + \cdots + \frac{1}{42} \times \frac{1}{80} \times 2.24$$

$$= \left(\frac{1}{6} + \frac{1}{12} + \frac{1}{20} + \frac{1}{30} + \frac{1}{42}\right) \times \left(\frac{1}{8} + \frac{1}{24} + \frac{1}{48} + \frac{1}{80}\right)$$

$$\times (2.82 + 2.76 + 2.18 + 2.24)$$

$$= \frac{70 + 35 + 21 + 14 + 10}{420} \times \left[\frac{30 + 10 + 5 + 3}{240}\right] \times 10$$

$$= \frac{5}{14} \times \frac{1}{5} \times 10$$

$$= \frac{5}{7}.$$

答：$\frac{5}{7}$

5. 解 根据题目的规定先确定每个带圈的方格及它前后的方格所必须连接的折线，可得图 6-12 (a).

(a)　　　　　(b)

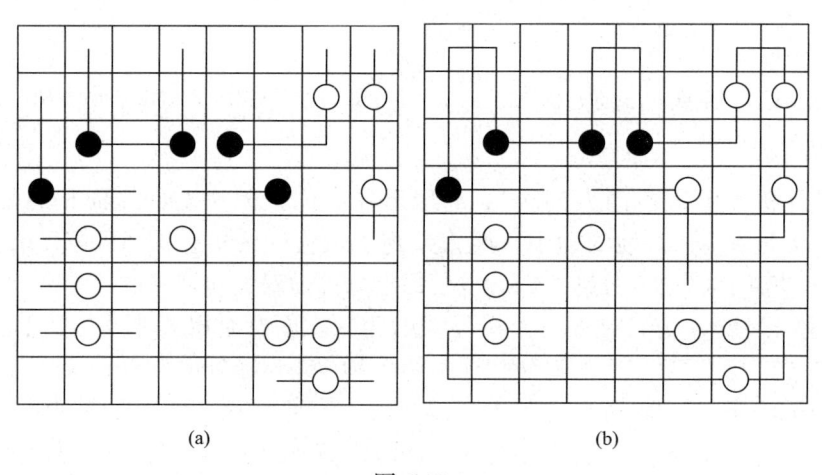

图 6-12

第 6 章　2008 年第 6 届国际小学数学竞赛

在图 6-12 (a) 基础上，再连接必须连接的线路，可得图 6-12 (b).

最后，根据图 6-12 (b) 所得的结果，继续加入必须连接的线段而完成全折线，如图 6-13 所示.

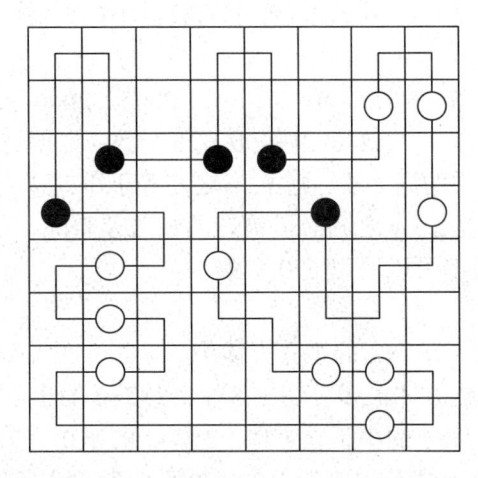

图 6-13

6．解　如图 6-9 所示，灰色小方格占四个角．白色方格组成两个 3×4 的矩形，其中一个是三行四列；一个是四行三列．如果棋子全部放置在白色方格中，则每个矩形里必各有三枚棋子，在每个矩形里放棋子有 4×3×2 种方法，所以在白方格里共有 24×24=576 种方法放棋子.

如果棋子全部放置在灰色方格中，灰方格组成一个 4×4 的正方形和一个 3×3 的正方形，则可能在 4×4 的正方形内放置 3 枚棋子，在 3×3 的正方形内放置 3 枚棋子或在 4×4 的正方形内放置 4 枚棋子，在 3×3 的正方形内放置 2 枚棋子.

若 4×4 的正方形内有 3 枚棋子且在 3×3 的正方形内有 3 枚棋子，先确定哪行不放棋子，有 4 种选择，再把 3 枚棋子放到 4×3 的正方形有 4×3×2 种选择；把 3 枚棋子放到 3×3 的正方形有 3×2×1 种方法，所以，共有 (4×4×3×2×1) × (3×2×1) =576 种.

若 4×4 的正方形内有 4 枚棋子且在 3×3 的正方形内有 2 枚棋子，则放棋子的方法共有 (4×3×2×1) × (3×3×2) =432 种.

综上，共有 576+576+432=1584 种方法.

答: 1584种

7. 解 首先，我们可以取 1、4、7、…、2008 等 670 个数，其中任意两数之和不能被 3 整除，而其差是 3 的倍数，所以，其中任意两数之和不能被这两数之差整除．

此外，将 1、2、3、…、2008 中的数自小到大按每三数一段，共可分为 670 段：

1、2、3|、4、5、6|、7、8、9|、…|、2005、2006、2007|、2008．

如果从 1、2、3、…、2008 中任取 671 个数，根据鸽笼原理必有两个数 x、y 取自上述 670 段中的同一段，则 x、y 之差等于 1 或 2，注意到 x、y 之差与 x、y 之和同奇偶，于是 x、y 之和必可被这两数之差整除．

综上所述，最多可以取出 670 个数．

答: 670 个

8. 解 可知在 7×7×7 的正立方体中，4×4×4 的小正立方体最多可切出 1 个、3×3×3 的小正立方体最多可切出 8 个、2×2×2 的小正立方体最多可切出 27 个．而每多 1 个 4×4×4 的小正立方体，2×2×2 的小正立方体个数至少减少 8 个或 3×3×3 的小正立方体至少减少 1 个；每多 1 个 3×3×3 的小正立方体，2×2×2 的小正立方体个数至少减少 1 个．

当我们决定了 4×4×4 与 3×3×3 小正立方体个数后，为了切出最少的小正立方体个数，2×2×2 的小正立方体个数必须尽可能多．因此可知：

(1) 1 个 4×4×4 的小正立方体、7 个 3×3×3 的小正立方体时：此时无法再切出 2×2×2 的小正立方体，故 1×1×1 的小正立方体个数为 343−1×64−7×27=90，合计有 1+7+90=98 个小正立方体．

(2) 1 个 4×4×4 的小正立方体、6 个 3×3×3 的小正立方体时：因此时可视为不切出在 (1) 内的其中 1 个 3×3×3 的小正立方体，在该位置改切 2×2×2 的小正立方体，故最多可切出 7 个 2×2×2 的小正立方体，所以 1×1×1 的小正立方体个数为 343−1×64−6×27−7×8=61，合计有 1+6+7+61=75 个小正立方体．

(3) 1 个 4×4×4 的小正立方体、5 个 3×3×3 的小正立方体时：因此时可视为不切出在 (1) 内的其中 2 个 3×3×3 的小正立方体，在该位置改切 2×2×2 的小正立方体，故最多可切出 11 个 2×2×2 的小正立方体，所以 1×1×1 的小正立方体个数为 343−1×64−5×27−11×8=56，合计有 1+5+11+56=73 个小正立方体．

(4) 1 个 4×4×4 的小正立方体、4 个 3×3×3 的小正立方体时：2×2×2 的小正

第 6 章　2008 年第 6 届国际小学数学竞赛

立方体个数最多为 27–1×8–4×1=15；若可切成，此时 1×1×1 的小正立方体个数为 343–1×64–4×27–15×8=51，合计有 1+4+15+51=71 个小正立方体. 如图 6-14 所示，此情况可以完成.

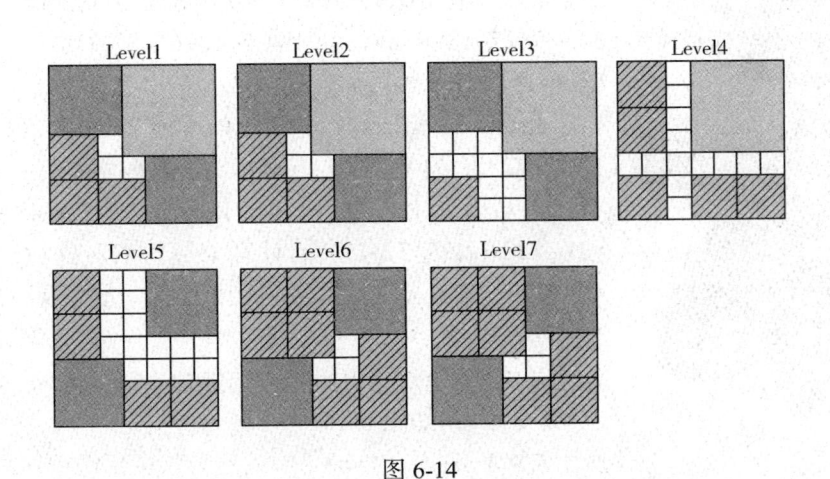

图 6-14

此后，每减少 k 个 3×3×3 的小正立方体时 (4≥k≥1)，2×2×2 的小正立方体个数最多为 27–1×8–(4–k)×1=15+k，即 1×1×1 的小正立方体个数最少为 343–1×64–(4–k)×27–(15+k)×8=51+19k，合计有 1+(4–k)+(15+k)+(51+19k)=71+19k 个小正立方体，都多于 71 个.

(5) 0 个 4×4×4 的小正立方体、8 个 3×3×3 的小正立方体时：此时无法再切出 2×2×2 的小正立方体，故 1×1×1 的小正立方体个数为 343–8×27=127，合计有 8+127=135 个小正立方体.

(6) 0 个 4×4×4 的小正立方体、7 个 3×3×3 的小正立方体时：因此时可视为不切出在 (5) 内的其中 1 个 3×3×3 的小正立方体，在该位置改切 2×2×2 的小正立方体，故最多可切出 8 个 2×2×2 的小正立方体，所以 1×1×1 的小正立方体个数为 343–7×27–8×8=90，合计有 7+8+90=105 个小正立方体.

(7) 0 个 4×4×4 的小正立方体、6 个 3×3×3 的小正立方体时：因此时可视为不切出在 (5) 内的其中 2 个 3×3×3 的小正立方体，在该位置改切 2×2×2 的小正立方体，故最多可切出 13 个 2×2×2 的小正立方体，所以 1×1×1 的小正立方体个数为 343–6×27–13×8=77，合计有 6+13+77=96 个小正立方体.

(8) 0 个 4×4×4 的小正立方体、5 个 3×3×3 的小正立方体时，因此时可视为不切出在 (5) 内的其中 3 个 3×3×3 小正立方体，在该位置改切 2×2×2 的小正立方体，故最多可切出 18 个 2×2×2 的小正立方体，所以 1×1×1 的小正立方体个数为 343−5×27−18×8=64，合计有 5+18+64=87 个小正立方体(图 6-15)．

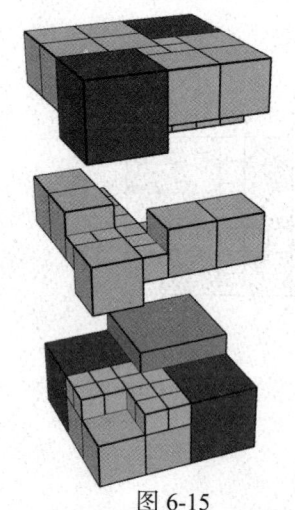

此后，每减少 k 个 3×3×3 的小正立方体时 (4≥k≥1)，2×2×2 的小正立方体个数最多为 27−(5−k)×1=22+k，即 1×1×1 的小正立方体个数最少为 343−(5−k)×27−(22+k)×8=32+19k，合计有 (5−k)+(22+k)+(32+19k)=59+19k 个小正立方体，都多于 71 个．故答案为 71．

答：71 个

图 6-15

9. **解** 令圆圈内所填入的数为 a、b、c、d、e、f、g、h、i、j，如图 6-16 所示．令 $X=a+g+j$，$Y=b+c+d+f+h+i$，并令 S 代表每个朝上三角形顶点上的数之和．由图 6-16 中可看出 $X+Y+e=45$，$X+Y=3S$，$Y+3e=3S$，易知 X、Y、e 均为 3 的倍数且 $X=3e$．

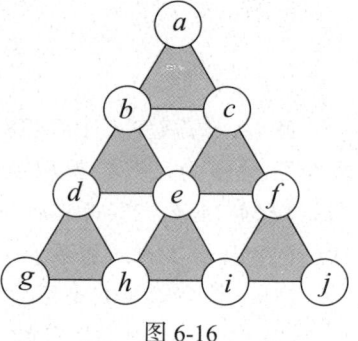

而 $6=1+2+3≤3e=X=a+g+j≤9+8+7=24$，所以 $2<e<8$，$e=3$ 或 6．

当 $e=3$，$X=9$，$Y=33$，$S=14$；当 $e=6$，$X=18$，$Y=21$，$S=13$．其解分别如图 6-17 所示，两组解是互补的，即在同位置圆圈内的数之和都等于 9．

图 6-16

第6章 2008年第6届国际小学数学竞赛

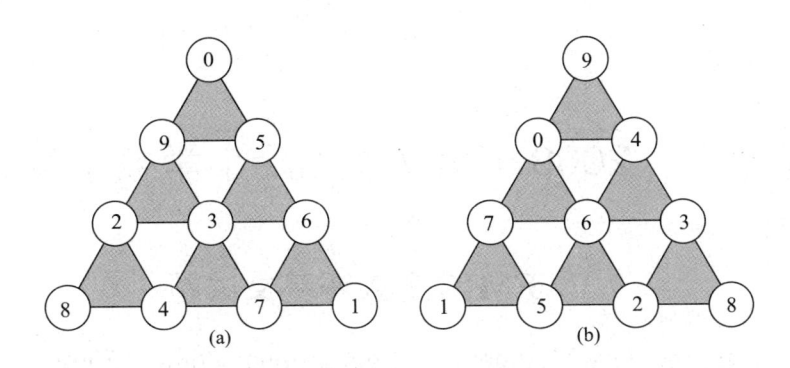

图 6-17

10. **解** 若青蛙每次都是向东跳，则共跳 $1^2+2^2+\cdots+19^2=2470$(cm)，超过目的地 $2470-2008=462$(cm). 可知必须有若干次向西跳. 因每将一个向东跳改为向西跳时，向东移动距离会减少该次跳动距离的 2 倍，因此必须从 1^2、2^2、$\cdots$、19^2 中找出和为 $462\div2=231$ 的距离向西跳. 因要使最后一次向西跳的距离最短，故要让找出的数中最大之数尽可能小. 因 $1^2+2^2+3^2+4^2+5^2+6^2+7^2+8^2=204<231$，故最大数至少为 9^2. 可发现 $1^2+6^2+7^2+8^2+9^2=3^2+4^2+5^2+6^2+8^2+9^2=231$ 都可以达成目的，故所有可能的 n 值中的最小值是 9.

答: 9

第 7 章　2009 年第 7 届国际小学数学竞赛

7.1　EMIC 个人赛英文试题

Elementary Mathematics International Contest 2009
30th November, 2009, Iloilo City, Philippines

Individual Contest

1. Find the smallest positive integer whose product after multiplica-tion by 543 ends in 2009.

2. Linda was delighted on her tenth birthday, 13 July 1991 (13/7/91), when she realized that the product of the day of the month together with the month in the year was equal to the year in the century: 13×7=91. She started thinking about other occasions in the century when such an event might occur, and imagine her surprise when she realized that the numbers in her two younger brothers' tenth birthdays would also have a similar relationship. Given that the birthdays of the two boys are on consecutive days, when was Linda's youngest brother born?

3. Philip arranged the number 1, 2, 3, ⋯, 11, 12 into six pairs so that the sum of the numbers in any pair is prime and no two of these primes are equal. Find the largest of these primes.

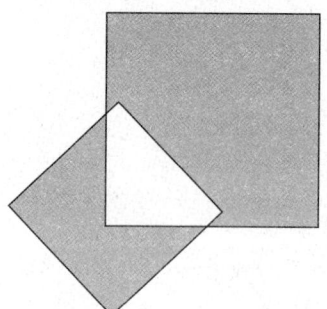

4. In the figure, $\frac{3}{4}$ of the larger square is shaded and $\frac{5}{7}$ of the smaller square is shaded. What is the ratio of the shaded area of the larger square to the shaded area of the smaller square?

5. Observe the sequence 1, 1, 2, 3, 5, 8, 13, ⋯, Starting from the third number, each number is the sum of the two previous numbers. What is the remainder when the 2009th

number in this sequence is divided by 8?

6. Ampang Street has no more than 15 houses, numbered 1, 2, 3 and so on. Mrs. Lau lives in one of the houses, but not in the first house. The product of all the house numbers before Mrs. Lau's house, is the same as that of the house numbers after her house. How many houses are on Ampang Street?

7. In the given figure, ABC is a right-angled triangle, where $\angle B=90°$, BC= 42 cm and AB=56 cm. A semicircle with AC as a diameter and a quarter-circle with BC as radius are drawn. Find the area of the shaded portion, in cm^2. $\left(\text{Use } \pi=\dfrac{22}{7}\right)$

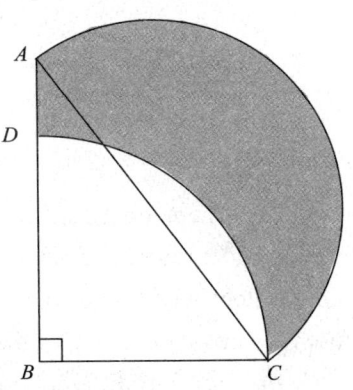

8. A number consists of three different digits. If the difference between the largest and the smallest numbers obtained by rearranging these three digits is equal to the original number, what is the original three-digit number?

9. The last 3 digits of some perfect squares are the same and non-zero. What is the smallest possible value of such a perfect square?

10. Lynn is walking from town A to town B, and Mike is riding a bike from town B to town A along the same road. They started out at the same time and met 1 hour after. When Mike reaches town A, he turns around immediately. Forty minutes after they first met, he catches up with Lynn, still on her way to town B. When Mike reaches town B, he turns around immediately. Find the ratio of the distances between their third meeting point and the towns A and B.

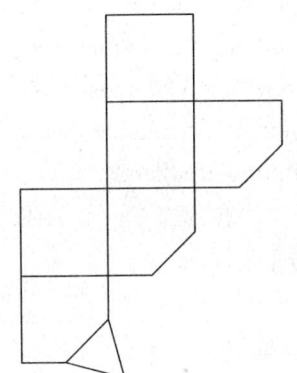

11. The figure shows the net of a polyhedron. How many edges does this polyhedron have?

12. In the figure, the centers of the five circles, of same radius 1 cm, are the vertices of the triangles. What is the total area, in cm^2, of the shaded regions? $\left(\text{Use } \pi=\dfrac{22}{7}\right)$

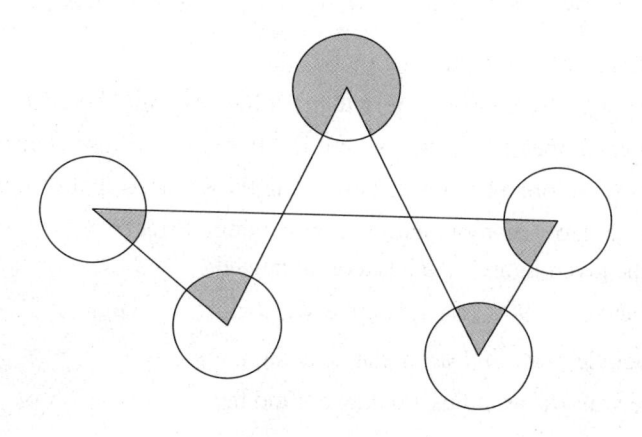

13. There are 10 steps from the ground level to the top of a platform. The 6th step is under repair and can only be crossed over but not stepped on. Michael walks up the steps with one or two steps only at a time. How many different ways can he use to walk up to the top of the platform?

14. For four different positive integers a, b, c and d, where $a < b < c < d$, if the product $(d-c) \times (c-b) \times (b-a)$ is divisible by 2009, then we call this group of four integers a 'friendly group'. How many 'friendly groups' are there from 1 to 60?

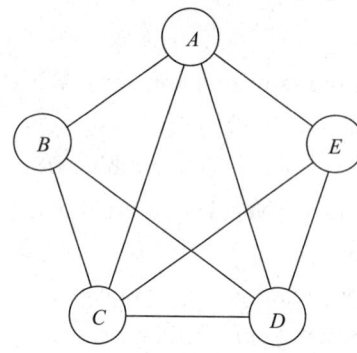

15. The figure shows five circles A, B, C, D and E. They are to be painted, each in one color. Two circles joined by a line segment must have different colors. If five colors are available, how many different ways of painting are there?

7.2 EMIC个人赛中文试题

2009年国际小学数学竞赛个人竞赛试题

1. 将一个正整数乘以543使得乘积的最末四位数为2009，请问满足条件的最小正整数是什么？

2. 小玲十岁的生日是1991年7月13日，她发现她十岁生日的日与月之

第 7 章　2009 年第 7 届国际小学数学竞赛

乘积恰好等于公元年的末两位数：13×7=91. 她开始思考在 20 世纪中是否还有其他的年月日满足这种情况. 令她惊讶的是，她发现她的两位弟弟的十岁生日时也都恰好具有此性质. 已知她的两位弟弟的生日正好是相邻的两天，请问小玲的最小弟弟出生的日期为何年何月何日？

3. 小菲将正整数 1、2、3、…、11、12 分为六对，使得每一对中的数之和都是素数，且这六个素数都互不相同. 请问这六个素数中最大的是什么？

4. 在图 7-1 中，大正方形的四分之三被涂上阴影；小正方形的七分之五被涂上阴影. 请问大正方形被涂上阴影部分的面积与小正方形被涂上阴影部分的面积之比为何？

5. 观察数列 1、1、2、3、5、8、13、…，它从第三项起每一项都等于前面两项之和. 请问此数列的第 2009 项除以 8 所得的余数是什么？

图 7-1

6. 安平街上的房屋总数不多于 15 间，它们依序编上 1、2、3、…的号码，刘女士住在其中一间房子，但不是第一间，已知房屋编号小于刘女士房屋编号的所有数的乘积恰等于房屋编号大于刘女士房屋编号的所有数的乘积. 请问安平街上共有多少间房屋？

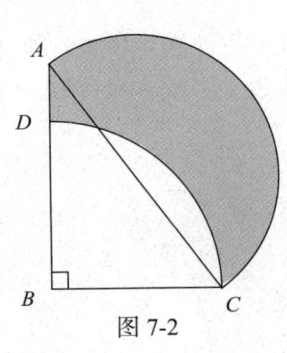

7. 在直角 △ABC 中，∠B=90°、BC=42 cm、AB=56cm，以 AC 为直径作一个半圆，以 BC 为半径作一个四分之一圆，如图 7-2 所示. 请问图 7-2 中阴影部分的面积为多少 cm²？$\left(令 \pi = \dfrac{22}{7}\right)$

8. 有一个三位数，它的各位数码都互不相同，将其各位数码重新排列组成新的三位数，若所得到的最大数与最小数之差正好等于原来的数，请问原来的三位数是什么？

图 7-2

9. 有一些完全平方数的最后三位数码都相同且不为 0，请问这些数中最小的是什么？

10. 小林从 A 地出发步行往 B 地，同时小明从 B 地出发骑自行车往 A 地走的是同一条路，1 h 后两人在途中相遇. 小明到达 A 地后立即返回，在第一次相遇后又经过 40 分钟，小明在途中追上小林. 小明到达 B 地后又立

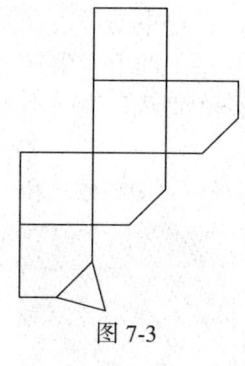

即返回，请问他们第三次相遇的地点到 A、B 两地的距离之比为何？

11. 如图 7-3 所示是一个多面体的展开图，请问这个多面体有多少条棱？

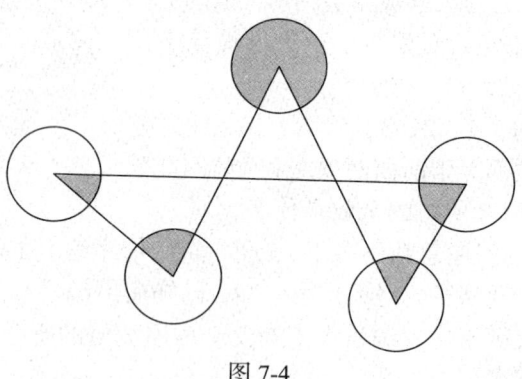

12. 如图 7-4 所示，五个半径为 1 cm 的圆之圆心分别在各个三角形的顶点处，请问阴影部分的面积总共为多少 cm²？$\left(\diamondsuit \pi = \dfrac{22}{7}\right)$

图 7-3

图 7-4

13. 从地面到高台顶有 10 级台阶，但第 6 级台阶正在维修，只能跨越过去而不能踩在此级台阶．小明由地面向上走，每次只能迈 1 级或 2 级台阶，请问小明可以有多少种不同的方式走到高台顶？

14. 将两两互不相同的四个正整数 a、b、c、d 从小到大排列 $a<b<c<d$，如果它们正好满足 $(d-c)\times(c-b)\times(b-a)$ 能被 2009 整除，我们则称这四个正整数为一组"好友数"．请问从 1 到 60 之间共有多少组"好友数"？

15. 欲将如图 7-5 所示的五个圆圈 A、B、C、D、E 分别涂上颜色，每个圆圈涂一种颜色．若要求有线段直接相连的两个圆圈必须涂上不同的颜色，现有五种不同颜色的染料可以使用，请问共有多少种不同的涂法？

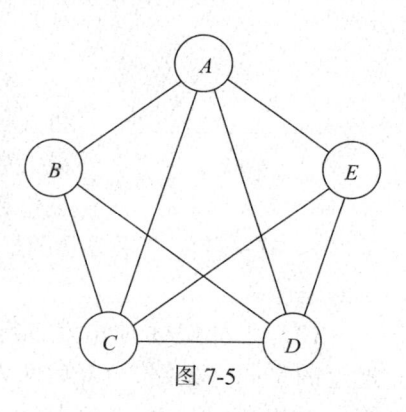

图 7-5

第 7 章 2009 年第 7 届国际小学数学竞赛

7.3 EMIC 个人赛试题解答与评注

2009 年国际小学数学竞赛个人竞赛试题解答

1. **解法 1** 若 543 为乘数，则设所求最小的正整数为 x，显然 x 的个位数必须为 3. 假设 x 的十位数为 a，则

$$
\begin{array}{r}
a\ 3 \\
\times\ \ 5\ 4\ 3 \\
\hline
?\ ?\ 9 \\
?\ ?\ 2\ \\
?\ 5\ \ \ \\
\hline
?\ 2\ 0\ 0\ 9
\end{array}
$$

因为 x 与 543 的乘积的十位数是 0，从而 $3\times 4=12$ 与 $3a$ 的个位数码之和的末位数为 0，所以 $a=6$.

假设 x 的百位数为 b，则

$$
\begin{array}{r}
b\ 6\ 3 \\
\times\ \ 5\ 4\ 3 \\
\hline
?\ ?\ 8\ 9 \\
?\ ?\ 5\ 2\ \\
?\ 1\ 5\ \ \ \\
\hline
?\ 2\ 0\ 0\ 9
\end{array}
$$

因为 x 与 543 的乘积的百位数是 0，从而 $5\times 3=15$、$4\times 6=24$ 与 $3b$ 的个位数码之和加上这些数 $4\times 3=12$、$3\times 6=18$ 与 $8+2=10$ 的十位数码之和，所得结果的末位数为 0，所以 $b=6$，因为 $663\times 543=360009$，所以 $x\neq 663$.

假设 x 的千位数为 c，则

$$
\begin{array}{r}
c\ 6\ 6\ 3 \\
\times\ \ \ \ 5\ 4\ 3 \\
\hline
?\ ?\ 9\ 8\ 9 \\
?\ ?\ 6\ 5\ 2\ \\
?\ 3\ 1\ 5\ \ \ \\
\hline
?\ 2\ 0\ 0\ 9
\end{array}
$$

因为 x 与 543 的乘积的千位数是 2，从而 5×6=30、4×6=24 与 3c 的个位数码之和加上这些数 5×3=15、4×6+1=25、3×6+1=19 和 9+5+5+1=20 的十位数码之和，所得结果的末位数为 2，所以 $c=4$. 因为 4663×543=2532009，所以 $x=4663$.

解法 2 若 543 为被乘数，则设所求最小的正整数为 x，显然 x 的个位数必须为 3. 假设 x 的十位数为 a，则

```
        5  4  3
    ×      a  3
    ─────────────
        1  6  2  9
    ?  ?  ?  A
    ─────────────
    ?  2  0  0  9
```

因为 x 与 543 的乘积的十位数是 0，故知 $2+A$ 之值的末位数为 0，即 $A=8$，故 $a=6$. 但因 63×543=34209，所以 $x \neq 63$.

假设 x 的百位数为 b，则

```
           5  4  3
    ×      b  6  3
    ─────────────
           1  6  2  9
        3  2  5  8
    ?  ?  ?  B
    ─────────────
    ?  ?  2  0  0  9
```

因为 x 与 543 的乘积的百位数是 0，故知 $(6+5+B)+1$ 之值的末位数为 0，即 $B=8$，所以 $b=6$；但因 663×543=360009，所以 $x \neq 663$.

假设 x 的千位数为 c，则

```
              5  4  3
    ×      c  6  6  3
    ─────────────
              1  6  2  9
           3  2  5  8
        3  2  5  8
    ?  ?  ?  C
    ─────────────
    ?  ?  ?  2  0  0  9
```

136

第7章 2009年第7届国际小学数学竞赛

因为 x 与 543 的乘积的千位数是 2,故知 $(1+2+5+C)+2$ 之值的末位数为 2,即 $C=2$,所以 $c=4$. 因为 $4663×543=2532009$,所以 $x=4663$.

答：4663

2．解 在 20 世纪中,小玲十岁的生日之后还有以下日期满足这种特殊的关系,以日/月/年的形式表示：

23/4/1992	24/4/1996	8/12/1996
31/3/1993	16/6/1996	11/9/1999
19/5/1995	12/8/1996	9/11/1999

所以她的两位弟弟的十岁生日只能在 1992 年 4 月 23 日和 1996 年 4 月 24 日．因此小玲的最小弟弟出生于 1986 年 4 月 24 日．

答：1986年4月24日

3．解 观察可得 $11+12=23$ 是最大的素数,下面说明这六个素数中必须含有 23．由条件可知这六个不同的素数的和等于 $1+2+…+11+12=78$,且每个素数都不超过 23,而这些素数只能是 3、5、7、11、13、17、19、23 中的六个．若它们都小于 23,则这六个素数的和最大只能为 $5+7+11+13+17+19=72<78$,所以这六个素数中必须含有 23．而 $23=12+11$,剩下的十个数之总和为 55 必须配对成五个素数．若它们都小于 19,则这五个素数的和最大只能为 $5+7+11+13+17=53<55$,所以这五个素数中必须含有 19．而 $19=10+9$,剩下的八个数之总和为 36 必须配对成四个素数．而 $8+7=15<17$,故这些素数只能是 3、5、7、11、13 中的四个．而 $5+7+11+13=36$,故这四个素数只能是 5、7、11、13. 可以按以下两组方式配对：$1+6=7$、$2+3=5$、$4+7=11$、$5+8=13$ 或 $1+4=5$、$2+5=7$、$3+8=11$、$6+7=13$.

答：23

4．解 假设图中没有涂上阴影部分的面积为 $2x$. 由题目条件可得

(1) 大正方形的面积为 $8x$,从而大正方形被涂上阴影部分的面积为 $6x$;

(2) 小正方形的面积为 $7x$,从而小正方形被涂上阴影部分的面积为 $5x$.

因此所求比例为 $6x:5x=6:5$.

答：6：5

5．解

数列	1	1	2	3	5	8	13	21	34	55	89	144	233	377	610
余数	1	1	2	3	5	0	5	5	2	7	1	0	1	1	2

题目所给的数列是斐波那契数列，这个数列除以 8 的余数形成另外一个周期为 12 的数列.

2009=12×167+5，所以第 2009 项与第 5 项的余数相同为 5. 所以原数列的第 2009 项除以 8 的余数是 5.

答: 5

6. 解 若刘女士住的房号小于 7，则因小于 7 的数中没有任何一个数有素因子 7，故街上至多只有 6 间房子，此时均无符合条件的房屋数.

若刘女士住的房号大于 7，则因 14 是除了 7 以外唯一有素因子 7 的数，故街上至少有 14 间房子. 此时再由小于 15 的数中除了 11 及 13 以外没有任何一个数有素因子 11 及 13，可知刘女士不可能同时住在 11 及 13 号房.

因此刘女士住的房号必为 7. 此时因 1×2×3×4×5×6=720 恰为 8×9×10，故安平街上共有 10 间房屋.

答: 10 间

7. 解 根据勾股定理可得到 $AC^2 = AB^2 + BC^2 = 4900$ (cm²)，因此可得 AC=70 (cm)，以 AC 为直径的半圆的面积为

$$\frac{1}{2} \times \pi \times \left(\frac{1}{2} AC\right)^2 = \frac{1}{2} \times \frac{22}{7} \times 35 \times 35 = 1925 \,(\text{cm}^2),$$

且 △ABC 的面积为 $\frac{1}{2} \times AB \times BC = 1176$ (cm²).

而四分之一圆 DBC 的面积为

$$\frac{1}{4} \times \pi \times BC^2 = \frac{1}{4} \times \frac{22}{7} \times 42 \times 42 = 1386 \,(\text{cm}^2),$$

所以阴影部分的面积为 1925+1176−1386=1715 (cm²).

答: 1715 cm²

8. 解 设三位数 $\overline{xyz}$ 经过重新排列后所得到的最大三位数为 $\overline{abc}$ ($a>b>c$)，则最小的三位数是 $\overline{cba}$. 因为 $\overline{xyz} = \overline{abc} - \overline{cba} = 99(a-c)$，所以 $\overline{xyz}$ 是 99 的倍数，而是 99 倍数的三位数只有 9 个: 198、297、396、495、594、693、792、891、990. 经验证，易知只有 495 符合题意.

答: 495

9. 解 一个完全平方数的末位数只能是 0、1、4、5、6、9. 当其末位数为 1、4、5、9 时，其十位数必须是偶数；当其末位数为 6 时，其十位数必须是奇数. 所以当完全平方数的末三位数码都相同且不为 0 时，这三位数

第7章 2009年第7届国际小学数学竞赛

码只能是 444，又 444 不是平方数，易知 $1444=38^2$ 为完全平方数，它是这些数中最小的.

答：1444

10. 解 关注于两人第一次相遇到小明追上小林之间的路程，可得知小明行驶 40 分钟的路程，小林要步行 (60+60+40) =160 分钟，故小明的速度是小林的 4 倍，AB 之距离小林需要步行 5 h.

第三次相遇时，小林和小明所走过的路程之和是 AB 的距离的 3 倍．由题目条件可知，他们 1 h 所走过的路程之和为 AB 的距离，所以第三次相遇时小林共步行 3 h，故第三次相遇点与 A 地、B 地的距离比为 $3:2$.

答：$3:2$

11. 解法 1 把这个多面体构造出来如图 7-6 所示，可得多面体一共有 15 条棱.

解法 2 在展开图中的各条边段，如果它是两个面的公共边，则它对应多面体的一条棱，如果它不是两个面的公共边，则两条边段才对应多面体的一条棱，所以多面体一共有 $6+\dfrac{18}{2}=15$ 条棱.

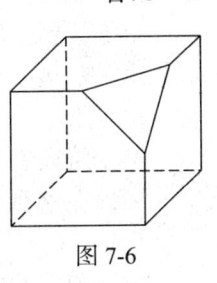

图 7-6

答：15条

12. 解 分别给图形中的角标上序号，则阴影部分的面积可以表示为

$$\pi \times \dfrac{\angle 1+\angle 2+\angle 3+\angle 4+(360°-\angle 5)}{360°}.$$

在图形中，$\angle 1+\angle 2+\angle 6=180°$，$\angle 3+\angle 4+\angle 7=180°$，$\angle 5+\angle 8+\angle 9=180°$，且 $\angle 6=\angle 8$，$\angle 7=\angle 9$．所以

$$\angle 1+\angle 2+\angle 3+\angle 4+\angle 6+\angle 7=360°,$$
$$\angle 1+\angle 2+\angle 3+\angle 4+\angle 8+\angle 9=360°,$$
$$\angle 1+\angle 2+\angle 3+\angle 4+(180°-\angle 5)=360°,$$
$$\angle 1+\angle 2+\angle 3+\angle 4+(360°-\angle 5)=540°,$$

所以阴影部分的面积为 $\pi \times \dfrac{540°}{360°}=\dfrac{22}{7}\times\dfrac{3}{2}=\dfrac{33}{7}\ \text{cm}^2$.

答：$\dfrac{33}{7}\ \text{cm}^2$

13. 解 因为第 6 级台阶正在维修，只能越过去而不能踩，并且小明每次只能迈 1 级或 2 级，所以小明只能上到第 5 级台阶然后越过第 6 级台阶到达第

7级台阶再继续往上走.

故这个过程可以分成两个阶段,第一阶段上5级台阶,第二阶段上3级台阶.

用递推的方法,只有1级台阶时,只有1种方法可上;

有2级台阶时,只有2种方法可上(迈两次1级或一次2级);

有3级台阶时,如果第一步迈1级台阶,那么剩下2级台阶有2种方法;如果第一步迈2级台阶,那么剩下1级台阶有1种方法,所以3级台阶有2+1=3种方法可上;

有4级台阶时,如果第一步迈1级台阶,那么剩下3级台阶有3种方法,如果第一步迈2级台阶,那么剩下2级台阶有2种方法,所以4级台阶有3+2=5种方法可上;

有5级台阶时,如果第一步迈1级台阶,那么剩下4级台阶有5种方法;如果第一步迈2级台阶,那么剩下3级台阶有3种方法,所以5级台阶有5+3=8种方法可上.

第二阶段有3种方法.

所以在题目条件下,小明共有8×3=24种方法.

答: 24

14. **解** $2009=7×7×41$,假设 a、b、c、d(其中 $a<b<c<d$)为1到60的一组"好友数".所以这四个数的任意两个之差小于60.因为 $(d-c)×(c-b)×(b-a)$ 能被2009整除,所以 $d-c$、$c-b$、$b-a$ 中必有一个等于41,并且剩下的两个都是7的倍数(因剩下的两个差不可能是49的倍数,否则存在两个数之差至少为41+49=90).

如果 $d-c=41$,则只能有 $c-b=7$、$b-a=7$(因为如果其中一个大于或等于14,那么 $d-a$ 将大于41+14+7=62).这时 $d-a=55$,并且当 a 和 d 确定时,b 与 c 也确定了.所以这种情况一共有5组"好友数":

$(a, b, c, d) = (1, 8, 15, 56)$、$(2, 9, 16, 57)$、$(3, 10, 17, 58)$、
$(4, 11, 18, 59)$、$(5, 12, 19, 60)$.

如果 $c-b=41$,则只能有 $d-c=7$、$b-a=7$.同理,这种情况一共有5组"好友数":

$(a, b, c, d) = (1, 8, 49, 56)$、$(2, 9, 50, 57)$、$(3, 10, 51, 58)$、
$(4, 11, 52, 59)$、$(5, 12, 53, 60)$.

如果 $b-a=41$,则只能有 $d-c=7$,$c-b=73$.同理,这种情况一共有5组"好友数":

$(a，b，c，d) = (1，42，49，56)$、$(2，43，50，57)$、$(3，44，51，58)$、
$(4，45，52，59)$、$(5，46，53，60)$.

综上所述，1 到 60 之间有 15 组"好友数".

答: 15

15. 解 由图可知圆圈 A、C、D、E 中，两两圆圈都有线段连接，所以圆圈 A、C、D、E 所涂的颜色必须两两不同，这就需要用四种不同的颜色. 同样圆圈 A、B、C、D 所涂的颜色必须两两不同. 所以有两种涂色情况:

(1) 用五种颜色分别给五个圆圈涂色，每个圆圈的都互不相同. 所有不同的涂法其实是这五种颜色的一个排列，所以有 $5×4×3×2×1=120$ 种.

(2) 用四种颜色分别给五个圆圈涂色，且 B 和 E 所涂的颜色相同. 这等价于用四种颜色分别给圆圈 A、B、C、D 涂色，每个圆圈的都互不相同. 先从五种颜色中选出四种颜色，有 5 种选法. 然后用选出的四种颜色分别给圆圈 A、B、C、D 涂色，不同的涂法其实是这四种颜色的一个排列，有 $4×3×2×1=24$ 种. 故所有不同的涂法有 $5×24=120$ 种.

综上所述，一共有 $120+120=240$ 种不同的涂法.

答: 240种

7.4 EMIC队际赛英文试题

Elementary Mathematics International Contest 2009
30th November，2009，Iloilo City，Philippines

Team Contest

1. Below is a 3×60 table. Each row is filled with digits following its own particular sequence. For each column，a sum is obtained by adding the three digits in each column. How many times is the most frequent sum obtained?

Row A	1	2	3	4	5	1	2	3	4	5	⋯	4	5
Row B	1	2	3	4	1	2	3	4	1	2	⋯	3	4
Row C	1	2	1	2	1	2	1	2	1	2	⋯	1	2

2. All surfaces of the T-shape block below is painted red. It is then cut into 1cm×1 cm×1 cm cubes. Find the number of 1 cm×1 cm×1 cm cubes with all six

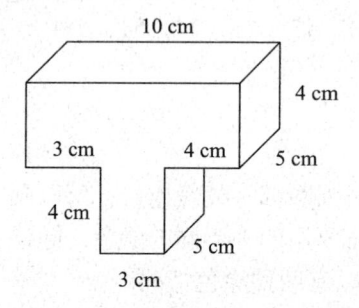

faces unpainted.

3. Kiran and his younger brother Babu are walking on a beach with Babu walking in front. Each of Kiran's step measures 0.8 meters while each of Babu's step measures 0.6 meters. If both of them begin their walk along a straight line from the same starting point (where the first footprint is marked) and cover a 100 meter stretch, how many foot-prints are left along the path? (If a footprint is imprinted on the 100 meter point, it should be counted. Consider two foot-prints as recognizable and distinct if one does not overlap exactly on top of the other)

4. Four 2×1 cards, shown on the right in the following figure, are to be placed on the board shown on the left below, without overlapping and such that the marked diagonals of any two cards do not meet at a corner. The cards may not be rotated nor flipped over. Find all the ways of arranging these cards that satisfy the given conditions.

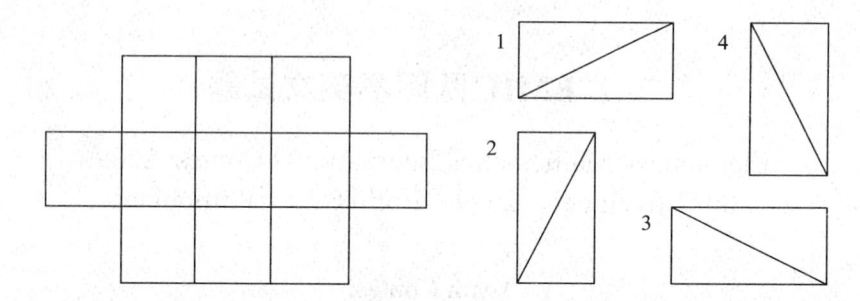

5. Water is leaking out continuously from a large reservoir at a constant rate. To facilitate repair, the workers have to first drain-off the water in the reservoir with the help of water pumps. If 20 pumps are used, it takes 5 full hours to completely drain-off the water from the reservoir. If only 15 pumps are used, it will take an hour longer. If the workers are given 10 hours to complete the job of draining-off the water, what is the minimum number of water pumps required for the job?

6. As shown in the following figure, we arranged the positive integers into a triangular shape so that the numbers above or on the left must be less than the

numbers below or on the right and each line has one more number than those above. Let us suppose a_{ij} stands for the number which is in the i-th line from the top and j is the count from the left in the triangular figure (e.g. $a_{43}=9$). If a_{ij} is 2009, what is the value of $i+j$?

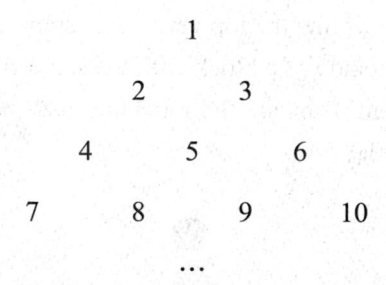

$$
\begin{array}{c}
1 \\
2 \quad 3 \\
4 \quad 5 \quad 6 \\
7 \quad 8 \quad 9 \quad 10 \\
\cdots
\end{array}
$$

7. In the figure below, the area of triangle ABC is 12 cm². $DCFE$ is a parallelogram with vertex D on the line segment AC and F is on the extension of line segment BC. If $BC = 3CF$, find the area of the shaded region, in cm².

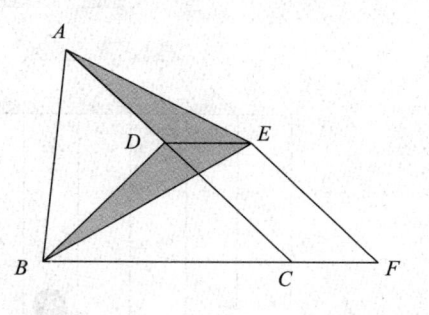

8. In the figure, the diameter AB of semi-circle O is 12 cm long. Points C and D trisect line segment AB. An arc centered at C and with CA as radius meets another arc centered at D and with DB as radius at point M. Take the distance from point M to AB as 3.464 cm. Using C as center and CO as radius, a semi-circle is constructed to meet AB at point E. Using D as center and DO as radius, another semi-circle is constructed to meet AB at point F. Find the area of the shaded region. (Use $\pi = 3.14$ and give your answer correct to 3 decimal places)

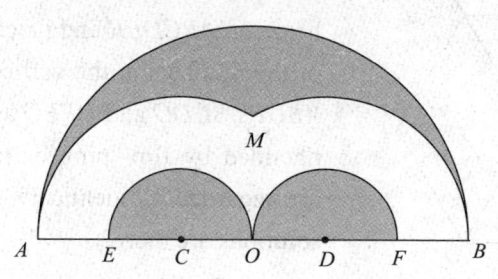

9. The following figure shows a famous model, designed by Galton, a British biostatistician, to test the stability of frequency. Some wooden blocks with cross-sections in the shape of isosceles triangles are affixed to a wooden board. There are 7 bottles below the board and a small ball on top of the highest block. As the small ball falls down, it hits the top vertices of some wooden blocks below and rolls down the left or right side of a block with the same chance, until it falls into a bottle. How many different paths are there for the small ball to fall from the top of the highest block to a bottle?

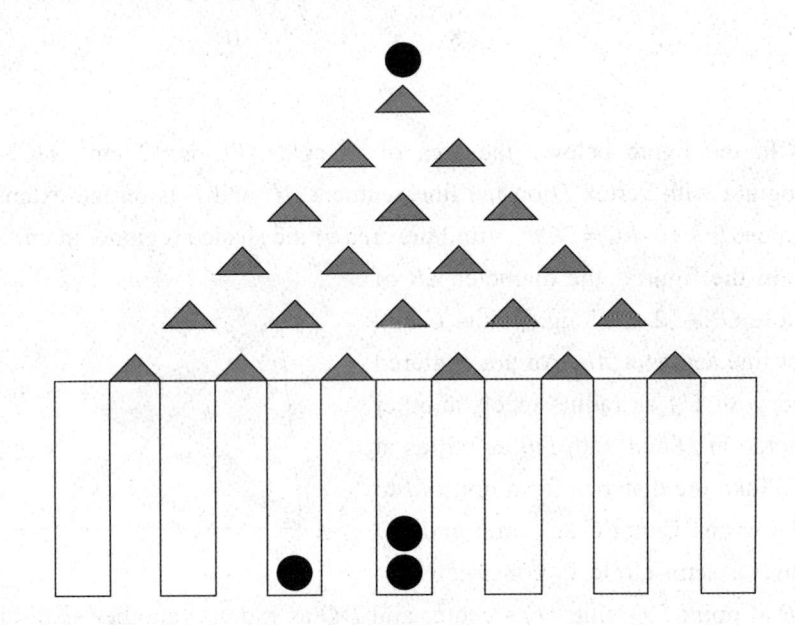

10. In the following figure, assign each of the numbers 1, 2, 3, 4, 5, 6, 7 to one of the six vertices of the regular hexagon ABCDEF and its center O so that sums of the numbers at the vertices of the rhombuses ABOF, BCDO and DEFO are equal. If solutions obtained by flip-ping or rotating the hexagon are regarded as identical, how many different solutions are there?

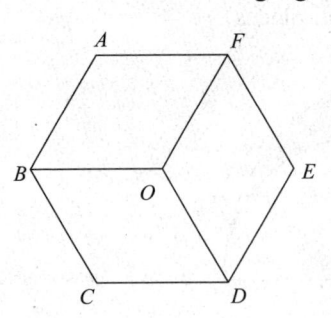

第7章 2009年第7届国际小学数学竞赛

7.5 EMIC队际赛中文试题

2009年国际小学数学竞赛队际竞赛试题

1. 下面是一个 3×60 的表格，每行按顺序填入一组数，然后求出每列的三个数之和．请问所有这些和之中，出现最多的和总共出现了几次？

行 A	1	2	3	4	5	1	2	3	4	5	...	4	5
行 B	1	2	3	4	1	2	3	4	1	2	...	3	4
行 C	1	2	1	2	1	2	1	2	1	2	...	1	2

2. 有一个 T 型木块，如图 7-7 所示，把它所有的表面全部都涂成红色，然后锯成 1 cm×1 cm×1 cm 的小立方体．请问六个面都没涂有红色的小正方体共有几个？

3. 小明和他的弟弟小亮在沙滩上散步，并且小亮走在前面．小明每一步长度为 0.8 m，而小亮每一步长度为 0.6m．如果他们按固定的步长从同一点（这一点记为他们的第一个脚印）开始沿着同一条直线往相同的方向走．请问 100m 内共留下多少个脚印？(如果有一个脚印刚好踩在 100 m 的点上，则这个脚印也计算在内．对于两个脚印，如果其中一个不是完全吻合地踩在另外一个上面，我们认为这是两个可辨别且不相同的脚印)

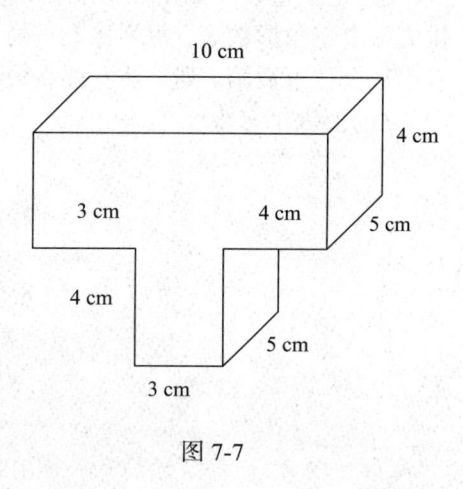

图 7-7

4. 图 7-8 中，把右边的四个 2×1 纸板放入左边的棋盘中，不能重叠，使得任意两个纸板中标出的对角线的端点不能重合，纸板不能旋转也不能翻转．请找出所有满足条件的放置方法．

图 7-8

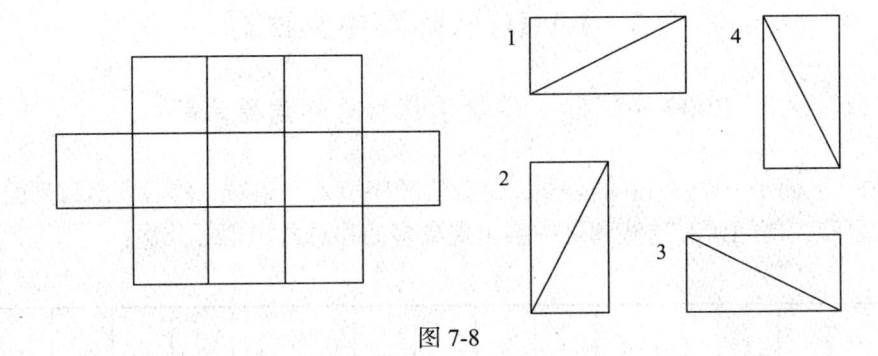

5. 一个大水池以固定的速率不断地往外漏水．为了方便维修，工人首先要用抽水机把水池的水抽干．如果用 20 台抽水机，则 5 个小时就可以把水池的水抽干．如果只用 15 台抽水机，则需要多用 1 个小时才可以把水池的水抽干．如果要求工人在 10 个小时内把水池的水抽干，请问至少需要几台抽水机？

6. 把正整数按如图 7-9 所示的方式排列，其原则是上小下大、左小右大排成一个三角形数表（每列比上一列多一个数），设 a_{ij} 表示位于这个三角形数表中从上往下数第 i 列、从左往右数第 j 个数（例如，$a_{43}=9$）．若 $a_{ij}=2009$，请问 $i+j$ 的值等于多少？

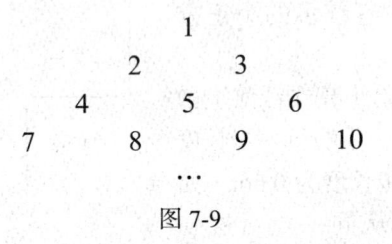

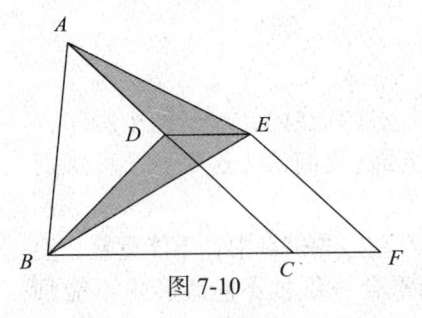

```
        1
      2   3
    4   5   6
  7   8   9   10
         ...
```

图 7-9

7. 已知 △ABC 的面积为 12 cm², 点 D 在线段 AC 上，点 F 在线段 BC 的延长线上，BC = 3CF，且 DCFE 是平行四边形．请问阴影部分的面积为多少 cm²（图 7-10）？

8. 如图 7-11 所示，半圆 O 的直径为 AB = 12 cm，点 C、D 为线段 AB 的三等分点．以 C 为圆心，CA 为半径所作的圆弧与以 D 为圆心，DB 为半径所作的圆弧相交于 M 点，且点 M 到 AB 的距离可视为 3.464 cm．以 C 为圆心，CO 为半径作半圆交 AB

图 7-10

第 7 章 2009 年第 7 届国际小学数学竞赛

于 E 点，以 D 为圆心，DO 为半径作半圆交 AB 于 F 点．请问阴影部分的面积为多少 cm²？（令 π = 3.14，答案需精确到小数点后三位）

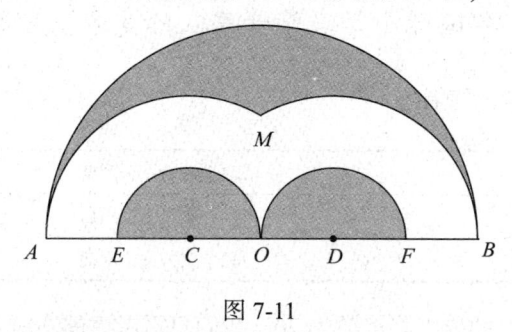

图 7-11

9. 图 7-12 是英国生物统计学家高尔顿（Galton）设计的一个著名的试验模型，用来验证频率的稳定性．在木板上固定着一些截面是等腰三角形的木块，下面放着 7 个瓶子．在最上面的木块上方放一个小球，小球往下落的过程中每次碰到等腰三角形的顶点后都以相同的可能性往左边滚落或往右边滚落，直到掉到瓶子里．请问小球从开始滚落到掉到瓶子里共有多少条不同的路线？

10. 将数 1、2、3、4、5、6、7 不重复地填写在如图 7-13 所示正六边形 ABCDEF 的六个顶点与中心点 O 上，使得图 7-13 中三个菱形 ABOF、BCDO、DEFO 的四个顶点上所填的数之和都相等．若将旋转、翻转的解答视为相同，请问共有几种不同的填写方法？

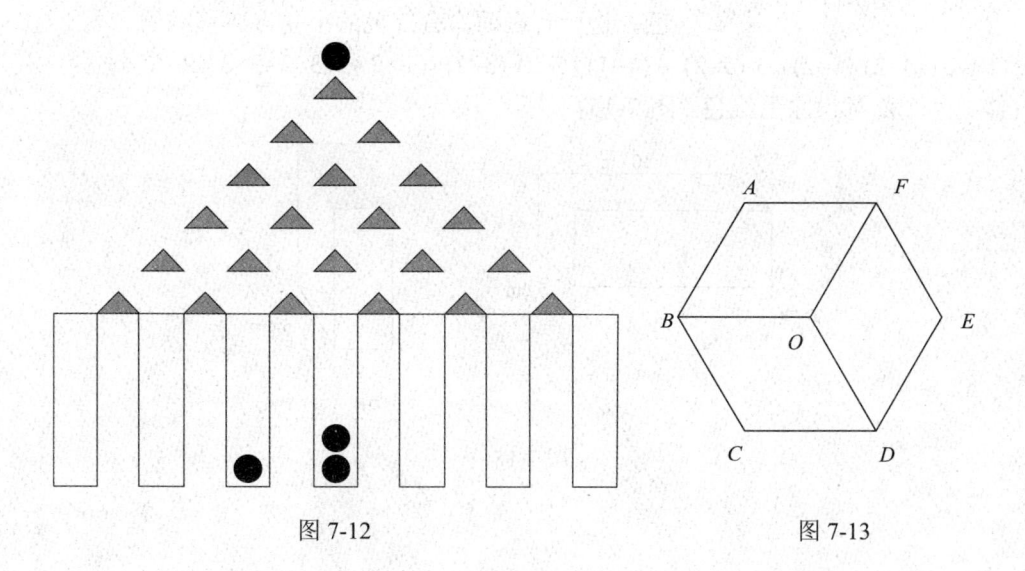

图 7-12   图 7-13

7.6 EMIC 队际赛试题解答与评注

2009 年国际小学数学竞赛队际竞赛试题解答

1. **解** 每行数的规律如下：

行 A	每5个数为一个周期
行 B	每4个数为一个周期
行 C	每2个数为一个周期

因为 5、4 和 2 的最小公倍数为 20，我们只需考虑前 20 行的和，它们分别是 3、6、7、10、7、5、6、9、6、9、5、8、5、8、9、7、4、7、8 和 11。在这些数中，7 出现的次数最多，出现了四次，所以 7 一共出现的次数为 60÷20×4=12 次。

答：12次

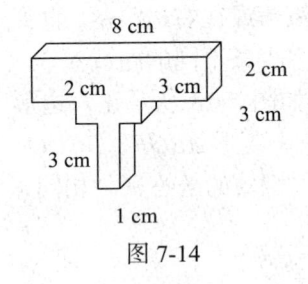

2. **解法 1** 锯下最外面一层涂有红色的小立方体，剩下如图 7-14 所示的形状没涂红色，其体积是 8×2×3+3×1×3+3×1×3=66(cm³)。所以，六个面都没涂有红色的小正方体有 66 个。

图 7-14

解法 2 将原 T 型木块切成 4×5×10 与 3×4×5 的两个长方体，可知它们的接缝处表面并未涂上红色，将所有表面涂有红色的小立方体移除后，剩下 (10−2)(4−2)(5−2)+3(5−2)+(4−1)(5−2)(3−2) = 8×2×3+3×3+3×3=66 个小立方体的六个面都没涂上红色 (图 7-15)。

(a)

(b)

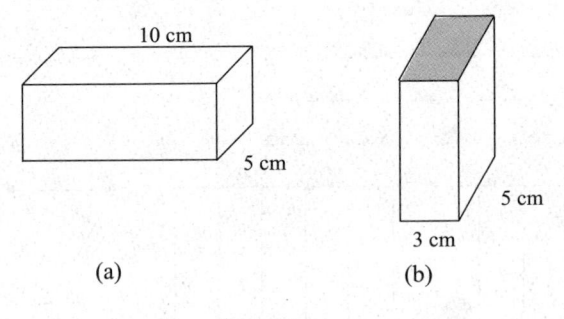

图 7-15

答：66个

第7章 2009年第7届国际小学数学竞赛

3. 解 $100=0.8\times125$,故小明留下的脚印数为 126 (包括开始的脚印).
$100=0.6\times166+0.4$,小亮留下的脚印数为 167 (包括开始的脚印).
$100=2.4\times41+1.6$,完全重叠的脚印数为 42 (包括开始的脚印).
所以 100 m 内一共留下 $126+167-42=251$ 个脚印.

答: 251 个

4. 解 将棋盘黑白相间涂色,纸板编号,如图 7-16 所示.

(a)

(b)

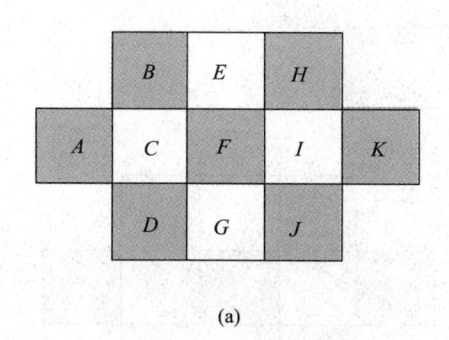

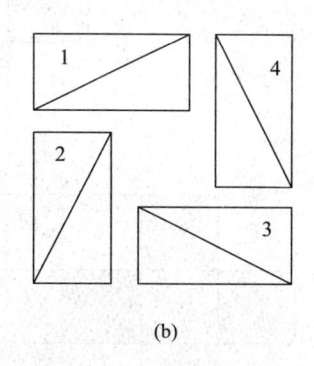

图 7-16

因每张纸板放入棋盘内一定都盖住一个黑色与一个白色小方格,现欲放入四张纸板,它们必须盖住这四个白色小方格.

由于棋盘是对称的. 不失一般性,我们可以从 C 处的小方格开始分析.

若在 BC 放置 2 号纸板,则 4 号纸板不能放在 HI 或 IJ 位置,否则没有足够位置放置 1 与 3 号纸板,即 4 号纸板只能放在 FG 位置,如图 7-17 所示.

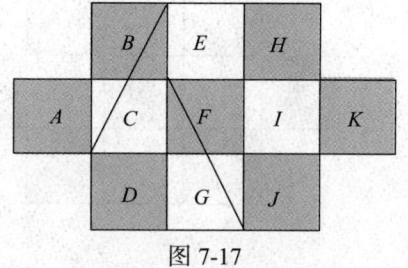

图 7-17

此时 1 号与 3 号纸板只能放置在 EH 或 IK 位置,但是无论 1 号或 3 号纸板都不能放在 EH 位置,故此情况无解.

若在 CD 放置 2 号纸板,则 4 号纸板不能放在 HI 或 IJ 位置,否则没有足够位置放置 1 与 3 号,即 4 号纸板只能放在 EF 位置,同上相同理由此情况无解.

若在 BE 放置 1 号纸板,则 4 号纸板不能放在 CD 或 HI 位置,也不能放在 IJ 位置,否则无法放置 1 与 3 号纸板,即 4 号纸板只能放在 FG 位置,如图 7-18 所示.

此时 2 号纸板只能放置在 HI 位置，3 号纸板只能放置在 AC 位置，故此情况有一解．因棋盘与纸板都是对称形式，故此解经翻转、旋转也是解答，如图 7-19 所示．

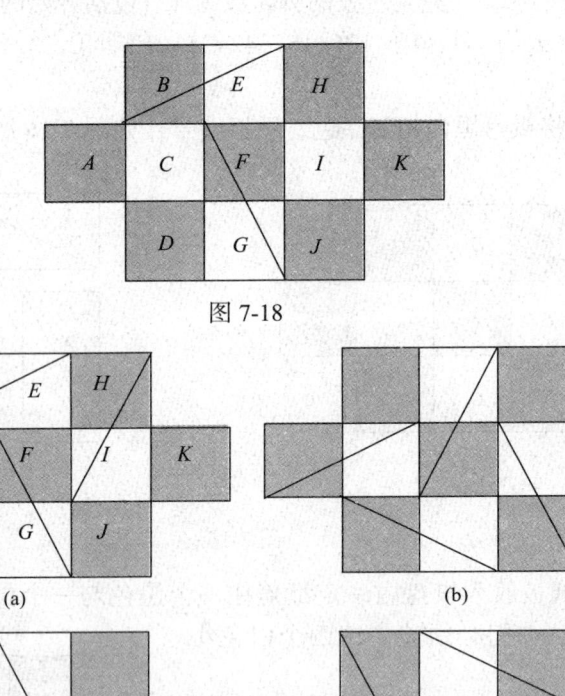

图 7-18

图 7-19

若在 CF 放置 1 号纸板，则无法再同时放入 2 与 4 号，故此情况无解．

若在 AC 放置 1 号纸板，则只能在 FG 放 2 号在 HI 放 4 号或在 EF 放 2 号在 IJ 放 4 号，前者无法再放入 3 号．后者唯有能在 DG 放置 3 号而得到解．而此解与上列解答相同，故共只有 4 组解．

答：4 组解，如图 7-19 所示

5. **解** 设 1 台抽水机 1 h 的抽水量为 1 个单位，则知

20 台抽水机×5 h=100 个单位、

第7章　2009年第7届国际小学数学竞赛

15 台抽水机×6 h=90 个单位.

故 1 h 漏掉的水量为 10 个单位.

而原来总水量为 20×5+10×5=150 个单位，所以在要求的 10 h 内共漏掉 10×10=100 个单位的水，所以至少需要 (150−100)÷10=5 台抽水机.

答: 5台

6. **解**　图 7-9 中前 n 列共有 $1+2+\cdots+n=\dfrac{n(n+1)}{2}$ 个数，即第 i 列的最后一个数是 $\dfrac{i(i+1)}{2}$. 如果 a_{ij}=2009，则 i (第 i 列) 是满足不等式 $\dfrac{i(i+1)}{2}\geqslant 2009$ 的最小正整数.

因为 $\dfrac{62\times 63}{2}=1953\leqslant 2009\leqslant 2016=\dfrac{63\times 64}{2}$，所以 i=63. 而第 63 列的第一个数是 $\dfrac{62\times 63}{2}+1=1954$，故 j= (2009−1954) +1=56，所以 $i+j$=63+56=119.

答: 119

7. **解**　因为 DCFE 是平行四边形，所以 DE//CF 且 EF//CD (图 7-20). 连接 CE，因为 DE//CF，即 DE//BF，所以
$$S_{\triangle DEB}=S_{\triangle DEC},$$
因此原来阴影部分的面积等于 △ACE 的面积.

连接 AF，因为 EF//CD，即 EF//AC，所以 $S_{\triangle ACE}=S_{\triangle ACF}$. 因为 $BC=3CF$，所以 $S_{\triangle ABC}=3S_{\triangle ACF}$. 故阴影部分的面积为 4 cm².

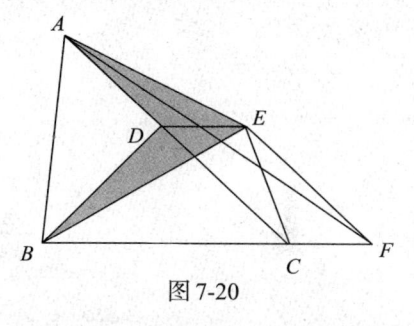

图 7-20

答: 4 cm²

8. **解**　连接 CM 与 DM (图 7-21).

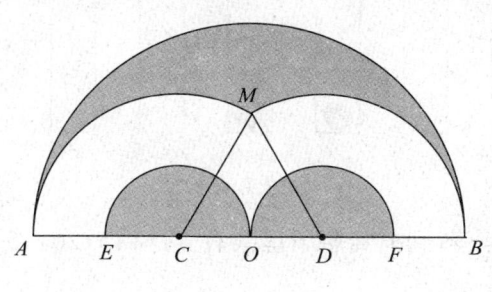

图 7-21

由题目条件可知 $CD=CM=DM$. 故 $\triangle CDM$ 是边长为 4 (cm)的等边三角形,所以 $\angle ACM = \angle BDM = 120°$.

因为半圆 C 和半圆 D 的半径都是 2 (cm),且点 M 到 AB 的距离为 3.464 (cm),所以等边 $\triangle CDM$ 的面积为

$$\frac{1}{2} \times 4 \times 3.464 = 6.928 \ (cm^2).$$

由此可知阴影部分的面积为

$$3.14 \times 6^2 \times \frac{1}{2} - 3.14 \times 4^2 \times \frac{120}{360} \times 2 - 6.928 + 3.14 \times 2^2 = 28.659 \ (cm^2).$$

答：28.659 cm^2

9. **解** 如图 7-22 所示,在每个等腰三角形的顶点处和每个瓶口处标上数,这些数表示小球从开始滚落到该位置的路线条数. 例如,小球从开始滚落到标有 2 的等腰三角形顶点处有两条路线.

第 1 条小球开始滚落撞到第二行的第 1 个等腰三角形的顶点后往右边滚落；第 2 条小球开始滚落撞到第二行的第 2 个等腰三角形的顶点后往左边滚落.

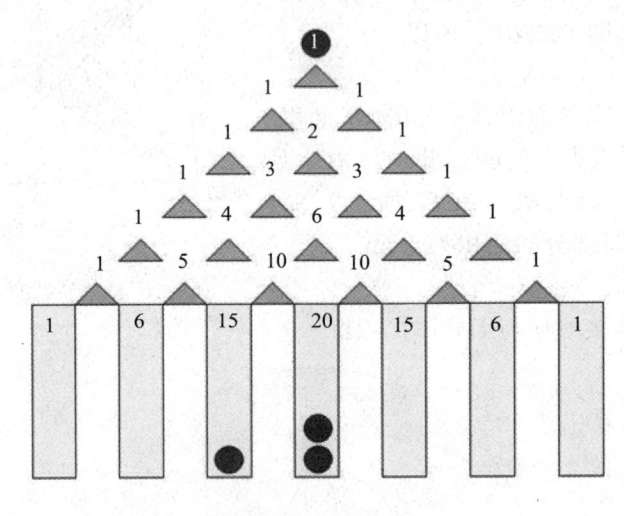

图 7-22

故小球从开始滚落到掉到瓶子里共有 1+6+15+20+15+6+1=64 条不同的路线.

答：64条

第 7 章　2009 年第 7 届国际小学数学竞赛

10. 解　因为 $A+B+O+F=B+C+D+O=D+E+F+O$，所以 $A+F=C+D$、$B+C=E+F$、$A+B=D+E$，即 $C-A=F-D$、$E-C=B-F$、$E-A=B-D$. 故 △ACE 相邻两个顶点上的数之差与 △DFB 相邻两个顶点上的数之差对应相等 (图 7-23).

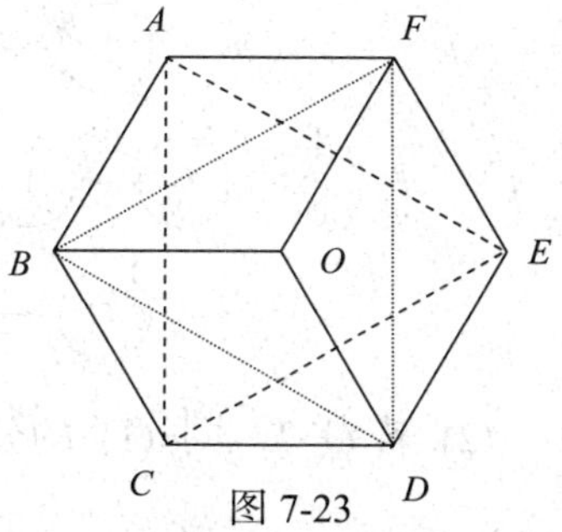

当把给定的三个数填写到 △ACE 的三个顶点时，若将旋转、翻转的解答视为相同，则只有一种填写方法. 不妨设 $A<C<E$.

我们先填中心点 O 上的数码，然后把剩下的六个数分成两组，每组三个数，分别填写到 $\{A, C, E\}$ 和 $\{D, F, B\}$ 这两组顶点上.

由上面可知，若填写好 $\{A, C, E\}$ 这组顶点上的数，则 $\{D, F, B\}$ 这组顶点上的数也就确定了.

故分情况来讨论点 O 上可能填入的数码：

(1) 若 $O=1$，则把 2、3、4、5、6、7 分成两组，并且把每组中的三个数从小到大排列.

因为 $C-A=F-D$、$E-C=B-F$、$E-A=B-D$，所以两组中相邻两个数之差必须对应相等.

如果 2 和 3 在同一组，容易验证只有 $\{2, 3, 4\}$、$\{5, 6, 7\}$ 这种分法符合要求. 如果 2 和 4 在同一组，容易验证只有 $\{2, 4, 6\}$、$\{3, 5, 7\}$ 这种分法符合要求. 如果 2 和 5 在同一组，那么 3 和 4 在另外一组，而 $5-2\neq 4-3$，显然不符合要求. 同样可以验证没有其他符合要求的分法. 所以这种情况共有 4 种填法：

$\{A, C, E\}=\{2, 3, 4\}$,　$\{A, C, E\}=\{5, 6, 7\}$,
$\{D, F, B\}=\{5, 6, 7\}$;　$\{D, F, B\}=\{2, 3, 4\}$.

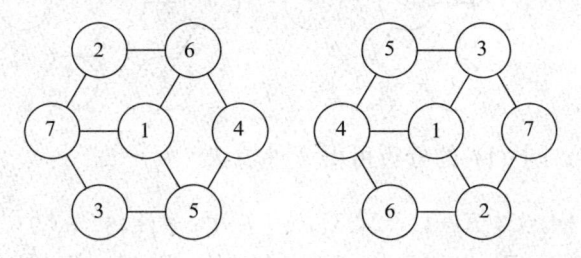

153

$\{A, C, E\} = \{3, 5, 7\}$, $\{A, C, E\} = \{2, 4, 6\}$,
$\{D, F, B\} = \{2, 4, 6\}$. $\{D, F, B\} = \{3, 5, 7\}$.

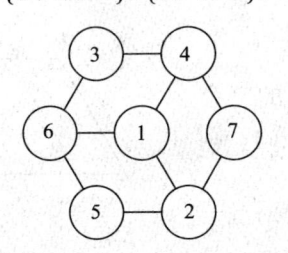

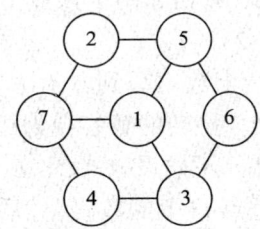

(2) 若 $O=2$，同 (1) 的分析可得 2 种填法:

$\{A, C, E\} = \{1, 4, 5\}$, $\{A, C, E\} = \{3, 6, 7\}$,
$\{D, F, B\} = \{3, 6, 7\}$, $\{D, F, B\} = \{1, 4, 5\}$.

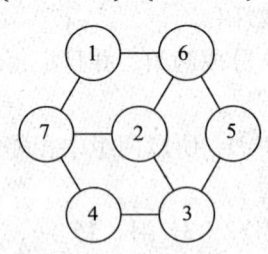

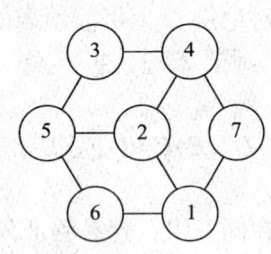

(3) 若 $O=3$，同 (1) 的分析可得 2 种填法:

$\{A, C, E\} = \{1, 4, 6\}$, $\{A, C, E\} = \{2, 5, 7\}$,
$\{D, F, B\} = \{2, 5, 7\}$, $\{D, F, B\} = \{1, 4, 6\}$.

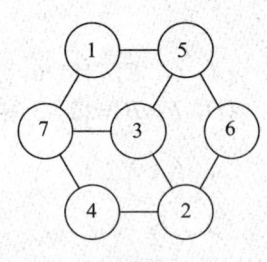

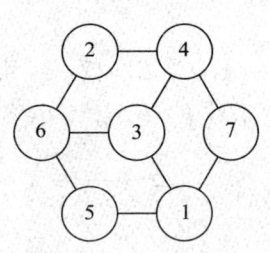

(4) 若 $O=4$，同 (1) 的分析可得 2 种填法:

$\{A, C, E\} = \{1, 2, 3\}$, $\{A, C, E\} = \{5, 6, 7\}$,
$\{D, F, B\} = \{5, 6, 7\}$, $\{D, F, B\} = \{1, 2, 3\}$.

第7章 2009年第7届国际小学数学竞赛

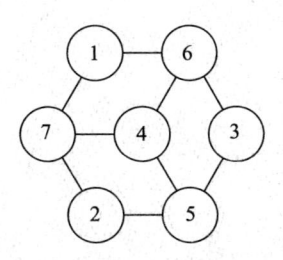

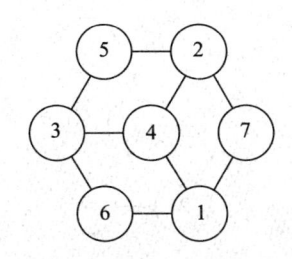

(5) 若 $O=5$,因为 1、2、3、4、5、6、7 是连续的 7 个整数,所以这种情况的分组方法和 $O=3$ 的情况一样. 容易得到这种情况有 2 种填法:

$\{A, C, E\}=\{1, 3, 6\}$, $\{A, C, E\}=\{2, 4, 7\}$,
$\{D, F, B\}=\{2, 4, 7\}$, $\{D, F, B\}=\{1, 3, 6\}$.

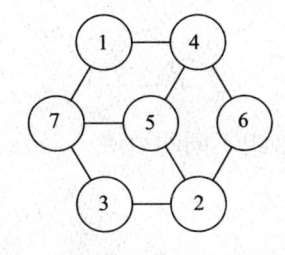

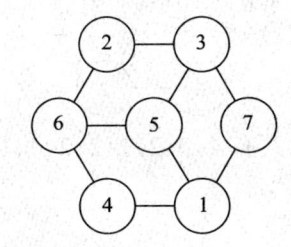

(6) 若 $O=6$,因为 1、2、3、4、5、6、7 是连续的 7 个整数,所以这种情况的分组方法和 $O=2$ 的情况一样. 容易得到这种情况有 2 种填法:

$\{A, C, E\}=\{3, 4, 7\}$, $\{A, C, E\}=\{1, 2, 5\}$,
$\{D, F, B\}=\{1, 2, 5\}$, $\{D, F, B\}=\{3, 4, 7\}$.

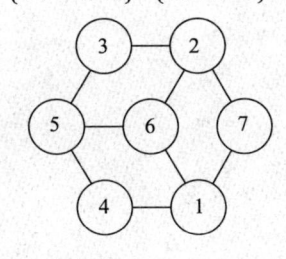

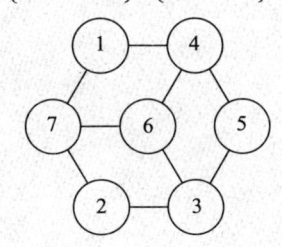

(7) 若 $O=7$,同样因为 1、2、3、4、5、6、7 是连续的 7 个整数,所以这种情况的分组方法和 $O=1$ 的情况一样. 共有 4 种填法:

$\{A, C, E\}=\{1, 2, 3\}$, $\{A, C, E\}=\{4, 5, 6\}$,
$\{D, F, B\}=\{4, 5, 6\}$, $\{D, F, B\}=\{1, 2, 3\}$.

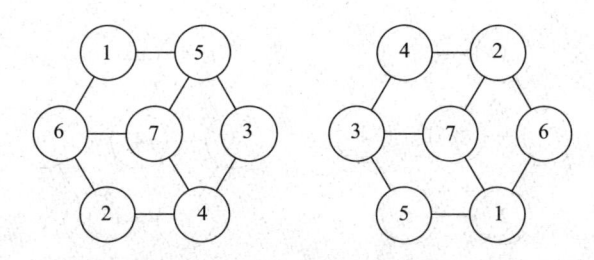

{A, C, E}={1, 3, 5}, {A, C, E}={2, 4, 6},
{D, F, B}={2, 4, 6}, {D, F, B}={1, 3, 5}.

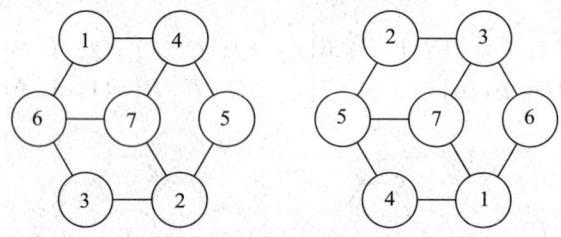

综上所述，共有 4+2+2+2+2+2+4=18 组不同的填法.

答：18组

第8章 2010年第8届国际小学数学竞赛

8.1 EMIC个人赛英文试题

Elementary Mathematics International Contest 2010
27th July, 2010, Incheon, Korea

Individual Contest

1. A computer billboard is displaying the three 'words': IMC 2010 INCHEON. A malfunction causes the initial 'letter' of each of the three words to be shifted to the end of that word every minute. Thus after 1 minute, the billboard reads MCI 0102 NCHEONI, and after 2 minutes, it reads CIM 1020 CHEONIN. After how many minutes will the original three words reappear for the first time?

2. What is the sum of the digits of the number $10^{2010} - 2010$?

3. By the notation d_n, we mean an n-digit number consisting of n times of the digit d. Thus $5_3=555$ and $4_3 9_5 8_1 3_6=444999998333333$. If $2_w 3_x 5_y + 3_y 5_w 2_x = 5_3 7_2 8_z 5_1 7_3$ for some integers w, x, y and z, what is the value of $w+x+y+z$?

4. A man weighs 60 kg plus one-quarter of his weight. His wife weighs 64 kg plus one-fifth of her weight. What is the absolute difference between the weights of the man and his wife in kg?

5. In quadrilateral $ABCD$, AB=6 cm, AD=4 cm, BC=7 cm and CD=15 cm. If the length of AC is an integer number of cm, what is this number?

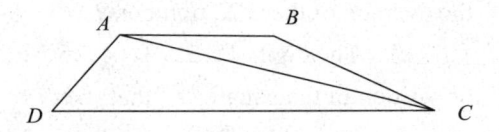

6. The speed of the current in the river is 1 km per hour. A man rows a boat at constant speed. He rows upstream for 3 hours, and rows downstream for 2 hours to return to his starting point. What is the distance, in km, between the starting point of

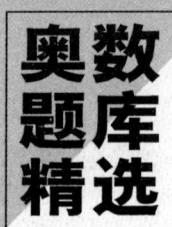

the boat and the point at which the boat turns around?

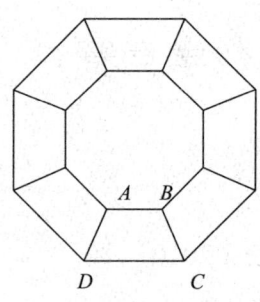

7. In the quadrilateral *ABCD*, *AB* is parallel to *DC* and *AD*=*BC*. If eight copies of this quadrilateral can be used to form a hollow regular octagon as shown in the diagram below, what is the measure of ∠*BAD*, in degree?

8. Let $\overline{abc}$, $\overline{def}$ be two different 3-digit numbers. If the difference $\overline{abcdef} - \overline{defabc}$ is divisible by 2010, what is the largest possible sum of these two 3-digit numbers?

9. What is the average of all different 9-digits numbers where each consists of the digit 5 five times and the digit 4 four times?

10. *ABCD* is a rectangle with *AB*=4 cm and *BC*=6 cm. *E*, *F*, *G* and *H* are points on the sides *AB*, *BC*, *CD* and *DA* respectively, such that *AE*=*CG*=3 cm and *BF*=*DH*=4 cm. If *P* is a point inside *ABCD* such that the area of the quadrilateral *AEPH* is 5 cm^2, what is the area the quadrilateral *PFCG*, in cm^2?

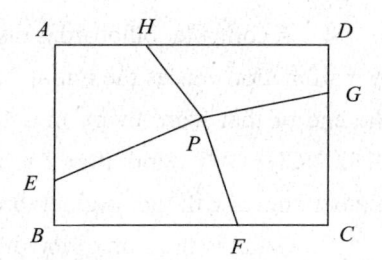

11. Narrow vegetable spring-rolls of length 8 cm are supposed to be made by rolling 8-cm bean sprouts inside 6 cm×8 cm rice papers into cylinders. Instead, the workers are provided with 6 cm bean sprouts. So they roll the rice paper the other way and get wide cylinders of length 6 cm. For either kind of spring rolls, there is an overlap of 1 cm in order for the rice paper to stick. What is the ratio of the volume of the 8 cm spring roll to the volume of the 6 cm spring roll?

12. The largest of 23 consecutive odd numbers is 5 times the smallest. What is the average of these 23 numbers?

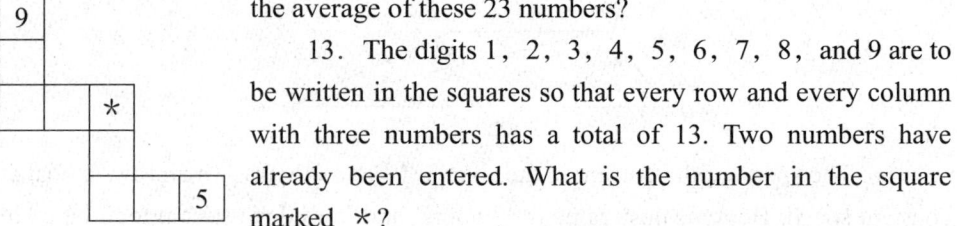

13. The digits 1, 2, 3, 4, 5, 6, 7, 8, and 9 are to be written in the squares so that every row and every column with three numbers has a total of 13. Two numbers have already been entered. What is the number in the square marked *?

14. In a test given in four subjects, each of five students obtained a score of *w*,

x, y or z in each individual subject, as shown in the table below. The total score of each student had been computed, as well as the class total for each subject except for one. What was the class total for Biology?

Student	Anna	Gail	Mary	Patty	Susie	Class Total
Algebra	w	z	w	z	y	416
Biology	w	x	y	y	z	?
Chemistry	x	y	y	w	x	428
Dictation	y	w	z	z	x	401
Individual Total	349	330	349	326	315	

15. What is the largest positive integer n which does not contain the digit 0, such that the sum of its digits is 15 and the sum of the digits of $2n$ is less than 20?

8.2 EMIC个人赛中文试题

2010年国际小学数学竞赛个人竞赛试题

1. 一个电子广告牌正在显示三个"单词"：IMC 2010 INCHEON. 由于系统出现故障导致每隔1分钟每个"单词"最前面的一个字符就被移到该单词的末尾. 即1分钟后，广告牌显示: MCI 0102 NCHEONI；再过1分钟后，广告牌显示: CIM 1020 CHEONIN. 请问几分钟后广告牌首次再度显示原来的三个"单词"？

2. 请问$10^{2010}-2010$的各位数码之和为多少？

3. 我们约定一种标记法：d_n表示各位数码都是d的n位数，例如，5_3=555和$4_3 9_5 8_1 3_6$=444999998333333. 若整数x、y、z和w满足$2_w 3_x 5_y+3_y 5_w 2_x=5_3 7_2 8_z 5_1 7_3$，请问$x+y+z+w$的值为多少？

4. 丈夫的体重等于他的体重的四分之一加上60 kg. 妻子的体重等于她的体重的五分之一加上64 kg. 请问丈夫与妻子的体重之差为多少千克？

5. 在四边形$ABCD$中，AB=6 cm，AD=4 cm，BC=7 cm和CD=15 cm. 已知AC的长度是整数（单位：cm），请问AC的长度为多少cm（图8-1）？

图 8-1

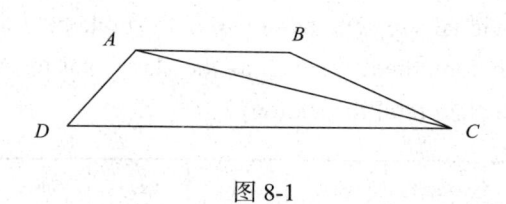

6. 一条河的水流速度是 1 km/h. 小明以固定的速度划一条小船. 他逆流划行了 3 h, 然后顺流划行返回原来的出发地点, 用了 2 h. 请问小明的出发地点与他开始返回的地点之间的距离为多少 km?

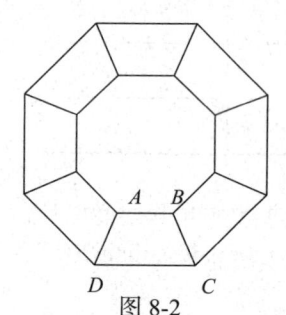

7. 在四边形 ABCD 中, AB//DC 且 AD=BC. 如果用八个与 ABCD 相同的四边形能够拼成一个空心的正八边形 (图 8-2), 请问 ∠BAD 为多少度?

图 8-2

8. 设 $\overline{abc}$、$\overline{def}$ 为两个不同的三位数, 满足 $\overline{abcdef} - \overline{defabc}$ 能被 2010 整除, 请问这两个三位数之和的最大值为多少?

9. 请问由四个 4 和五个 5 组成的所有不同的九位数之平均值为多少?

10. 点 E、F、G 和 H 分别在长方形 ABCD 的 AB、BC、CD 和 DA 边上, 点 P 在长方形的内部, 如图 8-3 所示. 已知 AB=4 cm, BC=6 cm, AE=CG=3 cm, BF=DH=4 cm, 且四边形 AEPH 的面积为 5cm². 请问四边形 PFCG 的面积为多少 cm²?

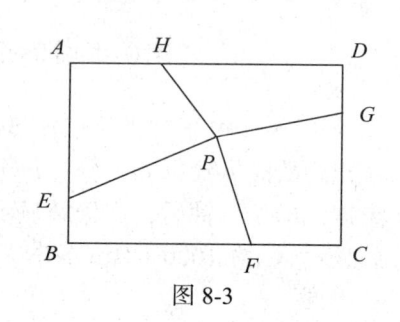

图 8-3

11. 长度为 8 cm 的素菜春卷的制作方法是: 用一张 6 cm × 8 cm 的春卷皮把长度为 8cm 的豆芽卷在里面, 外形呈圆柱状. 有一天, 菜商提供的豆芽的长度只有 6 cm. 于是他们用另一种方式来卷春卷皮, 得到长度为 6 cm 的宽圆柱. 如果这两种大小的春卷在相接处都重叠了 1cm 的春卷皮, 请问长度为 8 cm 的春卷与长度为 6 cm 的春卷的体积之比是多少?

12. 给定 23 个连续奇数, 其中最大的奇数是最小的奇数的 5 倍. 请问这 23 个奇数的平均值是多少?

第8章　2010年第8届国际小学数学竞赛

13. 把数 1，2，3，4，5，6，7，8 和 9 不重复地填入小方格内，每个小方格内恰填一个数，使得有三个小方格的每行和每列的三个数之和都为 13。有两个数已经填入小方格内．请问标记有 ＊ 处的小方格内所填的数是什么？

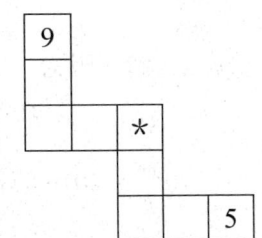

14. 有 5 名学生参加四个科目的考试，每名学生每科的得分是 w，x，y 或 z，如表 8-1 所示．每个学生四科的总分已经计算出来．除了生物这一科，其他科目的班级总分也已经计算出来，请问生物这一科的班级总分是多少？

表 8-1

学生	Anna	Gail	Mary	Patty	Susie	班级总分
代数	w	z	w	z	y	416
生物	w	x	y	y	z	?
化学	x	y	y	w	x	428
听写	y	w	z	z	x	401
个人总分	349	330	349	326	315	

15. 正整数 n 的各位数码都不为 0，且它们的和为 15，而 $2n$ 的各位数码之和小于 20．请问 n 的最大值为多少？

8.3　EMIC个人赛试题解答与评注

2010 年国际小学数学竞赛个人竞赛试题解答

1. **解**　正确的单词 "IMC" 每隔 3 分钟就出现一次，正确的单词 "2010" 每隔 4 分钟就出现一次，正确的单词 "INCHEON" 每隔 7 分钟就出现一次．因 3、4 和 7 的最小公倍数是 3×4×7=84，所以 84 分钟后广告牌首次再度显示原来的三个单词．

答：84

2. **解** 因为

$$10^{2010} - 2010 = \underbrace{100\cdots0}_{2010\text{个}0} - 2010 = \underbrace{99\cdots9}_{2006\text{个}9}7990,$$

所以 $10^{2010} - 2010$ 的各位数码之和为 $9\times2006+7+9+9=18054+25 =18079$.

答: 18079

3. **解** 首先,我们注意到这三个数的位数相同. 其次,我们发现加法中没有进位. 所以在和数中,前面的 3 个 5 只能由 2+3 得到,紧随其后的 2 个 7 只能由 2+5 得到,而接下来的 8 只能由 3+5 得到,这说明 y=3 和 w=5. 最后面的 3 个 7 只能由 5+2 得到,且它们前面的 5 只能由 3+2 得到,这说明 x=4 和 z=3. 由此可得 $w+x+y+z$=15. 完整的加式如下图所示.

```
    2 2 2 2 2 3 3 3 5 5 5
  + 3 3 3 5 5 5 5 5 2 2 2
  ─────────────────────────
    5 5 5 7 7 8 8 8 5 7 7 7
```

答: 15

4. **解** 由题目的条件可知丈夫的体重的 $\frac{3}{4}$ 等于 60(kg),所以他的体重为 80(kg). 妻子的体重的 $\frac{4}{5}$ 等于 64(kg),所以她的体重也为 80(kg). 从而丈夫与妻子的体重之差是 0(kg).

答: 0 kg

5. **解** 由三角不等式知,AC< $AB+BC$=6+7=13(cm),AC >CD–AD=15–4= 11(cm). 因为 AC 的长度是整数,所以 AC =12(cm).

答: 12 cm

6. **解** 小船在逆流中的速度与在顺流中的速度之比为 2:3=4:6= (5–1):(5+1). 所以小明在静水中划船的速度为 5(km/h). 因为小明逆流划行了 3 h,所以小明的出发地点与他开始返回的地点之间的距离为 (5–1)×3=12 (km).

答: 12 km

7. **解** 因为外面的八边形的八个内角之和为 (8–2)×180°=1080°,所以每个内角等于 1080°÷8=135°. 由题目条件可得四边形 $ABCD$ 是等腰梯形,所以 $\angle ADC$=$\angle BCD$. 由此可得 $\angle ADC$=135°÷2 =67.5°. 因为 $AB//DC$,所以 $\angle BAD$=180°–$\angle ADC$ =112.5°.

答: 112.5°

第8章 2010年第8届国际小学数学竞赛

8. 解
$$\overline{abcdef} - \overline{defabc} = (1000 \times \overline{abc} + \overline{def}) - (\overline{abc} + 1000 \times \overline{def})$$
$$= 999 \times (\overline{abc} - \overline{def})$$
$$= 3^3 \times 37 \times (\overline{abc} - \overline{def}),$$

且知 2010=2×3×5×67. 要想使得 $\overline{abcdef} - \overline{defabc}$ 能被 2010 整除，必须 $\overline{abc} - \overline{def}$ 能被 2×5×67=670 整除. 而 $\overline{abc} - \overline{def}$ 最多是三位数，且 $\overline{abc}$ 与 $\overline{def}$ 不同，所以 $\overline{abc} - \overline{def}$ =670.

故当 $\overline{abc}$ =999、$\overline{def}$ =329 时，$\overline{abc} + \overline{def}$ 取得最大值 999+329 =1328.

答：1328

9. **解法1** 考虑把所有的这些九位数用竖式求和，对于每一列，数码5与数码4的个数之比都为 5：4.

```
    5 5 5 5 5 4 4 4 4
    5 5 5 5 4 4 4 4 5
    5 5 5 4 4 4 4 5 5
    5 5 4 4 4 4 5 5 5
    5 4 4 4 4 5 5 5 5
    4 4 4 4 5 5 5 5 4
    4 4 4 5 5 5 5 4 4
    4 4 5 5 5 5 4 4 4
  + 4 5 5 5 5 4 4 4 4
  ─────────────────────
  4 5 5 5 5 5 5 5 5 1
```

所以全部的平均值等于上面九个数的平均值，也就是
4555555551÷9=506172839.

解法2 由四个 4 和五个 5 组成不同的九位数有 $\dfrac{9!}{4!5!}$=126 个. 这些九位数的每个数码上只能是 4 或 5. 选定某个数码，当该数码上是 4 时，这样的九位数有 $\dfrac{8!}{3!5!}$=56 个；当该数码上是 5 时，这样的九位数有 $\dfrac{8!}{4!4!}$=70 个（或 126−56=70 个）. 所以这 126 个九位数的平均值是

$$\frac{70\times 555555555+56\times 444444444}{126}$$

$$=\frac{10\times 5\times 111111111+8\times 4\times 111111111}{18}$$

$$=\frac{82\times 111111111}{18}$$

$$=\frac{41\times 111111111}{9}$$

$$=506172839.$$

答：506172839

10. **解法 1** 由题目的条件知 $S_{\triangle AEH}$=3(cm^2), $S_{\triangle EBF}$=2(cm^2), S_{ABCD}=24(cm^2). 所以 S_{EFGH}=24−(3+2)×2=14(cm^2). 因四边形 EFGH 是平行四边形，所以

$$S_{\triangle HEP}+S_{\triangle PFG}=\frac{14}{2}=7 \text{ (cm}^2\text{)}.$$

因 $S_{\triangle HEP}$=2(cm^2), 故 $S_{\triangle PFG}$=5(cm^2), 即 S_{PFCG}=5+3=8 (cm^2).

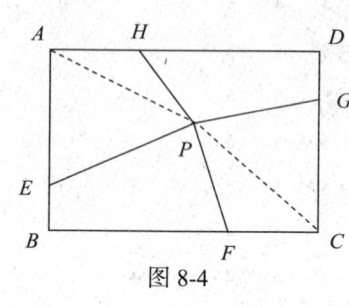

解法 2 连接 AP、CP（图 8-4）. 因 AE=CG=3(cm)、BC=6(cm), 故 $S_{\triangle AEP}+S_{\triangle CGP}=\frac{1}{2}\times 3\times 6=9$(cm^2). 因 BF=DH=4(cm)、BC=6(cm), 故 AH=CF=2(cm).

因 AB=4cm, 故 $S_{\triangle AHP}+S_{\triangle CFP}=\frac{1}{2}\times 2\times 4=4$(cm^2).

$S_{PFCG}+S_{AEPH}=S_{\triangle AEP}+S_{\triangle CGP}+S_{\triangle AHP}+S_{\triangle CFP}$=9+4=13(cm^2). 因为 S_{AEPH}=5(cm^2), 所以 S_{PFCG}=13−5=8(cm^2).

图 8-4

答：8 cm^2

11. **解** 窄春卷底面的周长为 6−1=5 cm, 所以底面的半径为 $\frac{5}{2\pi}$(cm), 从而窄春卷的体积为 $8\times\left(\frac{5}{2\pi}\right)^2=\frac{50}{\pi^2}$(cm^3). 宽春卷底面的周长为 8−1=7(cm), 所以底面的半径为 $\frac{7}{2\pi}$(cm), 从而宽春卷的体积为 $6\times\left(\frac{7}{2\pi}\right)^2=\frac{147}{2\pi^2}$(cm^3). 所以它们的体积之比为 100：147.

第8章　2010年第8届国际小学数学竞赛

答：100∶147

12．解　令这 23 个奇数中最小的为 $2n+1$，其中 n 为非负整数，则最大的奇数为 $2n+45$．因 $2n+45=5(2n+1)$，故 $40=8n$ 或 $n=5$．因为这 23 个奇数是连续的，所以它们的平均值为 $[(2n+1)+(2n+45)]\div 2=2n+23$，即 33．

答：33

13．解　设另外三个拐角处的方格所填的数分别是 m，n 和 p，如图 8-5 (a) 所示．由题目的条件可知

$$13\times 4=1+2+3+4+5+6+7+8+9+m+n+p,$$

所以 $m+n+p=7$．因为 m，n 和 p 互不相同，所以 m，n 和 p 只能是 1，2，4 这三个数．显然 $m\neq 4$，否则它与 p 同一行的和会大于 13．如果 $p=4$，则最下一列中间的数也是 4，矛盾．所以 $n=4$，此时很容易地可完成全图唯一的解．

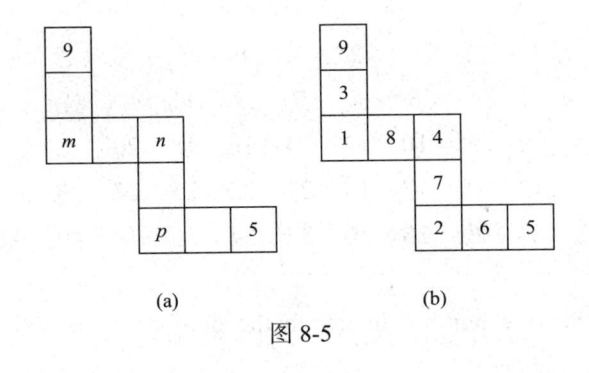

图 8-5

答：4

14．解　所有 5 名学生在四个科目中的总分是 $349+330+349+326+315=1669$．所以生物这一科的班级总分是 $1669-416-428-401=424$．这个结果是成立的，因为我们可取 $w=90$，$x=75$，$y=94$ 和 $z=71$．

答：424

15．解　为了使 n 取得的最大值，则 n 的各数位上不能有数码 2，3 或 4．因为如果我们把数码 2，3 或 4 分别换成 11，111 和 1111，这样不会改变 n 和 $2n$ 的各位数码之和，但 n 的值会增大．同样地，n 的各数位上不能有数码 6，7，8 或 9，因为它们分别可以换成 51，511，5111 和 51111．因为 n 的各位数码之和为 15，所以数码 1 的个数是 5 的倍数，但不能大于或等于 10，否则 $2n$ 的各位数码之和至少为 20．故 n 的最大值为 5511111．

答：5511111

165

8.4 EMIC队际赛英文试题

Elementary Mathematics International Contest 2010
27th July, 2010, Incheon, Korea

Team Contest

1. Pat is building a number triangle so that the first row has only one number, and each subsequent row has two more numbers than the preceding one. Starting from 1, the odd numbers are used in order in the odd-numbered rows. Starting from 2, the even numbers are used in order in the even-numbered rows. Thus her triangle starts off as follows.

$$
\begin{array}{ccccccccc}
 & & & & 1 & & & & \\
 & & & 2 & 4 & 6 & & & \\
 & & 3 & 5 & 7 & 9 & 11 & & \\
 & 8 & 10 & 12 & 14 & 16 & 18 & 20 & \\
13 & 15 & 17 & 19 & 21 & 23 & 25 & 27 & 29 \\
22 & 24 & 26 & 28 & 30 & 32 & 34 & 36 & 38 & 40 & 42 \\
 & & & & \cdots & & & &
\end{array}
$$

Determine the row number in which the number 2010 will appear in Pat's number triangle.

2. In a faulty calculator, only the keys 7, −, ×, ÷ and = work. If you press 7 after 7, you will get 77, and so on. As soon as an operation key is pressed, the preceding operation, if any, will be performed. When the = key is pressed, the final answer will appear. Find a sequence of key pressing which produces the final answer 34.

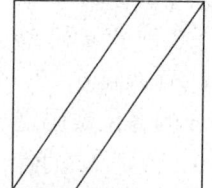

3. A square is divided into three parts of equal area by two parallel lines drawn from opposite vertices, as shown in the diagram below. Determine the area of the square, in cm^2, if the distance between the two parallel lines is 1 cm?

4. John and Mary live in the same building which has ten apartments on each floor. The apartments are numbered consecutively, with 1 to 10 on the first floor, 11 to 20 on the second floor, 21 to 30 on the third floor, and so on.

166

第 8 章 2010 年第 8 届国际小学数学竞赛

The number of Mary's apartment is equal to John's floor number, and the sum of their apartment numbers is 239. Determine the number of John's apartment.

5. Three couples went shopping in a mall. The following facts were known.

(1) Each person spent a whole number of dollars.

(2) The three wives spent $2408 among them.

(3) Lady A spent $400 plus half of what Lady B spent.

(4) Lady C spent $204 more than Lady A.

(5) Mr. X spent four times as much as his wife.

(6) Mr. Y spent $8 more than his wife.

(7) Mr. Z spent one and a half times as much as his wife.

(8) The three couples spent altogether $8040.

Determine the three husband-wife pairs.

6. A nine-digit number contains each of the digits 1, 2, 3, 4, 5, 6, 7, 8 and 9 exactly once, and every two adjacent digits of this nine-digit number form a two-digit number which is the product of two one-digit numbers. Determine this nine-digit number.

7. Sixteen students, labelled A to P, are writing a five-day examination. On each day, they write in four rooms, with four of them in a room. No two students are to be in the same room for more than one day. The published schedule, as shown in the diagram below, contains smudges, and unreadable entries are replaced by Xs. Replace each X by the correct letter.

Room	Day 1				Day 2				Day 3				Day 4				Day 5			
1	A	B	C	D	X	G	I	P	X	X	X	M	X	H	I	X	X	G	X	X
2	E	F	G	H	X	X	X	N	D	F	X	O	X	E	J	X	B	X	J	O
3	I	J	K	L	C	E	L	X	X	H	L	P	A	X	K	X	A	X	X	M
4	M	N	O	P	D	X	K	X	X	X	K	X	B	X	X	X	C	F	X	X

8. A 1×4 alien spaceship is going to land on a 7×7 airfield, occupying 4 of the 49 squares in a row or a column. Mines are placed in some of the squares, and if the alien space ship lands on a square with a mine, it will blow up. Determine the smallest

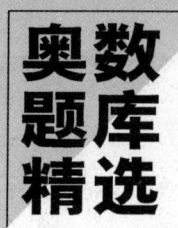

number of mines required to guarantee that the alien spaceship will be blown up, wherever it lands on this airfield. Show where the mines should be placed.

9. All but one of the numbers from 1 to 21 are to be filled into the squares of a 4×5 table, one number in each square, such that the sum of all the numbers in each row is equal to a number, and the sum of all the numbers in each column is equal to another number. Find all possible values of the number which is deleted, and find a way of filling in the table for each number that was deleted.

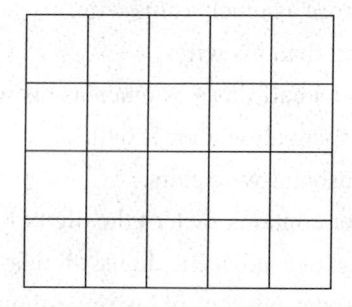

10. Each of the six pieces shown in the diagram below consists of two to five isosceles right triangles of the same size. A square is to be constructed, without overlap, using n of the six pieces. For each possible value of n, give a construction.

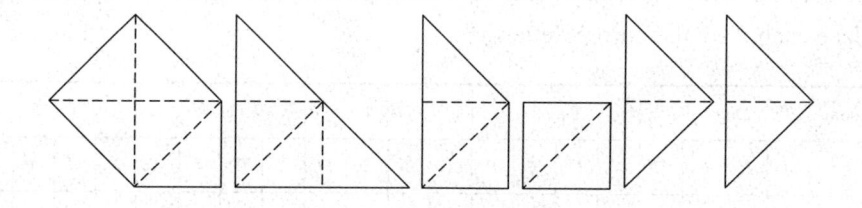

8.5　EMIC队际赛中文试题

2010年国际小学数学竞赛队际竞赛试题

1. 小白构造了一个三角形数阵，其中第一列只有一个数，接下来的每一列都比上一列多两个数. 从1开始，所有奇数按顺序排在奇数列上；从2开始，

第8章 2010年第8届国际小学数学竞赛

所有偶数按顺序排在偶数列上．他所构造的三角形数阵的前面几列如图 8-6 所示．

```
                    1
                 2  4  6
              3  5  7  9 11
           8 10 12 14 16 18 20
        13 15 17 19 21 23 25 27 29
     22 24 26 28 30 32 34 36 38 40 42
                    …
```

图 8-6

请问 2010 出现在这个三角形数阵的第几列？

2. 在一个部分损坏的计算器上，只有 7、−、×、÷、= 这些按键能正常使用．如果您按下 7 后接着再按一次 7，您将得到 77，依此类推．当按下一个运算键时，如果前面有未执行的运算，则开始执行前面的这个运算．当按下"="键时，将显示最终结果．请设计一个按键的序列使得这个计算器最终产生的结果为 34．

3. 从正方形的一组相对顶点引出的两条并行线把正方形划分为三等份，如图 8-7 所示．已知这两条并行线的距离为 1 cm，请问正方形的面积为多少 cm²？

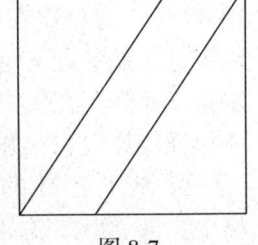

图 8-7

4. 约翰和玛丽住在同一栋大厦，此大厦的每层楼都有 10 套房间．这些房间的编号是连续的，第一层的编号是 1 号至 10 号，第二层的编号是 11 号至 20 号，第三层的编号是 21 号至 30 号，依此类推．已知玛丽家的房号等于约翰的家所在的楼层数，且他们的房号之和为 239．请问约翰家的房号是什么？

5. 有三对夫妻在一个商场购物，我们得知以下的事实：

(1) 每个人所花的钱的数目都是整数 (单位为元)．

(2) 三位女士总共花掉 2408 元．

(3) A 女士花的钱比 B 女士所花的钱的一半多 400 元．

(4) C 女士比 A 女士多花 204 元．

(5) X 先生所花的钱是他的妻子所花的钱的 4 倍．

(6) Y 先生比他的妻子多花 8 元．

(7) Z 先生所花的钱是他的妻子所花的钱的 $\frac{3}{2}$ 倍.

(8) 这三对夫妻总共花掉 8040 元.

请问 X 先生、Y 先生和 Z 先生的太太分别是谁？

6. 一个九位数所包含的数码恰好是 1、2、3、4、5、6、7、8、9 各一个，且这个九位数的任意两个相邻数码所组成的两位数都可以表示为两个一位数的乘积. 请问这个九位数是什么？

7. 十六名学生分别用字母 A 至 P 表示，他们同时参加了五天的考试. 考场一共有四间教室，每四名学生在一间教室. 对于任何两名学生，他们在同一间教室考试的天数都不多于一天. 考试日程表不小心被弄污了，看不清的学生代号用字母 X 代替，如表 8-2 所示. 请把每个字母 X 替换成正确的字母.

表 8-2

教室	第1天				第2天				第3天				第4天				第5天			
1	A	B	C	D	X	G	I	P	X	X	X	M	X	H	I	X	X	G	X	X
2	E	F	G	H	X	X	X	D	F	X	O	X	E	X	J	X	B	X	J	O
3	I	J	K	L	C	E	L	X	X	H	L	P	A	X	K	X	A	X	X	M
4	M	N	O	P	D	X	K	X	X	K	B	X	X	X	C	F	X	X		

8. 一架 1×4 的外星人宇宙飞船准备降落在一个 7×7 的飞机场上，它将占用 49 个小方格中在同一行或同一列的 4 个小方格. 我们在某些小方格内埋入地雷，如果宇宙飞船降落在埋有地雷的小方格上，则它将会被炸毁. 无论这架宇宙飞船降落在飞机场内的什么位置，请问至少要在多少个小方格内埋入地雷才保证能炸毁它？并请标出埋入地雷的小方格之位置.

9. 从 1 至 21 的整数中删除一个数，把剩下的数不重复地填入 4×5 的小方格中，每个小方格内恰只填一个数，使得每一行的所有数之和都相等；每一列的所有数之和也都相等. 求出所有可能被删除的数，并对每个被删除的数，给出一个满足上述条件的填表方式.

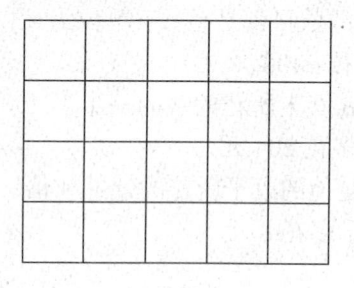

10. 下面的六张纸板 (图 8-8) 分别是由 2 至 5 个大小相同的等腰直角三角形所组成．利用这六张纸板中的 n 张能够拼成一个正方形 (纸板不能重叠)，请对每个可能的 n 值，给出一个拼图．

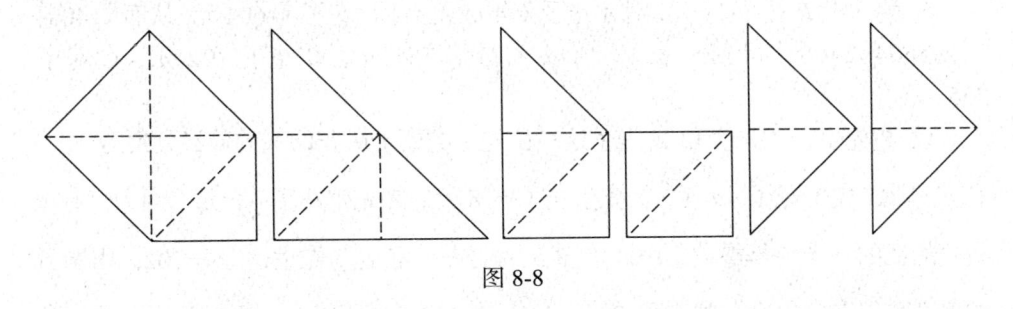

图 8-8

8.6 EMIC 队际赛试题解答与评注

2010 年国际小学数学竞赛队际竞赛试题解答

1. **解** 从 1 至 2010，一共有 1005 个偶数，且它们出现在偶数列上．这些偶数列上的数之个数分别为 3、7、11、…个，第 $2n$ 列有 $4n-1$ 个数．而 $3+7+11+\cdots+(4n-1) = n(2n+1)$，如果 $n=22$，则 $n(2n+1) = 990<1005$；如果 $n=23$，则 $n(2n+1) =1081>1005$．所以 2010 出现在这个三角形数阵的第 $2n=46$ 列．

答：第46列

2. **解** $777 \div 7 - 77 = 34$．

答：$777 \div 7 - 77 = 34$

3. **解** 令这个正方形为 $ABCD$，且 $BF//ED$ (图 8-9)．因为 $\triangle AFB$ 与平行四边 $BEDF$ 有相同的面积和高，所以 $AF=2DF$．设 $AB=3x$(cm)，则 $AF=2x$(cm)，且利用勾股定理，得到 $BF=\sqrt{13}x$(cm)．$\triangle AFB$ 的面积为 $3x^2$ (cm²)，等于 $BEDF$ 的面积 $\sqrt{13}x$ (cm²)，即 $x = \dfrac{\sqrt{13}}{3}$．从而 $ABCD$ 的面积为 $9x^2 = 13$ (cm²)．

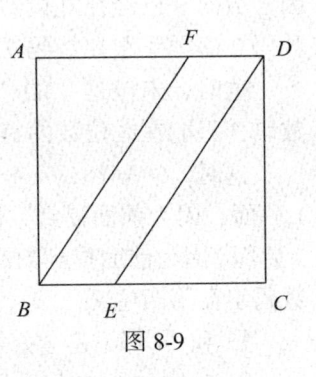

答：13 cm²

图 8-9

4. **解** 设约翰的家所在的楼层数为 a，则他的房号为 $10(a-1)+b$，其中 b 为整数且 $1 \leqslant b \leqslant 10$．由题目的条件可知玛丽家的房号为 a，我们得到 $10(a$

−1)+ b+a=239，化简可得 11a=249−b．所以 239≤11a≤248，而只有 242 是 11 的倍数，因此 a=22 和 b=7．所以约翰家的房号是 217．

答：217．

5. 解 设 B 花了 $2x$ 元，则 A 花了 $x+400$ 元，且 C 花了 $x+604$ 元．从而 $x+400+2x+x+604=2408$，得到 $x=351$．所以 A 花了 751 元，B 花了 702 元，C 花了 955 元．

设 X 先生，Y 先生和 Z 先生这三位先生的妻子所花的钱的数目分别为 a，b 和 c，则 X 先生花了 $4a$ 元，Y 先生花了 $b+8$ 元，Z 先生花了 $\frac{3}{2}c$ 元．因为只有 B 所花的钱的一半还是整数，由此可知 B 的丈夫一定是 Z 先生，即 $c=702$．由题目的条件可得三位先生一共花了 $8040-2408=5632$ 元，所以 $4a+b+2+\frac{3}{2}c=5632$．从这个式子中消去 $a+b+c=2408$ 和 $\frac{1}{2}c=351$，可得 $3a=2865$，所以 $a=955$．由此可知 C 的丈夫是 X 先生，A 的丈夫是 Y 先生．

答：X 先生的太太是 C、Y 先生的太太是 A、Z 先生的太太是 B．

6. 解 如果一个两位数可以表示为两个一位数的乘积，则我们称这个两位数为"好数"．因为没有"好数"的首位为 9，所以数码 9 只能在这个九位数的最后一位．

末位数是 9 的"好数"只有 7×7=49，所以数码 4 在第八位．

首位数是 8 的"好数"只有 9×9=81，且首位是 7 的"好数"只有 9×8=72，因为数码 9 已经在九位数的最后一位，所以数码 1 必须紧跟在数码 8 的后面，数码 2 必须紧跟在数码 7 的后面．

这时，末位是 7 的"好数"只有 9×3=27，但 7 不能跟在 2 的后面，所以数码 7 只能在九位数的首位且数码 2 在第二位．

这时，6×3=18，7×4=28 和 8×6=48 都是"好数"，但数码 8 不能跟在数码 1 后面，因为前面提到数码 1 必须跟在数码 8 的后面；数码 8 也不能跟在数码 4 后面，因为前面提到数码 9 跟在数码 4 后面．所以数码 8 在九位数的第三位，数码 1 在第四位．

13 和 34 都不是"好数"，所以数码 3 在第六位．

而 5×3=15 是"好数"，但 53 不是"好数"，所以数码 5 不在第五位．

因为 8×2=16 与 9×7=63 都是"好数"，所以我们可以把数码 6 放在第五位．

最后，因为 7×5=35 和 9×6=54 都是"好数"，所以数码 5 在第七位．

第8章 2010年第8届国际小学数学竞赛

这个九位数是 728163549.

答：728163549

7. 解 通过观察可以发现第 2 天的第三行、第 3 天的第四行、第 4 天的第三行和第 5 天的第一行都只有一个 X. 所以这些 X 只能分别是 J、N、L、D. 因为 B 和 D 第 5 天都在教室 2，因此第 2 天第一行的第一个 X 是 B 而第二个 X 是 A；依同样的方法观察可知出其余的 X 所代表的学生并得到下面这个日程表8-3.

表 8-3

教室	第1天				第2天				第3天				第4天				第5天			
1	A	B	C	D	B	G	I	P	C	G	J	M	C	H	I	N	D	G	L	N
2	E	F	G	H	A	F	J	N	D	F	I	O	D	E	J	P	B	H	J	O
3	I	J	K	L	C	E	L	O	A	H	L	P	A	G	K	O	A	E	I	M
4	M	N	O	P	D	H	K	M	B	E	K	N	B	F	L	M	C	F	K	P

8. 解 图 8-10 (a) 说明了如果我们把地雷埋在标了黑圆圈的方格内，则外星人的宇宙飞船无论这架宇宙飞船降落在飞机场内的什么位置将会被炸毁. 因为这架宇宙飞船有 12 种不重叠的方式可以降落在飞机场上，故放地雷的小方格少于 12 个不能保证炸毁这架宇宙飞船，如图 8-10 (b) 所示.

(a) (b)

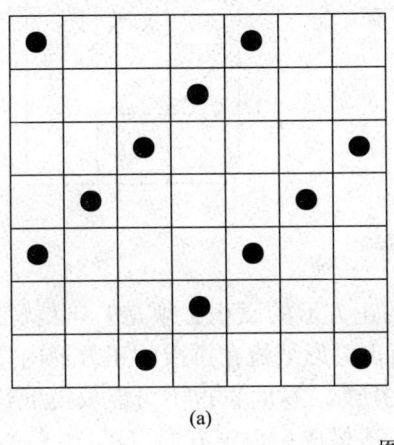

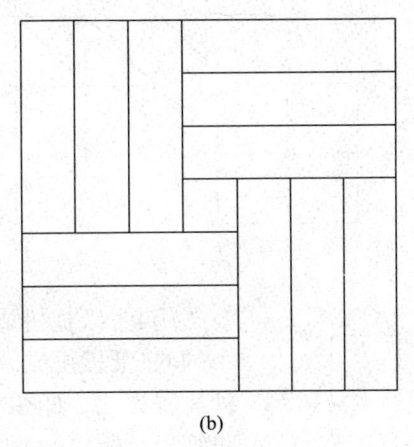

图 8-10

答：12个

9. 解 设 S 为每一行的所有数之和，T 为每一列的所有数之和，则表格中的所有数之和为 $4S=5T$. 这说明表格中的所有数之和是 4 和 5 的公倍数，所以必须是 20 的倍数. 因为 $1+2+\cdots+21=231$，所以删除掉的数必须是 11. 图 8-11

173

给出了一个满足要求的填表方式.

21	4	5	15	10
20	3	6	14	12
1	18	16	7	13
2	19	17	8	9

图 8-11

答: 11

10. **解** 设每个小等腰直角三角形的面积为 1, 则这六张纸板的面积分别为 5、4、3、2、2 和 2. 能用这些纸板拼成的正方形的面积必须是完全平方数或完全平方数的两倍, 即 1、2、4、8、9、16 或 18. 面积为 2、4、8、16 和 18 的正方形可以分别用 1、2、3、5 和 6 张给定的纸板拼成, 如图 8-12 所示.

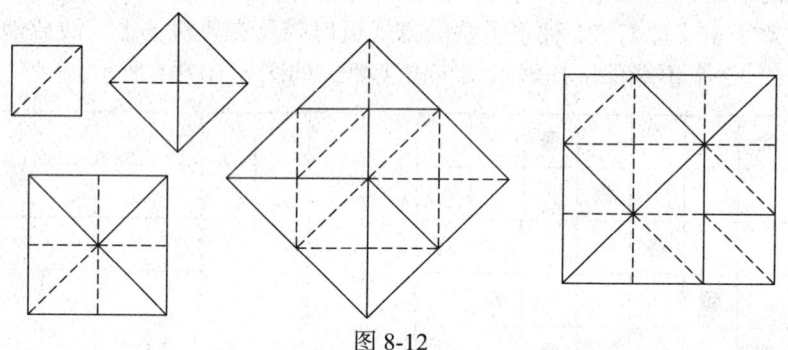

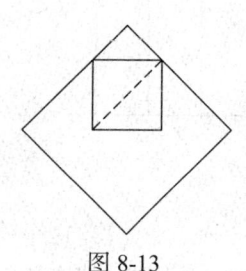

图 8-12

用 4 张纸板拼成的正方形的面积必须是 9, 也就是用最小的 4 张纸板拼成. 而正方形纸板在拼成的正方形内只有一种放置方式, 如图 8-13 所示. 这时再也不可能放得下其他三张纸板. 所以 $n=4$ 张无法拼成一个正方形.

图 8-13

第9章 2011年第9届国际小学数学竞赛

9.1 EMIC个人赛英文试题

Elementary Mathematics International Contest 2011
20th July, 2011, Bali, Indonesia

Individual Contest

1. For any two numbers a and b, $a*b$ means $a+b-\dfrac{2011}{2}$. Calculate: $1*2*3*\cdots*2010*2011$.

2. Suppose 11 coconuts have the same cost as 14 pineapples, 22 mango have the same cost as 21 pineapples, 10 mango have the same cost as 3 bananas, and 5 oranges have the same cost as 2 bananas. How many coconuts have the same cost as 13 oranges?

3. A girl calculates $\dfrac{1+2}{3}+\dfrac{4+5}{6}+\cdots+\dfrac{2011+2012}{2013}$ and a boy calculates $1+\dfrac{1}{2}+\dfrac{1}{3}+\cdots+\dfrac{1}{671}$. What is the sum of their answers?

4. What is the first time between 4:00 and 5:00 that the hour hand and the minute hand are exactly 10° apart?

5. Two squirrels, Tim and Kim, are dividing a pile of hazelnuts. Tim starts by taking 5 hazelnuts. Thereafter, they take alternate turns, each time taking 1 more hazelnut than the other in the preceding turn. If the number of hazelnuts to be taken is larger than what remains in the pile, then all remaining hazelnuts are taken. At the end, Tim has taken 101 hazelnuts. What is the exact number of hazelnuts at the beginning?

6. In how many ways can we pay a bill of $500 by a combination of $10, $20 and $50 notes?

7. The least common multiple of the numbers 16, 50 and A is 1200. How many

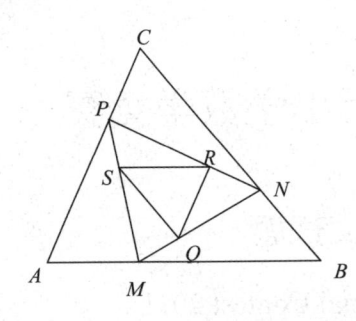

positive integers A have this property?

8. In the figure below, $\dfrac{AM}{MB} = \dfrac{BN}{NC} = \dfrac{CP}{PA} = \dfrac{1}{2}$ and $\dfrac{MQ}{QN} = \dfrac{NR}{RP} = \dfrac{PS}{SM} = \dfrac{1}{2}$. If the area of $\triangle ABC$ is 360 cm^2, what is the area of $\triangle QRS$, in cm^2?

9. In a 2×3 table, there are 10 rectangles which consist of an even number of unit squares.

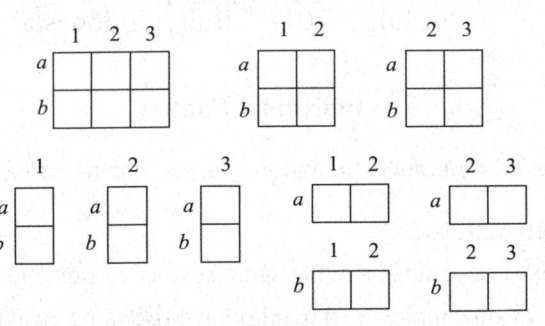

How many rectangles are there in a 6×9 table which consist of an even number of unit squares?

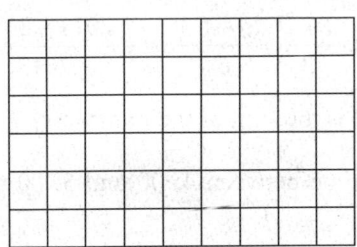

10. Find the smallest positive common multiple of 4 and 6 such that each digit is either 4 or 6, there is at least one 4 and there is at least one 6.

11. We have two kinds of isosceles triangles each with two sides of length 1. The acute triangle has a 30° angle between the two equal sides, and the right triangle has a right angle between the two equal sides. We place a sequence of isosceles triangles around a point according to the following rules. The n-th isosceles triangle is a right isosceles triangle if n is a multiple of 3, and an acute isosceles triangle if it is not. Moreover, the n-th and $(n+1)$-st isosceles triangles

share a common side, as shown in the diagram below. What is the smallest value of $n>1$ such that the n-th isosceles triangle coincides with the 1-st one?

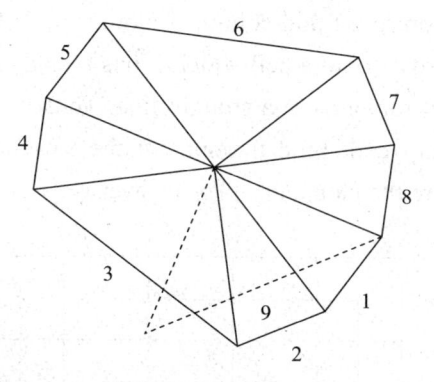

12. When the digits of a two-digit number are reversed, the new number is at least 3 times as large as the original number. How many such two-digit numbers are there?

13. In the quadrilateral $ABCD$, $AB=CD$, $\angle BCD=57°$, and $\angle ADB +\angle CBD=180°$. Find the value of $\angle BAD$.

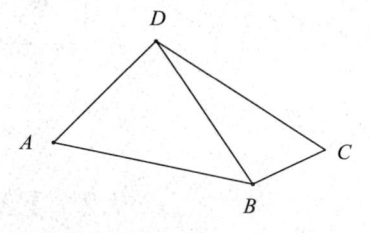

14. Squares on an infinite chessboard are being painted. As shown in the diagram below, three squares (lightly shaded) are initially painted. In the first step, we paint all squares (darkly shaded) which share at least one edge with squares already painted. The same rule applies in all subsequent steps. Find the number of painted squares after one hundred steps.

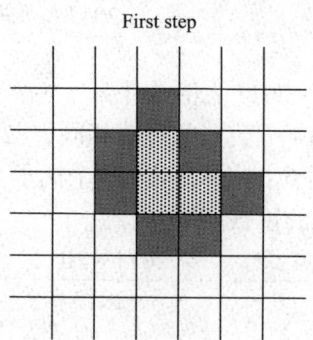

15. The rows of a 2011×4024 chessboard are numbered from 1 to 2011 from bottom to top, and the columns from 1 to 4024 from left to right. A snail starts crawling from the cell on row 1 and column 1 along row 1. Whenever it is about to crawl off the chessboard or onto a cell which it has already visited, it will make a left turn and then crawl forwards in a straight line. Thus it follows a spiraling path until it has visited every cell. Find the sum of the row number and the column number of the cell where the path ends. (The answer is 3+2=5 for a 4×5 table)

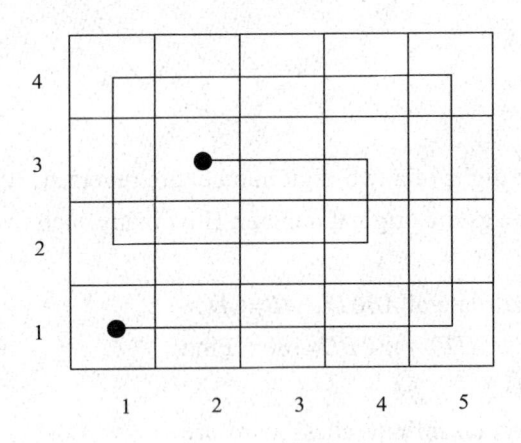

9.2 EMIC个人赛中文试题

2011年国际小学数学竞赛个人竞赛试题

1. 对任意两个数 a 和 b，我们规定
$$a*b = a+b-\frac{2011}{2}.$$
请问 $1*2*3*\cdots*2010*2011$ 之值是什么？

2. 假设11个椰子与14个菠萝的价钱相同，22个芒果与21个菠萝的价钱相同，10个芒果与3根香蕉的价钱相同，5个橘子与2根香蕉的价钱相同. 请问13个橘子与多少个椰子的价钱相同？

3. 小明在计算 $\frac{1+2}{3}+\frac{4+5}{6}+\cdots+\frac{2011+2012}{2013}$，小亮在计算 $1+\frac{1}{2}+\frac{1}{3}+\cdots+$

第9章 2011年第9届国际小学数学竞赛

$\frac{1}{671}$，请问他们计算得到的结果之和为多少？

4. 请问在 4:00 到 5:00 之间时针和分针首次夹角为 10°是什么时刻？

5. 两只松鼠甜甜与金金分一堆榛果．它们轮流拿榛果，由甜甜先开始拿走 5 个榛果，接下来规定每只松鼠每一次拿走的榛果数量要比之前另一只松鼠刚拿走的榛果数量多 1 个．如果要拿走的榛果数量多于所剩下的榛果数量，则拿光所有剩下的榛果．依照上述方式分完这堆榛果后，已知甜甜总共拿到 101 个榛果，请问这堆榛果最初共有多少个？

6. 用面值为 10 元、20 元和 50 元的纸币来支付 500 元，请问总共有多少种不同的支付方式？

7. 已知 16、50、A 三个数的最小公倍数为 1200．请问正整数 A 共有多少种可能的值？

8. 在图 9-1 中，已知 $\frac{AM}{MB} = \frac{BN}{NC} = \frac{CP}{PA} = \frac{1}{2}$ 且 $\frac{MQ}{QN} = \frac{NR}{RP} = \frac{PS}{SM} = \frac{1}{2}$，如果 △ABC 的面积为 360 cm²，请问△QRS 的面积为多少 cm²？

9. 在 2×3 的方格表中，由偶数个单位正方形组成的长方形有 10 个，如图 9-2 所示．

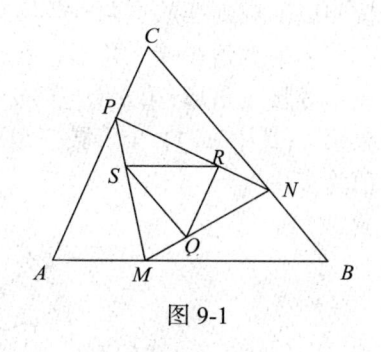

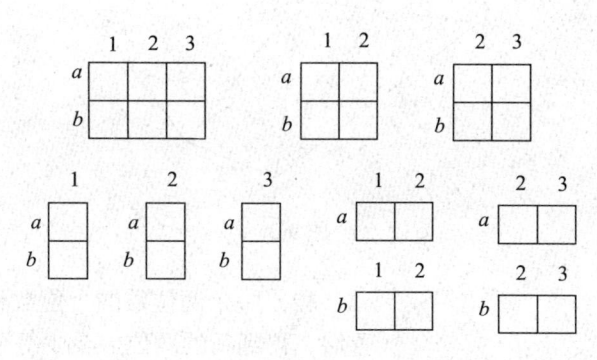

图 9-1

图 9-2

在 6×9 的方格表（下表）中，请问由偶数个单位正方形组成的长方形有多少个？

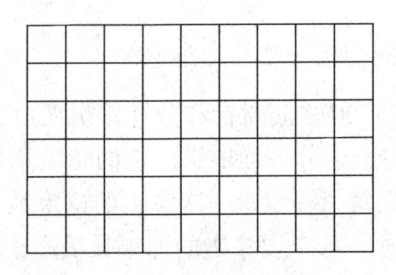

10. 已知正整数 n 是 4 与 6 的公倍数，n 的数码全都是 4 或 6，且数码 4 与 6 各至少有一个．请问满足上述条件的最小 n 值是什么？

11. 我们有两种等腰三角形，它们的腰长都为 1，其中一种等腰三角形的顶角为 30°，另一种等腰三角形的顶角为直角．我们将它的顶角围绕着一个点按照以下规则摆放这两种等腰三角形：当 n 为 3 的倍数时，第 n 个摆放的等腰三角形为直角等腰三角形；当 n 不为 3 的倍数时，第 n 个摆放的等腰三角形为锐角等腰三角形；第 n 个与第 $n+1$ 个等腰三角形有一条公共边，如图 9-3 所示．如果第 n (其中 $n>1$) 个等腰三角形与第 1 个等腰三角形完全重合，请问 n 的最小值为多少？

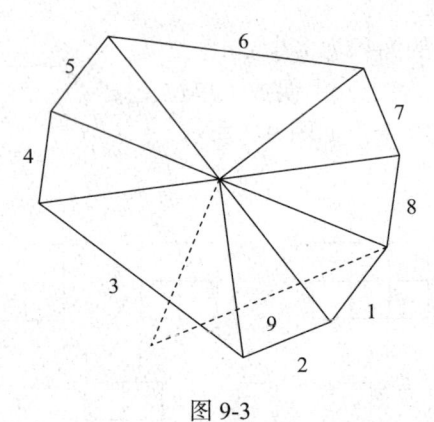

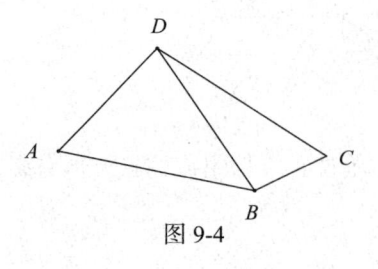

图 9-3

12. 一个两位数的个位数和十位数交换位置后，得到新的两位数至少等于原来的两位数的 3 倍．请问这样的两位数有多少个？

13. 在四边形 $ABCD$ 中（图 9-4），$\angle BCD=57°$，$AB=CD$，且 $\angle ADB + \angle CBD = 180°$．请问 $\angle BAD$ 为多少度？

图 9-4

第9章 2011年第9届国际小学数学竞赛

14. 我们对一个无限大的棋盘的格子进行涂色. 如图 9-5 所示, 有三个格子 (颜色较浅的格子) 在开始的时候已经涂色. 在第 1 步中, 我们给所有与已涂色的格子至少有一条公共边的格子涂色 (图 9-5 中颜色较深的格子). 接下来的每一步都采用同样的方式进行涂色. 经过 100 步涂色后, 请问这个棋盘上总共有多少个格子已被涂色?

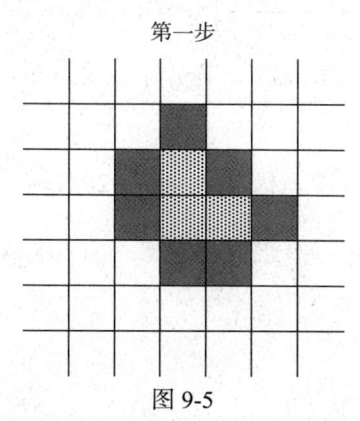

第一步

图 9-5

15. 在一个 2011×4024 的棋盘上, 从下到上每列分别标上从 1 至 2011 的编号, 从左到右每行分别标上从 1 至 4024 的编号. 一只蜗牛从位于第 1 列第 1 行的格子开始沿着第 1 列爬行. 每当蜗牛快要爬出棋盘或遇到已经爬过的格子时, 它必须向左拐, 然后沿着直线继续爬行. 这样, 它沿着一个螺旋状的路径爬行, 直到它爬完所有的格子为止. 请问蜗牛最后停留的格子之行的编号与列的编号之总和为多少? (图 9-6 为 4×5 棋盘的示例, 蜗牛最后停留的格子所在的行的编号与列的编号之总和为 2+3=5)

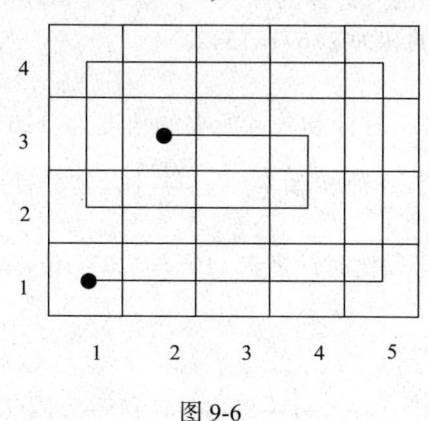

图 9-6

181

9.3　EMIC个人赛试题解答与评注

2011年国际小学数学竞赛个人竞赛试题解答

1. **解**　$a*b*c = \left(a+b-\dfrac{2011}{2}\right)*c = a+b+c-2011$.

$a_1*a_2*\cdots*a_n = a_1+a_2+\cdots+a_n-\dfrac{2011}{2}\times(n-1)$ （$n=2$、3、4、$\cdots$），

$1*2*3*\cdots*2010*2011 = (1+2+3+\cdots+2011)-\dfrac{2011}{2}\times 2010$

$= \dfrac{2011\times 2012}{2} - 2011\times 1005$

$= 2011$.

答：2011

2. **解**　可知 1 个橘子与 $\dfrac{2}{5}$ 根香蕉的价钱相等、1 根香蕉与 $\dfrac{10}{3}$ 个芒果的价钱相等、1 个芒果与 $\dfrac{21}{22}$ 个菠萝的价钱相等、1 个菠萝与 $\dfrac{11}{14}$ 个椰子价钱相等. 因此 1 个橘子与 $\dfrac{2}{5}\times\dfrac{10}{3}\times\dfrac{21}{22}\times\dfrac{11}{14} = 1$ 个椰子价钱相等，故 13 个橘子与 13 个椰子价钱相等.

答：13 个

3. **解**　观察可知两人计算的算式中，每一个依序对应的项之和都为 2，故知两人计算的结果的和为 $2\times 671 = 1342$.

答：1342

4. **解**　4：00 时，时针和分针所夹的角度为 120°. 因分针每分钟转动 $6° = \left(=\dfrac{360°}{60}\right)$、时针每分钟转动 $\dfrac{1}{2}° \left(=\dfrac{30°}{60}\right)$，其分针每分钟比时针多走了 $6° - \dfrac{1}{2}° = 5.5°$. 因分针必须比时针多走 110° (=120°−10°)，故需 $\dfrac{110°}{5.5°} = 20$ 分钟. 因此所求时间为 4：20.

答：4：20

5. **解**　观察知 $101 = 5+7+9+11+13+15+17+19+5$. 因此金金拿走 $6+8+10+12+$

第 9 章　2011 年第 9 届国际小学数学竞赛

14+16+18+20=104，故最初共有 101+104=205 个榛果.

答：205个

6. 解　可令使用 x 张 10 元纸币、y 张 20 元纸币与 z 张 50 元纸币，则知 $10x+20y+50z=500$，即 $x+2y+5z=50$，其中 x、y、$z \geq 0$.

(1) 若 $z=0$，则 $x+2y=50 \Rightarrow x = 50-2y$ 且 $0 \leq y \leq 25$，故共有 26 种.

(2) 若 $z=1$，则 $x+2y=45 \Rightarrow x = 45-2y$ 且 $0 \leq y \leq 22\frac{1}{2}$，故共有 23 种.

(3) 若 $z=2$，则 $x+2y=40 \Rightarrow x = 40-2y$ 且 $0 \leq y \leq 20$，故共有 21 种.

(4) 若 $z=3$，则 $x+2y=35 \Rightarrow x = 35-2y$ 且 $0 \leq y \leq 17\frac{1}{2}$，故共有 18 种.

继续相同的计算方式，可知合计共有 26+23+21+18+16+13+11+8+6+3+1= 146 种.

答：146种

7. 解　可知 $16 = 2^4$、$50 = 2 \times 5^2$，因此 16 与 50 的最小公倍数为 400，且有 $1200 \div 400 = 3$. 故知 A 的素因子分解式里恰有一个 3 且至多有 4 个 2 与至多 2 个 5. 因此 A 的可能值有 $(4+1) \times (2+1) = 15$ 种.

答：15种

8. 解　连接 M 点与 C 点，则知 $S_{\triangle AMC} = \frac{1}{2} S_{\triangle ABC}$ 以及 $S_{\triangle AMP} = \frac{2}{3} S_{\triangle AMC}$，故 $S_{\triangle AMP} = \frac{1}{3} \times \frac{2}{3} S_{\triangle ABC} = \frac{2}{9} S_{\triangle ABC}$（图 9-7）.

同理，$S_{\triangle BNM} = \frac{2}{9} S_{\triangle ABC}$、$S_{\triangle CPM} = \frac{2}{9} S_{\triangle ABC}$，故

$S_{\triangle PMN} = (1 - \frac{2}{9} \times 3) S_{\triangle ABC} = \frac{1}{3} S_{\triangle ABC}$.

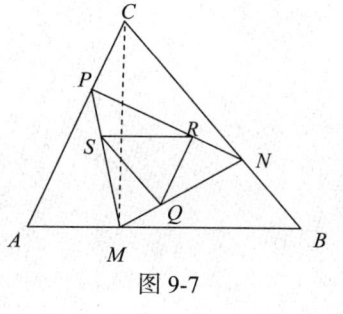

图 9-7

同理，$S_{\triangle QRS} = \frac{1}{3} S_{\triangle PMN}$. 故可得 $S_{\triangle QRS} = \frac{1}{9} S_{\triangle ABC} = 40 \text{ (cm}^2)$.

答：40 cm²

9. 解法 1　可知长方形至少有一个维度必为偶数. 若铅直方向为偶数，则共有 $(5+3+1) \times (9+8+\cdots+2+1) = 405$ 个长方形；若水平方向为偶数，则共有 $(6+5+4+3+2+1) \times (8+6+4+2) = 420$ 个长方形；若铅直与水平方向都为偶数，则共有 $(5+3+1) \times (8+6+4+2) = 180$ 个长方形. 因此合计有 405+420−180=645 个

长方形.

解法2 在方格表中，共有 (6+5+4+3+2+1)×(9+8+…+2+1)=945 个长方形. 因只有长与宽皆为奇数的长方形才是由奇数个单位正方形组成的，故知共有 (6+4+2)×(9+7+5+3+1)=300 个这样的长方形，因此所求的长方形共有 945−600=645 个.

答：645 个

10. **解** 答案为 4464. 可知末两位数必为 44、46、64 或 66. 因是 4 的倍数，故末两位数必须是 4 的倍数，所以可删去 46 与 66，即末位数必为 4. 因此数也必是 3 的倍数，故知数码和必为 3 的倍数；再因现在至少有一个数码是 4，故知此数至少需有 3 个数码是 4，且因至少有一个 6，故知满足条件的最小 n 值是 4464.

答：4464

11. **解** 如图 9-8 所示，可知 $n=23$.

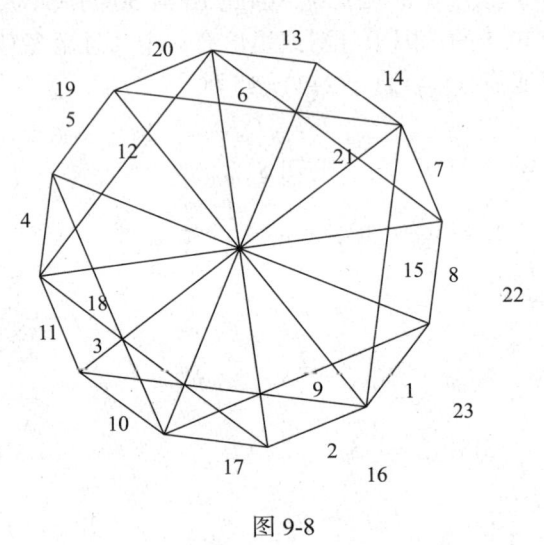

图 9-8

答：23

12. **解** 令此两位数为 $\overline{ab}=10a+b$，则知 $10b+a \geq 3(10a+b)$，即 $7b \geq 29a$. 因 a 与 b 都为数码，故可得 $a \leq 2$. 若 $a=2$，则 $7b \geq 58$，即 $b \geq \frac{58}{7}=8\frac{2}{7}$，故知 $b=9$；若 $a=1$，则 $7b \geq 29$，即 $b \geq \frac{29}{7}=4\frac{1}{7}$，故知 $b=9$、8、7、6 或 5. 因

184

此共有 6 个这样的数：29、15、16、17、18、19.

答：6个

13. **解** 如图 9-9 所示，将 △BCD 以 BD 的中垂线镜射，则知 ∠ADB+∠C'DB=180°，故 ADC'是一条直线，因此 △ABC' 为等腰三角形，故 ∠BAD= 57°.

答：57°

14. **解** 观察可知，开始时，仅有 2 列有格子被涂色，每操作一次则增加 2 列，因此最后共有 202 列有格子被涂色. 而每一次操作，我们在每一列已涂色的格子两端各新增加 1 个涂色的格子，且在最上方已涂色的格子上方新增加 1 个涂色的格子以及在最下方已涂色的格子下方新增加 2 个涂色的格子，因此共有 3+3×100+2×(2+4+…+200) = 20503 个格子已被涂色.

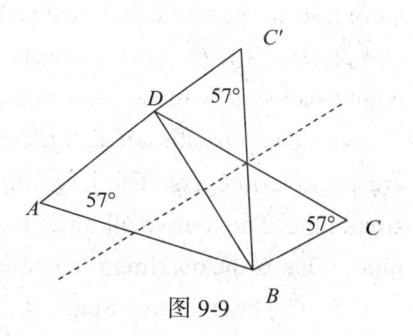

图 9-9

答：20503个

15. **解** 由对称性可知，这只蜗牛最后停留的列数为第 1006 列，且在该列，将由第 1005 行出发并最后停留在第 4024−1005=3019 行，即停留在第 1006 列、第 3019 行的格子上，因此所求为 1006+3019=4025.

答：4025

9.4 EMIC队际赛英文试题

Elementary Mathematics International Contest 2011
20th July，2011，Bali，Indonesia

Team Contest

1. There are 18 bags of candies. The first bag contains 1 piece. The second bag contains 4 pieces. In general, the k-th bag contains k^2 pieces. The bags are to be divided into three piles, each consisting of 6 bags, such that the total number of pieces inside the bags in each pile is the same. Find one way of doing so.

2. There are eight positive integers in a row. Starting from the third, each is the sum of the preceding two numbers. If the eighth number is 2011, what is the largest

possible value of the first one?

3. O is the centre of a circle. A light beam starts from a point A_0 on the circle, hits a point A_1 in the circle and then reflects to hit another point A_2 on the circle, where $\angle A_0A_1O = \angle A_2A_1O$. Then it reflects to hit another point A_3, and so on. If A_{95} is the first point to coincide with A_0, how many different choices of the point A_1 can there be?

4. The capacities of a large pipe and four identical small pipes, in m^3 per hour, are positive integers. The large pipe has a capacity of 6 m^3 per hour more than a small pipe. The four small pipes together can fill a pool 2 hours faster than the large pipe. What is the maximum volume of the pool, in m^3?

5. The boys in Key Stage II, wearing white, are playing a soccer match against the boys in Key Stage III, wearing black. At one point, the position of the players on the field are as shown in the diagram below. The ball may be passed from one team member, in any of the eight directions along a row, a column or a diagonal, to the first team member in line. The ball may not pass through an opposing team member. The goalkeeper of Stage II, standing in front of his goal on the right, has the ball. Pass the ball so that each member of the white team touches the ball once, and the last team member shoots the ball into the black team's net.

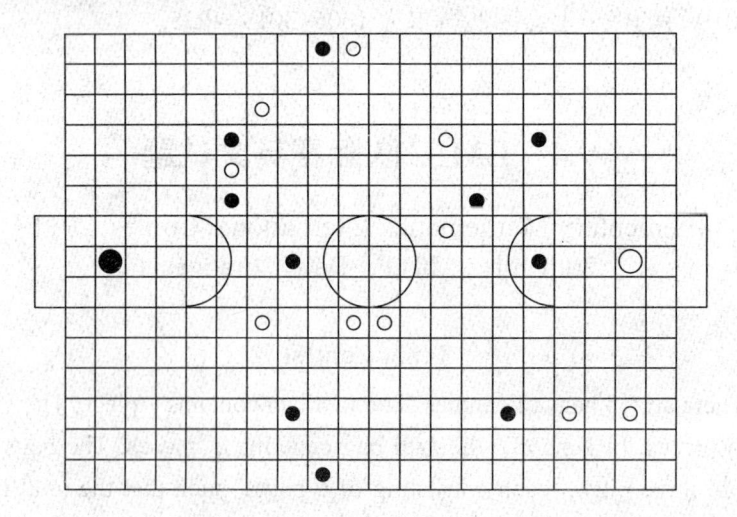

6. A palindrome is a positive integer which is the same when its digits are read in reverse order. In the addition 2882+9339=12221, all three numbers are palindromes. How many pairs of four-digit palindromes are there such that their sum is a five-

digit palindrome? The pair (9339, 2882) is not considered different from the pair (2882, 9339).

7. Place each of 1, 2, 3, 4, 5, 6 and 7 into a different vacant box in the diagram below, so that the arrows of the box containing 0 point to the box containing 1. For instance, 1 is in box *A* or *B*. Similarly, the arrows of the box containing 1 point to the box containing 2, and so on.

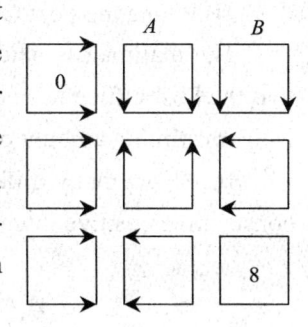

8. On calculators, the ten digits are displayed as shown in the diagram below, each consisting of six panels in a 3×2 configuration.

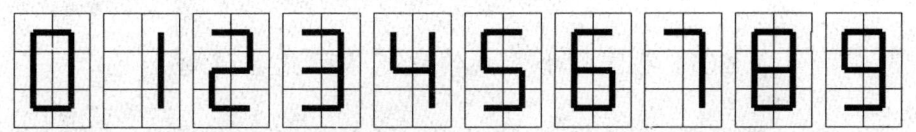

A calculator with a two-dimensional display was showing the subtraction of a three-digit number from another three-digit number, but the screen was malfunctioning so that only one panel of each digit was visible.

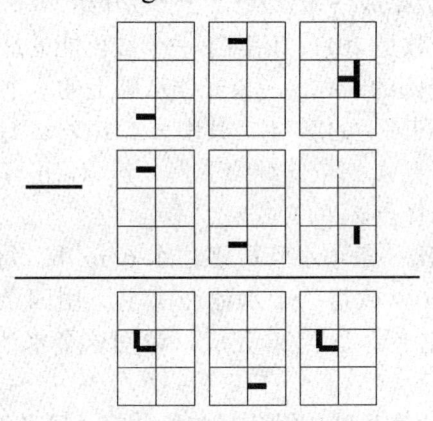

What is the maximum value of the three-digit difference?

9. Six villages are evenly spaced along a country road. It takes one hour to ride on a bicycle from one village to the next. Mail delivery is once a day. There are six packets of letters, one for each village. The mailman's introductions are as follows:

(1) Ask the Post Office van to drop you off at the village on the first packet and deliver it.

(2) Ride the bicycle non-stop to the village on the second packet and deliver it.

(3) Repeat the last step until all packets have been delivered.

(4) Phone the Post Office van to pick you up.

The mailman is paid 20000 rupiah an hour on the bicycle. Taking advantage that the Post Office has no instructions on how the packets are to be ordered, what is the maximum amount of money he can earn in a day?

10. How many different ways can 90 be expressed as the sum of at least two consecutive positive integers?

9.5 EMIC 队际赛中文试题

2011 年国际小学数学竞赛队际竞赛试题

1. 有 18 袋糖果，第 1 袋内有 1 颗糖、第 2 袋内有 4 颗糖、…、第 k 袋内有 k^2 颗糖．现欲将这些袋子分为三堆，每堆都有六袋，且使得每堆糖果的总数都相等．请找出一种满足要求的分法．

2. 有八个正整数排成一列，从第三个数开始，每个数都等于它的前面两个数之和．若第八个数是 2011，请问第一个数可能的最大值是多少？

3. 点 O 是一个圆的圆心，一束光线从圆上的一个点 A_0 射出，碰到圆上的点 A_1 后反射并碰到圆上的点 A_2，其中 $\angle A_0A_1O = \angle A_2A_1O$．此光线接着反射并碰到圆上的另一个点 A_3，依此继续下去．若 A_{95} 正好第一次与 A_0 重合，请问圆周上有多少种选择点 A_1 的方式？

4. 一条大水管比一条小水管可多注水 6 m³/h，每条水管的注水量都是正整数（单位：m³/h）．欲将一个水池注满水，用四条相同的小水管同时注水可比大水管单独注水要提早 2h 完成．请问这个水池的最大可能容量为多少 m³？

5. 甲、乙两队比赛足球，甲队穿白色球衣、乙队穿黑色球衣．在某一时刻，球员在球场上所在的位置如图 9-10 所示，每队的队员可沿着水平、铅垂或与水平线夹角为 45°等八个方向将球传给他的队友，但是球不可以穿过对方球员所在的方格．甲队的守门员站在右侧球门的正中央，目前球正在他的手上．请画出一条传球的路径，使得甲队守门员在将球传出后，所有白色球员都接触到球一次，且由最后一位球员将球射进乙队的球门内 (图 9-10)．

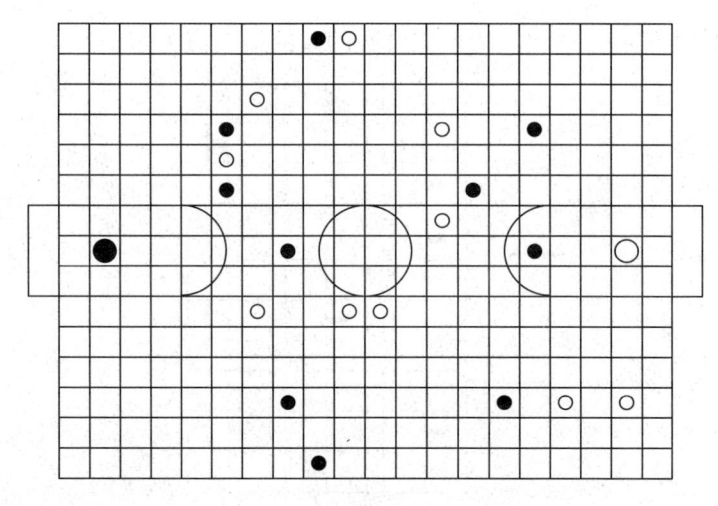

图 9-10

6. 回文数是指一个正整数从左侧读起与从右侧读起它的数值相同. 例如, 在加式 2882+9339=12221 中, 所有三个数都是回文数. 请问共有多少对四位数的回文数, 使得它们的和成为五位数的回文数? (注: 我们将数对 (9339, 2882) 与 (2882, 9339) 视为相同的一对回文数)

7. 在图 9-11 中, 将数码 1、2、3、4、5、6、7 分别不重复地填入一个不同的空白方格内, 使得填有 0 的方格上的箭头指向填有 1 的方格. 例如, 1 应该填入方格 A 或方格 B 中. 同样地, 填有 1 的方格上的箭头指向填有 2 的方格, 依此类推.

8. 在计算器的屏幕上所显示的十个数码如图 9-12 所示, 每个数码都是在 3×2 方格表内的图案.

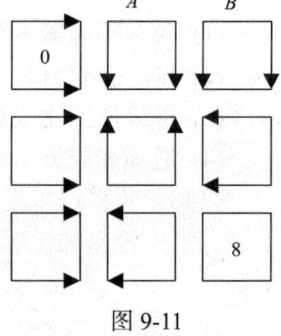

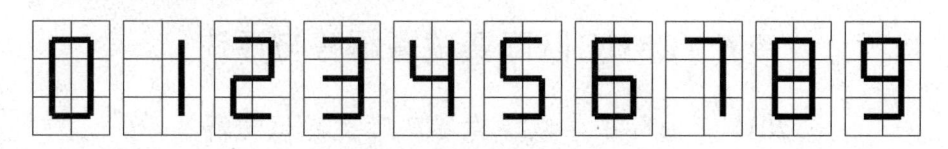

图 9-11

图 9-12

有一台宽屏幕计算器的屏幕上显示着一个三位数减另一个三位数的减法算式, 但因为屏幕显示器发生故障, 每位数码只有一个小方格内的图案显示出来，如图 9-13 所示．请问这两个三位数的差的最大值为多少？

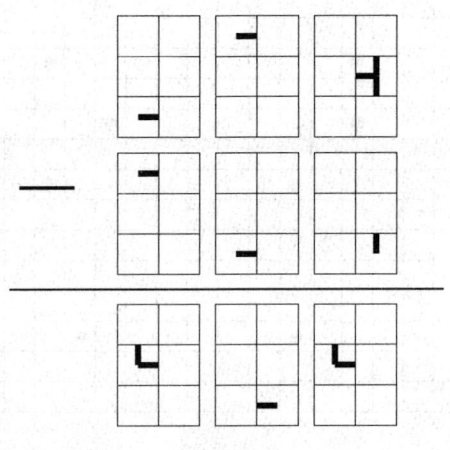

图 9-13

9. 在一条直线的公路上有六个村庄，任两个相邻的村庄的距离都相等，邮局每天派人投递一次邮包．从一个村庄骑车到另一个相邻的村庄要费时 1 h．现有六个邮包要投递，每个村庄各有一个邮包．邮差的工作指南有以下规定：

(1) 要求邮局派卡车将您送到第一个邮包所在的村庄并将它投递出．

(2) 接着您骑自行车投递第二个邮包，中途不可停留．

(3) 继续依上述步骤直到将所有的邮包全部投递完为止．

(4) 通知邮局派卡车来把您接回．

当邮差骑自行车投递邮包时，邮局支付他 20000 Rp/h．的工资．利用邮局并没有规定投递邮包顺序的漏洞，请问邮差投递这六个邮包最多可以赚得多少工资？

10. 请问共有多少种不同的方法可将 90 表示为至少两个连续正整数的和？

9.6 EMIC 队际赛试题解答与评注

2011 年国际小学数学竞赛队际竞赛试题解答

1. **解** 可知共有 1+4+9+16+25+36+49+64+81+100+121+144+169+196+225+256+289+324=2109 颗糖，因此每堆内要有 703 颗糖．

第9章 2011年第9届国际小学数学竞赛

不失一般性,可假设第一堆中有324颗糖的袋子;因703-324=379,我们可再将有289颗糖的袋子分在第一堆中;再因379-289=90,我们也可将有81颗糖的袋子分在第一堆中,此时可再将90-81=9颗糖的袋子置入第一堆里.

接着假设第二堆中有256颗糖与225颗糖这两个袋子;因703-256-225=222,我们可再将有196颗糖的袋子分在第二堆中;因222-196=26,我们也可将有25颗糖的袋子分在第二堆中,此时可再将26-25=1颗糖的袋子置入第二堆里.

此时尚未分堆的袋子为169、144、121、100、64、49、36、16与4颗糖的袋子,可先将这些袋子视为第三堆.此时为了满足每一堆各有6袋的条件,且可观察出289+81=370=169+121+64+16、196+1=197=144+49+4,故可以将第一堆中有289、81颗糖的这两个袋子与第三堆中有169、121、64、14颗糖的袋子互换、将第二堆中有196、1颗糖的这两个袋子与第三堆中有144、49、4颗糖的袋子互换.故知第一堆中的袋子为装有324、169、121、64、16与9颗糖的袋子、第二堆中的袋子为装有256、225、144、49、25与4颗糖的袋子、第三堆中的袋子为装有289、196、100、81、36与1颗糖的袋子.

答:第一堆为装有324、169、121、64、16与9颗糖的袋子、第二堆为装有256、225、144、49、25与4颗糖的袋子、第三堆为装有289、196、100、81、36与1颗糖的袋子

注:共有以下42组答案(表9-1).

表 9-1

			第1堆						第2堆						第3堆			
1	4	9	144	256	289	16	25	49	64	225	324	36	81	100	121	169	196
1	4	9	144	256	289	16	49	64	81	169	324	25	36	100	121	196	225
1	4	9	144	256	289	16	64	81	121	196	225	25	36	49	100	169	324
1	4	9	169	196	324	16	25	36	81	256	289	49	64	100	121	144	225
1	4	9	169	196	324	16	25	81	100	225	256	36	49	64	121	144	289
1	4	9	169	196	324	16	36	49	121	225	256	25	64	81	100	144	289
1	4	36	49	289	324	9	25	100	144	169	256	16	64	81	121	196	225
1	4	36	49	289	324	9	64	121	144	169	196	16	25	100	225	256	
1	4	49	100	225	324	9	64	121	144	169	196	16	25	36	81	256	289

续表

第1堆						第2堆						第3堆					
1	9	16	64	289	324	4	25	49	144	225	256	36	81	100	121	169	196
1	9	16	64	289	324	4	49	81	144	169	256	25	36	100	121	196	225
1	9	16	196	225	256	4	25	81	100	169	324	36	49	64	121	144	289
1	9	16	196	225	256	4	36	49	121	169	324	25	64	81	100	144	289
1	9	16	196	225	256	4	64	81	121	144	289	25	36	49	100	169	324
1	9	49	64	256	324	4	16	25	144	225	289	36	81	100	121	169	196
1	9	49	64	256	324	4	16	81	144	169	289	25	36	100	121	196	225
1	9	64	144	196	289	4	16	81	121	225	256	25	36	49	100	169	324
1	9	64	144	196	289	4	25	81	100	169	324	16	36	49	121	225	256
1	9	64	144	196	289	4	36	49	121	169	324	16	25	81	100	225	256
1	16	25	81	256	324	4	9	36	169	196	289	49	64	100	121	144	225
1	16	25	81	256	324	4	9	100	169	196	225	36	49	64	121	144	289
1	16	25	81	256	324	4	36	49	100	225	289	9	64	121	144	169	196
1	16	36	169	225	256	4	9	49	121	196	324	25	64	81	100	144	289
1	16	36	169	225	256	4	64	81	121	144	289	9	25	49	100	196	324
1	16	49	144	169	324	4	9	64	81	256	289	25	36	100	121	196	225
1	16	121	144	196	225	4	9	64	81	256	289	25	36	49	100	169	324
1	16	121	144	196	225	4	25	81	100	169	324	9	36	49	64	256	289
1	25	36	121	196	324	4	9	64	81	256	289	16	49	100	144	169	225
1	25	36	121	196	324	4	16	81	144	169	289	9	49	64	100	225	256
1	25	36	121	196	324	4	49	81	144	169	256	9	16	64	100	225	289
1	25	81	144	196	256	4	36	49	100	225	289	9	16	64	121	169	324
1	25	81	144	196	256	4	36	49	121	169	324	9	16	64	100	225	289
1	36	64	121	225	256	4	16	81	144	169	289	9	25	49	100	196	324
1	36	64	121	225	256	4	25	81	100	169	324	9	16	49	144	196	289
1	36	64	144	169	289	4	9	49	121	196	324	16	25	81	100	225	256
1	36	64	144	169	289	4	16	81	121	225	256	9	25	49	100	196	324
1	36	81	100	196	289	4	9	121	144	169	256	16	25	49	64	225	324
1	36	81	100	196	289	4	25	49	144	225	256	9	16	64	121	169	324
1	49	64	121	144	324	4	9	36	169	196	289	16	25	81	100	225	256
1	49	64	121	144	324	4	9	100	169	196	225	16	25	36	81	256	289
1	64	100	144	169	225	4	9	49	121	196	324	16	25	36	81	256	289
1	81	100	121	144	256	4	9	36	169	196	289	16	25	49	64	225	324

2．**解**　令首两个数依序为 a 与 b，则可知接下来的数依序为 $a+b$、$a+2b$、

第9章 2011年第9届国际小学数学竞赛

$2a+3b$、$3a+5b$、$5a+8b$ 及 $8a+13b=2011$. 故知

$a=251-b+\dfrac{3-5b}{8}$. 因 a 为正整数,且为了要使 a 尽可能大,故要使 b 尽可能小且 $3-5b$ 要被 8 整除,由此可知 b 为奇数.

当 $b=1$ 时,$3-5b=-2$,不可被 8 整除,故不符合;

当 $b=3$ 时,$3-5b=-12$,不可被 8 整除,故不符合;

当 $b=5$ 时,$3-5b=-22$,不可被 8 整除,故不符合;

当 $b=7$ 时,$3-5b=-32$,可被 8 整除,符合,故知 b 的最小值发生在 $b=7$,此时 $a=(2011-7\times13)\div8=240$.

答:240

3. 解 若 A_0 是一个圆内接正 95 边形的一个顶点,则 A_1 为其余 94 个顶点之一. 注意到 $95=5\times19$. 若此光束的路径构成一个正五边形或正五角星形,则 A_5 将会与 A_0 重合,A_{95} 也会与 A_0 重合. 若此光束的路径构成一个正十九边形或正十九角星形,则 A_{19} 将会与 A_0 重合,A_{95} 也会与 A_0 重合. 同样地,此光束的路径构成一个正九十五边形或正九十五角星形,则 A_{95} 将会第一次与 A_0 重合. 因此选择点 A_1 的方式有 $95-19-5+1=72$ 种.

答:72种

4. 解 假设大水管注入 x m³/h 且需花费 y h 注满水池,则可知小水管注入 $x-6$ m³/h 且四条小水管共需花费 $y-2$h 注满水池. 故由水池容量可以得到 $xy=4(x-6)(y-2)=4xy-8x-24y+48$. 化简后可得知 $0=3xy-8x-24y+48=x(3y-8)-8(3y-8)-16$,即 $(3y-8)(x-8)=16$. 为了使 $3y-8$ 整除 16,我们可知 $y=2$、3、4 或 8. 此时可得表 9-2.

表 9-2

y	3y − 8	x − 8	x	xy
2	−2	−8	0	0
3	1	16	24	72
4	4	4	12	48
8	16	1	9	72

因此水池最大的可能容量为 72 m³.

答:72 m³

5. 解 如图 9-15 所示,将白色的甲队球员从 1 号编到 11 号. 图 9-14 中并绘出所有可传球的路径,其中以粗线所绘出的即为必须用到的传球路径.

图 9-14

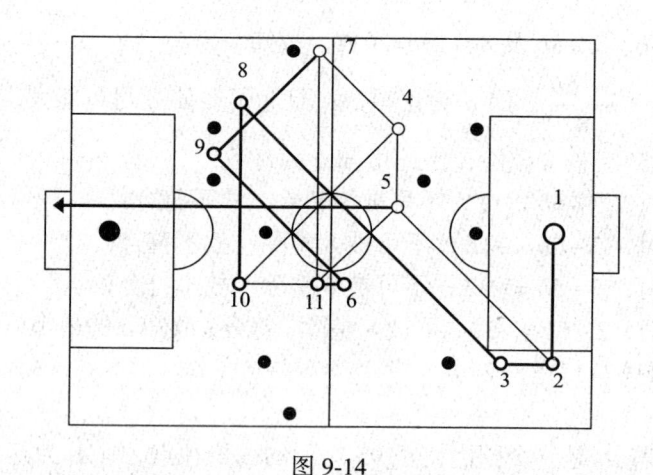

可知开始的传球路径必为 1—2—3—8—10.

若 10 号直接传给 4 号，则 4 号不可直接传给 5 号，这是因为 5 号是唯一可以将球射进对方球门内的球员，即 5 号必须是最后一个接到球的球员，故可知接下来的传球路径为 4—7—9—6—11—5.

若 10 号直接传给 11 号，则可知接下来的传球路径为 11—6—9—7—4—5.

故知共有两条满足题意的传球路径:

1—2—3—8—10—4—7—9—6—11—5、1—2—3—8—10—11—6—9—7—4—5

6. **解** 可判断出五位数的和之首位数必为 1，故其末位数也必为 1. 令它们分别为 $\overline{ABBA}$、$\overline{CDDC}$ 与 $\overline{1EFE1}$. 因此我们可将算式写成如下的加式:

$$\begin{array}{r} A\ B\ B\ A \\ +C\ D\ D\ C \\ \hline 1\ E\ F\ E\ 1 \end{array}$$

可知 $A+C=11$，因此数对 (A, C) 必为 $(2, 9)$、$(3, 8)$、$(4, 7)$、$(5, 6)$、$(6, 5)$、$(7, 4)$、$(8, 3)$ 与 $(9, 2)$ 其中之一. 而由被加数与加数的对称性可知数对 (A, C) 有 4 种选择. 此时再由和的千位数知 $E=1$ 或 $E=2$.

若 $E=1$，则 $B+D=0$ 且由此知 $B=D=0$. 若 $E=2$，则 $B+D=11$ 且可知共有 8 种选择.

因此合计共有 $4\times(1+8)=36$ 对.

答: 36 对

第9章 2011年第9届国际小学数学竞赛

7. 解 如图9-15所示,将每一个方格由上而下、由左至右依序标记上字母 A 到 I,则知 $A=0$ 且 $I=8$.

故可得知 $C=7$ 或 $G=7$. 若 $C=7$,则 $A=6$,与题意矛盾,因此知 $G=7$,且据此可得 $H=6$ 与 $B=5$. 接着便可得知 $C=1$、$F=2$ 且 $D=3$ 与 $E=4$. 完整填法如图9-15所示.

图9-15

8. 解 可令此减法算式为

$$\begin{array}{r} A\ B\ C \\ -\ D\ E\ F \\ \hline G\ H\ I \end{array}$$

可由观察知 A、$E=3$、5、9,B、$D=2$、3、7,$C=3$、4、8、9,$F=1$、4、7,G、$I=4$、5、9 且 $H=2$. 由 A、D、G 的可能值可判断出 $G=5$、$A=9$ 以及 $D=3$ 且 A 有借位 1 到十位数. 再由 $H=2$ 可知 $B=2$ 以及 $E=9$,并且 B 有借位 1 到个位数. 故可知 $C=3$、$F=4$ 及 $I=9$,即所求为 529. 如图9-16所示即为完整的减法算式.

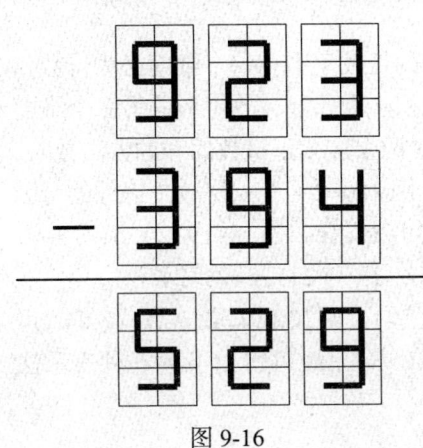

答: 529

图9-16

9. 解 这六个村庄依序从 1 号编到 6 号,则邮差若按照 3,6,1,5,2,4 或 3,5,1,6,2,4 的顺序投递邮包,最多可赚得 340000 Rp.的工资,这是因为邮差两个投递方式分别花费 3+5+4+3+2=17 h 与 2+4+5+4+2=17 h.

现证明无法再多: 可知在此数在线共有 15 条线段,其长度分别为 5、4、4、3、3、3、2、2、2、2、1、1、1、1 与 1. 为了从中选取五条线段使其总长度为 18,必须选择长度为 5 的线段,而两条长度为 4 的线段必须全选或三条长度为 3 的线段必须全选.

若两条长度为 4 的线段全选,则邮差路径必包含 2—6—1—5,此时无论如何安排 3、4 的投递顺序,其总长度皆无法超过 17.

若三条长度为 3 的线段全选,则邮差路径必包含 3—6—1—4 以及 2—5,此时无论如何安排这两条路径投递顺序,其总长度仍无法超过 17.

故总长度为 18 或以上都不可能完成,即最多为 17,故至多可赚得

195

340000 Rp.

答：340000 Rp

10. 解法 1 至少两个连续正整数的和可几何地视为一组阶梯．如果我们将两组全等的阶梯并在一起，可以拼成一个矩形，中间锯齿状的分割线是由横线（单位水平直线）与竖线（单位铅垂直线）交错组合而成．因分割线的第一条单位线段与最后一条单位线段都必是竖线，因此其中央可能是竖线或横线．例如，在图 9-17 中，因为 9=4+5=2+3+4，前者中央为横线而后者中央为竖线．

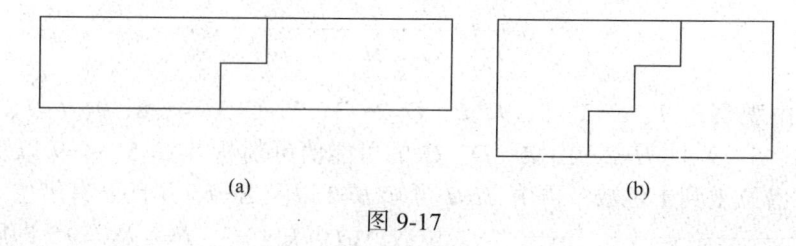

图 9-17

由中央具有横线或竖线的情况可知该矩形的长或宽中有一个维度必为奇数，再因矩形是由两组全等的阶梯组成可知矩形面积必为偶数，故矩形的另一个维度必为偶数．因此要找出将一个整数 n 表示为至少两个连续正整数的和的方法数时，即相当于找出 $2n$ 的除了 1 以外的奇因子个数．因 $180=2^2 \times 3^2 \times 5$，故 1 以外的奇因子为 3、5、9、15 与 45，故共有五种表示法：29+30+31，16+17+18+19+20，6+7+8+9+10+11+12+13+14，2+3+4+5+6+7+8+9+10+11+12+13 与 21+22+23+24．

解法 2 令 $90=a+(a+1)+\cdots+(a+k)$，其中 $k \geqslant 1$，则知 $180=(2a+k) \cdot (k+1)$．可知在 $2a+k$ 与 $k+1$ 恰只有一个数为奇数且 $2a+k>k+1$，故可得以下共 5 种表示法（表 9-3）．

表 9-3

2a+k	k+1	k	a	90
60	3	2	29	29+30+31
40	4	3	21	21+22+23+24
36	5	4	16	16+17+18+19+20
20	9	8	6	6+7+8+9+10+11+12+13+14
15	12	11	2	2+3+4+5+6+7+8+9+10+11+12+13

答：5种

第10章 2012年第10届国际小学数学竞赛

10.1 EMIC个人赛英文试题

Elementary Mathematics International Contest 2012
25th July, 2012, Taipei, Taiwan, China

Individual Contest

1. In how many ways can 20 identical pencils be distributed among three girls so that each gets at least 1 pencil?

2. On a circular highway, one has to pay toll charges at three places. In clockwise order, they are a bridge which costs $1 to cross, a tunnel which costs $3 to pass through, and the dam of a reservoir which costs $5 to go on top. Starting on the highway between the dam and the bridge, a car goes clockwise and pays toll-charges until the total bill amounts to $130. How much does it have to pay at the next place if he continues?

3. When a two-digit number is increased by 4, the sum of its digits is equal to half of the sum of the digits of the original number. How many possible values are there for such a two-digit number?

4. In the diagram below, OAB is a circular sector with $OA=OB$ and $\angle AOB = 30°$. A semicircle passing through A is drawn with centre C on OA, touc-hing OB at some point T. What is the ratio of the area of the semicircle to the area of the circular sector OAB?

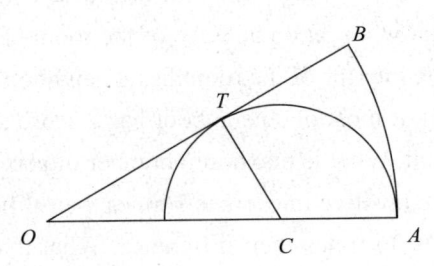

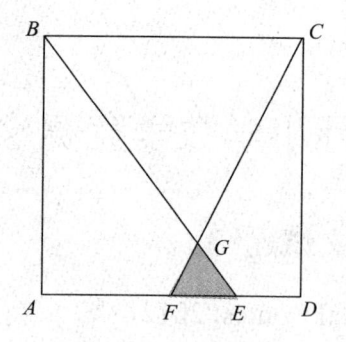

5. *ABCD* is a square with total area 36 cm². *F* is the midpoint of *AD* and *E* is the midpoint of *FD*. *BE* and *CF* intersect at *G*. What is the area, in cm², of triangle *EFG*?

6. In a village, friendship among girls is mutual. Each girl has either exactly one friend or exactly two friends among themselves. One morning, all girls with two friends wear red hats and the other girls all wear blue hats. It turns out that any two friends wear hats of different colours. In the afternoon, 10 girls change their red hats into blue hats and 12 girls change their blue hats into red hats. Now it turns out that any two friends wear hats of the same colour. How many girls are there in the village? (A girl can only change her hat once)

7. The diagram below shows a 7×7 grid in which the area of each unit cell (one of which is shaded) is 1 cm². Four congruent squares are drawn on this grid. The vertices of each square are chosen among the 49 dots, and two squares may not have any point in common. What is the maximum area, in cm², of one of these four squares?

8. The sum of 1006 different positive integers is 1019057. If none of them is greater than 2012, what is the minimum number of these integers which must be odd?

9. The desks in the TAIMC contest room are arranged in a 6×6 configuration. Two contestants are neighbours if they occupy adjacent seats along a row, a column or a diagonal. Thus a contestant in a seat at a corner of the room has 3 neighbours, a contestant in a seat on an edge of the room has 5 neighbours, and a contestant in a seat in the interior of the room has 8 neighbours. After the contest, a contestant gets a prize if at most one neighbour has a score greater than or equal to the score of the contestant. What is maximum number of prize-winners?

10. The sum of two positive integers is 7 times their difference. The product of the same two numbers is 36 times their difference. What is the larger one of these

two numbers?

11. In a competition, every student from school A and from school B is a gold medalist, a silver medalist or a bronze medalist. The number of gold medalist from each school is the same. The ratio of the percentage of students who are gold medalist from school A to that from school B is 5∶6. The ratio of the number of silver medalists from school A to that from school B is 9∶2. The percentage of students who are silver medalists from both school is 20%. If 50% of the students from school A are bronze medalists, what percentage of the students from school B are gold medalists?

12. We start with the fraction $\frac{5}{6}$. In each move, we can either increase the numerator by 6 or increases the denominator by 5, but not both. What is the minimum number of moves to make the value of the fraction equal to $\frac{5}{6}$ again?

13. Five consecutive two-digit numbers are such that 37 is a divisor of the sum of three of them, and 71 is also a divisor of the sum of three of them. What is the largest of these five numbers?

14. $ABCD$ is a square. M is the midpoint of AB and N is the midpoint of BC. P is a point on CD such that $CP=4$ cm and $PD=8$ cm, Q is a point on DA such that $DQ=3$ cm. O is the point of intersection of MP and NQ. Compare the areas of the two triangles in each of the pairs (QOM, QAM), (MON, MBN), (NOP, NCP) and (POQ, PDQ). In cm^2, what is the maximum value of these four differences?

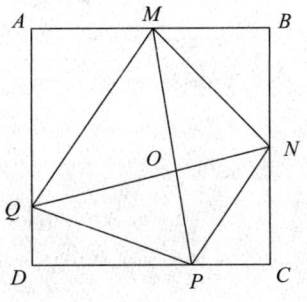

15. Right before Carol was born, the age of Eric is equal to the sum of the ages of Alice, Ben and Debra, and the average age of the four was 19. In 2010, the age of Debra was 8 more than the sum of the ages of Ben and Carol, and the average age of the five was 35.2. In 2012, the average age of Ben, Carol, Debra and Eric is 39.5. What is the age of Ben in 2012?

10.2　EMIC个人赛中文试题

2012年国际小学数学竞赛个人竞赛试题

1. 把20支完全相同的铅笔分给三个女孩，每人至少有一支，请问共有多少种分法？

2. 在一条环形高速公路上共有三个收费站，按顺时针方向它们分别位于一座桥、一条隧道和一条水库大坝上，且它们的收费标准分别是1元、3元和5元．一个人驾驶汽车从大坝和桥之间的某处开始沿顺时针方向在高速公路上行驶，当他所交的费用总和为130元时，请问他在下一个收费站需要交多少元？

3. 一个两位数加上4以后各位数码之和等于原来两位数的各位数码之和的一半，请问这样的两位数共有多少个？

4. 如图10-1所示，扇形 OAB 满足 $OA=OB$ 和 $\angle AOB = 30°$，点 C 在 OA 上，以 C 为圆心、CA 为半径作半圆与 OB 相切于点 T. 请问半圆的面积与扇形 OAB 面积之比为多少？

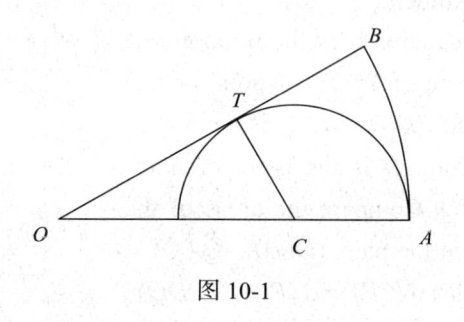

图 10-1

5. 在一个面积为36 cm^2 的正方形 $ABCD$ 中，点 F 是 AD 边的中点，点 E 是线段 FD 的中点．BE 与 CF 相交于点 G. 请问△EFG 的面积为多少 cm^2（图10-2）？

6. 在一个村庄里，女孩子之间的朋友关系是相互的，每个女孩恰好与她们之中的一个或两个女孩是朋友．一天早上，有两个朋友的女孩都戴红色帽子，其他女孩戴蓝色帽子，结果每对朋友戴的帽子的颜色不同．到了下午，10个原来戴红色帽子的女孩改戴蓝色帽子，且12个原来戴蓝色帽子的女孩改戴红色帽子,结果现在每对朋友戴的帽子的颜色相同. 请问这个村庄共有多少个女孩?

7. 在一个 7×7 的点阵中,每个单元格 (其中一个如图 10-3 所示中的阴影部分) 的面积为 1 cm². 在这个点阵中画出四个大小相同的正方形,使得每个正方形的顶点都选自这 49 个格点,且任何两个正方形 (包括它们的边界) 没有共同点. 请问其中一个正方形面积的最大值是多少 cm²?

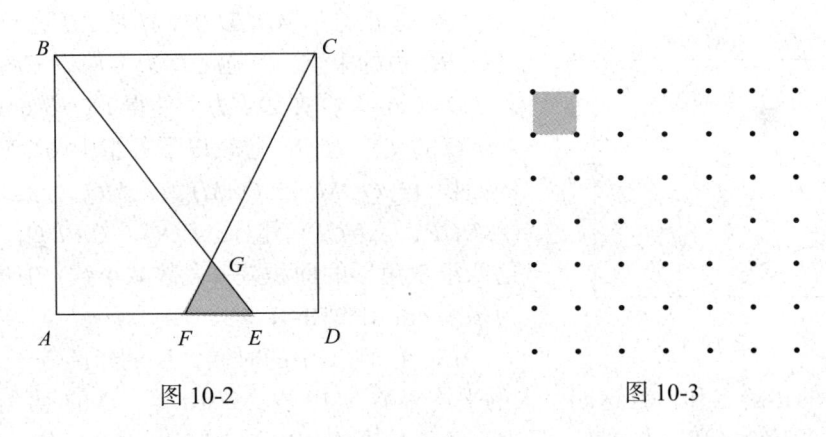

图 10-2

图 10-3

8. 已知 1006 个互不相同的正整数之和为 1019057,且每个数都不超过 2012,请问这些整数中至少有多少个奇数?

9. 在台湾数学竞赛中,试场的桌子排成 6 行 6 列. 如果两个参赛选手的座位在同一行、或同一列、或对角在线相邻,那么把他们称为邻桌. 这样,坐在试室角落的参赛选手有 3 个邻桌,坐在试室边上的参赛选手有 5 个邻桌,坐在试室中间的参赛选手有 8 个邻桌. 比赛结束后,如果一个参赛选手的邻桌最多有一个的得分不低于他的得分,那么这个参赛选手将获奖. 请问获奖选手的人数至多为多少?

10. 已知两个正整数之和是它们差的 7 倍,且这两个正整数的乘积是它们差的 36 倍. 请问这两个数中较大那个是多少?

11. 在一次比赛中,来自 A 校和 B 校的每位学生都获得了一枚奖牌 (金、银、或铜). 两所学校获得金牌的学生一样多,且 "A 校获得金牌的学生占该校学生的百分比" 与 "B 校获得金牌的学生占该校学生的百分比" 之比为 5∶6. "A 校获得银牌的学生数" 与 "B 校获得银牌的学生数" 之比为 9∶2,两校获得银牌的学生占两校所有学生的 20%. 如果 A 校有 50%的学生获得铜牌,请问 B

校获得金牌的学生占该校学生的百分之几?

12. 我们从 $\frac{5}{6}$ 开始操作,每一次操作将分子加上 6 或将分母加上 5,但不能同时加. 请问至少经过几次操作才能使得到的分数又等于 $\frac{5}{6}$?

13. 已知五个连续的两位数满足 37 能整除其中三个数之和,且 71 也能整除其中三个数之和. 请问这五个数中最大的数是多少?

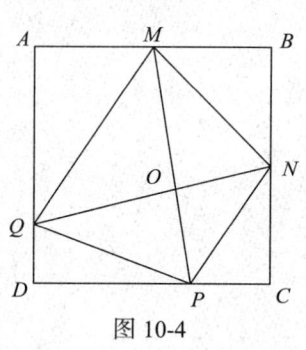

14. 在正方形 ABCD 中,M 是 AB 边的中点,N 是 BC 边的中点,P 在 CD 边上使得 CP= 4cm 且 PD=8 cm,Q 在 DA 边上使得 DQ=3 cm,MP 与 NQ 的交点为 O. 比较以下各组中两个三角形的面积:(△QOM,△QAM)、(△MON,△MBN)、(△NOP,△NCP) 和 (△POQ,△PDQ),请问这四组三角形的面积差 (大数减小数) 中最大值为多少 cm² (图 10-4) ?

图 10-4

15. C 刚出生的时候,E 的年龄等于 A、B 和 D 的年龄之和,且这四个人的平均年龄为 19 岁. 2010 年,D 的年龄比"C 与 B 的年龄之和"大 8 岁,且这五个人的平均年龄为 35.2 岁. 2012 年,B、C、D 和 E 的平均年龄为 39.5 岁. 请问 2012 年 B 的年龄为多少岁?

10.3 EMIC个人赛试题解答与评注

2012 年国际小学数学竞赛个人竞赛试题解答

1. **解法 1** 第一个女孩可有 1 支到 18 支铅笔. 若她得到 1 支,则第二个女孩可有 1 支到 17 支铅笔;接着以此类推,而第三个女孩则拥有剩下的铅笔. 因此共有 $18+17+\cdots+1 = \frac{19 \times 18}{2} = 171$ 种分法.

解法 2 可将 20 支铅笔如下排成一行:

| | | | | | | | | | | | | | | | | | | | |

将它们分给三位女孩,即将此铅笔划分为三堆,划分的方法为从 19 个间

第 10 章 2012 年第 10 届国际小学数学竞赛

隙中取 2 个分开,即共有 $\frac{19 \times 18}{2} = 171$ 种分法.

答:171种

2. **解** 因 1+3+5=9,故知每绕一圈需交 9 元. 而将 130 除以 9 后,所得之商为 14 而余数为 4,因此知在他所交的费用总和为 130 元后,已绕了此高速公路 14 圈且还多付了 4 元,即经过了桥与隧道. 因此下一个收费站为在水库大坝上,需交 5 元.

答:5元

3. **解** 可知此两位数加上 4 后必有进位,因此个位数为 6、7、8 或 9. 若个位数是 6,则会进位 1 至十位数,即数码和会减少 5,故原来两位数的数码和为 2×5=10,故此两位数为 46,验算可知 46 的数码和为 10 且 46+4=50 的数码和为 5,恰为 10 的一半;利用相同方式来继续讨论个位数为 7、8、9 的情形,可知 37、28、19 都满足题意,因此共有 4 个这样的两位数.

答:4个

4. **解** 令 OA=OB 为 6 单位,则由半径为 6 单位的圆之面积为 $\pi \times 6^2 = 36\pi$ 平方单位可知圆心角为 30° 的扇形面积为 $36\pi \times \frac{30°}{360°} = 3\pi$ 平方单位. 而 △COT 为正三角形的一半,因此 OC=2CT=2CA,即 OA=3CT. 因 OA=6 单位,故 CT=2 单位且半圆的面积为 $\frac{1}{2}\pi \times 2^2 = 2\pi$ 平方单位. 因此所求之比为 2∶3.

答:2∶3

5. **解** 由 ED=EF 知 △GED 的面积与 △EFG 的面积相同 (图 10-5);而由 AF=2EF 知 △GAF 的面积是 △EFG 面积的 2 倍;再由 △GBC 与 △EFG 为两个相似三角形且 BC=4EF 知 △GBC 的面积是 △EFG 面积的 16 倍. 因此 △EFG 的面积是 △ADG 与 △BCG 面积总和的 $\frac{1}{1+1+2+16} = \frac{1}{20}$,而 △ADG 与 △BCG 的面积总和为正方形 ABCD 的一半,因此 △EFG 的面积是正方形 ABCD 的 $\frac{1}{40}$,故 △EFG 的面积是 0.9 cm².

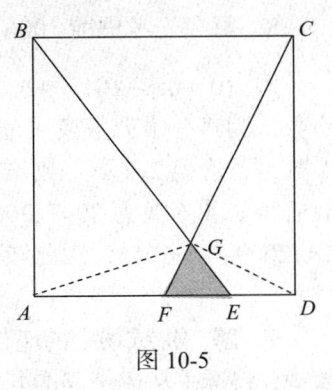

图 10-5

答:0.9 cm²

6. **解** 考虑只有一个朋友的女孩. 在早上时,她会戴着蓝色帽子而她唯一的朋友会戴着红色帽子,且这朋友的另一个朋友会戴着蓝色帽子,此友谊关系便停在此而不会再延伸. 故知村庄里的女孩子可依此关系分成好几个三人一组的小团体,每一组都是由一个女孩子与另两位女孩子有友谊关系,但这两位女孩子之间彼此并不认识. 到了下午,因每对朋友戴的帽子颜色都相同,因此同一组中的三位女孩子所戴的帽子颜色也都相同,此即为每一组里戴红色帽子的改戴蓝色帽子,或是两位戴蓝色帽子的女孩都改戴红色帽子,故知有 10 组戴红色帽子的改戴蓝色帽子且有 12÷2=6 组戴蓝色帽子的女孩都改戴红色帽子,因此共有 10+6=16 组,即合计有 16×3=48 个女孩.

答:48个

7. **解** 因正方形的顶点都选自这 49 个格点,故知正方形的边长为整数 cm 或是由勾股定理可知为两个正整数之和的平方根 cm. 不论是何种情形,其面积皆必为整数 cm^2. 因此点阵的总面积为 36(cm^2),故一个正方形面积至多为 9(cm^2),且不可能为 6 或 7(cm^2). 但可知其值也不可能为 9(cm^2),否则不同的正方形在边界上会有共同的点;其值也不可能为 8(cm^2),因为我们也无法将两个面积为 8(cm^2)的相同正方形放到此点阵中而在边界上没有共同的点;故此值最大为 5(cm^2),可如图 10-6 所示放置.

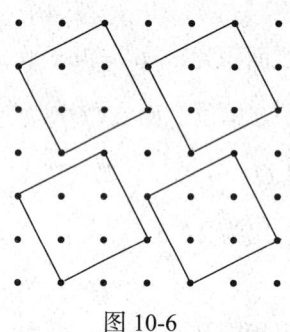

图 10-6

答:$5\ cm^2$

8. **解** 先考虑前 1006 个偶数的和,其值为 $\dfrac{1006\times(2+2012)}{2}=1013042$.

因 1019057−1013042=6015,故知我们需将其中一些偶数换成数量相同的奇数. 因将一个偶数换成奇数至多增加 2011−2=2009,故我们至少要换多于 1 个数. 若恰换 2 个数,则增加的值必为偶数,不合,因此至少需换三个数. 此时若将 2、4、6 换为 2007、2009、2011,则增加的值恰为 2007+2009+2011−2−4−6=3×(2009−4)=6015. 因此知这些整数中至少有 3 个奇数.

答:3个

9. **解** 将试场中的座位分成 9 个区域,每个区域都是 2×2. 在每一个区域中,将选手从成绩高的开始安排座位,则可知每一个区域中成绩第三或第四的都无法获奖,因为至少有两个邻桌的成绩不低于他. 所以可知至多有 2×9=18

第 10 章 2012 年第 10 届国际小学数学竞赛

位选手获奖,若成绩如图 10-7 所示,则可如图方式安排座位使第一行、第三行与第五行的选手都获奖.

40	50	60	70	80	90
10	10	10	10	10	10
40	50	60	70	80	90
10	10	10	10	10	10
40	50	60	70	80	90
10	10	10	10	10	10

图 10-7

答: 18 位

10. **解法 1** 假设两正整数之差为 1,则其和为 7. 若将 2 倍的较小数加到差里,则可得到和,故可知较小数为 3 而较大数为 4,此时乘积为 12,为差的 12 倍. 因现已知乘积为差的 36 倍,且 36÷12=3,故实际上较小数为 3×3=9 而较大数为 3×4=12.

解法 2 令两数为 a、b,且 $a>b$,则知 $\dfrac{a+b}{ab}=\dfrac{7}{36}$,即

$$\dfrac{1}{b}+\dfrac{1}{a}=\dfrac{7}{36}=\dfrac{6}{36}+\dfrac{1}{36}=\dfrac{4}{36}+\dfrac{3}{36},$$

故 $a=36$、$b=6$ 或 $a=12$、$b=9$. 但是当 $a=36$、$b=6$ 时,其差为 30、和为 42,故不符合,而 12+9=21≠7(12−9) 且 12×9=36 (12−9),故只有 $a=12$、$b=9$ 符合,即最大的数为 12.

答: 12

11. **解** 假设 A 校得到 9 个银牌,则 B 校得到 2 个银牌,因此合计共有 9+2=11 个银牌,故两校总参赛学生数为 11÷20%=55. 因两校获得金牌的学生数相同而"A 校获得金牌的学生占该校学生的百分比"与"B 校获得金牌的学生占该校学生的百分比"之比为 5:6,故知 A 校与 B 校的参赛学生比为 6:5,因此 A 校有 $55 \times \dfrac{6}{6+5}=30$ 位学生而 B 校有 55−30=25 位学生. 现因 A 校铜牌

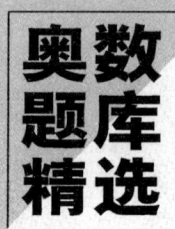

学生数为30×50%=15，故知两校获得金牌的学生数都为30-15-9=6位，故知 B 校获得金牌的学生占该校学生的 6÷25=24%.

答：24%

12. **解** 因为最后的分数之值未改变，故知分子、分母增加的数之比仍为 5：6. 因在分子增加了 $6s$ 而在分母增加了 $5t$，因此 $6s$ 之值必为 25 的倍数而 $5t$ 之值必为 36 的同等倍数，故知操作次数至少为 25+36=61 次.

答：61次

13. **解** 在五个连续的整数中，最大的三个数之和仅比最小的三个数之和多 6，因此我们考虑 37 的倍数与 71 的倍数至多差 6 的情形. 可知 37×2-71=3 及 37×4-71×2=6. 在后者中，148 必为最大的三个连续整数之和，故 148 必为 3 的倍数，矛盾；而在前者中，可知 71 < 23+24+25=72 < 74，因此这五个数中的最小数不可大于或等于 23 且最大数不可小于或等于 25，因此这五个数必为 22、23、24、25、26，即最大数为 26. 因这五个连续正整数仅为两位数，故不需再考虑 31 与 71 更大的倍数，否则其和将会太大.

答：26

14. **解** 可知 $AM=MB=BN=NC=6$(cm) 以及 $AQ=9$(cm). 故可得知四边形 $ABNQ$ 的面积为 $\frac{1}{2} \times 12 \times (9+6) = 90$(cm^2)，也由此可得知△$QMN$ 的面积为 $90 - \frac{1}{2} \times 9 \times 6 - \frac{1}{2} \times 6 \times 6 = 45$(cm^2). 而四边形 $QNCD$ 的面积为 12×12-90=54(cm^2)，因此△NPQ 的面积为 $54 - \frac{1}{2} \times 3 \times 8 - \frac{1}{2} \times 6 \times 4 = 30$(cm^2). 同理，△$PQM$ 的面积为 45(cm^2) 而△MNP 的面积为 30(cm^2). 因此可得知 $QO:ON$=45：30=3：2，故△QOM 的面积为 $45 \times \frac{3}{3+2} = 27$(cm^2)，此即与△$QAM$ 的面积相同. 而△MON 的面积为 45-27=18(cm^2)，此即与△MBN 的面积相同. 同理，△NOP 的面积为 $30 \times \frac{2}{3+2} = 12$(cm^2)，此即与△$NCP$ 的面积相同. 最后，△POQ 的面积为 30-12=18(cm^2)，此比△PDQ 的面积多 18-12=6 (cm^2)，因此所求最大的差为 6(cm^2).

答：6 cm^2

15. **解** 可知在 C 出生前一刻，A、B、D、E 的年龄总和为 19×4=76. 到了 2010 年，五人的年龄总和为 35.2×5=176，因此可知在 2010 年，C 的年纪为 (176-76)÷5=20 岁，故他出生于 1990 年. 而在 2012 年，B、C、D、E 的年龄

总和为 39.5×4=158，故知在 2010 年，此四人的年龄总和为 158-2×4=150，故可得知 A 的年龄为 26 岁．因 E 在 1990 年时的年龄为 76÷2=38，故知 E 在 2010 年时为 58 岁，且 B、C、D 的年龄总和为 176-26-58=92，故可得知 D 在此时的年龄为 (92+8) ÷ 2=50 岁，且 B 的年龄为 92-50-20=22 岁．因此 B 在 2012 年时为 22+2=24 岁．

答: 24岁

10.4　EMIC队际赛英文试题

Elementary Mathematics International Contest 2012
25th July 2012 Taipei，Taiwan，China

Team Contest

1. Each of the nine circles in the diagram below contains a different positive integer. These integers are consecutive and the sum of numbers in all the circles on each of the seven lines is 23. The number in the circle at the top right corner is less than the number in the circle at the bottom right corner. Eight of the numbers have been erased. Restore them.

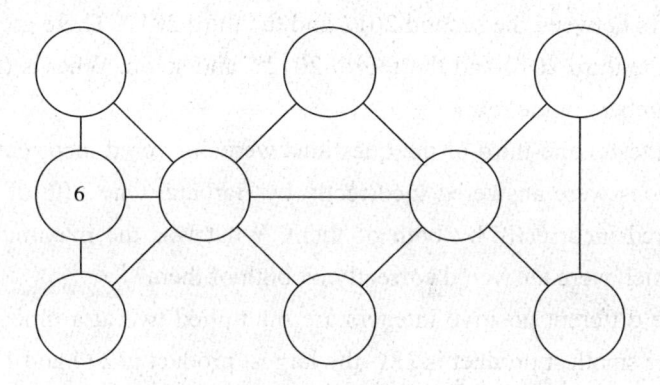

2. A clay tablet consists of a table of numbers，part of which is shown in the diagram below on the left. The first column consists of consecutive numbers starting from 0. In the first row，each subsequent number is obtained from the preceding one by adding 1. In the second row，each subsequent number is obtained from the preceding one by adding 2. In the third row，each subsequent number is

obtained from the preceding one by adding 3, and so on. The tablet falls down and breaks up into pieces, which are swept away except for the two shown in the diagram below on the right in magnified forms, each with a smudged square. What is the sum of the two numbers on these two squares?

0	1	2	3	4	5	
1	3	5	7	9	11	
2	5	8	11	14	17	
3	7	11	15	19	23	
4	9	14	19	24	29	
5	11	17	23	29	35	

?	2012	2023

2012
2683
?

3. In a row of numbers, each is either 2012 or 1. The first number is 2012. There is exactly one 1 between the first 2012 and the second 2012. There are exactly two 1s between the second 2012 and the third 2012. There are exactly three 1s between the third 2012 and the fourth 2012, and so on. What is the sum of the first 2012 numbers in the row?

4. In a test, one-third of the questions were answered incorrectly by Andrea and 7 questions were answered incorrectly by Barbara. One fifth of the questions were answered incorrectly by both of them. What was the maximum number of questions which were answered correctly by both of them?

5. Five different positive integers are multiplied two at a time, yielding ten products. The smallest product is 28, the largest product is 240 and 128 is also one of the products. What is the sum of these five numbers?

6. The diagram below shows a square *MNPQ* inside a rectangle *ABCD* where $AB - BC = 7$ cm. The sides of the rectangle parallel to the sides of the square. If the total area of *ABNM* and *CDQP* is 123 cm^2 and the total area of *ADQM* and *BCPN* is 312 cm^2, what is the area of *MNPQ* in cm^2?

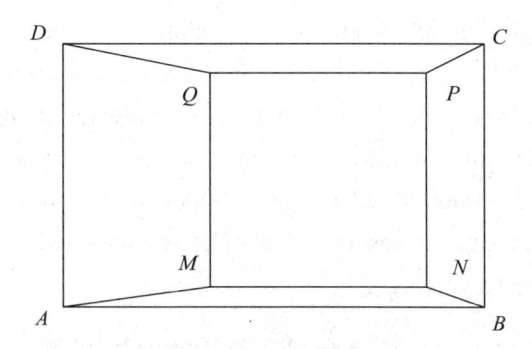

7. Two companies have the same number of employees. The first company hires new employees so that its workforce is 11 times its original size. The second company lays off 11 employees. After the change, the number of employees in the first company is a multiple of the number of employees in the second company. What is the maximum number of employees in each company before the change?

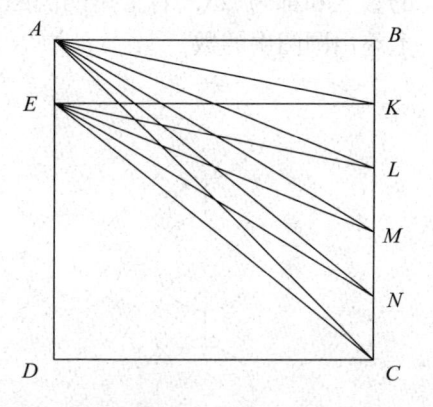

8. ABCD is a square. K, L, M and N are points on BC such that BK=KL=LM=MN=NC. E is the point on AD such that AE=BK. In degrees, what is the measure of
$\angle AKE + \angle ALE + \angle AME + \angle ANE + \angle ACE$.

9. The numbers 1 and 8 have been put into two squares of a 3×3 table, as shown in the diagram below. The remaining seven squares are to be filled with the numbers 2, 3, 4, 5, 6, 7 and 9, using each exactly once, such that the sum of the numbers is the same in any of the four 2×2 subtable shaded in the diagram below. Find all possible solutions.

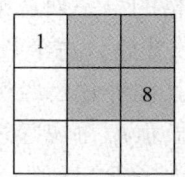

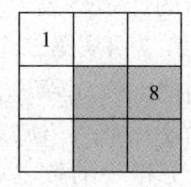

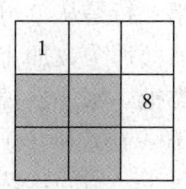

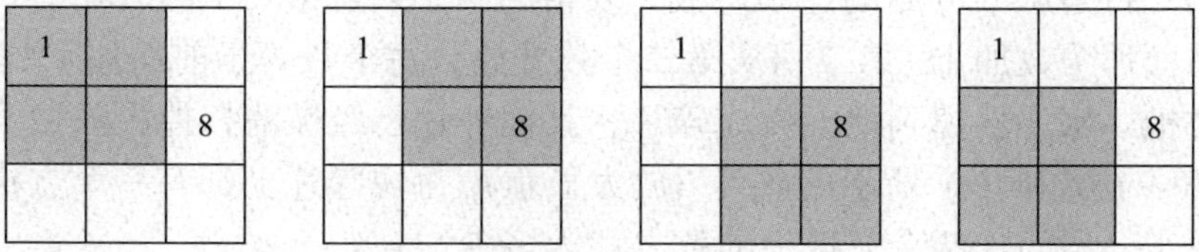

10. At the beginning of each month, an adult red ant gives birth to three baby black ants. An adult black ant eats one baby black ant, gives birth to three baby red ants, and then dies (Also, it is known that there are always enough baby black ants to be eaten). During the month, baby ants become adult ants, and the cycle continues. If there are 9000000 red ants and 1000000 black ants on Christmas day, what was the difference between the number of red ants and the number of black ants on Christmas day a year ago?

10.5 EMIC队际赛中文试题

2012 年国际小学数学竞赛队际竞赛试题

1. 下面的九个圆圈中各填有一个不同的正整数,其中八个数已经被擦掉. 这九个整数是连续的,且每条直线 (图 10-8 中共有七条) 上的所有圆圈中的数之和都为 23. 右上角的圆圈中的数小于右下角的圆圈中的数. 请重新填上空白圆圈中的数.

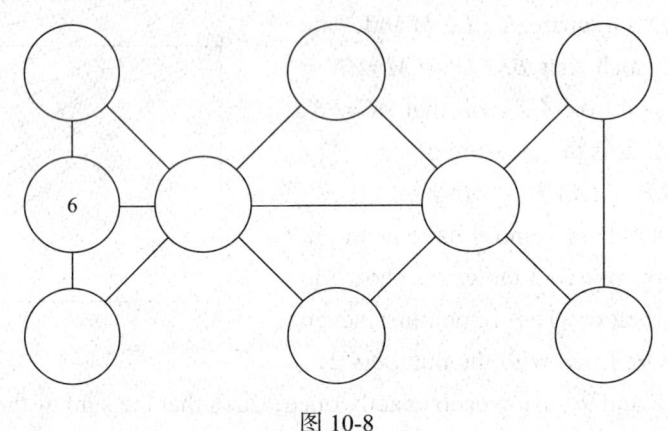

图 10-8

2. 一块水泥板上面画有一个数字表格,其中一部分如图 10-9 (a) 所示. 表格的第一行是从 0 开始的连续整数. 表格的第一列从第二个数开始,每个数等于前面那个数加 1;第二列从第二个数开始,每个数等于前面那个数加 2;依此类推. 水泥板掉到地上摔成碎片,其他碎片已经被清扫掉,只留下两块如图 10-9 (b) 和 (c) 所示的碎片 (放大显示),每块碎片上都有一个方格上的数涂污了,请问这两个方格中的数之和为多少?

第 10 章 2012 年第 10 届国际小学数学竞赛

0	1	2	3	4	5
1	3	5	7	9	11
2	5	8	11	14	17
3	7	11	15	19	23
4	9	14	19	24	29
5	11	17	23	29	35

(a)

?	2012	2023

(b)

2012
2683
?

(c)

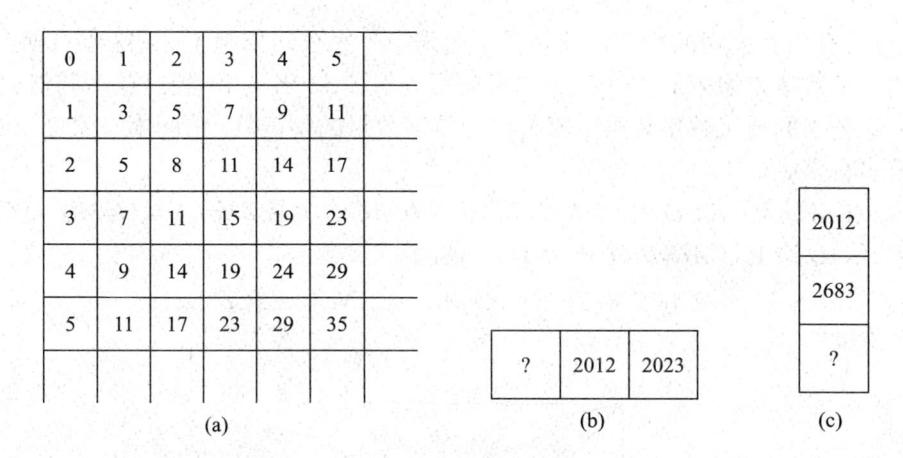

图 10-9

3. 有一列数，每个数是 2012 或者 1，其中第一个数是 2012. 第一个 2012 与第二个 2012 之间恰好有一个 1；第二个 2012 与第三个 2012 之间恰好有两个 1；第三个 2012 与第四个 2012 之间恰好有三个 1；依此类推. 请问这列数的前 2012 个数之和为多少？

4. 在一次考试中，小明答错了三分之一的题目，小亮答错了 7 道题. 有五分之一的题目他们俩都答错了. 请问他们俩都答对的题目至多有几题？

5. 五个互不相同的正整数两两相乘得到 10 个乘积，其中最小的乘积为 28，最大的乘积为 240，且 128 也是其中一个乘积. 请问这五个整数之和为多少？

6. 如图 10-10 所示，正方形 MNPQ 在长方形 ABCD 内，且长方形的边与正方形的边平行，$AB - BC = 7$ cm. 如果梯形 ABNM 与 CDQP 的面积的和为 123 cm², 且梯形 ADQM 与 BCPN 的面积的和为 312 cm². 请问正方形 MNPQ 的面积为多少 cm²？

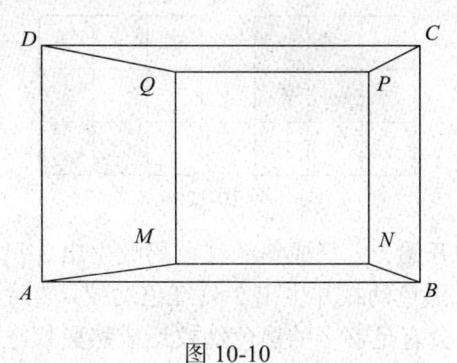

图 10-10

7. 有两家公司的员工数量相同，后来第一家公司招聘了一些新员工使得它的员工数量是原来的 11 倍．第二家公司辞退了 11 名员工，经过这个调整后，第一家公司的员工数量是第二家公司的员工数量的整倍数．请问第一家公司原本至多有多少员工？

8. 在正方形 ABCD 中，点 K、L、M 和 N 在 BC 边上且 BK=KL=LM=MN=NC，点 E 在 AD 边上且 AE=BK（图 10-11）．请问

$$\angle AKE + \angle ALE + \angle AME + \angle ANE + \angle ACE$$

为多少度？

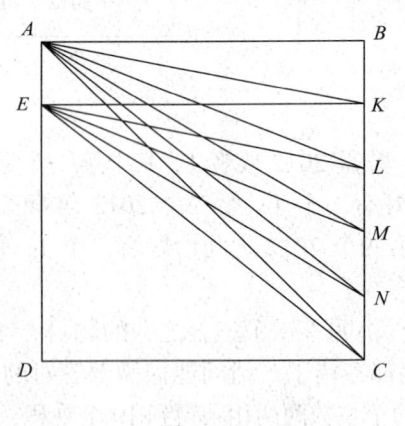

图 10-11

9. 如图 10-12 所示，数 1 和 8 已经填入 3×3 表格的两个方格中，把数 2、3、4、5、6、7 和 9 分别填入剩下的七个方格中，每个数仅填一次且每个方格仅填一个数，使得每个 2×2 表格（图 10-12 的阴影部分）中的之和都相等．请求出所有的填法．

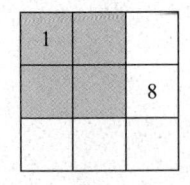

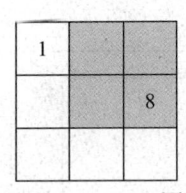

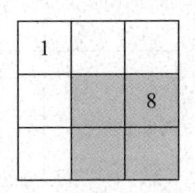

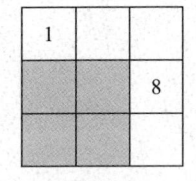

图 10-12

10. 在每个月的开始，一只成熟的红色蚂蚁生出 3 只黑色幼蚁，一只成熟的黑色蚂蚁吃掉 1 只黑色幼蚁并生出 3 只红色幼蚁，然后这只成熟的黑色蚂蚁死掉（已知每个月都会有足够多的黑色幼蚁让成熟黑蚁吃掉）．过了一个月，幼

蚁都成了成熟的蚂蚁, 如此不断持续下去. 如果今年的圣诞节有 9000000 只红色蚂蚁和 1000000 只黑色蚂蚁, 请问去年圣诞节时红色蚂蚁与黑色蚂蚁的数量之差是多少?

10.6 EMIC 队际赛试题解答与评注

2012 年国际小学数学竞赛队际竞赛试题解答

1. **解** 可知除了中间两个圆圈外, 每一个圆圈都有两条直线经过. 而中间这两个圆圈内所填的数之总和为 23−6=17, 因此所填入的九个连续整数之总和为 (7×23−17)÷2=72, 故这九个连续整数的中间数为 72÷9=8, 也就是说这九个连续整数为 4、5、6、7、8、9、10、11、12. 再由最右边的垂直线上仅有两个圆圈可知填入这两个圆圈内的数为 11 与 12, 并由右上角的圆圈中的数小于右下角的圆圈中的数可得右上角圆圈内的数为 11、右下角圆圈内的数为 12, 且经过右上角圆圈的另一条在线圆圈内之数的总和为 12、经过右下角圆圈的另一条在线圆圈内之数的总和为 11. 现因已知填入 6 的圆圈位置, 故可知 11=4+7; 而 12=5+7=4+8, 因此中间两个圆圈里位于右边的圆圈内所填的数为 4 或 7. 此时因中间这两个圆圈内所填的数之总和为 17, 故中间两个圆圈里位于右边的圆圈内所填的数不可为 4, 因此填入此圆圈内的数为 7 而填入中间这两个圆圈内另一个圆圈的数为 10, 接着便可利用唯一性将其余的圆圈内所填之数求出, 如图 10-13 所示.

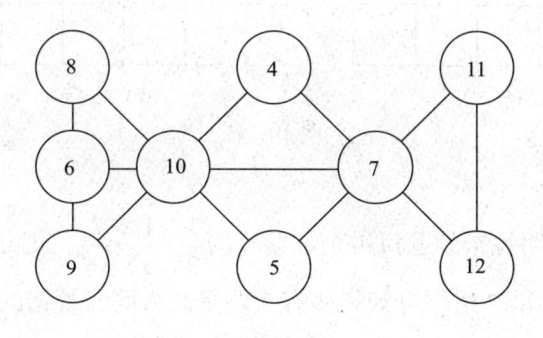

图 10-13

2. **解** 可知在第一块水泥板碎片上被涂污的数为 2012−(2023−2012)=2001. 观察可得知完整的水泥板上的数是以左上至右下的主对角线为对称轴对称

填入数的，因此第二块水泥板碎片上被涂污的数为2683+(2683−2012)=3354，故知所求为2001+3354=5355.

答：5355

3. **解** 将此数列上的数依以下方式依序填入一个阶梯形式的表.

将首2个数填在由上而下第一列、接下来的3个数填在第二列、接下来的4个数填在第三列、接着以此类推，如图10-14 (a) 所示. 再来我们先计算前四列的数之总和. 复制这一个表格而做出另一个阶梯形式的表，旋转180度后与原先的表格可拼成一个矩形，如图10-14 (b) 所示. 此时可知这个矩形的内行数比列数多3，因此共有4×7=28个数，所以原先的表格有28÷2=14个数. 而矩形的内行数比列数多3这一个性质并不会随着列数变化而改变，且依此方式包含此数列前2012个数的最小矩形内的数应尽可能接近2×2012=4024，故由61×64=3904、62×65=4030可知当取列数为61的阶梯形式的表时，共有3904÷2=1952个数. 为了求出前2012个数之和，还必须加入部分第62列上的数，所以可以得知在前2012个数内，共有62个2012及2012−62=1950个1，因此前2012个数之和为62×2012+1950=126694.

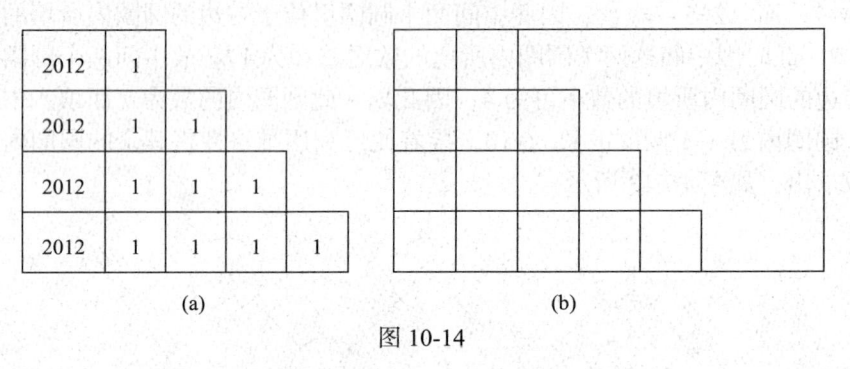

2012	1			
2012	1	1		
2012	1	1	1	
2012	1	1	1	1

(a)

(b)

图 10-14

答：126694

4. **解** 仅小明答错的题目占全部题目的 $\frac{1}{3}-\frac{1}{5}=\frac{2}{15}$，因此总题数为15的倍数；再由小亮答错7道题可知最多有7题是两人同时答错的，因此总题数最多为 $7\div\frac{1}{5}=35$ 题. 为了求出两人都答对的题目至多有几题，故取总题数的最大可能值，即30题. 此时共有 $30\times\frac{1}{5}=6$ 题是两人同时答错的，因此仅小亮答

第 10 章　2012 年第 10 届国际小学数学竞赛

错的题目为 7−6=1 题、仅小明答错的题目是 $30 \times \frac{2}{15} = 4$ 题,故共有 30−6−1−4=19 题是两人都答对的.

答: 19

5. 解　可知 28 是最小的两个正整数相乘之积而 240 是最大的两个正整数相乘之积. 因此最小的两个正整数为 1 与 28、2 与 14 或 4 与 7,即第二小的正整数不会小于 7,所以可推得第二大的正整数不会小于 9,故可知最大的两个正整数为 10 与 24、12 与 20 或 15 与 16,即第二大的正整数不会大于 15. 所以可再推得第二小的正整数不会大于 13,因此最小的两个正整数为 4 与 7. 而 128 不可被 7 以及 10、12、15 这几个可能为第二大的数所整除,且最小的数,4,也不可能是两数乘积为 128 的其中一数,否则另一数必为 32,都大于任何一个最大数的可能值,因此 128 必为最大数与第三大数的乘积,此时再由 20、24 皆不可整除 128 可得知最大数为 16,因此这五个正整数为 4、7、8、15、16,其和为 50.

答: 50

6. 解　如图 10-15 所示,将正方形移至中间并画出补助线,并将此图视为在长方形内部挖去一个正方形区域. 则可推得涂上阴影部分的区域与未涂上阴影部分的区域之面积差为 312−123=189 cm²。此结果并不会随着我们将位于图 10-15 中四个角落的八个全等的三角形互相抵消而改变,且剩余的部分为两个涂上阴影的矩形与两个未涂上阴影的矩形,其中每一个矩形的长之长度与 MN 等长. 因此若将两个涂上阴影的矩形沿等长的边合并成一个矩形、将两个未涂上阴影的矩形沿等长的边合并成一个矩形,则这两个合并后的矩形长都是 MN 而宽之差为 7,因此 MN=189÷7=27 (cm),故正方形 MNPQ 的面积为 $27^2 = 729$ (cm²).

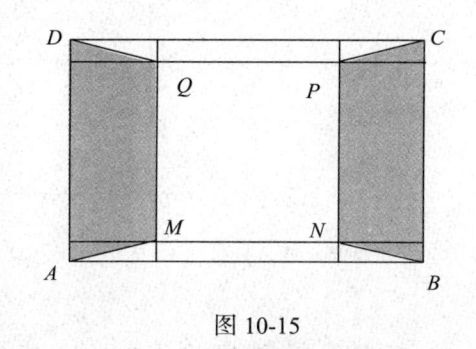

图 10-15

答: 729 cm²

7. 解　若两家公司原来的员工数都不是 11 的倍数. 在经过调整后,第二家公司的现有员工数整除原先的员工数,故知第二家公司的现有员工数一定会整除调整前后的员工数之差,此差即为 11. 因原来的员工数不是 11 的倍数，故第二间公司经过调整后的员工数也不是 11 的倍数，故可得知第二间公司经过调整后的员工数为 1，所以两家公司原来的员工数为 12．若两家公司原来的员工数都是 11 的倍数，则将每一间公司的员工都分成 11 组人数相同的小组．此时经过调整后第二间公司每一个小组的员工数必整除原先每一组员工数的 11 倍，因此其值必为 11 的因子：若为 1，则原先每一组员工数为 2 且每一间公司员工总数为 22；若为 11，则原先每一组员工数为 12 且每一间公司员工总数为 132．因此原本至多有 132 位员工．

答：132 位

8. 解 因四边形 $EABK$、$EAKL$、$EALM$、$EAMN$ 与 $EANC$ 都有一组对边是平行且相等，故可知都是平行四边形（图 10-16），因此可得知 $\angle AKE = \angle KAB$、$\angle ALE = \angle LAK$、$\angle AME = \angle MAL$、$\angle ANE = \angle NAM$ 及 $\angle ACE = \angle CAN$．

故 $\angle AKE + \angle ALE + \angle AME + \angle ANE + \angle ACE = \angle BAC = 45°$．

图 10-16

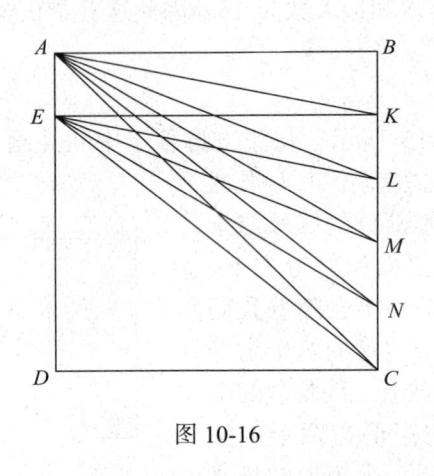

答：45°

9. 解 考虑前两个表格图 10-17 (a) 和 (b) 内的阴影部分，可知位于 1 正下方与 8 正上方的两个格子内之数的差必为 8−1=7，此时仅有 9 与 2 可满足，因此 1 正下方的数为 9 而 8 正上方的数为 2，如图 10-17 所示．接着考虑最后两个表格图 10-17 (c) 和 (d) 内的阴影部分，可知位于 9 正下方与 8 正下方的两个格子内之数必是两个连续正整数，因此其为 3 与 4、4 与 5、5 与 6 或 6 与 7，如图 10-17 所示．接着可将图 10-17 (a) ~ (c) 剩下的部分都填入数字而完成．而在最后一个情形时图 10-17 (d)，因在第二行中，最上方的数与最下方的数之差必为 6−1=5=7−2，但此时能填入的数字为 3、4、5，其差最大为 2，故不符合．因

第 10 章　2012 年第 10 届国际小学数学竞赛

此仅有三个答案.

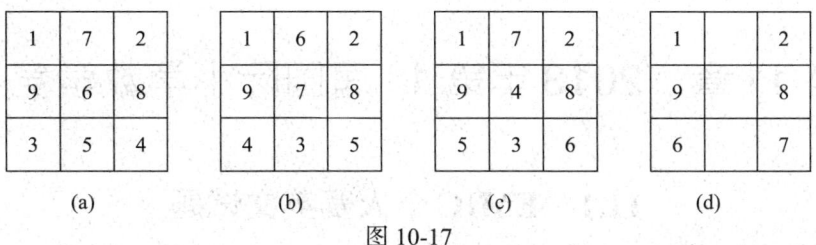

1	7	2
9	6	8
3	5	4

(a)

1	6	2
9	7	8
4	3	5

(b)

1	7	2
9	4	8
5	3	6

(c)

1		2
9		8
6		7

(d)

图 10-17

10. 解　以两个月为一个周期来考虑. 在第一个月后, 新的红蚂蚁数量为原先黑蚂蚁数量的 3 倍; 在第二个月后, 新的红蚂蚁数量为第一个月后存活的黑色幼蚁的 3 倍, 而此数量即为 3 倍的原先红蚂蚁数量再减去原先黑蚂蚁数量. 因此经过两个月后, 增加的红蚂蚁数量为原先红蚂蚁数量的 9 倍, 换句话说, 新的红蚂蚁数量为两个月前的红蚂蚁数量之 10 倍. 而在第一个月后, 新的黑蚂蚁数量是 3 倍的原先红蚂蚁数量再减去原先黑蚂蚁数量, 在第二个月初出生的黑色幼蚁数量为原先红蚂蚁数量的 3 倍与 9 倍的原先黑蚂蚁数量. 在这些蚂蚁之中, 有 3 倍的原先红蚂蚁数量再减去原先黑蚂蚁数量的黑色蚂蚁被吃掉, 因此新的黑蚂蚁数量为两个月前的黑蚂蚁数量之 10 倍. 在一年后, 这样的周期共经过六次, 因此蚂蚁增加了 6 次, 即此时数量变为原先数量的 1000000 倍. 因今年的圣诞节有 9000000 只红色蚂蚁和 1000000 只黑色蚂蚁, 故去年圣诞节时有 9 只红色蚂蚁与 1 只黑色蚂蚁, 其差为 8.

答: 8

第11章 2013年第11届国际小学数学竞赛

11.1 EMIC个人赛英文试题

Elementary Mathematics International Contest 2013
2nd July, 2013, Burgas, Bulgaria

Individual Contest

1. In a sequence of squares, the 1st one has side length 1 cm. The side length of each subsequent square is equal to the length of a diagonal of the preceding square. The diagram below illustrates the construction of the 2nd and 3rd squares. What is the side length, in cm, of the 11th square?

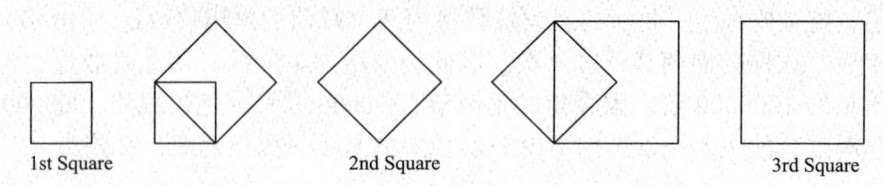

1st Square   2nd Square   3rd Square

2. Twenty girls stood in a row facing right. Four boys joined the row, but facing left. Each boy counted the number of girls in front of him. The numbers were 3, 6, 15 and 18 respectively. Each girl also counted the number of boys in front of her. What was the sum of the numbers counted by the girls?

3. The diagram below on the left shows ten advertisements A, B, C, D, E, F, G, H, I and J in the ten boxes on a 2×5 billboard, on a certain day. Each day, the advertisements move from box to box following a fixed pattern. On the day after, they appear as in the diagram below on the right. How many days will it take before all the advertisements return to their starting positions together for the first time?

第 11 章 2013 年第 11 届国际小学数学竞赛

A	B	C	D	E
F	G	H	I	J

G	A	E	F	B
I	C	J	D	H

4. Each side of a square of side length 10 cm is divided into three equal parts. Some of these division points are connected to the verti- ces of the square, as shown in the diagram below. What is the area, in cm^2, of the shaded region?

5. Two opposite corner dots from a 4×4 array have been removed, as shown in the diagram below. How many different squares can be formed using four of these 14 dots as vertices?

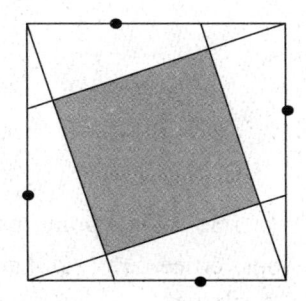

6. How many positive integers under 1000 with units digit 9 can be expressed as the sum of a power of 2 and a power of 3? Note that 1 is both a power of 2 and a power of 3.

7. Alice replaces each of the 2008 numbers 6, 7, 8, ⋯, 2012, 2013 with the sum of its digits. Brian replaces each of Alice's numbers with the sum of its digits, and Colin replaces each of Brian's numbers with the sum of its digits. What is the number which Colin obtains most frequently?

8. What is the smallest positive integer which is 2 times the square of some positive integer and also 5 times the fifth power of some other positive integer?

9. Every positive integer can be expressed as a sum of distinct powers of 2. Note that 1 and 2 are powers of 2. How many three-digit numbers are sums of exactly 9 distinct powers of 2?

10. In triangle ABC, D is the midpoint of BC and E is the midpoint of CA. AD and BE are perpendicular to each other. The diagram below shows the point G where they intersect. This point is called the centroid of ABC, and has the property that $AG=2DG$ and $BG=2EG$. What is the value of $\dfrac{BC^2+AC^2}{AB^2}$?

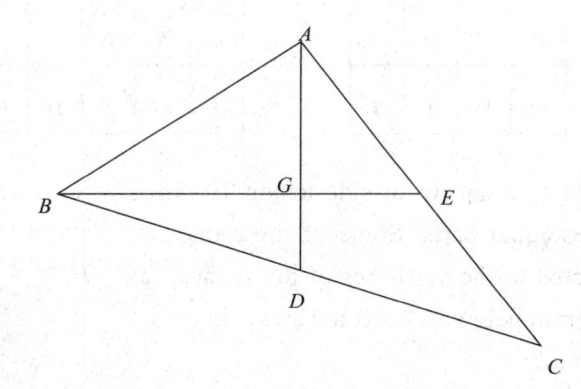

11. O is a point inside a quadrilateral $ABCD$ such that its distances from the four vertices are $1, 2, 4$ and 7 cm in some order. What is the maximum area, in cm^2, of $ABCD$?

12. From the product $1 \times 2 \times \cdots \times 2013$, what is the smallest number of factors we must remove in order for the units-digit of the product of the remaining factors to be 9?

13. A positive integer is said to be strange if in its prime factorization, all powers are odd. For instance, 22, 23 and 24 form a block of three consecutive strange numbers because $22 = 2^1 \times 11^1$, $23 = 23^1$ and $24 = 2^3 \times 3^1$. What is the greatest length of a block of consecutive strange numbers?

14. Half of the squares in an 8×8 board are shaded, as shown in the diagram below. What is the total number of 2×2, 4×4 and 6×6 subboards such that half of the squares in each are shaded?

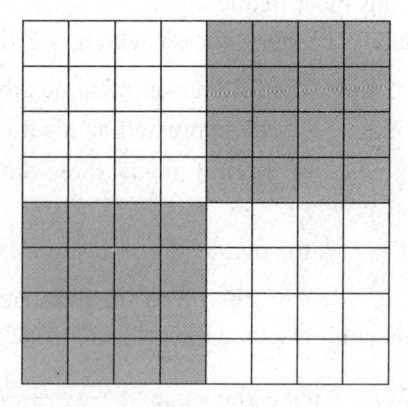

15. A positive integer with at most 9 digits is said to be good if its units digit is

0 or 1, its tens digit is 0, 1 or 2, its hundreds digit is 0, 1, 2 or 3, its thousands digit is 0, 1, 2, 3, or 4, and so on. Thus the first ten good numbers are 1, 10, 11, 20, 21, 100, 101, 110, 111 and 120. What is the 100 th good number?

11.2 EMIC个人赛中文试题

2013 年国际小学数学竞赛个人竞赛试题

1. 在以下一系列的正方形中 (图 11-1), 第一个正方形的边长为 1 cm, 之后每个正方形的边长都等于前一个正方形对角线的长度. 下图为所作出第二个、第三个正方形的例子. 请问第十一个正方形的边长为多少 cm?

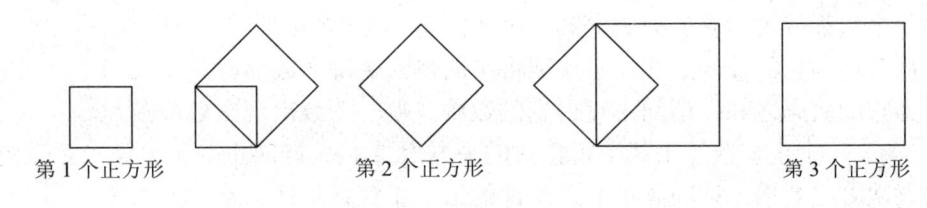

第 1 个正方形　　　　第 2 个正方形　　　　第 3 个正方形

图 11-1

2. 有二十位女孩站成一排且都面朝右边,四位男孩插入队伍中,但都面朝左边. 每位男孩都计算共有多少位女孩在他的前面, 所得的结果分别为 3、6、15、18. 每位女孩也都计算有多少位男孩在她的前面. 请问这些女孩所得的结果之总和是多少?

3. 图 11-2 (a) 中显示某一天十个广告 A、B、C、D、E、F、G、H、I、J 在 2×5 屏幕的 10 个格子中. 每一天, 这些广告都依照固定的模式从一个格子移到另一个格子. 次日, 它们的位置变成为图 11-2 (b). 请问要经过多少天所有的广告才能第一次同时都回到初始的位置?

A	B	C	D	E
F	G	H	I	J

(a)

G	A	E	F	B
I	C	J	D	H

(b)

图 11-2

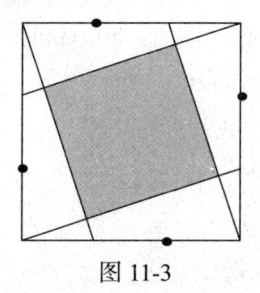

4. 将边长为 10 cm 的正方形之边长三等分．将某些分割点与顶点相连，如图 11-3 所示，请问阴影部分的面积为多少 cm²？

5. 图 11-4 是从 4×4 格点移除两个相对角落的点．利用这 14 个点中的四个点为顶点，请问共可以构成多少个不同的正方形？

6. 在 1000 以下且个位数为 9 的正整数中，请问共有多少个数可被表示为一个 2 的次幂与一个 3 的次幂之和？（注：1 可同时被表示为 2 的次幂或 3 的次幂）

7. 小艾将以下 2008 个正整数 6、7、8、…、2012、2013 中每个数都替换为它的数码之和，小伯则将小艾得到的每个数都替换为它的数码之和，小克则将小伯得到的每个数都替换为它的数码之和．请问小克得到的数中，哪一个数出现次数最多？

8. 一个正整数等于某个正整数的平方之 2 倍，同时也等于另一个正整数的五次方之 5 倍．请问满足上述条件的最小正整数是什么？

9. 每一个正整数都可以被表示为 2 的不同次幂之和，请问共有多少个三位数可以被表示为恰有九个 2 的不同次幂之和？(注：1 和 2 都是 2 的次幂)

10. 在 △ABC 中，点 D 为 BC 边之中点、点 E 为 CA 边之中点．线段 AD 与 BE 互相垂直，图 11-5 中标出其交点 G，这个点称为 △ABC 的重心，且具有 AG=2DG、BG=2EG 的性质．请问 $\dfrac{BC^2+AC^2}{AB^2}$ 的值是什么？

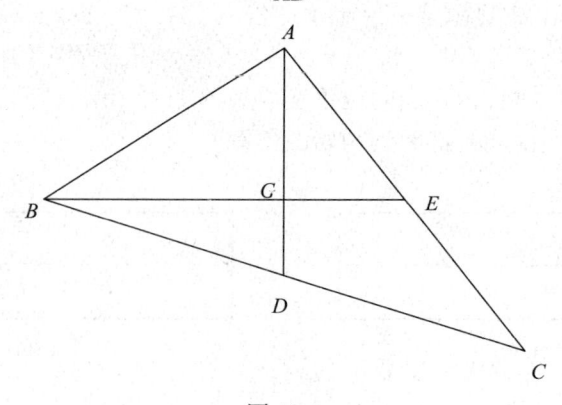

图 11-5

第 11 章　2013 年第 11 届国际小学数学竞赛

11. 点 O 为四边形 $ABCD$ 内的一个点，使得 O 点与四个顶点之距离依某种顺序分别为 1 cm、2 cm、4 cm、7 cm. 请问四边形 $ABCD$ 可能的最大面积为多少 cm^2？

12. 从乘式 $1×2×\cdots×2013$ 中，请问至少要删除多少个数才能使所得的乘积之个位数为 9？

13. 一个数经过标准素因子分解后，如果所有素因子的次数都是奇数，称此数为"怪数". 例如，因为 $22=2^1×11^1$、$23=23^1$、$24=2^3×3^1$，所以 22、23、24 三个数就构成一串长度为 3 的连续怪数. 请问一串连续的"怪数"其长度的最大值是多少？

14. 将 8×8 方格表的一半区域如图 11-6 所示的方式涂上阴影. 请问在图 11-6 中共有多少个 2×2、4×4、6×6 的子方格表使得每个子方格表中一半数量的小正方形被涂上阴影？

15. 一个正整数最多有 9 个数码且个位数是 0 或 1；十位数是 0、1、2 之一；百位数是 0、1、2、3 之一；千位数是 0、1、2、3、4 之一，依此规律继续下去，则称此数为一个"好数". 例如，首十个好数分别为 1、10、11、20、21、100、101、110、111、120. 请问第 100 个"好数"是什么？

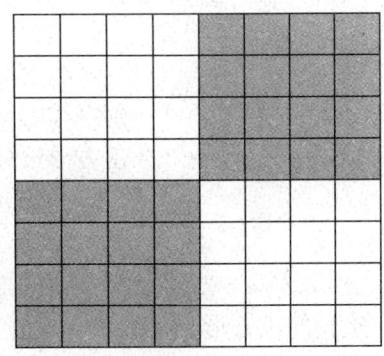

图 11-6

11.3　EMIC 个人赛试题解答与评注

2013 年国际小学数学竞赛个人竞赛试题解答

1. **解**　如图 11-7 所示，可发现第三个正方形的边长是第一个正方形的边长之 2 倍. 同样地，第五个正方形边长是第三个正方形的边长之 2 倍，并可依此类推. 因为 $\frac{11-1}{2}=5$，故可得知第十一个正方形的边长为第一个正方形的边长之 $2^5=32$ 倍，即 32 cm.

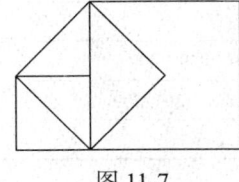

图 11-7

答：32 cm

2．解 可知每位男孩计算在他面前的女孩人数之总和为 3+6+15+18=42．若男孩与女孩互相面对面，则他们都会计算到对方；否则他们都不会计算到对方．因此这些女孩计算在她面前的男孩人数之总和也必是 42．

答：42

3．解 观察可知，广告 A、B、E、C 及 G 为每 5 天一循环；广告 D、I 及 F 为每 3 天一循环而广告 H、J 为每 2 天一循环，因此所有的广告经过 5×3×2=30 天后才能第一次同时回到初始的位置．

答：30天

4．解 如图 11-8 所示，可将虚线部分的两个三角形分别平移后与另两个三角形组成两个 1×3 的矩形，此 10×10 的正方形被分割成十个全等的小正方形，其中阴影部分占了 4 个，因此阴影部分的面积为原正方形面积的 40%，即 40(cm^2)．

图 11-8

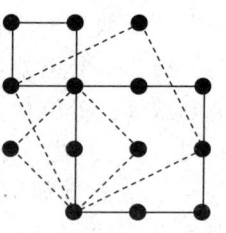

答：40 cm^2

5．解 观察可知共可构成如图 11-9 所示的四种不同边长的正方形，其中 1×1 的正方形共有 7 个、2×2 的正方形共有 2 个、$\sqrt{2}\times\sqrt{2}$ 的正方形共有 4 个、$\sqrt{5}\times\sqrt{5}$ 的正方形共有 2 个，合计 7+2+4+2=15 个．

答：15个

图 11-9

6．解 小于 1000 之 2 的次幂有 1、2、4、8、16、32、64、128、256 及 512，这些数的个位数只能是 1、2、4、6 与 8，而小于 1000 之 3 的次幂有 1、3、9、27、81、243 及 729，这些数的个位数只能是 1、3、7 与 9．表 11-1 列出满足条件的所有数，共有 10 个数．

表 11-1

2的次幂	3的次幂	满足条件的数
1		
2、32、512	27	29、59、539
4、64		
16、256	3、243	19、259、499
8、128	1、81	9、89、129、209
	9、729	

答：10个

7. **解** 可知小艾所得的数最大为 1+9+9+9=28，因此小伯所得的数最大为 1+9=2+8=10，从而小克所得到的数都是一位数，此数不为 9 时，恰与小艾所得的数被 9 除之后所得之非 0 余数相同；而若小艾所得的数被 9 除之后所得之余数为 0，则小克所得到的数为 9。因可以观察出这些数是从 6 开始并结束于 6 的数，且每 9 个数一循环，故知数码 6 比其他的数码都多出现 1 次，即 6 出现次数最多。

答：6

8. **解** 可知这一个正整数的素因子分解式中必有 2 与 5，因为要求出最小值，故可假设没有其他的素因子存在。因这一个正整数是某个正整数的平方之 2 倍，故知 2 的次数必为奇数而 5 的次数必为偶数；又因这一个正整数是另一个正整数五次方的 5 倍，故知 2 的次数必为 5 的倍数而 5 的次数必是除 5 后余数为 1 的数。因此可推知最小值为 $2^5 5^6 = 500000$。

答：500000 或 $2^5 5^6$

9. **解** 可知 $1023 = 1 + 2 + 2^2 + 2^3 + \cdots + 2^9$，故要删去其中一项而得到三位数。而观察后知可删除的数必须大于 23，即为 2^5、2^6、2^7、2^8 或 2^9，因此共有 5 个这样的数。

答：5 个

10. **解** 可令 $EG=x$ 而 $DG=y$，则知 $BG=2x$、$AG=2y$。接着由勾股定理可以得知

$$AB^2 = (2x)^2 + (2y)^2 = 4(x^2 + y^2),$$
$$AE^2 = x^2 + (2y)^2 = x^2 + 4y^2,$$
$$BD^2 = (2x)^2 + y^2 = 4x^2 + y^2.$$

因此

$$BC^2 + AC^2 = (2BD)^2 + (2AE)^2$$
$$= 4(4x^2 + y^2) + 4(x^2 + 4y^2)$$
$$= 20(x^2 + y^2),$$

故 $\dfrac{BC^2 + AC^2}{AB^2} = 5$。

答：5

11. **解** 当给定三角形的两条边时，在这两条边彼此互相垂直的情况下这个三角形的面积最大。因此我们不妨假设四边形 ABCD 的对角线 AC 与 BD 互相垂直并交于 O 点，则我们考虑将 1、2、4、7 两两配对，使所得两对的和之

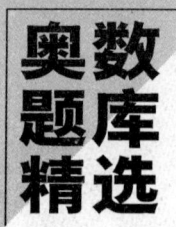

乘积尽可能大.

因 $(1+2)(4+7) = 33 < (1+4)(2+7) = 45 < (1+7)(2+4) = 48$，故知四边形 $ABCD$ 可能的最大面积为 $48÷2=24(cm^2)$.

答: 24 cm^2

12. 解 为了要使所得的乘积之个位数为 9，我们必须删除个位数为 0、2、4、5、6、8 的所有数，截至 2010 为止，这样的数共有 $6×201=1206$ 个．又因 $1×3×7×9$、$11×13×17×19$、…、$2001×2003×2007×2009$ 这 201 个乘积的个位数都是 9，且由 $9×9=81$ 及 $1×9=9$ 可以判断出截至 2010 为止，所有剩下的数之乘积的个位数为 9．接着因 2012 需被删除知只剩最后两个数仍需考虑: 2011、2013. 我们可以保留 2011 而必须删除 2013，因此至少要删除 $1206+1+1=1208$ 个数.

答: 1208个

13. 解 首先注意到 $29 = 29^1$、$30 = 2^1×3^1×5^1$、$31 = 31^1$、$32 = 2^5$、$33 = 3^1×11^1$、$34 = 2^1×17^1$、$35 = 5^1×7^1$ 构成一串长度为 7 的连续的怪数，接着证明其长度不可能超过 7．在八个连续的正整数中，必有一个数可被 4 整除但不能被 8 整除，此数不为怪数，所以一串连续的怪数其长度的最大值是 7.

答: 7

14. 解 可知 2×2 的子方格表必须位于第 4 列与第 5 列，或者是位于第 4 行与第 5 行，因此共有 13 个这样的子方格表；

可知 4×4 的子方格表必须位于第 3、4、5、6 列，或者是位于第 3、4、5、6 行，因此共有 9 个这样的子方格表；

可知 6×6 的子方格表必须位于第 2、3、4、5、6、7 列，或者位于第 2、3、4、5、6、7 行，因此共有 5 个这样的子方格表.

以上合计共 $13+9+5=27$ 个.

答: 27个

15. 解 观察可知第一个两位数的好数是位于这列数的第 2 位、第一个三位数的好数是位于这列数的第 6 位．又观察到 $2=1×2$ 及 $6=1×2×3$．事实上，第一个四位数的好数是位于这列数的第 $1×2×3×4=24$ 位、第一个五位数的好数是位于这列数的第 $1×2×3×4×5=120$ 位，因此我们所要找的数是一个四位数．又因为 $100=24×4+4$，商为 4 余数也为 4，故知首位数为 4，而所求之数为 4020.

答: 4020

11.4 EMIC队际赛英文试题

Elementary Mathematics International Contest 2013
2nd July, 2013, Burgas, Bulgaria

Team Contest

1. A 5×5 farm contains the houses of six farmers A, B, C, D, E and F, as shown in the diagram below. The remaining 19 squares are to be distributed among them. Farmer D will get 5 of these squares, farmers A and F will get 4 each and farmers B, C and E will get 2 each. The farmers can only take squares that are in the same row or column as their houses, and their squares must be connected either directly to their houses or via other squares which they get. On the diagram provided for you to record your answer, enter A, B, C, D, E or F in each blank square to indicate which farmer gets that square.

2. Mei feng wrote a short story in five days. The number of words written in each day is a positive integer. Each evening, she recorded the total number of words she had written so far. Then she divided her first number by 1×2, her second number by 2×3, her third number by 3×4, her fourth number by 4×5 and her last number by 5×6. The sum of these five fractions is 5. What is the minimum number of words in Mei feng's short story?

3. The diagram below shows nine circles each tangent to all its neighbours. One of the circles is labeled 1. The remaining circles are to be labeled with 1, 2, 3, 3, 3, 4, 4 and 4, such that no two tangent circles have the same label. In how many different ways can this be done?

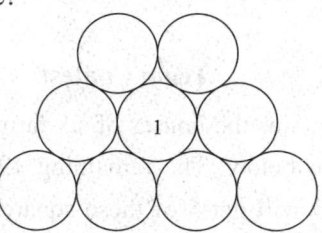

4. In the diagram below, triangles ABC and CDE have the same area, and F is the point of intersection of CA and DE. Moreover, AB is parallel to DE, AB=9 cm and EF=6 cm. What is the length, in cm, of DF?

5. A shop has 350 souvenirs which cost 1, 2, 3, ⋯, 349 and 350 dollars respectively. Daniela has 50 two-dollar bills and 50 five-dollar bills but no other money. She wants to buy one souvenir, and insists on paying the exact amount (without any change). How many of these 350 souvenirs can be the one she chooses?

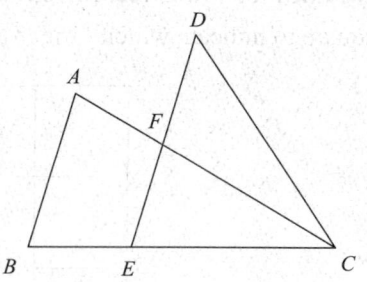

6. The sum of 1997 positive integers is 2013. What is the positive difference between the maximum value and the minimum value of the sum of their squares?

7. The number 16 is placed in the top left corner square of a 4×4 table. The remaining 15 squares are to be filled in using exactly once each of the numbers 1, 2, ⋯, 15, so that the sum of the four numbers in each row, each column and each diagonal is the same. What is the maximum value of the sum of the six numbers in the shaded squares shown in the diagram below?

8. Two corner squares are removed from a 7×8 rectangle in the three ways shown in the diagram below. We wish to dissect the remaining part of the rectangle into 18 copies of either the 1×3 or the 3×1 rectangle. For each of the three cases, either give such a dissection or prove that the task is impossible.

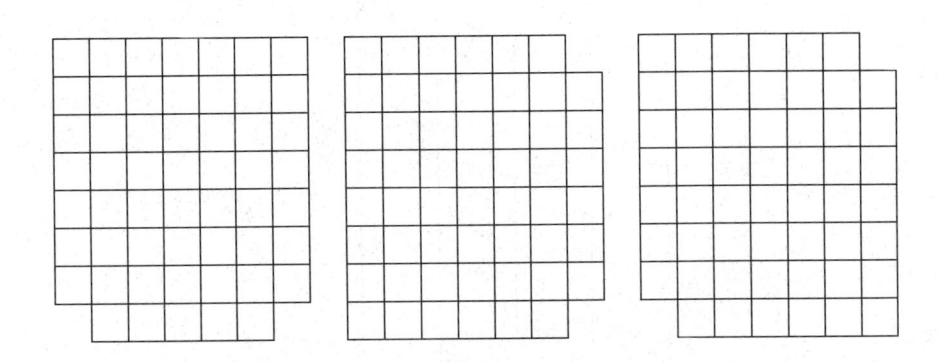

9. The 9 squares in the diagram below are to be filled in using exactly once each of the digits 0, 1, ⋯, 8, so that the equation is correct. What is the minimum value of the positive difference of the two three-digit numbers on the left side of the equation?

□ + □□ + □□□ + □□□ = 9 9 9

10. Each ten-digit numbers in which each digit is 1, 2 or 3 is painted in exactly one of the colours red, green and blue, such that any two numbers which differ in all ten digits have different colours. If 1111111111 is red and 1112111111 is blue, what is the colour of 1231231231?

11.5　EMIC队际赛中文试题

2013年国际小学数学竞赛队际竞赛试题

1. 一个 5×5 的农场中有六间农夫的房舍 A、B、C、D、E、F，如图 11-10 所示. 将剩下的 19 块小方田分配给他们，农夫 D 将获得 5 块小方田；农夫 A 与 F 各获得 4 块小方田；农夫 B、C、E 各获得 2 块小方田. 每位农夫所分配到小方田必须与他们的房舍在同一行或同一列，并且必须与房舍直接相连或通过他所分配到的小方田与房舍相连在一起. 请在最底下图形的每个小方格内填写 A、B、C、D、E、F，以指出这块小方田是由哪位农夫分得.

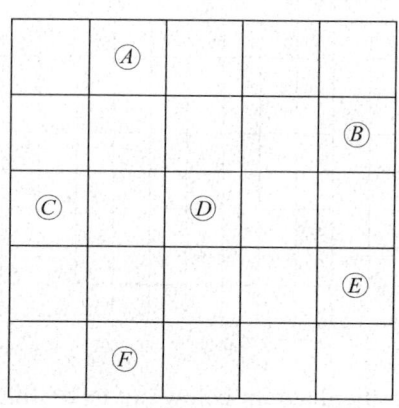

图 11-10

2. 小梅在五天中写了一短篇故事，每天她都写正整数个字．每天晚上，她将截至当时所写的总字数记录下来．她将第一个数除以 1×2、将第二个数除以 2×3、将第三个数除以 3×4、将第四个数除以 4×5、将第五个数除以 5×6，最后她所得到的这五个分数的总和为 5．请问小梅所写的这篇故事至少共有多少个字？

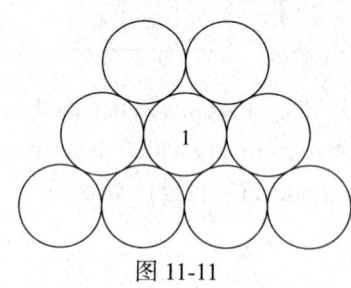

图 11-11

3. 有九个圆都与其相邻的圆互相相切，如图 11-11 所示，其中一圆内已标记数码 1．剩下的圆将分别标记数码 1、2、3、3、3、4、4、4，使得任两个相切的圆所标记的数码都不相同．请问共有多少种不同的标记方法？

4. 图 11-12 中，△ABC 与 △CDE 的面积相等，点 F 为线段 CA 与 DE 之交点．已知 AB 平行于 DE、AB=9 cm、EF= 6cm，请问 DF 的长度为多少 cm？

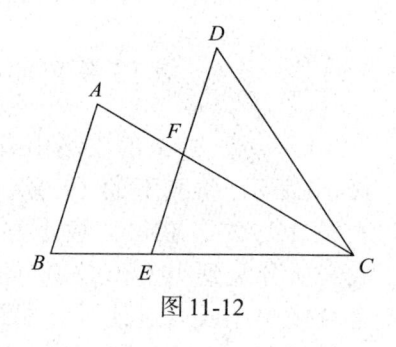

5. 某商店共有 350 个纪念品贩卖，其售价分别为 1、2、3、…、349、350 元．小丹共有 50 张两元与 50 张五元，此外没有其他的纸币．她坚持只想购买一个她恰好能用这些纸币支付而不需找零的纪念品．请问这 350 个纪念品中，她可以有多少种选择？

6. 有 1997 个正整数之总和为 2013．请问它们的平方之和的最大值与最

图 11-12

小值相差 (取正值) 多少?

7. 数 16 已经填入以下 4×4 方格表左上角的小方格内. 剩下的 15 个小方格内分别不重复地填入 1、2、3、⋯、15 之一个数,使得每行、每列、每条对角线在四个小方格内的数之总和都相等. 请问图 11-13 中六个涂上阴影的小方格内的数之总和的最大值是什么?

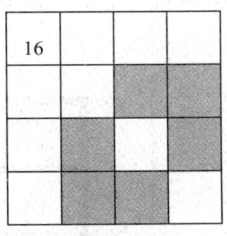

图 11-13

8. 从一个 7×8 的方格表中移除两个角落的小方格,如图 11-14 所示为三种不同的方式. 我们欲将方格表剩下的部分切为 18 片 1×3 或 3×1 的矩形. 对于以下三种情况中的每一种,请画出对应的切割方法或证明无论如何都不可能达成目的.

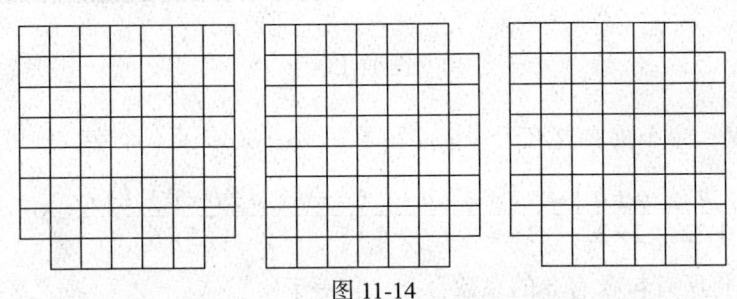

图 11-14

9. 在下列算式左侧的 9 个小方格内不重复地各填入一个数码 0、1、⋯、8,使得等式成立. 请问算式左侧的两个三位数之差 (取正值) 的最小值是什么?

☐ + ☐☐ + ☐☐☐ + ☐☐☐ = 999

10. 十位数的每位数码为 1、2、3 之一,现将这些十位数涂上红色、绿色或蓝色,使得任何两个数,如果它们的数码在十个数字上都互不相同,那么它们所涂的颜色不相同. 已知 1111111111 为红色、1112111111 为蓝色,请问 1231231231 是什么颜色?

11.6　EMIC 队际赛试题解答与评注

2013 年国际小学数学竞赛队际竞赛试题解答

1. 解　首先将唯一确定要分割给某位农夫的小方田标记出，如图 11-15 (a) 所示. 接下来不难分配剩下的小方田，而得到满足条件的分割图，如图 11-15 (b) 所示.

图 11-15

2. 解　令小梅在这五天中依序写了 a、b、c、d 及 e 个字，则可得知

$$\frac{a}{1\times 2}+\frac{a+b}{2\times 3}+\frac{a+b+c}{3\times 4}+\frac{a+b+c+d}{4\times 5}+\frac{a+b+c+d+e}{5\times 6}=5.$$

接着将所有包含有 a 的系数合并，它等于

$$\frac{1}{1\times 2}+\frac{1}{2\times 3}+\frac{1}{3\times 4}+\frac{1}{4\times 5}+\frac{1}{5\times 6}$$

$$=1-\frac{1}{2}+\frac{1}{2}-\frac{1}{3}+\frac{1}{3}-\frac{1}{4}+\frac{1}{4}-\frac{1}{5}+\frac{1}{5}-\frac{1}{6}$$

$$=1-\frac{1}{6}=\frac{5}{6}.$$

同样地，其他项分别为 $\frac{1}{3}$、$\frac{1}{6}$、$\frac{1}{12}$ 与 $\frac{1}{30}$. 因这些值的分母的最小公倍数为 60，故可以得到 $50a+20b+10c+5d+2e=300$，此时可以判断出 e 必可被 5

所整除，不妨令 $e=5f$，则有 $10a+4b+2c+d+2f=60$，此时可以判断出 d 必为偶数，不妨令 $d=2g$，则有 $5a+2b+c+g+f=30$. 而为了得到 $a+b+c+d+e$ 的最小值，我们必须使 a 的值尽可能的大。因 b、c、d 及 e 都为正整数，故可取 $a=5$，此时 $b=c=g=f=1$，因此 $d=2$ 而 $e=5$.

故小梅所写的这篇故事至少共有 $5+1+1+2+5=14$ 个字.

答：14个字

3. **解** 另一个 1 的位置一定是在角落的圆内，由对称性不妨假设位于左下角的圆内.

若右下角的圆内标记的数码为 2，则剩余的数码必须围绕中央的圆交错地填入，此只能有如图 11-16 所示的两种方式.

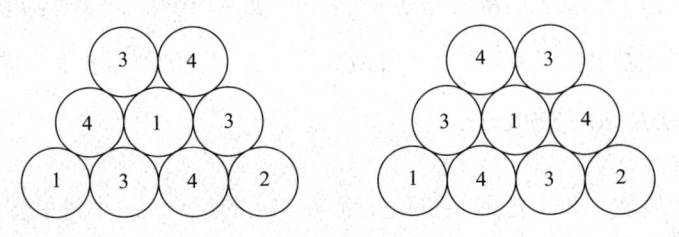

图 11-16

若右下角的圆内标记的数码为 3，则知三个 4 必须围绕中央的圆交错地填入，且 2 必须标记在与右下角的圆相切的另一个圆上，此只能有如图 11-17 所示的两种方式.

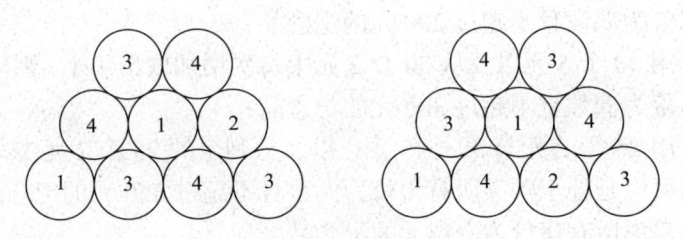

图 11-17

若右下角的圆内标记的数码为 4，则与前一种情况类似，也有另外的两种方式. 因 1 也可能在右下角的圆内，因此我们必须将所得的 2+2+2=6 种方式加倍，即共有 12 种不同的方式.

答：12种

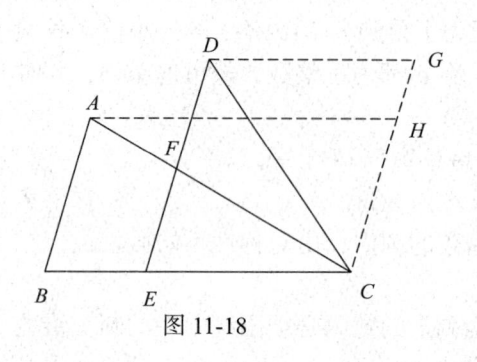

4. **解法 1** 如图 11-18 所示，画出平行四边形 DECG 及 ABCH. 可知点 H 必落在线段 CG 上. 由 $\frac{AB}{EF}=\frac{9}{6}=\frac{3}{2}$ 可知 CE= 2BE. 此时因平行四边形 ABCH 与 DECG 的面积相同，可以得知 CH=2HG.

因此 DE=GC=9+4.5=13.5，且据此可知 DF=DE−EF=13.5−6=7.5(cm).

解法 2 由 AB 平行于 DE 得知 ∠ABC = ∠DEC，因 △ABC 与 △CDE 的面积相等，由共角定理得知 AB×BC=DE×CE. 由 $\frac{AB}{EF}=\frac{9}{6}=\frac{3}{2}$ 可知 BC=$\frac{3}{2}$CE. 故 DE=$\frac{3}{2}$AB，即 DE=13.5(cm)，可得知 DF=DE−EF=7.5 (cm).

答：7.5 cm

5. **解** 显然小丹无法购买价值 1 元与 3 元的纪念品；小丹最多能花费 50×(2+5) = 350 元来购买纪念品. 小丹也无法购买价值 349 元与 347 元的纪念品，因为小丹无法恰好剩下 1 元与 3 元. 接着我们将验证小丹可以购买其他所有不超过 350 元的纪念品，因而她共有 346 种选择.

若小丹只用 2 元，则可以购买所有售价为偶数且不超过 100 元的纪念品；

若小丹用 20 个 5 元以及从 50 个 2 元中每次增加取出 1 个，则可以延伸至购买所有售价为偶数且不超过 200 元的纪念品；

若小丹用 40 个 5 元以及从 50 个 2 元中每次增加取出 1 个，则可以延伸至购买所有售价为偶数且不超过 300 元的纪念品；

若小丹用 25 个 2 元与 50 个 5 元，以及从剩余的 25 个 2 元中每次增加取出 1 个，则可以延伸至购买所有售价为偶数且不超过 350 元的纪念品.

接着来考虑所有售价为奇数元的纪念品.

若小丹用 1 个 5 元以及从 50 个 2 元中每次增加取出 1 个，则可以购买售价介于 5 元至 105 元之间所有奇数元的纪念品；

若小丹用 21 个 5 元以及从 50 个 2 元中每次增加取出 1 个，则可以购买售价介于 105 元至 205 元之间所有奇数元的纪念品；

第 11 章　2013 年第 11 届国际小学数学竞赛

若小丹用 41 个 5 元以及从 50 个 2 元中每次增加取出 1 个,则可以购买售价介于 205 元至 305 元之间所有奇数元的纪念品;

若小丹用 49 个 5 元与 30 个 2 元,以及从剩余的 20 个 2 元中每次增加取出 1 个,则可以购买售价介于 305 元至 345 元之间所有奇数元的纪念品.

此时我们证明了小丹共有 346 种选择.

答:346种

6. **解**　若两个正整数 a 与 b,其中 $2 \leqslant b \leqslant a$,当用 $b-1$ 与 $a+1$ 来替代这两个数时,其和仍不变,但由 $(a+1)^2+(b-1)^2-(a^2+b^2)=2a-2b+2>0$ 可知平方和会增加,故这 1997 个正整数的平方和之最大值发生在 $1996+(2013-1996)^2=2285$.

若两个正整数 a 与 b,其中 $a-b \geqslant 2$,则用 $a-1$ 与 $b+1$ 来替代这两个数时,其和仍不变,但由 $a^2+b^2-(a-1)^2-(b+1)^2=2a-2b-2>0$ 可知平方和会减少,故这 1997 个正整数的平方和之最小值发生在这些数都是 1 或 2,即 $(2×1997-2013)+(2013-1997)×4=2045$. 故所求之值为 $2285-2045=240$.

答:240

7. **解**　因 $1+2+3+\cdots+16=\dfrac{16×17}{2}=136$,故知和的常数为 $136÷4=34$. 在最上一列、最左一行及从左上至右下的对角线的 10 个数之总和为 $34×3-16×2=70$,因此六个涂上阴影的小方格内的数之总 $136-70=66$. 图 11-19 即为可得到最大值的一种填法.

16	2	3	13
5	11	10	8
9	7	6	12
4	14	15	1

图 11-19

答:66

8. **解**　后两种情形可以达成目的,如图 11-20 (a) 和 (b) 所示.

(a)   (b)

图 11-20

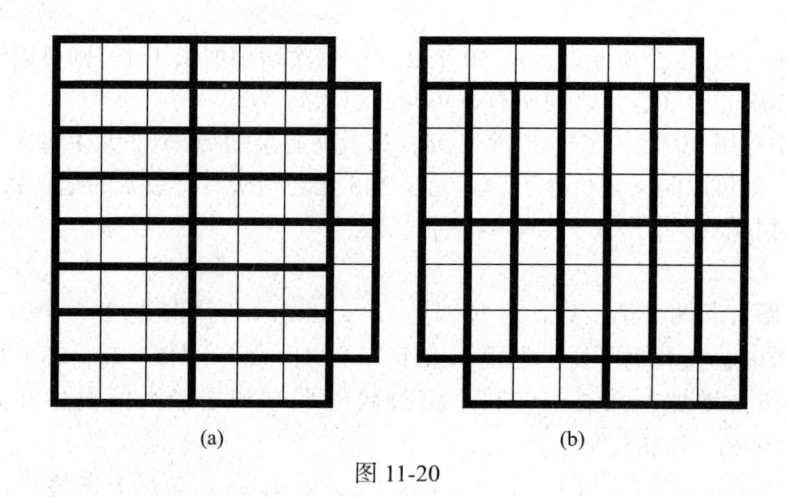

现考虑第一种情形. 在小方格内标记 1、2、3，如图 11-21 所示. 可知任何一片 1×3 或 3×1 的矩形，都会涵盖住一个标记 1 的正方形、一个标记 2 的正方形、一个标记 3 的正方形. 但现有 19 个小正方形标记 1、17 个小正方形标记 2、18 个小正方形标记 3，故证明此情况是不可能完成的.

1	2	3	1	2	3	1
2	3	1	2	3	1	2
3	1	2	3	1	2	3
1	2	3	1	2	3	1
2	3	1	2	3	1	2
3	1	2	3	1	2	3
1	2	3	1	2	3	1
	3	1	2	3		

图 11-21

9. 解 假设算式中两个百位数数码分别为 4 与 5，则接着考虑四个数的个位数之和，若其和为 9，则只能是 0+1+2+6，此时三个十位数数码之和为 3+7+8=18，不符合. 因此四个数的个位数之和必有进位，且可推知三个十位数数码之和为 8. 为要找出两个三位数之差的最小值，故百位数数码为 4 的十位数数码要尽可能大而百位数数码为 5 的十位数数码要尽可能小，所以可判断出取 8=0+1+7，此时四个数的个位数码之和为 2+3+6+8=19，此时可得到差为

第 11 章　2013 年第 11 届国际小学数学竞赛

502−478=24，此即为最小值，因为我们若选用其他的百位数数码，则其差必超过 100．

答：24

10．**解**　因为 1111111111 是红色并且 1112111111 是蓝色，故可以判断出 3323323323 与 3233233233 都是绿色，接着再由 1111111111 是红色并且 3233233233 是绿色可以判断出 2322322322 是蓝色，最后再由 3323323323 是绿色并且 2322322322 是蓝色可以判断出 1231231231 是红色．可知整体的配色方案是判断一个数为红色、蓝色或是绿色是依据这一个数的第四个数码为 1、2 或是 3，此由题目所给定的数据可以得知，且任两个十个数字都不相同的数在第四个数码一定不相同，故一定是不同的颜色．

答：红色

第 12 章 2014 年第 12 届国际小学数学竞赛

12.1 EMIC 个人赛英文试题

Elementary Mathematics International Contest 2014
23rd July, 2014, Daejeon City, Korea

Individual Contest

1. The age of Max now times the age of Mini a year from now is the square of an integer. The age of Max a year from now times the age of Mini now is also the square of an integer. If Mini is 8 years old now, and Max is now older than 1 but younger than 100, how old is Max now?

2. In a choir, more than $\frac{2}{5}$ but less than $\frac{1}{2}$ of the children are boys. What is the smallest possible number of children in this choir?

3. Each girl wants to ride a horse by herself, but there are only enough horses for $\frac{10}{13}$ of them. If the total number of legs of all the horses and girls is 990, how many girls will have to wait for their turns?

4. Clearly, $\frac{23}{30} = \frac{57}{78}$ is incorrect. However, if the same positive integer is subtracted from each of 23, 30, 57 and 78, then it will be correct. What is the number to be subtracted?

5. A team is to be chosen from 4 girls and 6 boys. The only requirement is that it must contain at least 2 girls. How many different teams may be chosen?

6. The product of five positive integers is 2014. How many different values are possible as their sum?

7. A cat has caught three times as many black mice as white mice. Each day, she eats 6 black mice and 4 white mice. After a few days, there are 60 black mice and 4 white mice left. How many mice has the cat caught?

8. M is the midpoint of the side CD of a square $ABCD$ of side length 24 cm. P is a point such that $PA=PB=PM$. What is the minimum length, in cm, of PM?

9. In a party, every two people shake hands except for Bob, who only shakes hands with some of the people. No two people shake hands more than once. If the total number of handshakes is 2014, with how many people does Bob shake hands?

10. The cost of a ticket for a concert is \$26 for an adult, \$18 for a youth and \$10 for a child. The total cost of a party of 131 people is \$2014. How many more children than adults are in the party?

11. Two overlapping squares with parallel sides are such that the part common to both squares has an area of 4 cm^2. This is $\frac{1}{9}$ the area of the larger square and $\frac{1}{4}$ of the area of the smaller square. What is the minimum perimeter, in cm, of the eight-sided figure formed by the overlapping squares?

12. The number of stars in the sky is $8\times 12+98\times 102+998\times 1002+\cdots+99\cdots98\times 100\cdots02$. In the last term, there are 2014 copies of the digit 9 in $99\cdots98$ and 2014 copies of the digit 0 in $100\cdots02$. What is the sum of the digits of the number of stars?

13. In a triangle ABC, D is a point on BC and F is a point on AB. The point K of reflection of B across DF is on the opposite side of AC to B. AC intersects FK at P and DK at Q. The total area of triangles AFP, PKQ and QDC is 10 cm^2. If we add to this the area of the quadrilateral $DFPQ$, we obtain $\frac{2}{3}$ of the area of ABC. What is the area, in cm^2, of triangle ABC?

14. After Nadia goes up a hill, she finds a level path on top of length 2.5 km. At the end of it, she goes down the hill to a pond. Later, she goes back along the same route. Her walking speed is 5 kph, but it decreases to 4 kph going up the hill, and increases to 6 kph going down the hill. Her outward journey takes 1 hour 36 minutes but her return journey takes 1 hour 39 minutes. She does not stop anywhere at any time. What is the length, in km, from start point to the pond?

15. Five colours are available for the painting of the six faces of a cube. One colour is used to paint two of the faces, while each of the other four colours is used to paint one

face. How many differently painted cubes can there be? Two cubes painting the same colours on corresponding faces after rotation or flip are not considered to be different.

12.2 EMIC 个人赛中文试题

2014 年国际小学数学竞赛个人竞赛试题

1. 大宝现在的年龄乘以小宝明年同一日的年龄等于一个整数的平方，大宝明年同一日的年龄乘以小宝现在的年龄也等于一个整数的平方．若小宝现在的年龄为 8 岁，大宝的年龄大于 1 岁、小于 100 岁，请问大宝现在几岁？

2. 有一个合唱团，儿童团员中有超过 $\frac{2}{5}$ 但少于 $\frac{1}{2}$ 是男孩．请问此合唱团最少可能有多少位儿童团员？

3. 每位女孩都希望能独自骑一匹马，但现有的马只足够让她们人数的 $\frac{10}{13}$ 骑．已知所有马脚的数量与女孩脚的数量之总和为 990，请问共有多少位女孩目前没有马可骑？

4. 显然，$\frac{23}{30} = \frac{57}{78}$ 是错误的．但是，如果将 23、30、57 与 78 各减去一个相同的正整数，则它将变成正确的．请问减去的数是什么？

5. 从 4 位女孩与 6 位男孩中选出一支代表队．若要求代表队员中至少要有 2 位女孩，请问共有多少种不同的组队方法？

6. 五个正整数的乘积等于 2014．请问这五个数的和可能有多少种不同的值？

7. 一只猫捕获的黑鼠是白鼠的三倍．如果它每天都吃掉 6 只黑鼠与 4 只白鼠．经过数日后，还剩下 60 只黑鼠与 4 只白鼠．请问这只猫原先共捕获多少只老鼠？

8. 正方形 ABCD 的边长为 24 cm，点 M 是 CD 边上的中点，若点 P 满足 PA=PB=PM，请问 PM 的最小长度为多少 cm？

9. 在某次宴会上，除了小柏以外的每个人都互相各恰握一次手，而小柏只与部分的人握手，没有任两个人握手超过一次．已知握手总次数为 2014 次，请问小柏与多少人握手？

10. 音乐会入场券的票价为成人票每张 26 美元、青年票每张 18 美元、儿童票每张 10 美元．有一个社团共花费 2014 美元购买 131 张入场券，请问这个社团购买的儿童票比成人票多几张？

11. 将两个正方形以对应边互相平行的方式叠放，使重叠部分的面积为 4 cm^2. 已知重叠部分的面积占大正方形面积的 $\frac{1}{9}$、占小正方形面积的 $\frac{1}{4}$，请问这两个正方形叠放后所组成的八边形之周长的最小值为多少 cm？

12. 天空中星星的数量为 $8 \times 12 + 98 \times 102 + 998 \times 1002 + \cdots + 99\cdots98 \times 100\cdots02$，其中最后一项的 $99\cdots98$ 中有 2014 个 9、在 $100\cdots02$ 中有 2014 个 0. 请问星星数量的值的数码之和是什么？

13. 在 $\triangle ABC$ 中（图 12-1），点 D 在 BC 边上，点 F 在 AB 边上，点 B 以 DF 为对称轴的对称点为 K，且点 K 与点 B 在 AC 边的异侧. AC 边交 FK 于点 P，交 DK 于点 Q. 已知 $\triangle AFP$、$\triangle PKQ$、$\triangle QDC$ 的面积总和为 10 cm^2，且这三个三角形加上四边形 $DFPQ$ 的面积之总和为 $\triangle ABC$ 的面积的 $\frac{2}{3}$，请问 $\triangle ABC$ 的面积为多少 cm^2？

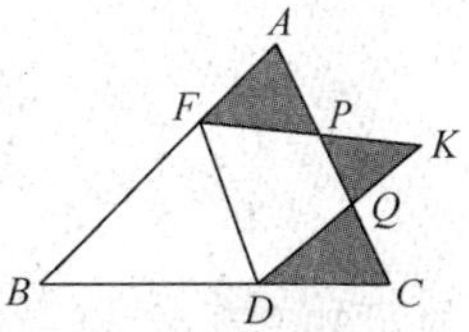

图 12-1

14. 小娜先走一段上坡的路，当她到达山顶后再走一段长为 2.5 km 的平路，接着再走一段下坡的路抵达一个池塘，稍后她便沿着原路返回. 已知她在平路上的速度为每小时 5 km、上坡的速度为每小时 4 km、下坡的速度为每小时 6 km. 若她从出发至抵达池塘共用了 1 小时 36 分钟，而返程则用了 1 小时 39 分钟，且途中没有任何停留. 请问从出发地点到池塘的总路程是多少 km？

15. 使用五种颜色将一个正六面体的表面涂色，其中某一种颜色涂两个面，而其他四种颜色各恰涂一个面. 请问共有多少种不同的涂色方法？（注：正六面体经旋转或翻转后，若一种涂色方法与另一种涂色方法相同，则视为是同一种涂色方法.)

12.3 EMIC 个人赛试题解答与评注

2014 年国际小学数学竞赛个人竞赛试题解答

1. **解** 因小宝现在的年龄 8 可以看成是 2 乘以一个平方数，故大宝一年之后的年龄也会是 2 乘以一个平方数；可知小宝一年之后的年龄 9 是一个平方数，故大宝现在年龄也会是一个平方数，且可推知其值为一个奇平方数. 介于 1 到 100 之间的奇平方数有 9、25、49、81，其中 9+1、25+1、81+1 都不是 2

乘以一个平方数,仅 $49+1=2\times 5^2$ 是 2 乘以一个平方数,故知大宝现在是 49 岁.

答: 49 岁

2. **解** 从分数 $\frac{0}{1}<\frac{1}{1}$ 开始,将相邻的两个分数之分子、分母分别相加而得到的新分数,其值会介于这两个分数之间,即 $\frac{0}{1}<\frac{1}{2}<\frac{1}{1}$. 继续操作下去,可得

$$\frac{0}{1}<\frac{1}{3}<\frac{1}{2}<\frac{2}{3}<\frac{1}{1},$$

$$\frac{0}{1}<\frac{1}{4}<\frac{1}{3}<\frac{2}{5}<\frac{1}{2}<\frac{3}{5}<\frac{2}{3}<\frac{3}{4}<\frac{1}{1} \text{ 与}$$

$$\frac{0}{1}<\frac{1}{5}<\frac{1}{4}<\frac{2}{7}<\frac{1}{3}<\frac{3}{8}<\frac{2}{5}<\frac{3}{7}<\frac{1}{2}<\frac{4}{7}<\frac{3}{5}<\frac{5}{8}<\frac{2}{3}<\frac{5}{7}<\frac{3}{4}<\frac{4}{5}<\frac{1}{1}.$$

故可知介于 $\frac{2}{5}$ 与 $\frac{1}{2}$ 之间,分母最小的分数为 $\frac{2+1}{5+2}=\frac{3}{7}$,因此合唱团中至少有 7 位儿童,且当恰有 7 位儿童时共有 3 位男孩.

答: 7 位

3. **解** 由比例关系知可将每 13 位女孩与每 10 匹马分为一组,每一组所有马腿的数量与女孩腿的数量之总和为 $13\times 2+10\times 4=66$. 现已知共有 990 条腿,故知共可分为 $990\div 66=15$ 组,因此可再推知共有 $(13-10)\times 15=45$ 位女孩目前没有马可骑.

答: 45 位

4. **解** 在减去这个相同的正整数之前与之后,其分子之差都等于 $57-23=34$、其分母之差都等于 $78-30=48$,故知在正确的等式中,这两个分数都应等于 $\frac{34}{48}=\frac{17}{24}$. 观察并计算后可得知 $\frac{23-6}{30-6}=\frac{17}{24}$、$\frac{57-6}{78-6}=\frac{51}{72}=\frac{17}{24}$,因此减去的数为 6.

答: 6

5. **解** 可知如果连全部女孩与男孩同时都不选择都当作一种组队方法,则所有的组队方法共有 $2^{10}=1024$ 种,其中一个女孩都不选择的组队方法有 $2^6=64$ 种、仅选择一位女孩的组队方法有 $4\times 2^6=256$ 种,因此满足题意的组队方法共有 $1024-64-256=704$ 种.

答: 704 种

6. **解** 将 2014 作质因子分解之后可得 $2014=2\times 19\times 53$. 此时可推知:

若这五个正整数中恰有 2 个 1,则这五个正整数为 1、1、2、19、53,其和仅有 1 个可能值;

第12章　2014年第12届国际小学数学竞赛

若这五个正整数中恰有 3 个 1，则因其余的两个正整数中，必恰有一个正整数是由这三个质因子中的两个素数相乘之值而另一个正整数为第三个素数，因此可再推知这五个正整数为

(1) 1、1、1、2×19、53；(2) 1、1、1、2×53、19；(3) 1、1、1、19×53、2.
故知其和会有 3 个可能值；

若这五个正整数中恰有 4 个 1，则这五个正整数为 1、1、1、1、2014，其和仅有 1 个可能值．

此时可判断出这五个可能值都不相等，因此共有 5 种不同的值．

答：5

7. **解**　此时如果这只猫再多吃一天，则会仅剩下 54 只黑鼠．接着逐日回溯过去，白鼠每回溯一天，会增加 4 只，而黑鼠会比白鼠再多增加 2 只，故可判断知需要回溯 54÷2=27 天才能使得黑鼠比白鼠多增加的数目与最后剩下的黑鼠数目相等．而由题意可知，开始时黑鼠是白鼠的 3 倍，即开始时黑鼠比白鼠多了 2 倍，因此可以得知实际上仅需回溯 27÷3=9 天即为开始的日子，因此这只猫原先捕获 4×9=36 只白鼠、3×36=108 只黑鼠，合计共捕获 36+108=144 只老鼠．

答：144 只

8. **解**　如图 12-2 所示，令 N 为 AB 的中点，则可知 AN=12(cm)．由对称性可判断出点 P 会落在 MN 之间使得 PA=PB．若点 P 愈靠近点 N，则 PA 愈短且 PM 愈长．因此可再判断知点 P 仅有一个可能的位置．而计算后可发现当 PN=9(cm)时，$PA^2 = 12^2 + 9^2 = 15^2$(cm)，PA=15(cm)，且 PM=24−9=15(cm)．故知所求为 15(cm)．

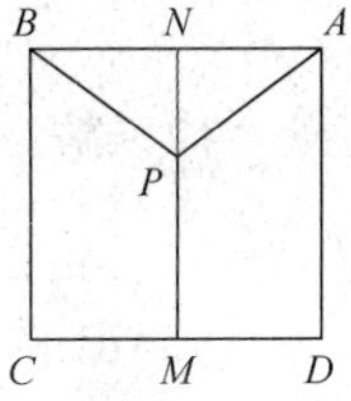

图 12-2

答：15 cm

9. **解**　若共有 63 人，则总握手次数至多为 $\frac{63 \times 62}{2}=1953$ 次，此数仍少于 2014；若共有 64 人，则握手总次数至多为 $\frac{64 \times 63}{2}=2016$ 次，此数比 2014 多了 2 次，此时可推知小柏只与 63−2=61 人握手；若共有 65 人，则握手总次数至多为 $\frac{65 \times 64}{2}=2080$ 次，此数比 2014 多了 66 次，此时可推知即使小柏没有与人握手，此时握手总次数是由 2080 降至 2016，仍比 2014 多了 2 次，故不合．因此可推知此宴会中共有 64 人参与，而小柏只与其中 61 人握手．

答：61 人

10. **解** 观察可知一张成人票与一张儿童票的总价与两张青年的票价相同，因此可将一张成人票与一张儿童票同时替换为两张青年票，且不会影响总价。若全部都是青年票，则总票价为 18×131=2358 美元，比现在实际的花费多了 2358–2014=344 美元，故可推得经过这样的替换后，仍有儿童票留着而无法被替换。因一张儿童票比一张青年票的票价少 $8，故知经过这样的替换后还有 344÷8=43 美元位儿童票无法被替换，此即为这个社团购买的儿童票比成人票多的张数。

答：43 位

11. **解** 可知大正方形的面积为 9×4=36(cm^2)，故其边长为 6(cm)；而小正方形的面积为 4×4=16(cm^2)，故其边长为 4(cm)。观察可知这两个正方形所组成的八边形周长为两个正方形的周长总和与重叠部分的矩形周长之差，其中重叠部分的矩形之面积为一定值。因此须使重叠部分的矩形之周长为最大值时才可求出所求之八边形周长的最小值，即须使重叠部分的矩形的长、宽之差愈大愈好，可推知重叠部分的矩形之长、宽差最大值发生在长为 4(cm)、宽为 1(cm)，如图 12-3 所示，因此所求为 4×(6+4)−2×(4+1)=30(cm)。

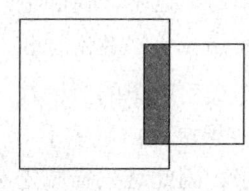

图 12-3

答：30 cm

12. **解** 天空中星星的颗数为

(10−2)(10+2) + (100−2)(100+2) + ⋯ + (100⋯00−2)(100⋯00+2)
= (100−4) + (10000−4) + ⋯ + (100⋯00−4)
= 1010⋯10100 − 4×2015
= 1010⋯10100 − 8060
= 1010⋯02040

且可观察出此数中数码 1 的个数为 2015−2=2013 个，因此其数码和为 2013+2+4=2019。

答：2019

13. **解** 为了方便起见，不妨用符号 [*] 来表示区域 * 的面积。则有

$$[DFPQ] = [ABC] − ([BDF] + [AFP] + [CDQ])$$
$$= [ABC] − ([DFK] + [AFP] + [CDQ])$$
$$= [ABC] − ([DFPQ] + [KPQ] + [AFP] + [CDQ])$$
$$= [ABC] − \frac{2}{3}[ABC]$$
$$= \frac{1}{3}[ABC]$$

因此可推知 $[KPQ]+[AFP]+[CDQ]=\frac{1}{3}[ABC]$．故有 $[ABC]=3\times10=30\,(\text{cm}^2)$．

答：30 cm²

14．**解** 可知小娜上坡时每 km 需费时 15 分钟、下坡时每 km 需费时 10 分钟，即上坡 1 km 与下坡 1 km 共需费时 25 分钟，而她走平路时去程与返程各分别费时 2.5÷5=0.5 小时，即 30 分钟．因她来回共费时 3 小时 15 分，故知来回的上坡与下坡共费时 $3\times60+15-30\times2=135$ 分钟，故知不是平路的路程共有 135÷25=5.4(km)，因此从出发地点到池塘的总路程是 5.4+2.5=7.9(km)．

答：7.9 km

15．**解** 可知所涂的两个面可能是相邻的两个面或相对的两个面，而涂这两个面的颜色共有 5 种选择．若已选定涂两面的颜色，则：

(1) 当这两个面是相对的两个面时，在其他的面中选出一个面并涂上另一个颜色，此时与该面相对的面共有 3 种涂色的选择，且无论另两个面如何涂色，经过旋转后都可变成相同的涂色方式；

(2) 当这两个面是相邻的两个面时，此时将这与两个面相对的面涂色方式共有 $\frac{4\times3}{2}=6$ 种，且对于每一种涂色法，再将最后另两个面的涂色方式共有 2 种．因此可以推知合计共有 $5\times(3+12)=75$ 种不同将此正六面体涂色的方法．

答：75 种

12.4　EMIC 队际赛英文试题

Elementary Mathematics International Contest 2014
23rd July，2014，Daejeon City，Korea

Team Contest

1. Exactly one pair of brackets is to be inserted into the expression
$$2\times2-2\times2-2\times2-2\times2-2\times2.$$
The left bracket must come before a 2 and the right bracket after a 2. Determine the largest possible value of the resulting expression.

2. Divide the 18 numbers 1, 2, ⋯, 18 into nine pairs such that the sum of the two numbers in each pair is the square of an integer.

3. The diagram below shows a right isosceles triangle partitioned into four

shaded right isosceles triangles and a number of squares. The side lengths of all the squares are positive integers. The smallest ten squares are of side length 1 cm. Determine the total area, in cm^2, of the four shaded triangles.

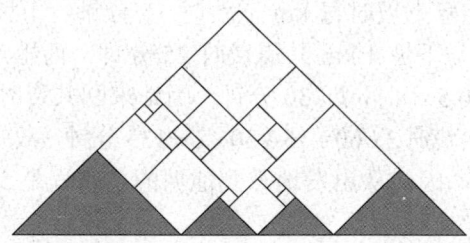

4. Each of the five families living in apartments 2, 3, 4, 6 and 12 in a building will adopt one of five cats, whose ages are 1, 2, 3, 4 and 6. The adopting family's apartment number must be divisible by the age of the cat. Find all possible adoption schemes.

	1-year-old	2-year-old	3-year-old	4-year-old	6-year-old
(1)					
(2)					
(3)					
(4)					
(5)					
(6)					
(7)					
(8)					
(9)					
(10)					
(11)					
(12)					
(13)					
⋮					

5. The positive integers 1, 2, ⋯, 2014 strung together form a very long multi-digit number 12345678910111213⋯201220132014. A seven-digit multiple of 11 is obtained by erasing all the digits before it and all the digits after it. Determine the smallest possible value of this seven-digit number, which may not start with the digit 0.

6. The diagram below shows a hexagonal configuration of 19 dots in an equilateral triangular grid.

(a) Determine the number of equilateral triangles of different sizes with all three vertices among the 19 dots. Draw an equilateral triangle of each size on the diagram.

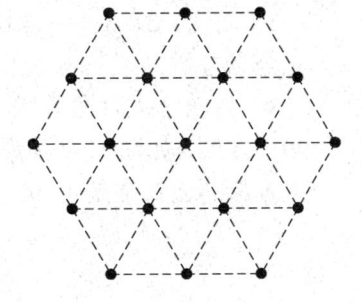

(b) Determine the number of equilateral triangles of each size.

7. Each of teams A, B, C, D and E plays against every other team exactly once. A win is worth 3 points, a draw 1 point and a loss 0 points. At the end of the tournament, no two teams have the same number of points. A has the highest number of points despite losing to B. Neither B nor C loses any game, but C has fewer points than D. How many points does E have?

8. P is a point inside a square $ABCD$ of side length 8 cm. What is the largest possible value of the area, in cm^2, of the smallest one among the six triangles PAB, PBC, PCD, PDA, PAC and PBD?

9. A sequence of 2014 two-digit numbers is such that each is a multiple of 19 or 23, and the tens digit of any number starting from the second is equal to the units digit of the preceding number. If the last number in the sequence is 23, determine the first number in the sequence.

10. There are ten real coins all of the same weight. There is a fake coin which is heavier than a real coin, and another fake coin which is lighter than a real coin. You cannot tell the coins apart. Explain how, in four weighing using a balance, you may determine whether the total weight of the two fake coins is greater than, equal to or less than the total weight of two real coins?

12.5 EMIC队际赛中文试题

2014年国际小学数学竞赛队标竞赛试题

1. 在算式 2×2−2×2−2×2−2×2−2×2 中恰好添加一个括号，左括号必须在某个 2 之前、右括号必须在某个 2 之后．请问添加括号后算式最大的可能值是多少？

2. 将 1、2、3、…、18 等十八个数分为 9 对，使得每对的两个数之和都为完全平方数.

3. 将一个大直角等腰三角形分割为四个涂上阴影的小直角等腰三角形与一些正方形，如图 12-4 所示. 已知每个正方形的边长都是正整数，且最小的十个正方形的边长都是 1 cm. 请问四个涂上阴影的三角形的总面积是多少 cm^2？

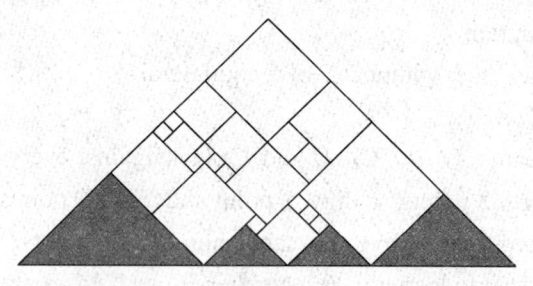

图 12-4

4. 五户家庭所住公寓的门牌号码分别是 2，3，4，6 与 12 号. 他们各收养了一只猫，这些猫的年龄分别是 1、2、3、4、6 岁. 若要求收养家庭的门牌号码必须被所收养的猫的年龄整除. 请列出表 12-1 所有可能的收养方案.

表 12-1

方案	1岁的猫	2岁的猫	3岁的猫	4岁的猫	6岁的猫
(1)					
(2)					
(3)					
(4)					
(5)					
(6)					
(7)					
(8)					
(9)					
(10)					
(11)					
(12)					
(13)					
⋮					

5. 将正整数 1、2、3、…、2014 依序接连写在一起，变成一个非常长的多位数 12345678910111213…201220132014．从中选出一段七位数并删除在此数之前与之后的所有数码，使得此七位数可被 11 整除．若此七位数的首位数码不能为 0，请问此七位数的最小可能值是多少？

6. 如图 12-5 所示是一个由 19 个正三角格子点所构成的六边形图形．

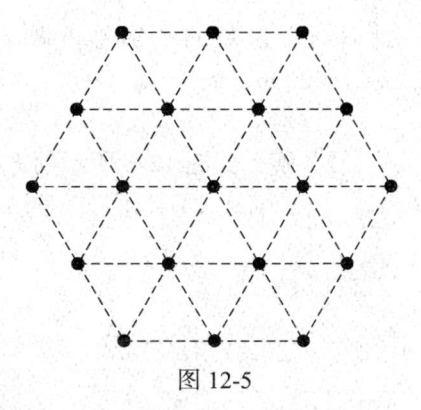

(1)请问三个顶点都在这 19 个格点上的正三角形有多少种不同的边长？在图中画出每种边长的正三角形，每种只需画出一个．

(2)请问在此图上各种不同边长的正三角形分别有多少个？

图 12-5

7. 五支球队 A、B、C、D、E 都恰互相比赛一场，赢队可得 3 分、输队得 0 分、平手则各得 1 分．比赛结束后，结果任何两队的总得分都不相同，虽然 A 队的总得分最高但被 B 队打败，B 队与 C 队都没有输过任何一场，且 C 队的总得分少于 D 队．请问 E 队的总得分为多少分？

8. 点 P 在边长为 8 cm 的正方形 $ABCD$ 之内部．请问六个 △PAB、△PBC、△PCD、△PDA、△PAC、△PBD 之中面积最小的三角形之最大值是多少 cm^2？

9. 有一个数列，它是由 2014 个两位数所构成的，每个两位数都是 19 或 23 的倍数，且数列中从第二个数开始，每个数的十位数码都等于前一个数码的个位数码．已知此数列的最末一个数为 23，请问此数列的第一个数是什么？

10. 有十枚重量相同的真币，同时有一枚比真币重的假币与另一枚比真币轻的假币，但我们无法从外观分辨它们．请问如何用没有刻度的天平最多秤四次，即可确定这两枚假币的总重量比两枚真币的总重量重、轻或相等？

12.6　EMIC 队际赛试题解答与评注

2014 年国际小学数学竞赛队标竞赛试题解答

1. **解**　观察可知，若在括号内没有任何的减号，则该式的值为−12．因此为了要使算式的值最大，在括号内至少要包含一个减号，且括号内的取值必须为尽可能小的负数．综合以上观察，可考虑算式 2×2−2×(2−2×2−2×2−2×2)=24，此时对于末端的右括号再做一个修正即可得最大值 2×2–2×(2–2×2–2×2–2)×2=36.

答：36

2. 解 如图 12-6 所示的方式，在每一个方格内分别填入这些数字，且若两个数字之和为一个平方数，则在两个方格间用一条直线连接．此时可发现，有三个数字分别都只有另一个数字可使其和为平方数：(18, 7)、(17, 8)与(16, 9)．接着继续观察所做的表格便可得知其余六对数为 (2, 14)、(11, 5)、(4, 12)、(13, 3)、(6, 10)与 (15, 1)．

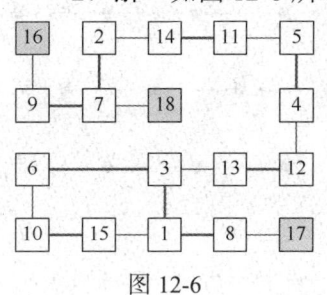

图 12-6

答：(18, 7)，(17, 8)，(16, 9)，(2, 14)，(11, 5)，(4, 12)，(13, 3)，(6, 10)，(15, 1)

答：见图 12-6

【评注】 学生或许仅得到部分的配对．若是利用有系统的推理方法但有些许瑕疵而得出其答案，至多可给 30 分；若仅给配对而没有提供推理方法，每给出一个正确的配对可得 2 分，若给出不正确的配对，每个不正确的配对倒扣 2 分．

3. 解 由最小的正方形边长为 1(cm) 便可以得知其余各个正方形的边长，再利用这些正方形的边长便可以得知所有阴影部分的等腰直角三角形的两股长，即可得知其总面积为 $\frac{1}{2}(9^2+4^2+4^2+7^2)=81(\text{cm}^2)$.

答：81 cm^2

4. 解 可知 1 岁的猫都可能是任一户所饲养的，而 4 岁的猫只可能被门牌号码为 4 号与 12 号的家庭所饲养．因此可考虑以下两种情况．

情况 1：4 岁的猫被门牌号码为 12 号的家庭所饲养：

此时 6 岁的猫只可被门牌号码为 6 号的家庭所饲养，而 3 岁的猫只可被门牌号码为 3 号的家庭所饲养．因此 2 岁的猫可能被门牌号码为 2 号或 4 号的家庭所饲养，而 1 岁的猫被另一户所饲养．故知此情况共有两种可能的饲养方案．

情况 2：4 岁的猫被门牌号码为 4 号的家庭所饲养：

此时 6 岁的猫只可被门牌号码为 6 号或 12 号的家庭所饲养，而无论是何种情况，6 号与 12 号这两户中的另一户可能饲养的猫都是为 1 岁、2 岁或 3 岁这三种，且一旦决定了另一户所饲养的猫，最后 2 户所饲养的猫也随之决定，故知共有 2×3×1=6 种可能的饲养方案．

第 12 章 2014 年第 12 届国际小学数学竞赛

综上所述，共有 2+6=8 种可能的饲养方案，如表 12-2.

表 12-2

1岁的猫	2岁的猫	3岁的猫	4岁的猫	6岁的猫
4号	2号	3号	12号	6号
2号	4号	3号	12号	6号
12号	2号	3号	4号	6号
2号	12号	3号	4号	6号
3号	2号	12号	4号	6号
6号	2号	3号	4号	12号
2号	6号	3号	4号	12号
3号	2号	6号	4号	12号

答：见表 12-2

【评注】学生或许得到不完整的饲养方案．若是利用有系统的推理方法但有些许瑕疵而得出其答案，至多可给 30 分；若仅给饲养方案而没有提供推理方法，每给出一个正确的配对可得 3 分，若给出错误方案，每个错误方案倒扣 3 分，直到 0 分为止．

5. **解** 为了要得到最小值，考虑首位数码为 1，且首位数码 1 之后连续出现数码 0 的个数要尽可能多．由数的形成规则可知，1 之后连续两个 0 会首次出现在 100，与接下来四个数码所形成的七位数为 1001011，且此数恰为 11 的倍数；而比这一个数小的数必为首位数码 1 之后连续三个 0，此数会出现在 1000，与接下来三个数码所形成的七位数为 1000100，但此数不为 11 的倍数．故所求的最小值为 1001011．

答：1001011

6. **解** (1) 如图 12-7 所示，共有 6 种不同边长的正三角形．

(2) 直接观察可知边长最长的三角形共有两个；

观察边长次长的三角形，可知此类正三角形的三个顶点分别为大正六边形不相邻的三边的中点，故知共有两个这样的正三角形；

现观察边长第三长的三角形，可知此类

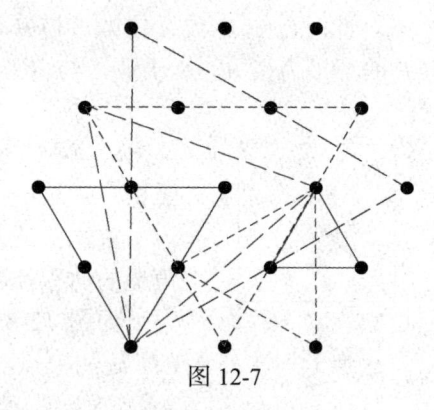

图 12-7

正三角形的三个顶点中，必有一个恰为最大正六边形的顶点，且最大正六边形的每一个顶点恰为两个这一类不同正三角形的顶点，故知共有 12 个这样的正三角形；

接着观察边长第四长的正三角形，对于每找到一个两个顶点在上方、一个顶点在下方的三角形，都有另一个一个顶点在上方、两个顶点在下方的三角形会对应出现．直接计算，可知两个顶点在上方、一个顶点在下方的此类三角形共有 6 个，故知合计共有 12 个这样的正三角形；

现观察边长次短的正三角形，可知此类每一个正三角形的内心皆为大正六边形内部的点，且大正六边形每一个内部的点恰为两个这一类不同正三角形的内心，故知共有 14 个这样的正三角形；

最后观察边长最短的正三角形，直接记数可知知共有 24 个这样的正三角形．

【评注】(1)得到正确答案，给 10 分；若答案为 4，则给 5 分；若答案为 3，则给 2 分；其余的答案，不给分．

(2)每得到一种大小的三角形个数，给 5 分．较简单的情况可不要求计算过程，但对于较复杂的情况，若不利用有系统的推理方式，则不容易计算出正确个数．

7. **解** 可知 A 得分最高的情况必发生在被 B 击败、与 C 平手且击败 D、E 的情况，即得 3+3+1=7 分的时候；而因 B 没有输过任何一场且击败 A，故 B 的得分至少为 3+1+1+1=6 分．此时再由任何两队的总得分不相同可判断出 A 即为得 7 分、B 即为得 6 分，即 B 与 C、D、E 都是平手的情况．

此时已知 C 与 A、B 都是平手，故 C 得分至少为 4 分且少于 D 的得分，因此再由 A、B 的得分可判断出 D 得 5 分、C 得 4 分，即 C 与 D、E 也是平手．

此时已知 D 被 A 击败、与 B、C 平手且共得 5 分，因此 D 必击败 E．所以 E 的赛果为被 A、D 击败，与 B、C 平手，因此 E 的得分为 2 分．

答：2 分

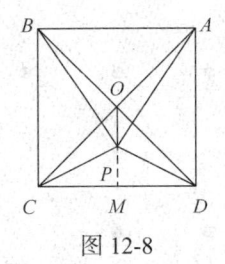

8. **解** 为了方便起见，不妨用符号 [*] 来表示区域 * 的面积．

首先验证存在一点 P 使得这六个三角形中的每一个三角形的面积都至少为 8(cm²)．

如图 12-8 所示，令点 O 为正方形的中心，而点 M 为 CD 边的中点，接着取点 P 为 MO 的中点，此时可以得知

图 12-8

$[PBC]=[PDA]$ 且 $[PAB]$ 的值大于 $[PCD]$，并可进一步计算得知 $[PAC]=[PBD]=2[POD]=[PCD]=\frac{1}{2}PM\times CD=8(\text{cm}^2)$．

若存在一点 P 使得这六个三角形中的每一个三角形的面积都大于 $8(\text{cm}^2)$，可假设点 P 落在 $\triangle OCD$ 内，则有

$$16=[PCD]+[POC]+[POD]$$
$$=[PCD]+\frac{1}{2}[PAC]+\frac{1}{2}[PBD]$$
$$>8+4+4$$
$$=16$$

此为矛盾的结果，即这样的点 P 不存在．故可推知这六个三角形中面积最小的三角形之最大值是 $8(\text{cm}^2)$．

答：8 cm^2

【评注】若仅由观察一个特例但没有给出最大值的证明而得到答案，得 20 分；若给出有意义但不完整的证明，可至多再给予 10 分；若所给的答案较小，且有给出例子及有意义的证明，至多给予 10 分．

9．**解** 可知在两位数中，19 与 23 的倍数有 19、23、38、46、57、69、76、92 与 95，其中仅 (57, 76, 69, 95) 可形成一个依题意规则循环重复出现的数列，而 19 与 46 只有可能是此数列的第一个数、38 只有可能为此数列的最后一个数，且此仅发生在 38 的前两个数依序为 92、23 时．现已知第 2014 个数为 23，故第 2013 个数为 92，而第 2012 个数为 69，再由 2014=503×4+2 可以观察出 69 必为循环重复出现的数列中的第四个，即这一个循环重复出现的数列顺序应为 (95, 57, 76, 69)，故可以判断出这个数列的第一个数是 95．

答：95

10．**解** 可将这 12 个硬币每三个一组分成 A、B、C、D 四组．第一次秤重比较 A、B 两组之间的重量关系、第二次秤重比较 C、D 两组之间的关系．此时有三种情形．

情形 1：两次秤重都是平衡．

此时可以判断出两枚假币都在同一组内，且两枚假币的总重量与两枚真币的总重量相等．

情形 2：只有一次秤重是平衡．

不妨令 A 组与 B 组的重量相等、C 组的重量大于 D 组的重量，此时可以

判断出两枚假币一定在 C 组与 D 组中，此时只要将 A、B 两组都置于天平一侧，C、D 两组置于天平另一侧，便可判断出这两枚假币之总重量比两枚真币之总重量重、轻或相等.

情形 3：两次秤重都不平衡.

不妨令 A 组的重量大于 B 组的重量、C 组的重量大于 D 组的重量，此时无论重假币在 A 组中、轻假币在 D 组中，或是重假币在 C 组中、轻假币在 B 组中，只要第三次秤重比较 A、D 两组之间的关系便可得知此时是何种情况，最后一次秤重再将 A、D 两组都置于天平一侧，B、C 两组置于天平另一侧，便可判断出这两枚假币之总重量比两枚真币之总重量重、轻或相等.

【评注】若利用五次秤重判断出来，得 20 分. 若给出可行的四次秤重的判断方式，但有瑕疵而无法实际利用四次秤重判断出来，至多给予 20 分.

第13章 2015年第13届国际小学数学竞赛

13.1 EMIC个人赛英文试题

Elementary Mathematics International Contest 2015
29th July, 2015, Changchun, China

Individual Contest

1. Find the smallest four-digit number which has the same number of positive divisors as 2015.

2. Each students is asked to remove three of the first twenty-one positive integers $(1, 2, 3, \cdots, 21)$ and calculate the sum of the remaining eighteen numbers. The three numbers removed by each student contain two consecutive numbers, and no two students remove the same three numbers. At most how many students can correctly get 212 as the answer?

3. $ABCD$ is a rectangular house. A fence extends AB to E with $BE = 80$ m. A fence extends BC to F with $CF = 70$ m. A fence extends CD to G with $DG = 50$ m. A fence extends DA to H with $AH = 90$ m. Fences through E and G parallel to AD and fences through F and H parallel to AB are built, enclosing a rectangular plot with four rectangular gardens around the house. The sum of the perimeters of the four gardens is 2016 m. What is the perimeter, in m, of the house?

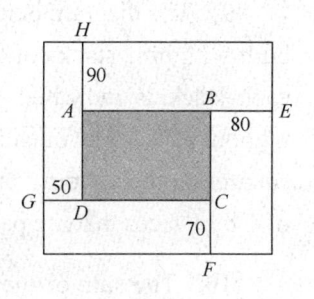

4. A certain community is divided into organizations, each organization is divided into associations, each association is divided into societies and each society is divided into clubs. The number of clubs in each society, the number of societies in each association and the number of associations in each organization are the same integer which is greater than 1. The community has a president, as does each

organization, association, society and club. If there are 161 presidential positions altogether, how many organizations are there in this community?

5. Each of the machines A and B can produce one bottle per minute. Machine A has to rest for one minute after producing 3 bottles and Machine B has to rest 1.5 minutes after producing 5 bottles. What is the minimum number of minutes for these two machines to produce 2015 bottles together?

6. The six digits 1, 2, 3, 4, 5 and 6 are used to construct a one-digit number, a two-digit number and a three-digit number. Each must be used only once and all six digits must be used. The sum of the one-digit number and the two-digit number is 47 and the sum of the two-digit number and the three-digit number is 358. Find the sum of all the three numbers.

7. E is a point on the side BC of a square $ABCD$ such that $BE = 20$ cm and $CE = 28$ cm. P is a point of the diagonal BD. What is the smallest possible value, in cm, of $PE + PC$?

8. In a group of distinct positive integers, the largest one is less than 36, and is equal to three times the smallest one. The smallest number is equal to two-thirds of the group average. At most how many numbers are there in this group?

9. The diagram below shows the top view of a structure built with nine stacks of unit cubes. The number of cubes in each stack is indicated. Each stack rises from the bottom without gaps. The outside surface, including the nine 1 by 1 squares on the bottom, are painted. What is the total number of 1 by 1 faces that are painted?

10. The sum of the digits of each of four different three-digit numbers is the same, and the sum of these four numbers is 2015. Find the sum of all possible values of the common digit sum of the four numbers.

11. There are three positive integers. The first is a two-digit number which consists of two identical digits. The second one is a two-digit number which consists of two different digits, and its units digit is the same as that of the first number. The third one is a one-digit number which consists of only one digit, which

is the same as the tens digit of the second number. Exactly two of these three numbers are prime numbers. In how many different ways can the three positive integers be chosen?

12. A positive integer is divided by 5. The quotient and the remainder are recorded. The same number is divided by 3. Again the quotient and the remainder are recorded. If the same two numbers in different order are recorded, find the product of all possible values of the original number.

13. E is a point of the side AB of a rectangle $ABCD$ such that $AE = 2EB$, and Z is the midpoint of the side BC. M and N are the midpoints of DE and DZ respectively. If the area of the triangle EMN is 5 cm^2, calculate the area, in cm^2, of the pentagon $MEBZN$.

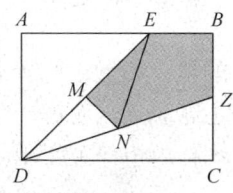

14. In how many ways can we divide the numbers $1, 2, 3, \cdots, 12$ into four groups, each containing three numbers whose sum is divisible by 3?

15. A number from $1, 2, 3, \cdots, 19$ is said to be a follower of a second number from $1, 2, 3, \cdots, 19$ if either the second number is 10 to 18 more than the first, or the first number is 1 to 9 more than the second. Thus 6 is a follower of 16, 17, 18, 19, 1, 2, 3, 4 and 5. In how many ways can we choose three numbers from $1, 2, 3, \cdots, 19$ such that the first is a follower of the second, the second is a follower of the third, and the first is also a follower of the third?

13.2　EMIC个人赛中文试题

2015年国际小学数学竞赛个人竞赛试题

1. 请问与2015的正因子个数相同的最小四位数是什么？

2. 每位学生从1、2、3、⋯、20、21这二十一个正整数中移除三个正整数并计算其余十八个正整数的和，且在被移除的三个正整数中，有两个数为连续的正整数．若没有两位学生移除的三个正整数完全相同，请问至多能有多少位学生所正确计算出的和为212？

3. 从矩形房子$ABCD$向外延长篱笆．延长篱笆AB至点E使得$BE = 80$ m、延长篱笆BC至点F使得$CF = 70$ m、延长篱笆CD至点G使得$DG = 50$ m、延长篱笆DA至点H使得$AH = 90$ m，接着经过点E、G分别筑平行于AD的篱

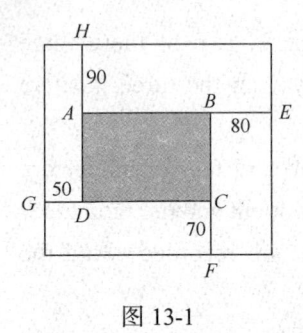

笆、经过点 F、H 分别筑平行于 AB 的篱笆，这几道篱笆在房子四周恰好围出了四块矩形花园，如图 13-1 所示．若这四块花园的周长总和为 2016 m，请问这栋房子的周长是多少 m？

4．有一个团体是由若干个组织所构成，而其中每一个组织都是由若干个协会所构成、每一个协会都是由若干个学会所构成、每一个学会都是由若干个俱乐部所构成．已知每一个学会内的俱乐部数量、每一个协会内的学会数量、每一个组织内的协会数量都相同且多于 1 个．若这一个团体有一个主席职务，而每一个组织、协会、学会及俱乐部也都各有一个主席职务，且整个团体内担任主席职务的总数有 161 个，请问这个团体内有多少个组织？

5．A、B 两台机器用一分钟各都可以制造出 1 个瓶子，但机器 A 每制造 3 个瓶子后就必须停机 1 分钟、机器 B 每制造 5 个瓶子后就必须停机 1.5 分钟．请问同时利用这两台机器制造 2015 个瓶子至少需花费多少分钟？

6．用 1、2、3、4、5 与 6 这六个数码各恰一次，构造出一个一位数、一个两位数、一个三位数．已知一位数与两位数的和为 47、两位数与三位数的和为 358，请问这三个数的总和是多少？

7．已知点 E 在正方形 ABCD 的边 BC 上（图 13-2），且 BE = 20 cm、CE = 28 cm．若点 P 是对角线 BD 上的一个点，请问 PE + PC 的最小可能值是多少 cm？

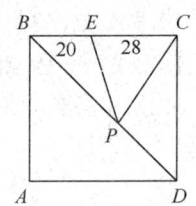

8．在一组相异的正整数中，最大的数小于 36，且恰为最小的数的三倍，而最小的数恰为这一组数的平均值的三分之二．请问这一组数中至多有多少个数？

9．如图 13-3 所示是一个立体结构的俯视图，它是由单位正立方体为基底并以面对面完全重合的方式叠合一些单位正立方体而组成的，且其底部都在同一平面上．图中每一个数即为每一个基底上所使用的单位正立方体个数．若将这个立体结构的表面涂上油漆（包括底部的九个 1×1 的正方形），请问在所有单位正立方体的面中，共有多少个 1×1 的表面被涂上油漆？

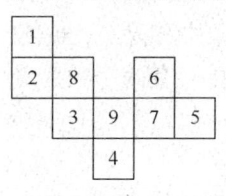

10．有四个相异的三位数，每个数的数码之和都相等，且这四个三位数之和为 2015．请问这四个三位数之数码和的所有可能值之和是多少？

11. 已知有三个正整数,第一个正整数是由两个相同数码所组成的两位数、第二个正整数则是由二个相异数码所组成的两位数,且其个位数码与第一个正整数的数码相同、第三个正整数则是由一个数码所组成的一位数且这个数码与第二个正整数的十位数数码相同. 若这三个正整数中恰有两个正整数是素数,请问满足上述条件的三个正整数共有多少种可能?

12. 将一个正整数除以 5,然后把所得的商与余数逐项记录下来,再将同一个正整数除以 3 后,同样地也把所得的商与余数逐项记录下来. 若两次记录的数都相同但顺序相反,请问原来正整数的所有可能值之乘积是多少?

13. 如图 13-4 所示,点 E 为矩形 $ABCD$ 的 AB 边上的一点,使得 $AE=2EB$ 且点 Z 为 BC 边的中点,而点 M 与 N 分别为线段 DE 与 DZ 的中点. 若△EMN 的面积为 5 cm^2,请问五边形 $MEBZN$ 的面积为多少 cm^2?

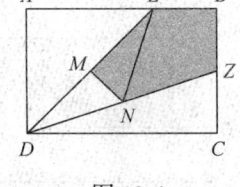

14. 将 1、2、3、⋯、12 分成四组,每一组恰有三个数且每一组内的数之和都可被 3 整除. 请问共有多少种不同的分组方法?

15. 从 1、2、3、⋯、19 中选出第一个数,并从 1、2、3、⋯、19 中选出第二个数,若第二个数比第一个数多 10—18,或少 1—9,则称第一个数是第二个数的"跟随数",例如 6 是 16、17、18、19、1、2、3、4 与 5 的"跟随数". 现从数 1、2、3、⋯、19 中任选三个数,使得第一个数是第二个数的"跟随数"、第二个数是第三个数的"跟随数"且第一个数也是第三个数的"跟随数". 请问共有多少种不同的选择方法?

图 13-4

13.3 EMIC个人赛试题解答与评注

2015 年国际小学数学竞赛个人竞赛试题解答

1. **解** 因 $2015=5 \times 13 \times 31$,故 2015 有三个相异的质因子且共有 $(1+1) \times (1+1) \times (1+1)=8$ 个正因子. 而有 8 个正因子的另一类数可写成一个素数的立方与另一个相异素数的积,或是一个素数的七次方. 可知最小的四位数 1000 都不属这三种情况,而次小的四位数 1001 则是 7、11 与 13 的乘积. 故所求的最小四位数是 1001.

答:1001

2. **解** 为使学生能正确计算出和 212 时,所移除的数之和为 $(1+2+\cdots+$

21)−212=19．此时被移除的两个连续正整数可能为(1, 2)、(2, 3)、(3, 4)、(4, 5)、(5, 6)、(6, 7)、(7, 8)、(8, 9)，且对应的第三个被移除的数依序为16、14、12、10、8、6、4、2．可发现在这八组数中，因(6, 7, 6)这组数中的 6 重复出现了两次，故必须排除．因此知至多有 7 位学生能正确计算出和为 212．

答：7

3．**解** 如图 13-5，可知这四块花园的周长总和之一半为 1008(m)，此即为 $(AH+AB+BE)+(BE+BC+CF)+(CF+CD+DG)+(DG+DA+AH)$ 之值，而将此式化简后即可得 $(AB+BC+CD+DA)+2(AH+BE+CF+DG)=AB+BC+CD+DA+2×290$，故可推得这栋房子的周长是 $1008−2×290=428$ (m)．

答：428m

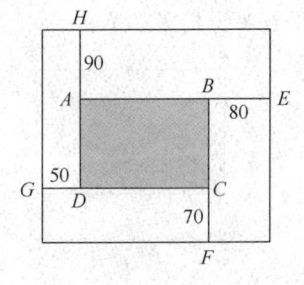

图 13-5

4．**解** 若题目中相同的数目是 2，则每一个组织内的主委职务共 $1+2+2^2+2^3=15$ 个；若此相同的数目为 3，则每一个组织内的主委职务共 $1+3+3^2+3^3=40$ 个；若此相同的数目为 4，则每一个组织内的主委职务共 $1+4+4^2+4^3=85$ 个．可知这一个团体除了主席以外，共 $161−1=160$ 个主委职务，因此由每一个组织内的主委职务数目必可整除 160 可判断出题目中相同的数目为 3，且共有 $160÷40=4$ 个组织．

答：4

5．**解** 可知机器 A 每 4 分钟可制造 3 个瓶子、机器 B 每 13 分钟可制造 10 个瓶子，因此可推得每 52 分钟机器 A 可制造 39 个瓶子、机器 B 可制造 40 个瓶子，合计共制造 $39+40=79$ 个瓶子．因 $2015=25×79+40$，所以在经过 $52×25$ 分钟后，仍需再制造 40 个瓶子．由两台机器的制造规律可推知再经过 25 分钟后，机器 A 制造了 19 个瓶子而机器 B 同时间也制造了 20 个瓶子，且在第 26 分钟，机器 A 继续制造 1 个瓶子而机器 B 开始休息，因此这两台机器制造 2015 个瓶子要花费 $25×52+26=1326$ 分钟．

答：1326 分钟

6．**解** 可以判断出所构造出的一位数与两位数之个位数码和至多为 $5+6=11$，而现已知此和的个位数码为 7，故此和即为 7，因此可判断出两位位数的首位数码为 4，且由两位数与三位数的和为 358 可再判断出三位数的首位数码是 3．再因两位数与三位数的和为 358 可以得知三位数的十位数码为 1，因此可以得知所求之和为 $310+40+(2+5+6)=363$，此时这三个数可取为 5、42 与 316．

260

第13章　2015年第13届国际小学数学竞赛

答: 363

7. 解　如图 13-6 所示，在边 AB 上取一点 F 使得 $AF=CE$，此时可以判断出点 F 与点 E 为以线段 BD 为对称轴的对称点. 再由三角不等式可得 $PE+PC=PC+PF \geqslant CF$，因此知 $PE+PC$ 的最小值发生在点 P 落在线段 CF 上时，且其值为 $CF=\sqrt{BC^2+BF^2}=\sqrt{20^2+48^2}=52$ (cm).

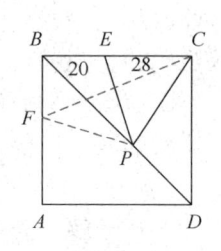

答: 52 cm

图 13-6

8. 解　可知最大数是 3 的倍数. 为了使这一组数的个数尽可能多，需使最大数尽可能地大，因此可令最大数为 33，此时最小数为 11 且知这一组数的平均值为 $11 \div \dfrac{2}{3}=\dfrac{33}{2}$. 接着若将 11 与 $\dfrac{33}{2}=16.5$ 之间的整数全部放到这一组数内，则这一组数中最小的六个数为 11、12、13、14、15、16，这些数比平均值少的量之总和为 18，而 33 比平均值大 $\dfrac{33}{2}$，故知可再加入的数比平均值多的量之总和为 $18-\dfrac{33}{2}=\dfrac{3}{2}$，即可判断仅能再加入 $\dfrac{33}{2}+\dfrac{3}{2}=18$ 才会满足题意，所以一组数中至多有 8 个数.

答: 8 个

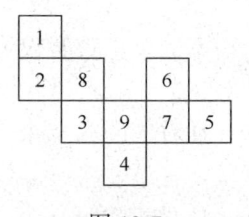

图 13-7

9. 解　如图 13-7 所示，可以判断出若从正面来看，可看到 $2+8+9+7+5=31$ 个单位正立方体；若从侧面来看，可看到 $1+8+9+4=22$ 个单位正立方体. 故连同底部的九个 1×1 的面，知从前、后、上、下、左、右这六个角度可看到 1×1 的面共有 $2\times(9+31+22)=124$ 个. 而由俯视图可得知在分别由六个正立方体与八个正立方体所组成的这两个长方体之间并没有其他的长方体，因此之间会有 $6\times 2=12$ 个面是六个角度都无法看见但仍涂上油漆的 1×1 的面，因此共有 $124+12=136$ 个 1×1 的面被涂上油漆.

答: 136 个

10. 解　可知当 2015 在除以 9 之后所得的余数为 8. 现因这四个相异的三位数之数码和都相等，故可判断知这四个三位数之数码和在除以 9 之后所得的余数都相等，且可推知这四个三位数之数码和在除以 9 之后所得的余数必为 2. 但因三位数的数码和至多为 27，且数码和为 2 的三位数仅有 200、101、110 这三个数，故可得知这四个三位数之数码和为 11 或 20. 若数码和为 11 时，可从先取最大数 920 开始考虑，此时其余三数的和为 $2015-920=1095$，接着取

261

560，此约略为一半的数，故其余两数的和为 $1095-560=535$，最后可再取 380，此时最后一数为 $535-380=155$，即可得一解 $920+560+380+155=2015$；若数码和为 20 时，可分别取百位数码为 2、3、4 时，数码和为 20 的最小数，此时即可得到另一解 $299+389+479+848=2015$. 因此知数码和为 11 与 20 时，这样的四个相异三位数都存在，故所求之值为 $11+20=31$.

答：31

11. **解** 若第一个正整数为素数，则第一个正整数必为 11.

(1) 若假设第三个正整数也是素数，则第二个正整数不为素数，因此由 21、51 不为素数可推知第三个正整数为 2 或 5，而 31、71 为素数可推知第三个正整数不可为 3 或 7.

(2) 若假设第三个正整数不是素数，则第二个正整数是素数，因此由 41、61 为素数可推知第三个正整数为 4 或 6，而 81、91 不为素数可推知第三个正整数不可为 8 或 9.

故此情况共有 4 种可能.

若第一个正整数不是素数，则另两个数必为素数. 现由第三个正整数为素数知：

(1) 若第三个正整数为 2，则第二个正整数可为 23 或 29，且对应的第一个正整数依序为 33 或 99；

(2) 若第三个正整数为 3，则由第一个正整数不可为 11 知第二个正整数仅可为 37，且对应的第一个正整数为 77；

(3) 若第三个正整数为 5，则第二个正整数可为 53 或 59，且对应的第一个正整数依序为 33 或 99；

(4) 若第三个正整数为 7，则第二个正整数可为 73 或 79，且对应的第一个正整数依序为 33 或 99；

故此情况共有 7 种可能.

所以像这样的三个正整数共有 $4+7=11$ 种可能.

答：11 种

12. **解** 可知在第二次记录中的商与第一次记录中的余数相同，故其可能值为 0、1、2、3 或 4，而在第一次记录中的商与第二次记录中的余数相同，故其可能值为 0、1 或 2，因此可得知这样的正整数至多为 $3\times5=15$. 现若分别在两个 3×5 的表格中依序填入 0 到 14，其中一个表格填数方式为逐列依序由左向右填数，如表 13-1、另一个表格为逐行依序由上至下填数，如表 13-2.

表 13-1

0	1	2	3	4
5	6	7	8	9
10	11	12	13	14

表 13-2

0	3	6	9	12
1	4	7	10	13
2	5	8	11	14

可发现仅有 0、7、14 会填在相同位置的格子内．因 0 不为正整数，故需将 0 舍去而得可能的值为 7 与 14，其乘积为 $7 \times 14 = 98$．

答：98

13. **解** 如图 13-8 利用符号 [ ] 来表示一个区域内的面积．连接 EZ．

因 $EM = DM$ 且 $ZN = DN$，故可得 $[DEZ] = 2[DEN] = 4[MEN] = 20\,(\text{cm}^2)$．

由 $\dfrac{BE}{BA} = \dfrac{1}{3}$ 且 $\dfrac{BZ}{BC} = \dfrac{1}{2}$ 可以得知 $\dfrac{[BEZ]}{[ABCD]} = \dfrac{1}{2} \times \dfrac{1}{3} \times \dfrac{1}{2} = \dfrac{1}{12}$；

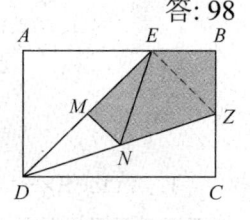

同样地，$\dfrac{[ADE]}{[ABCD]} = \dfrac{1}{3}$ 且 $\dfrac{[CDZ]}{[ABCD]} = \dfrac{1}{4}$，故有 $\dfrac{[DEZ]}{[ABCD]} = 1 - \dfrac{1}{12} - \dfrac{1}{3} - \dfrac{1}{4} = \dfrac{1}{3}$，即 $[ABCD] = 3 \times 20 = 60\,(\text{cm}^2)$．

因此可以推知 $[BEZ] = 5\,(\text{cm}^2)$ 以及 $[MEBZN] = [BEZ] + [MEN] + [NEZ] = 20\,(\text{cm}^2)$．

答：20 cm²

14. **解** 可先将这 12 个数依次被 3 除之后的情况分成三类：A 类为 3、6、9 与 12，即是 3 的倍数；B 类为 1、4、7 与 10，即是 3 的倍数加 1 的数；C 类为 2、5、8 与 11，即是 3 的倍数减 1 的数．此时可以判断知满足题意的分组方式有：

(1) 如果每一组中每一类的数都各有一个，则每一组内的数之和都可被 3 所整除．当 A 类的数分配到四个组后，B 类的数分配到这四组的不同方法数有 $4 \times 3 \times 2 \times 1 = 24$ 种、C 类也是 24 种，故此分配方式共有 $24 \times 24 = 576$ 种．

(2) 如果将每一类中各任选一数出来组成一组，每一类剩下的三数都自为一组，则每一组内的数之和也都可被 3 所整除．此分配方式共有 $4 \times 4 \times 4 = 64$ 种．

因此合计共有 $576 + 64 = 640$ 种分组的方法．

答: 640 种

15. 解 如果将数 1、2、3、…、19 以顺时针方向依序写在一个圆的圆周上,则每一个数都会是它以逆时针方向的前九个数的跟踪数. 此时第一个数可从这 19 个数中任选一个,而第二个数、第三个数则必须从第一个数的以逆时针方向的前九个数中选出,例如若第一个选的数是 6,且如果接着第二个数选的是 5 时,则第三个数只能从 4、3、2、1、19、18、17 与 16 中选出,一共有 8 个选择;而如果接着第二个数选的是 4 时,则第三个数能选择的数目就会减少 1;依此类推. 故知共有 $19 \times (8+7+6+5+4+3+2+1) = 684$ 种不同的选择方法.

答: 684 种

13.4 EMIC 队际赛英文试题

Elementary Mathematics International Contest 2015
29th July, 2015, Changchun, China

Team Contest

1. In the 9×9 table in the following diagram, some squares are shaded. Mark 9 of the squares with "X" so that there is a marked square in each row, each column and each of the nine 3×3 subtables defined by the double lines. Shaded squares may not be marked.

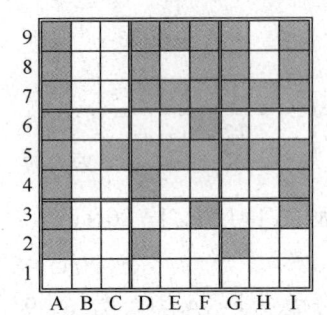

2. A 14×23 piece of paper is divided by grid lines into 1×1 squares. We wish to cut out square pieces of paper of different sizes along the grid lines. What is the largest number of pieces we can get? Prove that no larger value can work, and give an example to show that your answer can be realized.

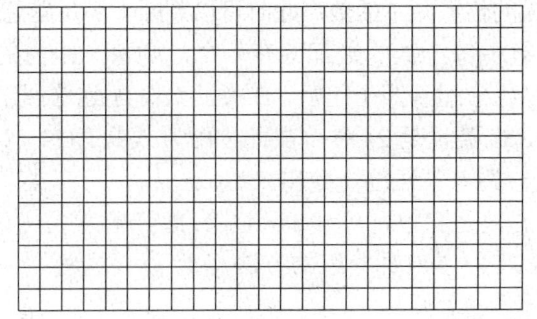

264

第 13 章 2015 年第 13 届国际小学数学竞赛

3. There is a machine with five slots. Each slots can receive two cards as input and in most cases will produce a new card as output. All cards have positive integers on them. The output from the +, −, × or ÷ slots is the sum, the difference, the product or the quotient. If the difference or the quotient is not a positive integer, there is no output. The output from the ~ slot is a number obtained by writing the second input immediately after the first input. For example, we get 102 if we input 10 and 2, or 210 if we input 2 and 10. All input cards are returned. Starting with two cards with the numbers 1 and 2, find a way of getting a card with the number 2015, using the machine only five times. Every time we use a slot it counts as a separate operation.

	1st time: Input cards	and	insert into the slot	, then get card
	2nd time: Input cards	and	insert into the slot	, then get card
	3rd time: Input cards	and	insert into the slot	, then get card
	4th time: Input cards	and	insert into the slot	, then get card
Answer:	5th time: Input cards	and	insert into the slot	, then get card

4. Twenty rabbits are hopping along the same path in the same direction, each at a different constant speed. The first rabbit leaves the starting point at noon. Each of the other rabbits leaves one minute after the preceding one. The second rabbit catches up with the first rabbit two minutes after it starts hopping. The third rabbit catches up with the second rabbit three minutes after it starts hopping. The pattern continues, so that the twentieth rabbit catches up with the nineteenth rabbit twenty minutes after it starts hopping. How many minutes past noon does the twentieth rabbit catch up with the first rabbit?

5. The diagram below shows ten circles each of radius 1 cm long. The four circles in the front row are tangent to their neighbours and their centres lie on the same line. For each of the six circles behind, the top semicircle runs between the highest points of two circles in the row in front. Calculate the area, in cm², of the

figure excluding the four circles in the front row. You may make take π to be 3.14.

6. A tennis club has six players numbered 1 to 6. Two of them are to be chosen to represent the club in a tournament. Five assistant coaches make the following recommendations: "#4 and #5", "#3 and #6", "#5 and #6", "#2 and #5" and "#1 and #3". The head coach ignores both players recommended by one of the assistant coaches, and chooses exactly one player from the recommendation of each of the other four. Which are the two chosen players?

7. The numbers 2, 3, 4, 5, 6, 7, 8 and 9 are to be put into four pairs such that the sum of the two numbers in each pair is a prime. How many different ways are there to split these numbers into four pairs?

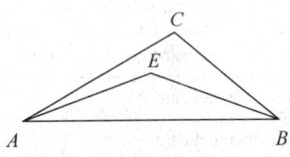

8. E is a point inside triangle ABC such that $AE = BE = BC$ and $\angle ABE = \angle CBE = 20°$. Find the measure, in degrees, of $\angle CAE$.

9. Find the largest number consisting of one copy of each of the digits 1 to 9, such that the sum of any two adjacent digits is a multiple of 5, 7 or 11.

10. A three-digit number does not contain the digit 9. When each digit is increased by 1, the product of the digits of the new number is three times the product of the digits of the original number. How many such numbers are there?

13.5 EMIC队际赛中文试题

2015年国际小学数学竞赛队标竞赛试题

1. 在如图 13-9 所示的9×9方格表中，部分的小方格被涂上了阴影．请在其余未涂上阴影的小方格中找出九个小方格，并在小方格内填入"X"，使得每一行、每一列以及每一个由双黑线所围成的3×3方格表内都各恰有一个"X"．

2. 一张14×23的纸片用网格线划分为1×1的小方格，如图 13-10 所示．现要沿着网格线将这一张方格表剪出一些边长互不相同的正方形纸片，请问最多可以剪出多少张正方形纸片？请证明不可能

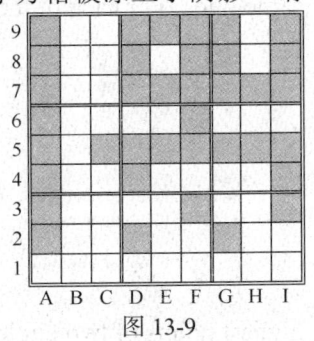

图 13-9

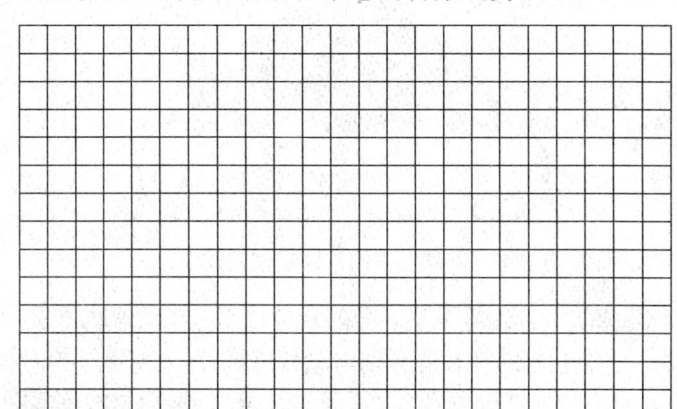

剪出更多张的正方形纸片并请给出一个您的答案之剪法.

图 13-10

3．一台机器上有五个插入槽，每个槽每次依序接收两张卡片作为输入，一般情况下会输出一张新的卡片．每张卡片上都印有一个正整数．此机器其中四个插入槽＋、－、×、÷分别输出卡片的和、差、积、商．若差或商不是一个正整数，则相应的槽不会输出卡片．此机器的另一插入槽～把输入的第二张卡片上的数连接在第一张卡片上的数后面，然后把所得的数打印在一张新卡片上并输出，例如：若输入为 10 与 2，则输出为 102；若输入为 2 与 10，则输出为 210．每次输入的卡片都会退还．若开始时仅有两张分别写有数 1 与 2 的卡片，请找出一种操作方式，使得仅用此机器五次，每次只操作一个插入槽，便可得到一张印有 2015 的卡片．

4．有二十只兔子从同一点开始沿着同一条路径、同一个方向跳跃，且每一只兔子的速度都不相同．已知第一只兔子在正中午时出发，接着每隔一分钟都有另一只兔子出发．若第二只兔子在它开始跳之后的 2 分钟追上第一只兔子、第三只兔子在它开始跳之后的 3 分钟追上第二只兔子、…，以此类推，直到第二十只兔子在它开始跳之后的 20 分钟追上第十九只兔子．请问从正中午开始过后几分钟，第二十只兔子追上第一只兔子？

5．有十个半径都是 1 cm 的圆依图 13-11 所示的方式排列，其中在最下面一行的四个圆之圆心都在同一条直线上，且每一个圆都与相邻的圆相切，而在上面的六个圆，每一个的上半圆都与在它下面的两个圆的最高点相连．请问图中的阴影部分之面积是多少 cm^2？取圆周率 π 之值为 3.14.

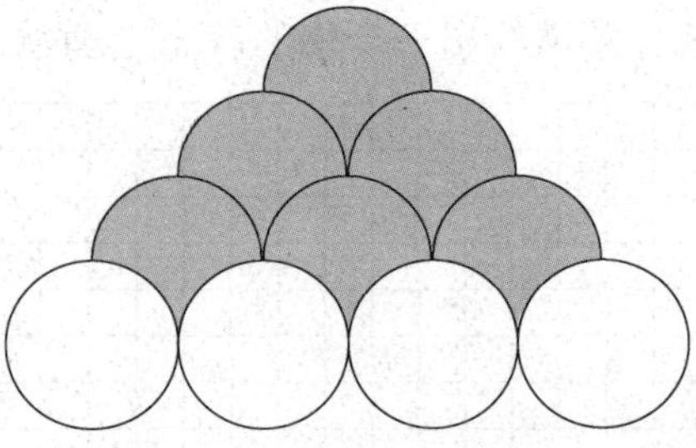

图 13-11

6. 在一个网球队中有编号 1 至 6 号的六位选手，此网球队将从中选出两位选手参加巡回赛．已知五名助理教练分别向总教练推荐："4 号与 5 号"、"3 号与 6 号"、"5 号与 6 号"、"2 号与 5 号"、"1 号与 3 号"．最后总教练驳回其中一位助理教练所推荐的两位选手，并且确定其余四位助理教练每人推荐的两位选手都恰有一位选手被选上，请问总教练选出的两位选手之编号是什么？

7. 将数 2、3、4、5、6、7、8、9 两两配成四对并将它们相加，若所得的和都是素数，请问共有多少种不同的配对方法？

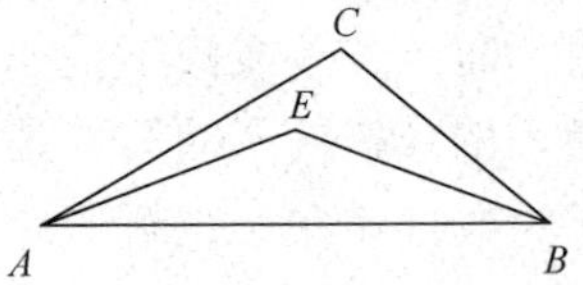

图 13-12

8. 如图 13-12 所示，在$\triangle ABC$的内部有一点E，满足$AE=BE=BC$与$\angle ABE=\angle CBE=20°$．请问$\angle CAE$是多少度？

9. 一个九位数是由数码 1 至 9 各一个所组成的，且在这个数中，相邻的任意两个数码之和都必为 5、7 或 11 的倍数．请问满足此条件的最大数是什么？

10. 一个三位数的三个数码都不为 9，每一个数码都增加 1 后得到一个新的数，且新的数之所有数码的乘积恰为原来的三位数的所有数码之乘积的三倍．请问满足上述条件的数共有多少个？

13.6 EMIC 队际赛试题解答与评注

2015 年国际小学数学竞赛队标竞赛试题解答

1. **解** 因 A1 是该行中唯一未涂上阴影的小方格、B5 是该列中唯一未涂上阴影的小方格且 E8 是所在的3×3子方格表内唯一未涂上阴影的小方格，故知这三个小方格都一定要填入"X"．此时由 E8 填入"X"可判断出 H9 也要填入"X"，因此 C7 是该列中唯一可填入"X"的小方格，如图 13-13 所示．

第 13 章　2015 年第 13 届国际小学数学竞赛

接着观察位于中间下方的 3×3 子方格表，此仅有两个可填入"X"的小方格．若在 F2 填入"X"，则一定也要在 D6 填入"X"，此时在第 I 列中无法填入任何一个"X"，故不合，因此知在中间下方的 3×3 子方格表中能填入"X"的小方格是 D3，此时可再依序推知需在 I2、F4 填入"X"，最后可再判断出 G6 也要填入"X"，此时即完成填表，如图 13-14 所示．

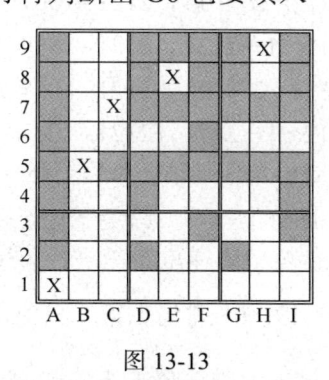

图 13-13　　　　　　　　　　图 13-14

2. 解　可知最小的 10 个完全平方数之和为 385，且此值大于 $14 \times 23 = 322$，故可判断出至多可剪出 9 张边长不相同的正方形纸片．再由 $8 + 7 > 14$ 可以判断出边长为 9、8、7 的正方形纸片在 14×23 的矩形中必须位于不同行上，但再因 $9 + 8 + 7 > 23$，故知边长为 9、8、7 的正方形纸片不可能同时剪出，所以至多只能剪出 8 张边长不相同的正方形纸片．而这 8 张边长不相同的正方形纸片可如图 13-15 所示之方式在 14×15 的矩形中剪出．

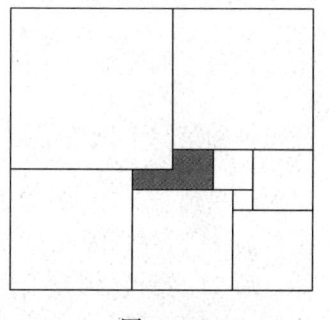

图 13-15

答：8

【评注】 证明所能剪出的不同边长之正方形纸片数量少于 10 张，得 10 分；证明所能剪出的不同边长之正方形纸片数量少于 9 张，得 10 分；举出一个恰可剪出 8 张不同边长之正方形纸片的剪法，得 20 分；只给出正确答案而无任何理由或说明，得 5 分．

3. 解　以下即为恰利用此机器五次后得到写有 2015 的卡片的操作方式：
$2 + 1 = 3$，$3 + 2 = 5$，$5 \times 3 = 15$，$15 + 5 = 20$，$20 \sim 15 = 2015$．
$2 + 1 = 3$，$3 + 2 = 5$，$1 \sim 5 = 15$，$15 + 5 = 20$，$20 \sim 15 = 2015$．
$2 + 1 = 3$，$3 \sim 1 = 31$，$31 + 3 = 34$，$34 + 31 = 65$，$31 \times 65 = 2015$．

269

$2+1=3$，$3\sim1=31$，$31\times2=62$，$62+3=65$，$31\times65=2015$．

$1\sim2=12$，$12+1=13$，$13\times12=156$，$156-1=155$，$155\times13=2015$．

$1\sim2=12$，$12+1=13$，$13\times12=156$，$13\times156=2028$，$2028-13=2015$．

$1\sim2=12$，$12+2=14$，$14\times12=168$，$168\times12=2016$，$2016-1=2015$．

$1\sim2=12$，$2\sim12=212$，$212\sim1=2121$，$212\div2=106$，$2121-106=2015$．

$1\sim2=12$，$2\sim12=212$，$212\div2=106$，$212\sim1=2121$，$2121-106=2015$．

$2\sim1=21$，$21\sim2=212$，$212\sim1=2121$，$212\div2=106$，$2121-106=2015$．

$2\sim1=21$，$21\sim2=212$，$212\div2=106$，$212\sim1=2121$，$2121-106=2015$．

4. 解 若令第一只兔子在正中午 12：00 时出发，则第二只兔子在 12：01 时出发且在 12：03 时追上第一只兔子．到此时为止，第二只兔子已经跳了 2 分钟而第一只兔子已经跳了 3 分钟，所以第二只兔子的速度是第一只兔子的速度的 $\frac{3}{2}$ 倍．而第三只兔子在 12：02 时出发且在 12：05 时追上第二只兔子．到此时为止，第三只兔子已经跳了 3 分钟而第二只兔子已经跳了 4 分钟，所以第三只兔子的速度是第二只兔子的速度的 $\frac{4}{3}$ 倍．依此类推，第四只兔子的速度是第三只兔子的速度的 $\frac{5}{4}$ 倍、第五只兔子的速度是第四只兔子的速度的 $\frac{6}{5}$ 倍、…，故可推知第二十只兔子的速度是第一只兔子的速度的 $\frac{3}{2}\times\frac{4}{3}\times\cdots\times\frac{21}{20}=\frac{21}{2}$ 倍．因第二十只兔子是在 12：19 出发，故 12：21 为它出发 2 分钟，此即第一只兔子出发后 21 分钟．因此第二十只兔子在 12：21 时追上第一只兔子，即正中午开始过后 21 分钟，第二十只兔子追上第一只兔子．

答案：21 分钟

【评注】 找出不同的兔子之间的速度关系，至多得 20 分；找出第一只兔子与第二十只兔子之间的速度关系，得 10 分；正确计算出所需时间，得 10 分；只给出正确答案而无任何理由或说明，得 5 分．

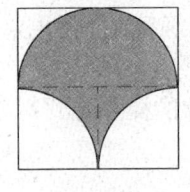

图 13-16

5. 解 可知阴影部分是由 6 个不完整的圆所构成的，且每一个都可被一个边长为 2(cm)的正方形正好完全盖住．观察后可发现，在每一个正方形中，上半部不在圆内部的区域面积都恰等于下半部在圆内部的区域面积，故可以判断出每一个不完整的圆之面积为 $2\times1=2(cm^2)$，所以图 13-16 中的阴影部分

270

第13章 2015年第13届国际小学数学竞赛

之面积是 $2 \times 6 = 12 \, (\text{cm}^2)$.

答：12cm²

6. 解 可知助理教练共建议了十个人次，其中有四个人次被采纳．观察可知，1号、2号与4号各被建议一次，3号、6号各被建议两次，5号被建议三次，因此可以判断出，被选出参赛的选手为3号以及6号，或是5号以及1号、2号、4号中的一位选手搭档参赛．但因3号与6号被一位助理教练同时建议，故不可能是这一对选手，且这一位助理教练所建议的选手都未被选上．而另四位助理教练中，共有三位助理教练推荐5号选手，因此这三位助理教练所推荐的另一位选手都未被选上，即4号、6号、2号都未被选上，再因已知3号选手也未被选上，故可得知另一位被选上的选手是1号选手．

答：1号与5号

【评注】 本题并无唯一的推理过程，且因仅15种选择选手的方式，学生甚至可利用穷举法验证出正确答案．给出正确答案，得10分；推理过程，至多30分，若推理过程不完整，可给予部分分数；只给出正确答案而无任何理由或说明，得10分．

7. 解 可知每一对数的两个数都恰为一个奇数与一个偶数，且观察可知6仅可与5或7配对．若6与5配对，则可将2、4与8写在一边，3、7与9写在另一边，此时可发现4可与任何一个奇数配对，但2、8都不可与7配对，因此4必须与7配对，此时剩下未配对的数共有2种配对方式．若6与7配对，则可将2、4与8写在一边，3、5与9写在另一边，此时可发现2、8可与任何一个奇数配对，但4不可与5配对，因此4有2种配对方式，且每一种4的配对方式中，此时剩下未配对的数共有 2 种配对方式．故知合计共有 $2 + 2 \times 2 = 6$ 种配对方式．

答：6种

8. 解 如图13-17所示，取点 D 使得 $BC = CD$、$\angle CBD = 20°$．此时可知 $\triangle AEB$ 与 $\triangle DCB$ 全等，故有 $BA = BD$．接着由 $\angle ABD = \angle ABE + \angle CBE + \angle CBD = 60°$ 可推知 $\triangle ABD$ 为正三角形，再因 $BC = CD$ 以及 $BA = AD$，故知 AC 为 $\angle BAD$ 的角平分线，所以 $\angle CAE = \angle CAB - \angle EBA = 30° - 20° = 10°$．

图 13-17

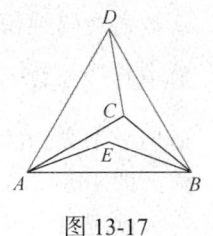

答：10°

【评注】 利用补助线造出所需的正三角形，至多20分；找出所需的全等三

271

角形关系,得 10 分;验证 AC 为角平分线并计算出正确的角度,得 10 分;只给出正确答案而无任何理由或说明,得 5 分.

9. 解 观察每一个数码与那一个数码之和会恰为 5、7、11 的倍数的情况后可得图 13-18,其中两个数码之间有线连接及代表这两个数码之和为 5、7、11 的倍数.

此时需找出一条恰经过每一个数码的路径,即汉米尔顿路径,而使这九个数码形成一个九位数,且要使这九位数尽可能大.因此不妨从 9 开始出发,且下一个数码取 6,此时因每一个数码仅可有偶数条线相连,故可将 9、5 之间的线以及 9、1 之间的线删去.接着若是从 6 走到 8,则可将其余未使用到与 6 相连的线删除,即 6、5 之间的线以及 6、1 之间的线都会被删除,此时可发现 5 与 1 都是只有一条线相连,故 5 与 1 都同时是这一个数的末位数码,所以不合(图 13-19).

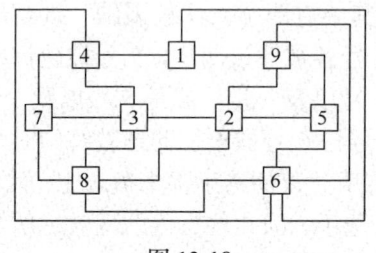

图 13-18

故知不可能是从 6 走到 8;接着观察若是从 6 走到 5,接下来必为从 5 走到 2,然后可接着依序取 8、7. 最后为了使 1 为末位数码,故可再依序取 3、4、1,即满足题意的最大数是 965287341.

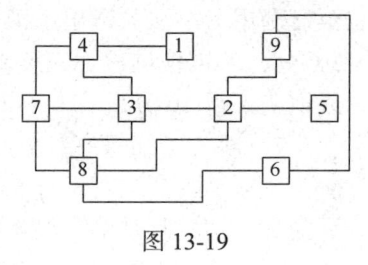

图 13-19

答: 965287341

10. 解 可知新数的数码乘积必为 3 的倍数,因此新数中必至少有一个数码为 3、6 或 9:

状况 1:若是新数中有一个数码为 6,则原来的数中有一个数码为 5,故新数之数码乘积也是 5 的倍数,所以新数中有一个数码为 5,据此可再得知原数中有一个数码为 4. 因 $\dfrac{6\times 5}{5\times 4}=\dfrac{1}{2}\times 3$,所以新数最后一个未知的数码必为原数最后一个未知的数码的 2 倍,此时仅 2 与 1 满足此条件,所以共有六个这样的数,即 145、154、415、451、514 与 541.

状况 2:若是新数中有一个数码为 9,则原来的数中有一个数码为 8. 现因 $9=3\times 3$ 故原数之数码乘积是 3 的倍数,所以原数中有一个数码为 3 或 6. 若原数中有一个数码为 6,则知新数中有一个数码为 7,据此可再得知原数中有

第 13 章　2015 年第 13 届国际小学数学竞赛

一个数码为 7，但此时因 $\frac{9\times 8\times 7}{8\times 7\times 6}=\frac{3}{2}\neq 3$，故不合，所以原数中必有一个数码为 3，此时知新数中有一个数码为 4，且有 $\frac{9\times 4}{8\times 3}=\frac{3}{2}$，故与前一个状况一样可判断出此时仅 2 与 1 满足此条件，所以共有六个这样的数，即 138、183、318、381、813 与 831．

状况 3：若是新数中有一个数码为 3，则原来的数中有一个数码为 2，故新数中另两个数码之乘积恰为原数中另两个数码之乘积的 2 倍．因已有 $\frac{3\times 2}{2\times 1}=3$，所以新数的数码都必大于 2．因 $\frac{4\times 4\times 3}{3\times 3\times 2}<3$，所以新数中必还有一个数码为 3．由 $\frac{3\times 3}{2\times 2}=\frac{3}{4}\times 3$ 可判断知新数中最后一个未知的数码必是 4，此时原数中最后一个未知的数码是 3，所以共有三个这样的数，即 223、232 与 322．

因此合计共有 $6+6+3=15$ 个这样的数．

答：15 个

【评注】 说明新数中至少有一个数码为 3、6 或 9，得 4 分；状况 1：至少有一个数码为 6 并找出此状况的 6 个数：145，154，415，451，514 与 541，12 分；状况 2：至少有一个数码为 9 并找出此状况的 6 个数：138，183，318，381，813 与 831，得 12 分；状况 3：至少有一个数码为 3 并找出此状况的 3 个数：223，232 与 322，得 12 分；只给出正确答案而无任何理由或说明，得 5 分；直接举出满足题意的数字而无其他说明，至多 15 分．（每举出 1 个正确数字可得 1 分）；若利用其他手法证明，视证明过程给予分数．

第14章 2016年第14届国际小学数学竞赛

14.1 EMIC个人赛英文试题

Elementary Mathematics International Contest 2016
17th August, 2016, Chiang Mai, Thailand

Individual Contest

1. *ABCDE* is a regular pentagon of side length 1 m. There are 5, 15, 14, 9 and 17 students at the vertices *A*, *B*, *C*, *D* and *E* respectively. The teacher wants the same number of students at each vertex, so some of the students have to walk to other vertices. They may only walk along the sides. What is the minimum total length, in m, the students have to walk?

2. A, B and C run a 200-m race in constant speeds. When A finishes the race, B is 40 m behind A and C is 10 m behind B. When B finishes, C still has to run another 2 seconds. How many seconds does B still have to run when A finishes?

3. With each vertex of a 1 cm by 1 cm square as centre, circles of radius 1 cm are drawn, as shown in the diagram below. How much larger, in cm^2, is the area of the shaded region than the area of a circle of radius 1 cm?（Take $\pi = 3.14$）

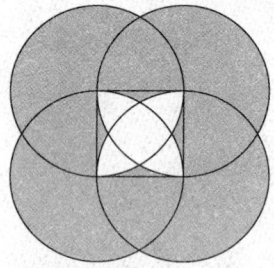

4. How many multiples of 18 are there between 8142016 and 8202016?

5. In a basketball game, a foul shot is worth 1 point, a field shot is worth 2 points and a long-range shot is worth 3 points. Stephen makes 8 foul shots and 14 others. If he had made twice as many field shots and half as many long-range shots, he would have

scored 7 extra points. How many points has Stephen actually scored?

6. John's running speed is twice his walking speed. Both are constant. On his way to school one day, John walks for twice as long as he runs, and the trip takes 30 minutes. The next day, he runs for twice as long as he walks. How many minutes does the same trip take on the second day?

7. Jimmy has some peanuts. On the first day, he eats 13 peanuts in the morning and one tenth of the rest in the afternoon. On the second day, he eats 16 peanuts in the morning and one tenth of the rest in the afternoon. If he has eaten the same number of peanuts on both days, how many peanuts will he have left?

8. The sum of 49 different positive integers is 2016. What is the minimum number of these integers which are odd?

9. The sum of 25 positive integers is 2016. Find the maximum possible value of their greatest common divisor.

10. $ABCD$ is the rectangle where AB=12 cm and BC=5 cm. E is a point on the opposite side of AB to C, as shown in the diagram below. If $AE=BE$ and the area of triangle AEB is 36 cm^2, find the area, in cm^2, of triangle AEC.

11. Anna starts writing down all the prime numbers in order, 235711…. She stops after she has written down ten prime numbers. She now removes 7 of the digits, and treats what is left as a 9-digit number. What is the maximum value of this number?

12. Three two-digit numbers are such that the sum of any two is formed of the same digits as the third number but in reverse order. Find the sum of all three numbers.

13. The sum of two four-digit numbers is a five-digit number. If each of these three numbers reads the same in both directions, how many different four-digit numbers can appear in such an addition?

14. When 2016 is divided by 3, 5 and 11, the respective remainders are 0, 1 and 3. Find the smallest number with the same properties that can be made from the digits 2, 0, 1 and 6, using each at most once.

15. Each student writes down six positive integers, not necessarily distinct, such that their product is less than or equal to their sum, and their sum is less than or equal to 12. If no two students write down the same six numbers, at most how

many students are there?

14.2 EMIC个人赛中文试题

2016年国际小学数学竞赛个人竞赛试题

1. 正五边形 ABCDE 的边长为 1 m. 已知在其顶点 A、B、C、D、E 上依序分别有 5、15、14、9、17 位学生，老师希望每个顶点上的学生人数都一样，因此有一些学生必须移动到其他的顶点上. 若学生移动时只能沿着正五边形的边走，请问学生们移动的总距离至少是多少 m？

2. 在一场 200 m 的赛跑中，A、B、C 三人都以匀速跑步. 当 A 抵达终点时，B 尚距离终点 40 m 且 C 在 B 后面 10 m；接着当 B 抵达终点时，C 仍需要再跑 2 秒才能抵达. 请问当 A 抵达终点时，B 还需要再跑多少秒才能抵达终点？

3. 以边长为 1 cm 的正方形之四个顶点为圆心，分别画出四个半径为 1 cm 的圆，如图 14-1 所示. 请问图中阴影部分的面积比半径为 1 cm 的圆之面积大多少 cm²？（取 $\pi = 3.14$）

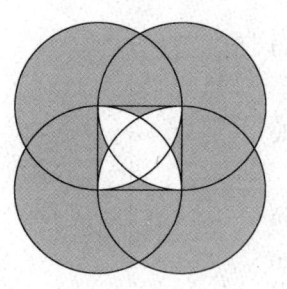

图 14-1

4. 请问从 8142016 到 8202016 总共有多少个整数是 18 的倍数？

5. 在篮球比赛中，罚球每投进一球得一分，而在三分线内每投进一球得二分、在三分线外每投进一球得三分. 在某场比赛小史罚球共投进 8 球、其余的投篮共投进 14 球. 若他投进二分球的球数变为原来的 2 倍、投进三分球的球数变为原来的一半，则他将比原来的得分多 7 分. 请问小史在这一场比赛中实际上得多少分？

6. 小强跑步的速度是走路的速度之两倍，且他跑步与走路的速度都维持不变. 小强从家到学校，某日他走路的时间是他跑步的时间之两倍，他总共费时 30 分钟. 第二天，他跑步的时间是他走路的时间之两倍. 请问第二天从家到学校他总共费时多少分钟？

7. 小杰有一堆花生. 第一天，他在早上吃 13 颗花生、下午再吃剩下花生的十分之一；第二天，他在早上吃 16 颗花生、下午再吃剩下花生的十分之一. 若这两天他所吃的花生之颗数一样多，请问最后他还剩下多少颗花生？

8. 已知有 49 个相异的正整数之和为 2016. 在这些正整数中，请问至少有多少个数是奇数？

9. 已知有 25 个正整数之和为 2016，请问这些数的最大公因子之最大可能值是什么？

10. 矩形 ABCD 中，AB=12 cm、BC=5 cm．点 E 与点 C 分别位于直线 AB 的异侧，使得 AE=BE，如图 14-2 所示．已知△AEB 的面积为 36 cm²，请问△AEC 的面积为多少 cm²？

11. 小安将所有的素数由小到大依序连在一起写下：235711…．在她写完第十个素数时停止，接着她移除其中七个数码后，剩下的九个数码由左至右可以视为一个九位数．请问这个九位数的最大可能值是什么？

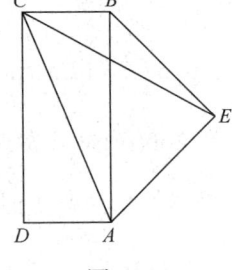

图 14-2

12. 有三个两位数，已知任意两个数之和都恰等于第三个数之两个数码交换顺序后所得到的二位数．请问这三个两位数的总和是什么？

13. 已知两个四位数的和为一个五位数．若这三个数之数码由左至右读与由右至左读都一样，请问有多少个相异的四位数可以出现在上述的加式中？

14. 当 2016 分别被 3、5、11 除时，具有所得的余数依序分别为 0、1、3 的性质．在由数码 2、0、1、6 都各至多出现一次所构成的数中，请问与 2016 具有相同性质的最小正整数是什么？

15. 教室里的每一位学生都写下六个正整数，这六个数不一定相异，并满足这六个数之和至多为 12 且六个数之和不小于六个数之积．若没有任何两位学生写下完全相同的六个数，请问教室内至多有多少位学生？

14.3 EMIC 个人赛试题解答与评注

2016 年国际小学数学竞赛个人竞赛试题解答

1. **解** 可知最终每个顶点上的学生人数为 (5+15+14+9+17)÷5=12 位，故顶点 A 必须移入 7 位学生、顶点 D 必须移入 3 位学生，而顶点 B 必须移出 3 位学生、顶点 C 必须移出 2 位学生、顶点 E 必须移出 5 位学生．此时即可判断出学生们移动的总距离至少是 7+3=10(m)=3+2+5 (m)，且此最小值是可以达成的．可知 B、C 之间不需要有学生移动，因此顶点 B 所移出的学生都必移入顶点 A、顶点 C 所移出的学生都必移入顶点 D，接着就可以判断出顶点 E 所移出的学生分别往顶点 A、D 移入 4 位与 1 位，如图 14-3 所示．

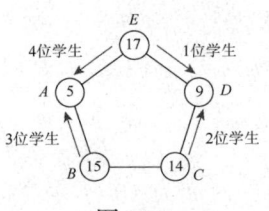

图 14-3

答:10(m)

2. **解** 可知当 A 跑 200(m)时，B 跑了 160(m)而 C 跑了 150(m). 故可推知当 B 再跑 40(m)时，C 跑了 $40 \times \dfrac{150}{160} = 37.5$ (m)，所以 C 在 2 秒内跑了 $50 - 37.5 = 12.5$ (m)，即可得知 C 跑 200(m)总共费时 $2 \times \dfrac{200}{12.5} = 32$ 秒，所以 B 跑 200(m)总共费时 $32 - 2 = 30$ 秒，而 A 跑 200(m)总共费时 $32 \times \dfrac{150}{200} = 24$ 秒，故当 A 抵达终点时，B 还需要再跑 6 秒才能抵达终点.

答: 6 秒

3. **解** 如图 14-4 所示，将位于中央正方形内的四块阴影区域分别往外平移至箭头所指的区域，此时可发现阴影部分可分割成四块边长皆为 1(cm) 的正方形区域与四块半径都是 1(cm)的四分之一圆区域，因此阴影部分的面积比半径为 1(cm)的圆之面积大 4(cm^2).

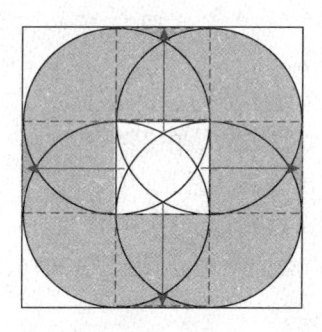

图 14-4

答: 4cm^2

4. **解法 1** 因 $8202016 - 8142016 = 60000$ 且有 $3333 \times 18 < 60000 < 3334 \times 18$，故可判断出会有 3333 或 3334 个整数是 18 的倍数. 而因 8142030 为偶数且其数码和为 18，故此范围内最小的 18 之倍数为 8142030，且因此数与 8142016 之差为 14，故可判断出此范围内不可能有 3334 个整数是 18 的倍数，即仅 3333 个整数是 18 的倍数.

解法 2 因 $8142016 = 18 \times 452334 + 4$、$8202016 = 18 \times 455667 + 10$，故可以得知此范围内共有 $455667 - 452334 = 3333$ 个整数是 18 的倍数.

答: 3333

5. **解** 若将三分线内每投进一球改为得 4 分、在三分线外每投进一球改为得 1.5 分，则假设的部分仍是会比原来的得分多 7 分，且对于小史所投进的 14 球，每投进一球就会多得 2 分或少得 1.5 分. 若每投进一球再多给予 1.5 分，则小史将共多得 $7 + 1.5 \times 14 = 28$ 分，且知小史每投进一球就会多得 3.5 分或 0 分，可得出小史在三分线内投进了 $\dfrac{28}{3.5} = 8$ 球，故此场比赛中他实际上得 $8 + 2 \times 8 + 3 \times (14 - 8) = 42$ 分.

答: 42 分

6. **解** 可知第一天小强走路的时间为 20 分钟、跑步的时间为 10 分钟. 因为跑步的速度是走路的速度之两倍，故可判断出走路的路程恰为整段路途的

第14章 2016年第14届国际小学数学竞赛

$\frac{1}{2}$、跑步的路程恰为整段路途的 $\frac{1}{2}$，故小强走完全程费时40分钟、跑完全程费时20分钟. 而在第二天，可判断出走路的路程恰为全程的 $\frac{1}{5}$、跑步的路程恰为全程的 $\frac{4}{5}$，因此跑步的时间为 $20 \times \frac{4}{5} = 16$ 分钟、走路的时间为 $40 \times \frac{1}{5} = 8$ 分钟，故第二天总共费时 $16 + 8 = 24$ 分钟.

答: 24 分钟

7. 解 可知在第一天早上后，剩下的花生数比原始的数量少了13颗；在第二天早上后，剩下的花生数比原始的数量减去第一天吃掉的数量再减去3颗后还少了13颗. 因小杰第二天早上比第一天早上多吃了3颗，所以小杰第二天下午比第一天下午少吃了3颗，因此可判断出 $3 \times 10 = 30$ 颗这个数量比第一天吃的数量还多3颗，即可推知小杰每天吃27颗花生，且他还剩下 $(27 - 16) \times 9 = 99$ 颗花生.

答: 99 颗

8. 解 因为2016为偶数，故知总共有偶数个相异的奇数. 因最小的45个偶数之和为 $2 + 4 + \cdots + 90 = 45 \times 46 = 2070 > 2016$，故知至多有43个偶数，因此至少有6个奇数，例如 $2 + 4 + \cdots + 86 + 1 + 3 + 5 + 7 + 9 + 99 = 2016$.

答: 6

9. 解 因每一个整数都不会小于这些数的最大公因子，故这些数的最大公因子不会超过 $\left[\frac{2016}{25}\right] = 80$ 且为2016的因子. 现因 $2016 = 2^5 \times 3^2 \times 7$，故这些数的最大公因子之最大可能值是72，例如这25个正整数为24个72与1个288.

答: 72

10. 解法1 分别在 CB、DA 的延长线上取点 G、F，使得 $CDFG$ 为矩形且点 E 落在 GF 上，如图14-5所示. 因 $\triangle AEB$ 的面积为 $36(\text{cm}^2)$，故 $BG = AF = 6(\text{cm})$、$GE = EF = 6(\text{cm})$. 由勾股定理可知 $AC = 13(\text{cm})$，因此

$[ACE] = [CGFD] - [CGE] - [ACD] - [AFE]$

$= 11 \times 12 - \frac{1}{2} \times 6 \times 11 - \frac{1}{2} \times 5 \times 12 - \frac{1}{2} \times 6 \times 6$

$= 51(\text{cm}^2)$

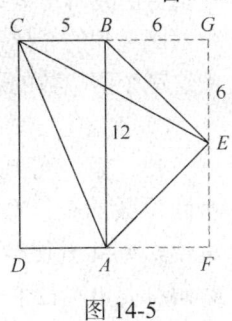

图14-5

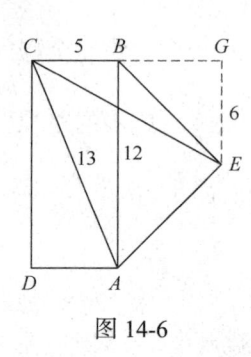

解法 2 由勾股定理可知 $AC=13$(cm). 现令点 G 为点 E 在直线 BC 上的垂足, 如图 14-6 所示. 因 $AE=BE$, 故知点 E 在线段 AB 的中垂线上, 即 $EG=\frac{1}{2}AB=6$ (cm). 因此知

$$[ACE]=[ABCD]+[ABE]-[BCE]-[ACD]$$
$$=5\times12+36-\frac{1}{2}\times5\times6-\frac{1}{2}\times5\times12$$
$$=51(\text{cm}^2).$$

图 14-6

解法 3 因 $AE=BE$, 故知点 E 在线段 AB 的中垂线上, 即 $[BCE]=\frac{1}{2}[ABC]$.

$$[ACE]=[ACBE]-[BCE]=[ABC]+[ABE]-\frac{1}{2}[ABC]$$
$$=\frac{1}{2}[ABC]+[ABE]=\frac{1}{2}\times\frac{1}{2}\times5\times12+36=51(\text{cm}^2).$$

答: 51cm^2

11. 解 可知在写下的数之前七个数码中, 最大的数码为 7, 故小安可将前三个数码 2、3、5 移除使得 7 为欲留下的九位数之首位数码; 接着明显可判断出需移除这个 7 之后的连续三个 1, 最后再将下一个 3 之后的数码 1 移除, 即可得到九位数的最大可能值 737192329.

答: 737192329

12. 解 由题意可得这三个数之间的三条算式相加, 可得知这三个两位数的十位数码之和的 20 倍与这三个两位数的个位数码之和的 2 倍相加所得之值, 恰等于这三个两位数的十位数码之和与这三个二位数的个位数码之和的 10 倍相加所得之值, 由此可得知这三个二位数的十位数码之和的 19 倍恰等于这三个两位数的个位数码之和的 8 倍, 因此这三个两位数的十位数码之和为 8、个位数码之和为 19, 故这三个两位数的总和是 $8\times10+19=99$, 例如取这三个两位数为 18、36、45.

答: 99

13. 解 可判断出这个五位数的首位数码与末位数码都必为 1, 因此这两个四位数的个位数码之和为 11. 若十位数码与百位数码在此加法计算中都没有进位, 则此五位数必为 11011, 此时即可判断出两个四位数的十位数码与百位数码都是 0, 且个位数码可能的组合为 (2, 9)、(3, 8)、(4, 7)、(5, 6), 故可得 8 个相异的四位数. 若十位数码与百位数码在此加法计算中都有进位, 则此五位数必为 12221, 此时即可判断出两个四位数的十位数码之和也是 11, 即其可

280

能的组合与个位数码可能的四个组合相同,故可得 $8 \times 8 = 64$ 个不同的四位数. 故总共有 $8 + 64 = 72$ 个相异的四位数.

答: 72 个

14. **解** 这四个数码所能构成的一位数中,3 的倍数为 0、6;这四个数码所能构成的两位数中,3 的倍数为 12、21、60. 这几个数除以 11 所得的余数都不是 3, 故不符合题意. 现观察这四个数码所能构成的三位数. 由 3 的倍数之数码和必为 3 的倍数可判断出所求之三位数必定同时包含有数码 1 与 2, 但若没有数码 0, 则奇数位数码之和减去偶数位数码之和所得的差都不可能为 3, 因此知所求之三位数必没有数码 6, 此时奇数位数码之和减去偶数位数码之和所得的差为 3 的情况有 102 与 201, 其中仅 201 被 5 除之后所得的余数为 1.

答: 201

15. **解** 因六个正整数之和至多为 12, 故这六个正整数之中的最大的数至多为 7. 此时可列出 14 组可写出的六个正整数如表 14-1 所示.

表 14-1

最大的数	其余的数
7	11111 (7<12)
6	21111 (12=12), 11111 (6<11)
5	21111 (10<11), 11111 (5<10)
4	21111 (8<10), 11111 (4<9)
3	31111 (9<10), 21111 (6<9), 11111 (3<8)
2	22111 (8<9), 21111 (4<8), 11111 (2<7)
1	11111 (1<6)

故知教室内至多有 14 位学生.

答: 14 位

14.4 EMIC 队际赛英文试题

Elementary Mathematics International Contest 2016
17th August, 2016, Chiang Mai, Thailand

Team Contest

1. Choose nine different ones of 1, 2, 3, 4, 5, 6, 7, 8, 9 and 10. Use each

of them exactly once to form three equations, using each of addition, subtraction, multiplication and division at most once. What is the smallest number that we can leave out?

1	2	3
4	5	6
7	8	9

2. The squares of a 3 by 3 table are labelled 1, 2, ···, 9 as shown. In how many ways can we shade five of the squares so that no row or column is completely shaded?

3. The diagram shows an 8 by 8 board. An ant visits each of the 64 squares once and only once. It crawls from one to another of two squares sharing at least one corner. The order in which the squares are visited is marked with numbers, starting from 1 and ending at 64. Some of the marked numbers have been erased. Restore these erased numbers.

	5			26	25		
		10	29		23		
2			31		37		
1	12	19	21		38	34
13		17	49		33	
59		16		50	47	40
		64			46		42
		55		53	52	45	43

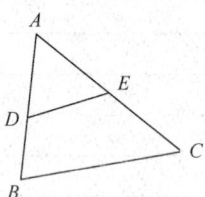

4. In triangle ABC, $AB=7$ cm and $AC=9$ cm. D is a point on AB such that $BD=3$ cm. E is a point on AC such that the area of the quadrilateral $BCED$ is $\frac{5}{7}$ of the area of triangle ABC. Find the length, in cm, of CE.

5. How many positive integers less than 100 are there such that the product of all positive divisors of such a number is equal to the square of the number?

6. A hat is put on the head of each of 33 children. Each hat is red, white or blue. Each can see the hats of all other children except his or her own. Willem sees three times as many red hats as blue hats. Maxima sees twice as many white hats as blue hats. What is the colour of Maxima's hat?

7. Mary has a three-digit number. The first two digits are the same but different from the third digit. Myra has a one-digit number. It is the same as the last digit of Mary's number. How many different four-digit numbers can be the product of Mary's and Myra's numbers?

8. A 4 m by 4 m window on a wall is to be boarded up with eight identical 1 m by 2 m or 2 m by 1 m wooden planks. In how many different ways can this be done? Two ways resulting in the same final diagram are not considered different.

第 14 章 2016 年第 14 届国际小学数学竞赛

9. The 6 by 6 table in the diagram below is divided into 17 regions, each containing a number. Each of the 36 squares contains one of the numbers 1, 2, 3, 4, 5 and 6. All six numbers appear in every row and every column. The number in a white region is the number in the only square of the region. The number in a yellow region is the difference when the number in one of the squares is subtracted from the number in the other square. The number in a green region is the quotient when the number in one of the squares is divided by the number in the other square. The number in a red region is the sum of the numbers in all the squares of the region. The number in a blue region is the product of the numbers in all the squares of the region. Fill in the 36 numbers.

3	24		5	5	
			60	3	12
1	1			150	
	24	3			
4		10		7	
	11				2

10. A polygon is said to be *convex* if each of its interior angles is less than $180°$. What is the maximum number of sides of a convex polygon which can be dissected into squares and equilateral triangles of equal side lengths? Justify your answer.

14.5 EMIC 队际赛中文试题

2016 年国际小学数学竞赛队标竞赛试题

1. 从 1、2、3、4、5、6、7、8、9、10 选取九个不同的数填入三条等式中，其中每一条等式都是从加、减、乘、除这四个运算中选取一个，并只能选一次. 若每一条等式的运算都彼此互不相同，请问没有被选到的数之最小值是多少？

1	2	3
4	5	6
7	8	9

图 14-7

2. 在 3×3 的方格表中分别填入 1、2、3、…、9，如图 14-7 所示. 现要将其中五个小方格涂上黑色，使得没有任何一列或任何一行上的三个小方格全都被涂上黑色. 请问总共有多少种不同的涂法？

3. 一只蚂蚁造访了一个 8×8 棋盘内的所有 64 个小方格，每一个小方格恰经过一次，这只蚂蚁可以任意爬行到与它所在的小方格至少有一个共同顶点的小方格内. 将开始出发的小方格标记 1，接着移动到上方的小方格标记 2，继续以此类推，最后移动到终点小方格标记 64，如图 14-8 所示. 但图中有一些

	5			26	25		
		10	29		23		
2			31		37		
1	12		19	21	38	34	
13			17	49	33		
59		16		50	47	40	
		64			46		42
		55		53	52	45	43

图 14-8

小方格内的数没有被标记出,请补上缺漏的数.

4. 如图 14-9 所示,△ABC 中,已知 AB=7 cm、AC=9 cm. 若点 D 在 AB 上使得 BD=3 cm 且点 E 在 AC 上使得四边形 BCED 的面积为 △ABC 的面积之 $\frac{5}{7}$,请问 CE 的长度为多少 cm?

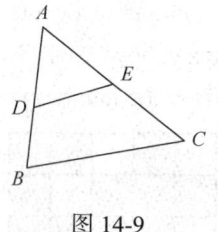

图 14-9

5. 小于 100 的正整数中,请问有多少个数的所有正因数之乘积恰好等于这一个数的平方?

6. 33 个小朋友的头上都戴有一顶帽子,帽子的颜色为红色、白色或蓝色其中一种. 每一个小朋友都可以看到其他人帽子的颜色,但是看不到自己帽子的颜色. 若小威看到的红色帽子数是蓝色帽子数的三倍、小马看到的白色帽子数是蓝色帽子数的二倍,请问小马所戴的帽子是什么颜色?

7. 小玛写下一个三位数,这个数的首两位数码相同但与个位数码相异. 小米写下一个一位数,这个一位数与小玛所写下的三位数之个位数码相同. 若将小玛与小米写下的数相乘,请问所得的乘积之可能值共有多少个相异的四位数?

8. 墙上有一个 4 m×4 m 的窗户,要利用八块全等的 1 m×2 m 或 2 m×1 m 之木板铺满窗户,请问共有多少种不同的铺法?若铺木板的顺序不同,但铺满后得到的图样相同视为相同的铺法.

9. 一个 6×6 的方格表被分割为如图 14-10 所示的 17 块区域,每块区域内都有一个数. 请在 36 个小方格内分别填入 1、2、3、4、5、6 中的一个数,使得每一列、每一行都恰出现这六个数各一次. 白色区域内仅有一个小方格,里面的数恰为此小方格内所填入的数、黄色区域(▨)内的数等于此区域中一个小方格内的数与另一个小方格内的数之差、绿色区域(▨)内的数等于此区域中一个小方格内的数被另一个小方格内的数整除后所得之商、红色区域(▨)内的数等于此区域中所有小方格内的数之和、蓝色区域(▨)内的数等于此区域中所有小方格内的数之乘积.

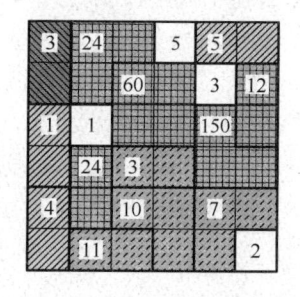

图 14-10

10. 若一个多边形的每一个内角都小于 180°,则称这个多边形为凸多边形. 已知有一个凸多边形可以被切成数块边长都相同的正方形与正三角形,请问这样的凸多边形最多能有多少条边?你必须证明不能再多.

第14章 2016年第14届国际小学数学竞赛

14.6 EMIC队际赛试题解答与评注

2016年国际小学数学竞赛队标竞赛试题解答

1. 解 首先注意到加式与减式之间可通过移项而改写成另一个运算,而乘式与除式也是,故都可视为同一种运算的等式;接着由$3\times 4=12>10$可判断出乘式中必有2.因此可知这三条简单等式必为一条乘式与两条加式,而其中一条加式可通过移项而改写成减式.

情况 1. 此乘式为$2\times 4=8$:此时可判断出另两条等式必分别有6与10中的一个数.因为$10=1+9=3+7$、$6=9-3=7-1=1+5$,故可能的组合仅有$10=3+7$与$6=1+5$,即没有被选到的数为9.

情况 2. 此乘式为$2\times 3=6$:此时可判断出另两条等式必分别有 1、5、7 与 9 中的两个数.因为$4=5-1=9-5$、$8=7+1=9-1$、$10=9+1$,故可能的组合仅有$4=9-5$与$8=7+1$,即没有被选到的数为10.

情况 3. 此乘式为$2\times 5=10$:此时可判断出另两条等式必分别有 1、3、7 与 9 中的二个数.因为$4=1+3=7-3$、$6=7-1=9-3$、$8=7+1=9-1$,故可能的组合有:

(i) $4=7-3$与$8=9-1$,即没有被选到的数为 6;

(ii) $6=9-3$与$8=7+1$,即没有被选到的数为 4.

故可以得知没有被选到的数之最小值是 4.

答: 4

2. 解法 1 若四个角落的方格都涂黑,则第五个涂黑的方格必为 5 号,此时仅有 1 种涂法.

若四个角落的方格有三个被涂黑,不妨令为1、3、7 号方格,则另两个被涂黑的方格必为 5、6、8 号中的两个方格,即有 3 种涂法.所以可以得知此情况共有$4\times 3=12$种涂法.

若四个角落的方格中,恰有两个位于同一列或同一行的方格被涂黑,不妨令为 1、3 号方格,则 8 号方格必被涂黑,而另两个被涂黑的方格必为 4、5、6 号中的两个方格,即有 3 种涂法.所以可以得知此情况共有$4\times 3=12$种涂法.

若四个角落的方格中,恰有两个位于对角的方格被涂黑,不妨令为 1、9 号方格.若 5 号方格没有被涂黑,则另三个被涂黑的方格必为 2、4、6、8 号中的三个方格;若 5 号方格被涂黑,则另两个被涂黑的方格必为 2、8 号中的一个方格,以及 4、6 号中的一个方格. 所以可以得知此情况共有 $(4+4) \times 2 = 16$ 种涂法.

若四个角落的方格中, 恰有一个被涂黑, 不妨令为 1 号方格, 则 6、8 号方格都必涂黑, 因此另两个被涂黑的方格必为 2、4 号方格. 所以可以得知此情况共有 $1 \times 4 = 4$ 种涂法.

因此总共有 $1 + 12 + 12 + 16 + 4 = 45$ 种不同的涂法.

解法 2　要将其中五个小方格涂上黑色且没有任何一行上的三个小方格全被涂上黑色, 因此这三行上被涂黑的小方格只能依照 2、2、1 个分配. 不妨假设第一行、第二行上都各有两个方格被涂上黑色, 又为满足三列上的三个小方格不全被涂上黑色, 则涂黑的情况只能如图 14-11 所示的 15 种涂法:

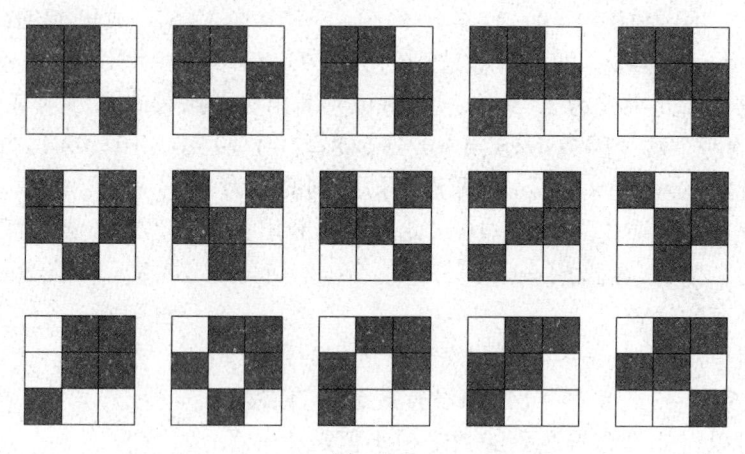

图 14-11

由于只有一个小方格被涂黑的列有三种可能的情况, 故共有 $15 \times 3 = 45$ 种不同的涂法.

解法 3　可知题目所要求之条件等价于每一列、每一行上的三个小方格都至少有一个没被涂上黑色. 因共有 4 个小方格没被涂上黑色, 故由抽屉原理知至少有一列有两个小方格没被涂上黑色、至少有一行有两个小方格没被涂上黑色.

情况 1. 在某一列上的三个小方格颜色都与其所在之该行上的另两个小方格颜色不同.

在此情况中, 让 1、2、6、9 没被涂上黑色是一种满足题意的涂法. 可判断出经过行、列的交换后, 共有 9 种这样的涂法.

情况 2. 与前一种情况相反, 在某一列上有一个小方格颜色与其所在之该行上的另两个小方格中的一个小方格颜色相同.

第 14 章 2016 年第 14 届国际小学数学竞赛

在此情况中, 让 1、2、5、9 没被涂上黑色是一种满足题意的涂法. 可判断出经过行、列的交换后, 共有 36 种这样的涂法.

因此总共有 9 + 36 = 45 种不同的涂法.

答: 45 种

【评注】恰建构出 45 个正确的涂色图形, 得 40 分; 建构出 45 个正确的涂色图形, 但有重复或错误的图形, 得 25 分; 建构出 30 至 44 个正确的涂色图形, 得 15 分; 建构出 15 至 29 个正确的涂色图形, 得 5 分.

3. **解** 分别由 21 与 23、31 与 33、53 与 55 的位置可得知 22、32、54 的位置, 接下来可以利用唯一性判断出 44、41、48、51、54、56、⋯的位置, 接着即可依序判断出其余格子所填之数, 如图 14-12 所示.

答: 见图 14-12

6	5	8	9	28	26	25	24
4	7	10	29	30	27	23	36
2	3	11	20	31	22	37	35
1	12	18	19	21	32	33	34
13	60	61	17	49	48	33	39
59	14	16	62	50	47	40	41
58	15	64	63	51	46	44	42
57	56	55	54	53	52	45	43

图 14-12

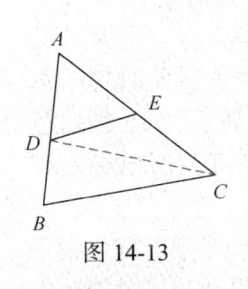

4. **解法 1** 如图 14-13 所示, 因 $AB=7$(cm)、$BD=3$(cm), 故知 $AD=4$(cm). 现连接 DC, 则可判断出 $\triangle ADC$ 的面积为 $\triangle ABC$ 的面积之 $\frac{4}{7}$, 因此 $\triangle DBC$ 的面积为 $\triangle ABC$ 的面积之 $\frac{3}{7}$. 因四边形 $BCED$ 的面积为 $\triangle ABC$ 的面积之 $\frac{5}{7}$, 所以 $\triangle DAE$ 的面积为 $\triangle ABC$ 的面积之 $\frac{2}{7}$, 且 $\triangle DEC$ 的面积也为 $\triangle ABC$ 的面积之 $\frac{2}{7}$. 因 $\triangle DAE$ 与 $\triangle DEC$ 为等高三角形且面积相等, 故 $AE=EC=\dfrac{AC}{2}=4\dfrac{1}{2}$(cm).

图 14-13

解法 2 由共角定理可知 $\dfrac{[ADE]}{[ABC]}=\dfrac{AD\times AE}{AB\times AC}$, 故可得 $1-\dfrac{5}{7}=\dfrac{4\times AE}{7\times 9}$, 即有 $AE=\dfrac{9}{2}$(cm), 因此 $EC=AC-AE=9-\dfrac{9}{2}=\dfrac{9}{2}=4\dfrac{1}{2}$(cm).

答: $4\dfrac{1}{2}$ cm

【评注】证明 $\triangle DEA$ 与 $\triangle DEC$ 的面积相同, 得 20 分; 试图计算出非显而易见的区域面积, 得 5 分; 连接 DC 或 BE, 得 5 分.

5. **解** 可知正整数 1 满足此条件. 而对于其他满足此条件的正整数, 都恰有四个正因数, 且可将这四个正因数两两分成二对, 每一对的数之积都恰为这一个正整数.这样的数都必为一个素数的立方,或是两个相异素数的乘积.可知小于 100 的正整数中,仅 $2^3 = 8$、$3^3 = 27$ 为一个素数的立方,而可表示为两个相异素数的乘积时,较小的素数之值至多为 7. 故得:

(1) 2 分别乘以 3、5、7、11、13、17、19、23、29、31、37、41、43、47;

(2) 3 分别乘以 5、7、11、13、17、19、23、29、31;

(3) 5 分别乘以 7、11、13、17、19;

(4) 7 分别乘以 11、13.

故总共有 $1+2+14+9+5+2=33$ 个数.

答: 33 个

6. **解** 若假设至少有 6 顶蓝色帽子,则在不考虑小威与小马所戴的帽子颜色时,可知小威至少看到 18 顶红色帽子、小马至少看到 12 顶白色帽子,此时帽子总数大于 33 顶,故不合;若假设至多有 4 顶蓝色帽子,则在不考虑小威与小马所戴的帽子颜色时,可知小威至多看到 15 顶红色帽子、小马至多看到 10 顶白色帽子,此时帽子总数小于 33 顶,故不合;因此可判断出在不考虑小威与小马所戴的帽子颜色时,恰有 5 顶蓝色帽子,因此小威至少看到 15 顶红色帽子、小马至少看到 10 顶白色帽子,此时可发现尚差 $33-5-15-10=3$ 顶帽子没有被计入,因此小威或小马中至少有一位戴着蓝色帽子. 若是小马戴着蓝色帽子,则小威看到 18 顶红色帽子,此时帽子总数大于 33 顶,故不合,因此必是小威戴着蓝色帽子,而小马看到 12 顶白色帽子. 因 $6+15+12=33$,故小马所戴的帽子已被计入,且可判断出必是红色帽子.

答: 红色帽子

【评注】直接说小马所戴的帽子是红色而无其他说明,得 0 分;讨论蓝色帽子数的情况,得 5 分;判断出在不考虑小威与小马所戴的帽子颜色时,恰有 5 顶蓝色帽子,得 20 分;说明小威戴着蓝色帽子但未判断出小马所戴的帽子颜色,得 30 分.

7. **解** 若首位数码为 1,则个位数码只能为 9

若首位数码为 2,则个位数码可为 5、6、7、8 或 9;

若首位数码为 3,则个位数码可为 4、5、6、7、8 或 9;

若首位数码为 4,则个位数码可为 3、5、6、7、8 或 9;

若首位数码为 5,则个位数码可为 2、3、4、6、7、8 或 9;

若首位数码为 6,则个位数码可为 2、3、4、5、7、8 或 9;

若首位数码为 7，则个位数码可为 2、3、4、5、6、8 或 9；
若首位数码为 8，则个位数码可为 2、3、4、5、6、7 或 9；
若首位数码为 9，则个位数码可为 2、3、4、5、6、7 或 8.
这些乘积都不相同，故总共有 1+5+6+6+7+7+7+7+7=53 个相异的四位数.

答：53 个

8. **解法 1** 可将之分成四块 2 m×2 m 的区域. 则有以下三种可能的情况：

情况 1：每一块区域都恰由两块木板铺满. 此时每一块区域内的木板都必同时水平放置或同时铅垂放置，因此共有 $2^4=16$ 种不同的铺法.

情况 2：仅有两块区域都恰由二块木板铺满. 可判断出此时这两块区域必相邻，共 4 种可能，且每一块区域内的木板都必同时水平放置或同时铅垂放置，而另外两块区域仅有一种放置方法，因此知共有 $4×2^2=16$ 种不同的铺法.

情况 3：不存在恰由两块木板铺满的区域. 可判断出原窗户中，中央的 2 m×2 m 的区域内有 2 种放置方法，而外围的区域也是有 2 种放置方法，因此知共有 2×2=4 种不同的铺法.

因不可能发生仅有一块区域是恰由两块木板铺满，或是恰有三块区域都恰由两块木板铺满，故总共有 16+16+4=36 种不同的铺法.

解法 2 容易验证若在 2×N 的窗户之情况下，铺法数即恰为第 N 个费氏数. 现考虑以下几种情况：

情况 1：将窗户分成两块 2×4 的区域，如图 14-14 所示. 因第四个费氏数为 5，故每一块区域都有 5 种不同的铺法，所以共有 25 种不同的铺法.

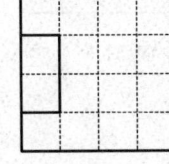

情况 2：有一块 2×1 的区域恰垂直位于中间左侧的位置，如图 14-15 所示. 此时共有以下两种铺法：

在图 14-16 的情况中，2×4 的区域有 5 种不同的铺法；在图 14-17 的情况中，此恰为 1 种铺法.

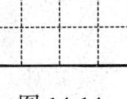

图 14-14

图 14-15

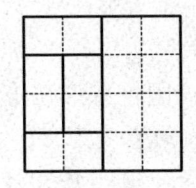

图 14-16

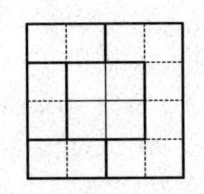

图 14-17

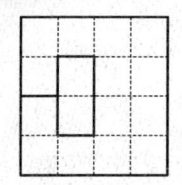

情况3：将情况2中的2×1区域恰往右平移1 m，如图14-18所示．此时若继续铺下去，可得1种不同的铺法．

情况4：将情况3中的2×1区域再恰往右平移1 m，如图14-19所示．此时若继续铺下去，可得4种不同的铺法．

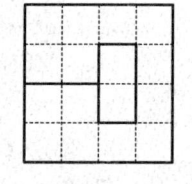

图14-18

情况5：将情况4中的2×1区域再恰往右平移1 m至中间右侧的位置，如图14-20所示．

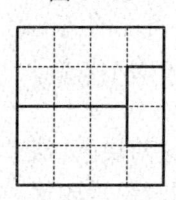

图14-19

此时若继续铺下去，无法得到与前面情况所得之不同的铺法．

故总共有 $25+5+1+1+4=36$ 种不同的铺法．

图14-20

答：36 种

【评注】 恰建构出36个正确的涂色图形，得40分；建构出36个正确的涂色图形，但有重复或错误的图形，得25分；建构出24至35个正确的涂色图形，得15分；建构出12至23个正确的涂色图形，得5分．

9. 解 可观察出，在红色区域中，有 $3=1+2$、$11=5+6$，且由7不能是 $1+3+3$ 知 $7=1+2+4$，以及由三个数组成的加式之和恰为10；在黄色区域中，有 $5=6-1$、$4=5-1=6-2$ 及由二个数组成的减式之差恰为 1；在蓝色区域中，有 $150=6×5×5$、$24=6×4$、$12=6×2=4×3$ 及由四个数组成的乘式之积恰为 60；在绿色区域中，有 $3=6÷2=3÷1$．利用这些算式及拉丁方阵的规则，即可得如图14-21所示的解．

答：见图14-21

图14-21

10. 解法1 可以利用以下三个步骤来组成一个凸12边形：

(1) 将六个正三角形拼成一个正六边形；
(2) 在此正六边形的每一条边上都往外放置一个正方形；
(3) 再加入六个正三角形即可补成一个完整的十二边形．

现验证13条边及以上的凸多边形是不可能的．因正方形与正三角形的每一个内角都是90°或60°，因此这样的凸多边形的内角至多为150°．若存在一个凸13边形是可以被拼出的，则其内角和至多为 $13×150°=1950°$，但凸13边形的内角和恒为 $(13-1)×180°=1980°$，故不合．而若边数继续增加，其误差只会更大,故不可能有 13 条边以上的凸多边形(图 14-22).

解法 2 可以利用以下三个步骤来组成一个凸 12 边形:

(1)将六个正三角形拼成一个正六边形;

(2)在此正六边形的每一条边上都往外放置一个正方形;

(3)再加入六个正三角形即可补成一个完整的十二边形.

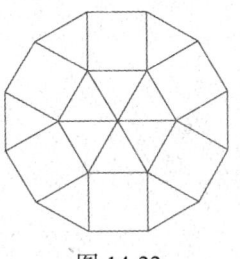

图 14-22

现验证 13 条边及以上的凸多边形是不可能的. 因正方形与正三角形的每一个内角都是 90° 或 60°,因此这样的凸多边形的外角至少为 30°. 若存在一个凸 13 边形是可以被拼出的,则其外角和至少为 $13 \times 30° = 390°$,而任意多边形的外角和恒等于 360°,故不合. 而若边数继续增加,其误差只会更大,故不可能有 13 条边以上的凸多边形(图 14-22).

答: 12

【评注】 求得边数下界,得 20 分;得到满足题意的 12 边形,得 20 分;得到满足题意的 11 边形,得 15 分;得到满足题意的 10 边形或 9 边形,得 10 分;得到满足题意的 8 边形或 7 边形,得 5 分;求得边数上界,得 20 分;若试图利用角度来讨论,得 5 分.